TAKING SIDES

Clashing Views
on Controversial Issues
in Mass Media and Society

Edited, Selected,
and with Introductions by

Alison Alexander
University of Massachusetts at Amherst

and

Jarice Hanson
University of Massachusetts at Amherst

The Dushkin Publishing Group, Inc.

Taking Sides ® is a registered trademark of
The Dushkin Publishing Group, Inc.

Library of Congress Catalog Card Number:
90-81841

Manufactured in the United States of America

First Edition, First Printing
ISBN: 0-87967-894-1

 Printed on Recycled Paper

The Dushkin Publishing Group, Inc.
Sluice Dock, Guilford, CT 06437

PREFACE

Comprehension without critical evaluation is impossible.
Friedrich Hegel (1770–1831)
German philosopher

Mass communication is one of the most popular college majors in the country, perhaps emerging from a belief in the importance of our communications systems as much as from a desire to work within the communications industry. This book, which contains thirty-six selections, presented in a pro and con format, addresses eighteen different controversial issues in mass communications and society. The purpose of this volume, and indeed of any course that deals with the social impact of media, is to create a literate consumer of media—someone who can walk the fine line between a naive acceptance of all media and a cynical disregard for any positive benefits it may offer.

The media today reflect the evolution of a nation that has increasingly seized on the need and desire for more leisure time. Technological developments have increased our range of choices—from the number of broadcast or cable channels we can select to the publications we can read that cater specifically to our individual interests and needs. New and improving technologies allow us to choose when and where to see a film (through the magic of the VCR), to create our preferred acoustical environment (by stereo, CD, or portable headphones), and to communicate over distances instantly (by means of computers and electronic mail). Because these many forms of media extend our capacities to consume media content, the study of mass media and society is the investigation of some of our most common daily activities. Since many of the issues in this volume are often in the news (or even *are* the news!), you may already have opinions on them. We encourage you to read the selections and discuss the issues with an open mind. Even if you do not initially agree with a position, or do not even understand how it is possible to make the opposing argument, give it a try. For we believe that thinking seriously about mass media is an important goal.

Plan of the book Our book is primarily designed for students in the introductory course in mass communication (sometimes called introduction to mass media or introduction to mass media and society). The issues are such that they can be easily incorporated into any media course regardless of how it is organized—thematically, chronologically, or by medium. The thirty-six selections have been taken from a variety of sources—books, journals, magazines, legal briefs, Senate testimony—and were chosen because of their usefulness in defending a position and for their accessibility to students.

i

Each issue in this volume has an issue *introduction*, which sets the stage for the debate as it is argued in the YES and NO selections. Each issue concludes with a *postscript* that makes some final observations about the selections, points the way to other questions related to the issue, and offers suggestions for further reading on the issue. The introductions and postscripts do not preempt what is the reader's own task: to achieve a critical and informed view of the issues at stake. In reading an issue and forming your own opinion you should not feel confined to adopt one or the other of the positions presented. Some readers may see important points on both sides of an issue and may construct for themselves a new and creative approach. Such an approach might incorporate the best of both sides, or it might provide an entirely new vantage point for understanding. At the back of the book (beginning on page 356) is a listing of all the *contributors to this volume*, which will give you additional information on the communication scholars, practitioners, policymakers, and media critics whose views are debated here.

Supplements An *Instructor's Manual with Test Questions* (multiple-choice and essay) is available through the publisher. And a general guidebook, called *Using Taking Sides in the Classroom*, which discusses methods and techniques for integrating the pro-con approach into any classroom setting, is also available.

Acknowledgments We wish to acknowledge the encouragement and support given to this project. We are particularly grateful to Mimi Egan, program manager of the Taking Sides series. And we thank our families (David, James, Katie, Jaime, and Tracy) for their patience and understanding during the period in which we prepared this book.

Alison Alexander
Jarice Hanson
University of Massachusetts, Amherst

CONTENTS IN BRIEF

CONTENTS

Social critic Michael Novak argues that television shapes the soul by affecting our perceptions of reality and that this reality is produced by an intellectual elite. Historian Walter Karp asserts that fears that media would result in a mass society are unfounded and that the messages the media offer us are not quite as oriented toward the status quo as the media critics would have us believe.

Professor John Downing states that "The Cosby Show" allows for the analysis of discourse about race in a racist society and he concludes that its treatment of sexism, the family, and social class has enabled it to convey positive messages to multiple audiences. Philosopher and media critic Michael Dyson argues that "The Cosby Show" has been successful in addressing major social problems, such as sexism, and so should not ignore the problems of racism, which he feels it currently does.

Author and children's advocate Marie Winn argues that television has a negative influence on children and their families. Dan Anderson, a professor of psychology, does not find evidence that television turns children into "zombies." He believes that television, used properly, can be a source of positive education and entertainment.

Author and communications professor Diana Meehan notes that there have been some changes in the portrayal of female characters in the popular media. The image of a strong, autonomous female has emerged and is an encouraging sign for those who advocate more varied gender portrayals. Communications instructor Elayne Rapping sees in Hollywood a reactionary backlash against feminist ideals that has resulted in portrayals of career women as mostly unhappy and neurotic, or even insane.

Janet Malcolm, *New Yorker* staff writer, investigates the relationship between Joe McGinniss, author of the nonfiction best-seller *Fatal Vision*, and his subject, Jeffrey MacDonald, and maintains that all journalists betray and manipulate their subjects. Martin Gottlieb, journalist and professor, argues against this claim by presenting his own interviews with prominent journalists—each of whom explores how he or she maintains professional distance from a subject.

Sociology professor James Rule argues that a legal infrastructure for privacy currently exists and calls for adherence to both the spirit and the letter of the Privacy Act. David Flaherty, a Canadian professor, warns that the individuals or corporations who are responsible for using new technologies do little to consider individual privacy as a primary goal to be maintained.

Former FCC chairman Mark Fowler and his legal assistant, Daniel Brenner, here articulate the most complete rationale for the deregulation of the communications industries. Senator Tim Wirth views deregulation as "not a goal" but a "means to an end" and therefore calls for greater governmental responsibility toward broadcast media.

Parents Music Resource Center (PMRC) requests in congressional testimony that Congress encourage the manufacturers of albums, cassette tapes, and compact discs to establish a rating system for their music. Musician Frank Zappa advocates protecting the musician's First Amendment right to free speech.

Judge Frank Easterbrook holds that an ordinance regulating pornography is an unconstitutional infringement on freedom of speech and press. Psychologist James Dobson is convinced of the devastation inflicted on victims of pornography and lists the ways in which pornography does harm.

Author and reporter Joe McGinniss is convinced that political campaigning is merely a matter of projecting the right image on the television screen to sell the politician to the public. Political scientists Thomas Patterson and Robert McClure explore the effects of political ads on television and conclude that the public is better informed and better able to make decisions as a result of exposure to televised political commercials.

William Rusher, publisher of the *National Review,* says that despite the number of media sources from which we have to choose, most information comes from "the media elite," a small corps reflecting a strongly liberal bias. Michael Robinson and Maura Clancey of the Media Analysis Project at George Washington University find little partisan bias in news reports, but do see a tendency to focus on negative issues.

Professor J. Fred MacDonald investigates media content during the Vietnam War and concludes that society was given a war agenda that reduced the struggle to issues of good versus evil. Author T. D. Allman examines the television documentary that supposedly told the "real" story of Vietnam and concludes that television indeed showed the real story—that Vietnam was about devastation rather than politics.

Hugh Malcolm Beville, a ratings pioneer, defends the credibility and utility of
ratings and argues that ratings provide networks with the information
necessary to make decisions about what the public wants. Todd Gitlin,
professor and popular author, attacks the misuse of ratings data, citing that
when high ratings are demanded of all new programs, cancellation decisions
are made too quickly and the public suffers.

Harvard Business School professor Theodore Levitt presents a philosophical
treatment of the human values of advertising and argues that embellishment
is expected by consumers. Professor Raymond Williams argues that advertising has surpassed its initial goal of selling goods and services and has
become involved with the teaching of social and personal values and exploits
the weaknesses of capitalist societies.

Ben Bagdikian, Pulitzer Prize-winning journalist and professor, contends
that only 23 corporations control America's mass media, with sobering
consequences. Professor Maxwell McCombs questions whether the marketplace of ideas becomes less diverse and responsive to local needs when
competition decreases and finds little evidence for this argument.

INTRODUCTION

Ways of Thinking About Mass Media and Society

Alison Alexander
and Jarice Hanson

Individuals in our society now spend over three hours a day viewing television, which is turned on in the average home over seven hours a day. Politics has emerged from the smoke-filled back room and is played out today in the media. Communications is now a multibillion-dollar industry. From these and other simple examples, we know that media have changed our society. We know that media have an impact, but our understanding of how and why is incomplete.

The dynamic relationship of media and society is very complex. As a result, there are no easy answers to understanding the web of relationships that ties media industries, content, production technologies, and meaning together. Furthermore, the media are not monolithic but are an enormously diverse set of messages, images, and ideas that can be said to originate *in* society and be sent back *to* society.

Many different groups are trying to understand the nature and impact of media systems, each from their own particular perspective. Practitioners must decide on a daily basis what the public will like, will buy, will find offensive, or will simply ignore. Critics are the informal watchdogs of the media and are committed to careful observation and evaluation of the content, practices, and potential influence of media. Social scientists are engaged in the attempt to test theoretical explanations against the observed realities, and each proceed from their own assumptions and goals, and with their own methods. Each provide different, and often contradictory, answers to the puzzling questions that are the focus of this book. Questions of media impact often cause heated debate; some defend, others criticize the media. By including selections from all of these perspectives, we have tried to provide a balanced approach to these debates, an approach that will allow you, the reader, to make an educated evaluation of the issues discussed.

DYNAMICS OF INTERACTION

Communication media are such integral components of our lives that it is easy to take them for granted. *Mass media* is not just a synonym for print, television, radio, or other electronic technologies. Mass media is a particular and special kind of communication that uses sophisticated secondary techniques to extend communication to situations in which face-to-face contact is impossible; that is, mass media provide indirect (or mediated) means by which the primary process of communication is carried out. In an attempt to understand the nature of the mass communication process, we seek to better comprehend both the nature of communication—such as who creates and sends the message, what is communicated, how, and with what result—and the role of the media as agents of the distribution of special types of messages—such as what changes as media "comes between" the sender(s) and the receiver(s) of the messages.

The United States today is rich in media technology. Government statistics report that at the end of 1989, 97.7 percent of American homes had at least one telephone; 98 percent of the homes had access to at least one television set; and 99.2 percent had at least one radio (although the average home had at least five different radio receivers!). Added to these forms of media that have traditionally been included in types of "mass" distribution technologies, we can consider as well the growth of cable television (68 percent of the population in 1989) and the video cassette recorder (VCR) market (55 percent at the end of 1989). Even satellite dishes and cellular phones are increasing in number and augmenting traditional distribution technologies.

Yet many of the questions about media and society remain the same, whatever technology is used. For example: How do audiences use a medium, and what is its influence? To answer that question, we begin by conceiving of groups of "receivers" or "users" as audiences. Audiences are involved in a dual task: receiving messages and producing meaning. The art of receiving is complex, for audiences as receivers of messages do not always perceive or comprehend a message in the exact way that the senders intended it to be received. Also, the audience *produces* meaning, and understanding the role of media in shaping the social reality of audiences (for example, the meanings they produce) is one of the key questions motivating current media research.

Surprisingly, we cannot even agree on what audiences are like. There are a number of dualities in our thinking about audiences: Audiences may be conceived of as active or as passive; they may be seen as having preconceived ideas or as totally responsive to the information provided by media. They may be seen as homogeneous or as fragmented; they may be seen as too intellectually limited to see that television could be harmful or to recognize the limitations of the medium in some cases (i.e., fantasy is entertainment) but not in others (i.e., believing that news is fact); or, on the other hand, they may be seen as critical and evaluative and not easily persuaded or influenced. You will see all these different characterizations of what "audiences" are in this volume.

These conceptions of audience are only part of an attempt to analyze the communication experience. We must also address the unique characteristics of how the medium is used to get a better perspective on the social character of the audience experience. For example, television is primarily a domestic medium. Much of television consumption is in the presence of others and will be discussed with others often in an informal setting such as the home. In realizing the special considerations of each medium, the environment in which it is used, and the conditions surrounding it, we can better understand how media consumption is integrated with everyday life.

NOTIONS Of MASS MEDIA AND THE INDIVIDUAL

The term *mass* implies much more than large numbers and has positive as well as negative connotations. A negative connotation is that of a "mob": unruly, ignorant, easily swayed, lacking in culture, intelligence, and rationality. The Oxford English Dictionary (OED) describes a *mass* as an aggregate in which individuality is lost. On the other hand, the term also supports a concept that denotes the solidarity of people organized to achieve important goals.

Traditional definitions of *mass media* maintained that the messages were created for the consumption of a large, heterogeneous, anonymous audience. Perhaps this definition has become dated because of the nature and amount of media today. Although much of the technology is still capable of catering to a mass audience, it can also be consumed in more intimate surroundings and is often programmed for specific functions by individuals. Video cassette recorders alter the nature of mass media somewhat by allowing the user to record a program in order to view it at a time of one's own choice. The added technology of the "fast forward" VCR button allows viewers to zap commercials or parts of a program not considered important or interesting. Where, then, does the "mass" nature of media fit?

The *mass society* perspective examines not only the nature of the audience as groups of people but also investigates the production of messages that reflect the interests of the dominant elite and provides what senders believe the mass audience will consume or at least tolerate. The mass society perspective has long held a bleak view of large audiences, which are described as acted upon (reactive rather than active) and heterogeneous (large numbers of different people are in the audience) but becoming increasingly homogeneous (in their susceptibility to persuasion). Because of the power of the producers of media messages, the mass society paradigm developed to understand better the political and economic implications of media created by few for the consumption of many. The saying "people only get what they want" is far too simplistic to address the dimensions of what constitutes media content. Decisions about what will be funded, produced, distributed, and marketed call into play a myriad of factors—from moral to economic. If indeed "people only got what they wanted," if only this one-dimensional agenda prevailed, then there would be no such phenomena as the flop, "the sleeper," or the cult media. The relationship of individuals, society, media industries, and time in history all play a part in acceptance or rejection of media content.

HOW MEDIA HAS BEEN STUDIED: FROM THE MAGIC BULLET TO THE INDIRECT EFFECT

Much of media research has been in search of theory. Theory is an organized common-sense refinement of everyday thinking, an attempt to establish a systematic view of a phenomenon in order to better understand that phenomenon. Theory is tested against reality to establish whether or not it is a good explanation. So, for example, a researcher might notice that what is covered by news outlets is very similar to what our citizens say are the important issues of the day. From such observation came agenda setting (the notion that media confers importance on the topics it covers, directing public attention to what is considered important).

Media researchers were faced with an initial view of the nature of humankind that was fundamental to the freedom of the press granted under the First Amendment. Libertarian theory undergirds press freedom and reflects normative and philosophical principles concerning the relation of press to society. These principles are used to evaluate how media, particularly the press, ought to operate: Media should promote a free marketplace of ideas from which rational individuals will come to know the truth. In our system, we assume that freedom of the press should follow the libertarian ideal—that is, to discover truth, check on government, and never be censored by that government. Our sense of social responsibility to that ideal suggests that media should encourage and promote a free and informed discussion of ideas.

Electronic communication challenged these notions of philosophy and individualism in decoding the content of message. The "magic bullet" theory was an early concept stating that media had a major direct effect on the receivers of the message, that the message intended by the senders was indeed injected into the passive receiver. In retrospect, this model seems simplistic, but when it was formulated, society had little experience with mass distribution of messages. The dominant modes of media at that time were print (a very individual experience from the perspective of the user), telephone (also an individual experience), film (viewed in confined environments), and radio (which was the "massest" of all media to that date but still consumed by the extension of the auditory sense rather than the more pervasive all-encompassing experience of watching television). The electronic media challenged past theories of the primacy of the written word and confused researchers seeking a linear, logical explanation for the impact of these new nonlinear, nonlogical media technologies.

The use of social science data to explore the effects of media on audiences strongly emphasized psychological schools of thought. It did not take long to see the limitations of the "magic bullet" theory, and researchers down-shifted from this all-powerful model of direct effect to a more reasonable belief in media's limited effects. How—and how much—then *did* media messages influence the attitudes, beliefs, and behaviors of audiences? The answer seemed to be that media primarily reinforced the status quo. Researchers concluded that media was not a primary cause of human action because more fundamental factors—patterns of thought, culture, and behavior having deep social and historical roots—prevailed.

As media research has matured, the theoretical and conceptual perspectives have increased. But in reevaluating media's influence on how an individual sees reality, one common factor is undeniable: the individuals within the "mass audience" each receive media messages subjectively. While some overarching characteristics of "mass" phenomena may be apparent, we can no longer say with certainty that every member of the audience will act, perceive, or internalize the same message in the same way.

Media research, then, has shifted from addressing specifically effects-oriented paradigms to exploring the nature of the institutions of media production themselves as well as the unique characteristics of each form of media as it contributes to what we know and how we use mediated information. Much of this research has provided a knowledge about the multidimensional aspects of media that transcends traditional social and behavioral methodologies.

Applying this knowledge to policy and personal decisions has served to integrate other fields of psychology, sociology, and popular culture with the perspectives provided by communication studies.

Other levels of analysis have focused on individual, family, group, social, cultural, and societal interpretations of frames of meaning, as well as economically and structurally derived positions of power, held or exercised by specific individuals within social frameworks. These concepts of power have become increasingly important as media becomes more pervasive throughout the world and various societies experience inequities in technologies, resources, and production skills.

Today we question the notions of past theories and models as well as definitions of "mass" and "society" and now place much of the emphasis of media dynamics in the perspective of global information exchange. A major controversy erupted in the early 1970s when many Third World countries disagreed with principles that sought to reify the industrialized nations' media. The New World Information Order noted the importance of media in carrying out developmental tasks within nations that have not had the economic and social benefits of industrialized countries, and it noted that emerging nations had different priorities that reflected indigenous cultures, which would sometimes be at odds with western notions of a free press. Their concerns dealt with power as imposed upon a nation from outside, using media as a vehicle for cultural dependency and imperialism.

THEMES OF CURRENT MASS MEDIA THEORY

In his text *Mass Communication Theory*, Dennis McQuail offers several themes that are currently at issue in mass media theory. Based on his list, we offer the following questions for debate about the influence of media:

1. Is media fragmenting or unifying? The central issue is whether media act as a central or unifying force for society or whether they fragment or decentralize. Beyond that are concerns as to whether these forces are positive or negative. For example, media may be seen as building national identity, political cohesion, or group solidarity. Alternatively, that centralizing force may be seen as promoting a stifling homogenization of taste and class. Fragmentation may be associated with privatization and loneliness (i.e., parasocial interaction—the substitution of mediated for real companionship) but may also be seen as promoting diversity, a cosmopolitan perspective, and providing opportunities for personal growth.

2. Is media a unique force for social change or does it primarily react to social forces? Here the question is whether media is an independent, unique force in social change (as such technological determinists such as Marshall McLuhan argue) or subordinate to evolving society and essentially reactive.

3. Whose interests do the media represent? The opposite poles of this issue can be described as concerns of dominance versus pluralism. Those who view media as an instrument in the hands of the dominant class see media as centralized, standardized, and controlled by a very few. A pluralistic position sees media as responding to demand from many groups in society, diverse and fragmented, with many different voices representing audiences or publics that freely choose which messages they are to receive.

SUMMARY

As the media have grown from infancy to maturity, we have developed numerous theories that seek to explain certain phenomena. We have improved our ability over time to unravel the complex set of interactions that ties the media and society together, but we need to continue to question past results, new practices and technologies, and our own evaluative measures. Theory helps us understand similarities, patterns, and generalizations, but we must not consider theory to be an easy answer for any of the difficult questions we encounter. All issues should be evaluated with regard to their time in history to better develop continuity in not only what we know but in how we come to know it.

PART 1

Mass Media's Role in Society

What are the consequences of our pleasures? Is media "mere entertainment," or are there serious side effects of our national preoccupation with television and other forms of mediated enjoyment? Do media merely reflect the social attitudes and concerns of our times, or are they also able to construct, legitimate, and reinforce social realities and attitudes? Should our concern be directed toward vulnerable populations such as children? Or, perhaps, is such concern our way of avoiding the more difficult issue of how media may truly influence us? Questions about the place of media within our technologically reliant society—both as a place for displaying our culture and as a force for cultural change—cannot be ignored.

Are American Values Shaped by the Mass Media?

Media Images of Blacks: Does "The Cosby Show" Adequately Address Issues of Race?

Is Television Harmful for Children?

Are Media Messages About Women Improving?

ISSUE 1

Are American Values Shaped by the Mass Media?

YES: Michael Novak, from "Television Shapes the Soul," in Sellars and Rivers, eds., *Mass Media Issues* (Prentice Hall, 1977).

NO: Walter Karp, from "Where the Media Critics Went Wrong," *American Heritage* (March 1988)

ISSUE SUMMARY

YES: Social critic and author Michael Novak argues that television shapes the soul by affecting our perceptions of reality and that, furthermore, this reality is produced by an intellectual elite, who are the writers, producers, and executives of the media industry, who represent only a small portion of our society.

NO: Historian Walter Karp asserts that fears in the 1950s that media would result in a mass society have proven to be unfounded, that individuals are resistant to the mass conformity and passivity that was feared, and that the messages the media offer us are not quite as oriented toward the status quo as the media critics would have us believe.

Can media fundamentally shape the interpretation of social reality? Arguments that media are powerful in the shaping of attitudes and opinions generally assume that the end result of such forces will be the homogenization of the American public. This homogenization is the logical consequence of a socialized viewer assaulted by years of consistent and limited messages. In American society, where access to the economic and cultural resources is limited, these messages are controlled by an elite group who own the media and are able to impose their perceptions and values on the rest of society. Thus, such conclusions of those who find the benefits of a popular medium like television to be overwhelmed by the attendant perils are formed by a view of society as a clash between unequal powers—the power of television's owners and programmers pitted against that of viewers lulled into receiving the medium's distorted view of reality through an uncritical acceptance of its messages.

Others disagree with this view and instead see the individual as resilient in the face of a barrage of media messages and quite capable of deciphering these messages for what they really are. And besides, they would add, the

2

individual is complex and subject to a whole host of influences (family, school, church, peers, culture, and so on), such that singling out the influence of television in shaping of the individual may be more difficult than at first it would appear.

These are not easy issues. Some days we hear of distorted news stories, see friends "dying" for the newest fashion, or hear of a new technology that will change our lives. Media is so pervasive that it is hard to believe it does not have important effects. Alternatively, few of us believe that media have personally made us buy products, harmed us, or holds a place of "prime importance" in our lives. Thus, our everyday lived experience is not one of media having an observable impact on us or on those around us. To attempt, however, to understand how media may shape the attitudes of ourselves, our friends, others in society, and the culture itself requires that we try to stand back from our personal experience to judge.

Michael Novak argues that "television is a molder of the soul's geography." His two major points are that television affects our perceptions of reality and that these effects spring from class bias. His argument implies that television does have the power to change fundamentally human consciousness and is explicit in stating that the media is dominated by an elite. In contrast, Walter Karp reflects on the fears prevalent in the early 1950s that television would generate "mass conformity, mass passivity, and loss of autonomy." Subsequent history, he argues, hardly supports that position but leads instead to the conclusion that commercial mass entertainment in this country is a wonderfully inefficient tool of mass persuasion. His position assumes that individuals are formed by a host of social pressures, with media only one among them—and in his mind, a rather inefficient one. Additionally, Karp argues for the "openness" of media messages and points to the Western and to comedic figures as providing messages that were much more than "nothing but entertainment and distraction."

YES

Michael Novak

TELEVISION SHAPES THE SOUL

For twenty-five years we have been immersed in a medium never before experienced on this earth. We can be forgiven if we do not yet understand all the ways in which this medium has altered us, particularly our inner selves, the perceiving, mythic, symbolic—and the judging, critical—parts of ourselves.

Media, like instruments, work "from the outside in." If you practice the craft of writing sedulously, you begin to think and perceive differently. If you run for twenty minutes a day, your psyche is subtly transformed. If you work in an executive office, you begin to think like an executive. And if you watch six hours of television, on the average, every day . . .?

Innocent of psychological testing and sociological survey, I would like to present a humanist's analysis of what television seems to be doing to me, to my students, to my children, and, in general, to those I see around me (including those I see on television, in movies, in magazines). My method is beloved of philosophers, theologians, cultural critics: try to *perceive*, make *distinctions, coax into the light* elusive movements of consciousness. It goes without saying that others will have to verify the following observations; they are necessarily in the hypothetical mode, even if some of the hypotheses have a cogency that almost bites.

Two clusters of points may be made. The first, rather metaphysical, concerns the way television affects our way of perceiving and approaching reality. The second cluster concerns the way television inflicts a class bias on the world of our perceptions—the bias of a relatively small and special social class.

TELEVISION AND REALITY

Television is a molder of the soul's geography. It builds up incrementally a psychic structure of expectations. It does so in much the same way that school lessons slowly, over the years, tutor the unformed mind and teach it "how to think." . . .

It is possible to isolate five or six ways in which television seems to affect those who watch it. Television series represent genres of artistic performance. They structure a viewer's way of perceiving, of making connections, and of following a story line. Try, for example, to bring to consciousness the difference between the experience of watching television and the experience of learning through reading, argument, the advice of elders, lectures in school, or other forms of structuring perception. The conventions of the various sorts of television series re-create different sorts of "worlds." These "worlds" raise questions—and, to some extent, illuminate certain features of experience that we notice in ourselves and around us as we watch.

Suppose that you were a writer for a television show—an action-adventure, a situation comedy, even a variety show. You would want to be very careful to avoid "dead" spots, "wooden" lines, "excess" verbiage. Every line has a function, even a double or triple function. Characters move on camera briskly, every line counts, the scene shifts rapidly. In comedy, every other line should be a laugh-getter. Brevity is the soul of hits.

Television is a teacher of expectations; it speeds up the rhythm of attention. Any act in competition with television must approach the same pace; otherwise it will seem "slow." . . .

But not only the pace is fast. Change of scene and change of perspective are also fast. In [an episode] of *Kojak*, [for example,] action in three or four parts of the city was kept moving along in alternating sequences of a minute or less. A "principle of association" was followed; some image in the last frames of one scene suggested a link to the first frames of the new scene. But one scene cut away from another very quickly.

The progression of a television show depends upon multiple logics—two or three different threads are followed si-

multaneously. The viewer must figure out the connections between people, between chains of action, and between scenes. Many clues are *shown*, not *said*. The viewer must detect them.

The logic of such shows is not sequential in a single chain. One subject is raised, then cut, and another subject is picked up, then cut. Verbal links—"Meanwhile, on the other side of the city . . ."—are not supplied.

In teaching and in writing I notice that for students one may swiftly change the subject, shift the scene, drop a line of argument in order to pick it up later—and not lose the logic of development. Students understand such a performance readily. They have been prepared for it. The systems of teaching which I learned in my student days—careful and exact exegesis proceeding serially from point to point, the careful definition and elucidation of terms in an argument and the careful scrutiny of chains of inference, and the like—now meet a new form of resistance. . . . [T]oday the minds and affections of the brighter students are teeming with images, vicarious experiences, and indeed of actual travel and accomplishments. Their minds race ahead and around the flanks of lines of argument. "Dialectics" rather than "logic" or "exegesis" is the habit of mind they are most ready for. I say this neither in praise nor in blame; pedagogy must deal with this new datum, if it is new. What are its limits and its possibilities? What correctives are needed among students—and among teachers?

The periodization of attention is also influenced by the format of television. For reasons of synchronized programming the ordinary television show is neatly divided into segments of approximately equal length, and each of these segments normally has its own dramatic rhythm so as to build to dramatic climax or sub-climax, with the appropriate degree of suspense or resolution . . . [T]he timing of television shows tutors their audience to expect a certain rhythm of development. The competitive pressures of television, moreover, encourage producers to "pack" as much action, intensity, or (to speak generally) entertainment into each segment as possible. . . .

Character is as important to successful shows as action; audiences need to "identify" with the heroes of the show, whether dramatic or comic. Thus in some ways the leisure necessary to develop character may provide a counter-tendency to the need for melodramatic rapidity. Still, "fast-paced" and "laugh-packed" and other such descriptions express the sensibility that television both serves and reinforces.

Television tutors the sensibilities of its audience in another way: it can handle only a limited range of human emotions, perplexities, motivations, and situations. The structure of competitive television seems to require this limitation; it springs from a practiced estimation of the capacity of the audience. Critics sometimes argue that American novelists have a long tradition of inadequacy with respect to the creation of strong, complicated women and, correspondingly, much too simple and superficial a grasp of the depths and complexities of human love. . . . If such critical judgments may be true of our greatest artists working in their chosen media, then, a fortiori, it is not putting down television to note that the range of human relations treated by artists on television is less than complete. The constraints under which television artists work are acute: the time available to them, the segmentation of this time,

and the competitive pressures they face for intense dramatic activity. To develop a fully complicated set of motivations, internal conflicts, and inner contradictions requires time and sensitivity to nuance. The present structure of television makes these requirements very difficult to meet.

This point acquires fuller significance if we note the extent to which Americans depend upon television for their public sense of how other human beings behave in diverse situations. The extent of this dependence should be investigated. In particular, we ought to examine the effects of the growing segregation of Americans by age. It does not happen frequently nowadays that children grow up in a household shared by three generations, in a neighborhood where activities involve members of all generations, or in a social framework where generation-mixing activities are fairly common. I have many times been told by students (from suburban environments, in particular) that they have hardly ever, or never, had a serious conversation with adults. . . . Their images of what adults do and how adults think and act were mainly supplied by various media, notably television and the cinema. The issue such comments raise is significant. Where *could* most Americans go to find dramatic models of adult behavior? In the eyes of young people does the public weight of what is seen on television count for more than what they see in their private world as a model for "how things are done"? Indeed, do adults themselves gain a sense of what counts as acceptable adult behavior from the public media?

If it turns out to be true that television (along with other media like magazines and the cinema) now constitutes a major source of guidance for behavior, to be placed in balance with what one learns from one's parents, from the churches, from one's local communities, and the like, then the range of dramatic materials on television has very serious consequences for the American psyche. While human behavior is to a remarkable extent diverse and variable, it tends to be "formed" and given shape by the attraction or the power of available imaginative materials: stories, models, symbols, images-in-action. The storehouse of imaginative materials available to each person provides a sort of repertoire. The impact of new models can be a powerful one, leading to "conversions," "liberations," or "new directions." The reservoir of acquired models exerts a strong influence both upon perception and upon response to unfamiliar models. If family and community ties weaken and if psychic development becomes somewhat more nuclearized or even atomized, the influence of television and other distant sources may well become increasingly powerful, moving, as it were, into something like a vacuum. Between the individual and the national source of image-making there will be little or no local resistance. The middle ground of the psyche, until recently thick and rich and resistant, will have become attenuated. . . .

Television also seems to conceive of itself as a national medium. It does not favor the varieties of accent, speech patterns, and other differences of the culture of the United States. It favors a language which might be called "televisionese"—a neutral accent, pronunciation, and diction perhaps most closely approximated in California.

Since television arises in the field of "news" and daily entertainment, television values highly a kind of topicality, instant reflection of trends, and an effort to be "with it" and even "swinging." It values the "front edge" of attention, and it dreads being outrun by events. Accordingly, its product is perishable. It functions, in a way, as a guide to the latest gadgets and to the wonders of new technologies, or, as a direct contrary, to a kind of nostalgia for simpler ways in simpler times. Fashions of dress, automobiles, and explicitness "date" a series of shows. (Even the techniques used in taping shows may date them.)

Thus television functions as an instrument of the national, mobile culture. It does not reinforce the concrete ways of life of individual neighborhoods, towns, or subcultures. It shows the way things are done (or fantasized as being done) in "the big world." It is an organ of Hollywood and New York, not of Macon, Peoria, Salinas, or Buffalo. . . . But, in general, television is an organ of nationalization, of homogenization—and, indeed, of a certain systematic inaccuracy about the actual, concrete texture of life in the United States.

This nationalizing effect also spills over into the news and the documentaries. The cultural factors which deeply affect the values and perceptions of various American communities are neglected; hence the treatment of problems affecting such communities is frequently oversimplified. This is especially true when matters of group conflict are involved. The tendency of newsmen is subtly to take sides and to regard some claims or behavior as due to "prejudice," others as rather more moral and commendable.

The mythic forms and story lines of the news and documentaries are not inconsonant with the mythic forms represented in the adventure stories and Westerns. "Good" and "evil" are rather clearly placed in conflict. "Hard-hitting" investigative reporting is mythically linked to classic American forms of moral heroism: the crimebuster, the incorruptible sheriff. The forces of law and progress ceaselessly cut into the jungle of corruption. There is continuity between the prime-time news and prime-time programming—much more continuity than is detected by the many cultivated Cyclopses who disdain "the wasteland" and praise the documentaries. The mythic structure of both is harmonious.

It should prove possible to mark out the habits of perception and mind encouraged by national television. If these categories are not decisive, better ones can surely be discerned. We might then design ways of instructing ourselves and our children in countervailing habits. It does not seem likely that the mind and heart tutored by many years of watching television (in doses of five or six hours a day) is in the same circumstance as the mind and heart never exposed to television. Education and criticism must, it seems, take this difference into account.

THE CLASS BIAS OF TELEVISION

Television has had two striking effects. On the one hand, as Norman Podhoretz has remarked, it has not seemed to prevent people from reading; more books are being published and mass marketed than ever before in American history. It is possible that television stimulates many to go beyond what television itself can offer.

Secondly, television works, or appears to work, as a homogenizing world to a national audience. In many respects, it could be shown, the overall ideological tendency of television productions—from the news, through the talk shows, to the comedy hours, variety shows, and adventure, crime, and family shows—is that of a vague and misty liberalism: belief in the efficacy of an ultimate optimism, "talking through one's problems," a questioning of institutional authorities, a triumph of good over evil. . . . In harmony with the images of progress built into both liberalism and capitalism, television seems, however gently, to undercut traditional institutions and to promote a restless, questioning attitude. The main product—and attitude—it has to sell is the new.

This attachment to the new ensures that television will be a vaguely leftist medium, no matter who its personnel might be. Insofar as it debunks traditions and institutions—and even the act of *representing* these in selective symbolic form is a kind of veiled threat to them—television serves the purposes of that large movement within which left and right (in America, at least) are rather like the two legs of locomotion: the movement of modernization. It serves, in general, the two mammoth institutions of modern life: the state and the great corporations. It serves these institutions even when it exalts the individual at the expense of family, neighborhood, religious organizations, and cultural groups. These are the only intermediate institutions that stand between the isolated individual and the massive institutions.

Thus the homogenizing tendencies of television are ambivalent. Television can electrify and unite the whole nation, creating an instantaneous network in which millions are simultaneously recipients of the same powerful images. But to what purpose, for whose use, and to what effect? Is it an unqualified good that the national grid should become so pre-eminent, superior to any and all local checks and balances? The relative national power and influence of state governors seems to have been weakened, for example; a state's two senators, by comparison, occupy a national stage and can more easily become national figures.

But in at least five other ways national television projects a sense of reality that is not identical to the sense of reality actual individuals in their concrete environments share. Taken together, these five ways construct a national social reality that is not free of a certain class and even ethnic bias. The television set becomes a new instrument of reality—of "what's happening" in the larger, national world, of "where it's at." In some sense what isn't on television isn't quite real, is not part of the nationally shared world, will be nonexistent for millions of citizens. . . .

[A]nyone who has participated in a large-scale event comes to recognize vividly how strait and narrow is the gate between what has actually happened and what gets on television. For the millions who see the television story, of course, the story is the reality. For those who lived through a strenuous sixteen-hour day on the campaign trail, for example, it is always something of a surprise to see what "made" the television screen—or, more accurately, what the television screen made real. That artificial reality turns out to have far more substance for the world at large than the lived sixteen hours. According to the ancient *maya*, the world of flesh and blood is an illusion. And so it is.

Television is a new technology and depends upon sophisticated crafts. It is a world of high profit. Its inside world is populated by persons in a high income bracket. Moreover, television is a world that requires a great deal of travel, expense-account living, a virtual shuttle between Los Angeles and New York, a taste for excellent service and high prestige. These economic factors seriously color television's image of the world.

The glitter of show business quickly spread to television. In the blossomy days when thinkers dreamed of an affluent society and praised the throwaway society, the shifting and glittering sets of television make-believe seemed like a metaphor for modern society. . . .

Moreover, the selling of products requires images of upward mobility. The sets, designs, and fluid metaphors of the shows themselves must suggest a certain richness, smoothness, and adequacy. It is not only that writers and producers understand that what audiences desire is escape. . . . It is also the case, apparently, that an inner imperative drives writers, producers, and sponsors to project their *own* fantasies. Not all Americans, by far, pursue upward mobility as a way of life. A great many teach their children to have modest expectations and turn down opportunities for advancement and mobility that would take them away from their familiar worlds.

The myths of the upwardly mobile and the tastes of the very affluent govern the visual symbols, the flow, and the chatter of television.

The class bias of television reality proceeds not only from the relative economic affluence of the industry and its personnel. It springs as well from the educational level. "Televisionese" sends a clear and distinct message to the people, a message of exclusion and superiority. . . .

Television is a parade of experts instructing the unenlightened about the weather, aspirins, toothpastes, the latest books or proposals for social reform, and the correct attitudes to have with respect to race, poverty, social conflict, and new moralities. Television is preeminently a world of intellectuals. Academic persons may be astonished to learn of it and serious writers and artists may hear the theme with withering scorn, but for most people in the United States television is the medium through which they meet an almost solid phalanx of college-educated persons, professionals, experts, thinkers, authorities, and "with it," "swinging" celebrities: i.e., people unlike themselves who are drawn from the top ten percent of the nation in terms of educational attainment. . . .

Television is the greatest instrument the educated class has ever had to parade its wares before the people. . . .

It is important to understand that the disdain for "popular culture" often heard in intellectual circles is seriously misplaced. Television, at least, more nearly represents the world of the educated ten percent than it reflects the world of the other ninety percent. At most, one might say in defense, the world of television represents the educated class's fantasies about the fantasies of the population. . . .

The interviews recorded by Robert Coles, for example, tend to show that persons of the social class represented by Archie Bunker are at least as complicated, many-sided, aware of moral ambiguities, troubled and sensitive, as the intellectuals who appear on television, in novels, or in the cinema. Artists who might use the materials of ordinary life for their creations are systematically separated from ordinary people by the economic conditions of creativity in the United States.

The writers, producers, actors, and journalists of television are [also] separated from most of the American population . . . by the culture in which their . . . lives are lived out. By "culture" I mean those implicit, lived criteria that suggest to each of us what is real, relevant, significant, meaningful in the buzzing confusion of our experience: how we select out and give shape to our world. The culture of prime-time television is, it appears, a serious dissolvant of the cultures of other Americans. The culture of television celebrates to an extraordinary degree two mythic strains in the American character: the lawless and the irreverent. On the first count, stories of cowboys, gangsters, and spies still preoccupy the American imagination. On the second, the myth of "enlightenment" from local standards and prejudices still dominates our images of self-liberation and sophistication. No doubt the stronghold of a kind of priggish righteousness in several layers of American history leads those who rebel to find their rebellion all too easy. It is as though the educated admonish one another that they "can't go home again" and that the culture against which they rebel is solid and unyielding.

But what if it isn't? What if the perception of culture on the part of millions is, rather, that chaos and the jungle are constantly encroaching and that the rule of good order is threatened in a dozen transactions every day—by products that don't work, by experts and officials who take advantage of lay ignorance, by muggings and robberies, by jobs and pensions that disappear, by schools that do not work in concert with the moral vision of the home?

Television keeps pressing on the barriers of cultural resistance to obscenities, to some forms of sexual behavior, and to various social understandings concerning work and neighborhood and family relationships. . . .

Television, and the mass media generally, have vested interests in new moralities. The excitement of transgressing inhibitions is gripping entertainment. There are, however, few vested interests wishing to strengthen the inhibitions which make such transgressions good entertainment. Television is only twenty-five years old. We have very little experience or understanding proportionate to the enormous moral stakes involved. It is folly to believe that *laissez-faire* works better in moral matters than in economic matters or that enormous decisions in these matters are not already being made in the absence of democratic consent. When one kind of show goes on the air others are excluded during that time. The present system is effectively a form of social control.

I do not advocate any particular solution to this far-ranging moral dilemma; I do not know what to recommend. But the issue is a novel one for a free society, and we do not even have a well-thought-out body of options from which to choose. In the vacuum a rather-too-narrow social class is making the decisions. The pressures of the free market (so they say) now guide them. Is that so? Should it be so?

Because of the structure and history of the social class that produces prime-time television, group conflict in the United States is also portrayed in a simplistic and biased way. The real diversity of American cultures and regions is shrouded in public ignorance. Occasional disruptions, like the rebellion of West Virginia miners against certain textbooks and the rebellion of parents in South Boston against what they perceived as downward mobility for their children and themselves, are as quickly as possible brushed from consciousness. America is pictured as though it were divided between one vast homogeneous "middle America," to be enlightened, and the enlighteners. In fact, there are several "middle Americas." . . .

It seems, moreover, that the social class guiding the destiny of television idealizes certain ethnic groups—the legitimate minorities—even while this class offers in its practices no greater evidence of genuine egalitarianism than other social classes. At the same time this class seems extremely slow to comprehend the experiences of other American cultures. One of the great traumas of human history was the massive migration to America during the last 100 years. It ought to be one of the great themes of high culture, and popular culture as well. Our dramatists neglect it.

Group conflict has, moreover, been the rule in every aspect of American life, from labor to corporate offices to neighborhoods to inter-ethnic marriages. Here, too, the drama is perhaps too real and vivid to be touched: *these* are inhibitions the liberal culture of television truly respects . . . Artists are still exploring the edges of how much reality can be given voice and how to voice it. These are difficult, even explosive, matters. Integrity and care are required.

It must seem odd to writers and producers to be accused of having a "liberal" bias when they are so aware of the limitations they daily face and the grueling battles they daily undergo. But why do they have these battles except that they have a point of view and a moral passion? We are lucky that the social class responsible for the creative side of television is not a reactionary and frankly illiberal class. Still, that it is a special class is itself a problem for all of us, including those involved in it.

NO
Walter Karp

WHERE THE MEDIA CRITICS
WENT WRONG

Way back when I was a teenager, it was common knowledge that the mass media—newly reinforced by television—were generating mass conformity, mass passivity, and mass "loss of autonomy." They were even producing a new kind of dismal American, a truly ominous being, grimly referred to as "mass man." In other words, it was common knowledge that the one thing we could not expect from the forthcoming 1960s—still hidden then in the womb of time—was exactly what we got from the turbulent era: a vast revival of political activity, a vast throwing off of the chains of conformity, and an exhibition of youthful autonomy so appalling to many a media critic that when last heard from they were blaming television for breeding unrest and political rebellion. Not since it was common knowledge that international trade made war obsolete (this was in 1914) had humankind's bottomless capacity for mischief proved so many reputable social thinkers so devastatingly wrong.

To find out why the early media critics had gone so far astray—for it is not easy to be completely wrong—I decided not long ago to return to the scene of the accident, by which I mean those anxious postwar years when "What Is Television Doing to Us?" (*The New York Times Magazine,* June 12, 1949) was a question to which every right-thinking American expected an unpleasant answer—and invariably got one. Whether it was the famed theologian Reinhold Niebuhr predicting in 1949 that "much of what is still wholesome in our lives will perish under the impact of this visual aid" or hack writers predicting the death of conversation and the onset of mass myopia ("Does Television Cause Eyestrain?" *House Beautiful,* August 1950), virtually the entire discussion of television's influence took place in an atmosphere of hand-wringing hysteria.

Curiously enough, this hysterical atmosphere had nothing directly to do with television itself. What inspired it was the unnerving national experience of wartime propaganda. Four years of "Rosie the Riveter," "Loose Lips Sink Ships," and "Uncle Joe" Stalin, combined with terrifying reports of Hitler's irresistible "big-lie technique," had persuaded a remarkable number of Americans that mass propaganda was a new power too great for "the masses" to withstand.

"Politically, a lever of frightening efficiency has been devised," warned Mahonri Sharp Young in the Spring 1948 issue of *The American Scholar.* "New techniques of mass persuasion are being designed to manipulate a supposedly spontaneous public opinion. The existence of radio's influence can hardly be doubted. Argument occurs only over its extent and its depth." Two issues later in the same learned journal, Joseph T. Klapper observed that it was now commonly believed that "never before" in human history "has public opinion lain so completely at the mercy of whoever may be in control" of the mass media. Now add the visual impact of television to this "frightening" power of radio, MGM, and *Life* magazine and the mass media truly looked like the new master and dictator of the world. They had become, warned the eminent critic Gilbert Seldes, "as powerful in shaping our lives as our schools, our politics, our system of government."

But was it? The power of the wartime propaganda rested on the fact that every means of persuasion had been concerted and coordinated to convey the same basic message: "V for Victory," "Beat the Axis," "E for Effort," win the war, and do your bit. If the mass media were really as powerful as the critics believed, then mass entertainment in peacetime America was not only a *potential* instrument of mass propaganda—which, of course, it is—but already the conveyer of concerted, coordinated mass propaganda. Beneath the surface of miscellaneous amusements, the mass media carried a propaganda message, and the early critics thought they knew exactly what it was. "The message is invariably that of identification with the *status quo,*" wrote T. W. Adorno, the social psychologist, in 1954. "These media have taken on the job of rendering mass publics conformative to the social and economic status quo," said Paul Lazarsfeld in his authoritative study *Radio and the Printed Page.* "The whole entertainment side of broadcasting which surrounds the communication of ideas," wrote Seldes, "tends to create a mood of consent and acceptance. It cannot afford to stir and agitate the mind." Agitation does not sell soap; agitation displeases the sponsors. Inevitably, wrote Lazarsfeld, "commercially-sponsored mass media indirectly but effectively restrain the cogent development of a genuinely critical attitude."

The very popularity of the mass media preserved the status quo. Popularity demanded the purveying of the "nationally common denominator of attitudes," and the early critics had few doubts about what Americans held in common: a view of life so shallow that, according to Adorno, "the 'message' of adjustment and unreflecting obedience seems to be dominant and all-pervasive today." Donald Duck was popular with the masses, observed Irving Howe, because he "has something of the SS man in him," and the American people, "having something of the SS man in us, naturally find [him] quite charming."

The mass media operated on the mass audience like a deadly opiate. They "expedited flight from unbearable reality," Leo Lowenthal pointed out in a 1950 issue of the *American Journal of Sociology.* "Wherever revolutionary tendencies show a timid head, they are mitigated and cut short by a false fulfilment of wish-dreams, like wealth, adventure, passionate love, power, and sensationalism in general."

A poisonous passivity was entering the national bloodstream. "Increasing dosages of mass communication may be inadvertently transforming the energies of men from active participation into passive knowledge," warned Lazarsfeld. "The occurrence of this narcotizing dysfunction can scarcely be doubted," and almost nobody did doubt it. Like an electronic vampire, the mass media sucked the life-force out of the people, robbing them of their inner strength. "The repetitiveness, the selfsameness, and the ubiquity of modern mass culture tend to make for automatized reactions," said Dr. Adorno, "and to weaken the forces of individual resistance." Gunther Anders, a radical, called this inner weakening "depersonalization." Ernest Van Der Haag, a conservative, called it "deindividualization." Whatever it was called, it was reducing Americans to a state of zombielike inner docility, especially the children, whose "strength and imagination" were being steadily sapped by television, according to Marya Mannes, the TV critic of the *Reporter* magazine.

Television shows were full of gunplay, fisticuffs, and crime stories. The inevitable result, said the critics, was that Americans were growing "callous" toward human suffering. News programs and variety shows mixed so many different things together, according to the critics, that the audience could make little sense of anything. Seeing Edward R. Murrow interview Krishna Menon, India's ambassador to the United States, in the first segment of "Person to Person" and Eva Gabor immediately following could only lead viewers to conclude, warned Murray Hausknecht, that the two were of "equal value." Early television was full of petty impostures. The hostess of a celebrity talk show, circa 1950, would hear the doorbell ring in her studio "living room" and exclaim, "Now who can that be?" as if the celebrities dropped in by surprise. This constant exposure to deception, warned Mannes, meant the "dulling of perception between true and false." The "senses" of the American people were becoming so "blunted" by television deceptions, warned Seldes, "they cannot tell truth from falsehood."

In short, whatever seemed likely to keep Americans in a state of vassalage the media effectively supplied—or so the students of "mass culture" insisted until a great democratic revival erupted in America for the first time in fifty years. Before the upheaval subsided, the alleged victims of the mass propaganda of "unreflecting obedience" had cast two Presidents—Johnson and Nixon—out of the White House.

Why had the great engine of passivity failed so badly, and why had the mass propaganda of conformity had so little effect? The answer is that commercial mass entertainment in America is a wonderfully inefficient tool of mass persuasion. The reason the early critics of the media failed to see this was that they assumed its efficiency in advance, made that "frightening efficiency" their starting point, and were blind to all evidence to the contrary.

The comedian Milton Berle is a good case in point. While the critics wrote of the media's "selfsameness" and their "stereotypes," the comic persona of the most dominating figure on television in those years was an outrageous egomaniac, so extravagantly shameless that nobody could have invented him except himself. So far from affirming "sanctioned attitudes," as the media were supposed to do, Berle trampled on every rule of decorum. Nor did he generate the required "mood of consent," since he was not only the most popular entertainer on television but also, as polls showed, the most widely detested one. I knew people who would drive nerve-racking miles on near-empty gas tanks just to avoid buying Texaco gasoline, the sponsor of the Berle show. To well-bred, right-thinking people, Berle's "message" was all too anarchic.

When Jackie Gleason supplanted Berle in public favor, the media critics did not modify by an iota their belief that the media "expedited flight from unbearable reality." Yet Gleason's Ralph Kramden in "The Honeymooners" was almost unbearably real. Envy and vanity made him a fool, and folly made him cruel and dishonest. The portrait was pitiless, as Seldes himself admitted, and the moral a harsh one, harsh yet profoundly humane: It takes strength and integrity just to be decent. Such was the weekly theme of an immensely popular television program while the critics were accusing the media of reproducing the smugness and intellectual passivity that seem to fit in with totalitarianism.

Blind to any virtues in popular things, the media critics took it for granted, noted Lowenthal in a survey of mass-culture studies, that the "media are estranged from values and offer nothing but entertainment and distractions." If something amused a vast number of Americans, it had to be degrading, or how else could it serve as mass propaganda?

In that bigoted spirit the critics could see nothing valuable, for example, in the American Western except infantile violence. According to Mannes, the entire genre could be summed up as "good

men and bad men who rode horses over magnificent country and decided issues by shooting each other." Yet it was the grand and terrible theme of the old-time Western that some issues could not be peaceably resolved: The dusty wooden cowboy town is in thrall to a tyrant, the local cattle baron, or the gambling casino owner; the sheriff is the tyrant's drunken tool; the churchgoing good folk are helplessly dithering. Nothing but armed insurrection can overthrow the tyranny and "clean up the town." Where is the message of subservience in that? Many Westerns could have been denounced as "subversive" had they not been so thoroughly American.

When a Senate judiciary subcommittee began investigating the influence of television on the juvenile crime rate in 1954, the senators saw precious little "narcotic dysfunction" generated by television. What worried them was television's all-too-stimulating incitement to mischief. Nor were they impressed by the media's power to "engineer consent." In its final report the subcommittee complained bitterly that television's judges, lawyers, and policemen were too often dishonest, incompetent, and stupid. Two decades later conservatives complained that big businessmen on television were too often portrayed as downright criminals. To the political leadership of America, the mass media have been, if anything, a little too *irreverent* for comfort.

Interestingly enough, the one truly prescient observation made in the 1950s about the impact of television was made by professional politicians. After seeing what the plot-ridden Republican National Convention looked like on television in 1952, politicians freely predicted that "TV would be the making of the direct Presidential primary," as Walter

Goodman reported in *The New Republic*. And so it was, although it took a rebellion against an unpopular war to complete the job television had begun.

The reason the politicians were right goes a long way toward explaining why the media critics were wrong. America's politicians understood television's menace to the old nominating system because they never lost sight of the central truth about American life: that the American people believe devoutly in democracy, that we hate to see it openly violated, that we love to see its values affirmed and triumphant, even in our "entertainment and distractions." That is why the mass media performed so poorly as an engine of social control and passive obedience. In America you cannot promote deference and successfully sell soap. You cannot promote servility and amuse a vast audience. The popular understanding of democracy may not be precise or exacting; but our love of democracy runs deep, and that love has done more to shape the media than the media have done to shape us. That was what the early critics overlooked so completely. Appalled by the power of mass propaganda, they concluded that the masses everywhere were empty and pliant and that Americans cherished nothing strongly enough to resist the designs of lawless ambition. That they were so largely in error is a truth well worth remembering in our darker hours.

POSTSCRIPT

Are American Values Shaped by the Mass Media?

Television is pervasive in American life. Yet the influence of television on society is difficult to ascertain. For example, a number of things have changed drastically since television was introduced in the 1950s—the election process, drug use, crime, lowering of SAT scores, the entry of many women into the work force. Did television cause all that? Of course not, but was it a contributing factor in these changes? How much influence did it have, and, most importantly, how could we answer questions about television or media influence?

One school of thought argues that television's primary effect is to reinforce the status quo. Does television contribute to the homogenization of society and promote middle-class values? Although television has certainly become a shared experience for many, how important it is in maintaining or changing the country's laws or norms remains to be established.

Yet some effects have been dramatically illustrated. For example, television is now the primary source of news for most Americans. Television's ability to bring events to millions of viewers may mean that television itself is a factor in determining the events (consider, for example, political terrorism and the role television plays in it).

Television has reshaped American politics but may have little influence on how people actually vote. Television has also altered the ways Americans spend their leisure time, ranking third behind sleep and work in the amount of time spent on it.

Dennis McQuail in *Mass Communication Theory: An Introduction*, 2nd edition, (Sage, 1987), provides an insightful review of mass communication theory with particular emphasis on the usefulness of theories of society for the understanding of the influence of mass communication. Robert Kubey and Mihaly Csikszentmihalyi in *Television and the Quality of Life: How Viewing Shapes Everyday Experience* (Erlbaum, 1990) examine audience activity and the place of media in the organization of everyday life.

17

ISSUE 2

Media Images of Blacks: Does "The Cosby Show" Adequately Address Issues of Race?

YES: John D. H. Downing, from " 'The Cosby Show' and American Racial Discourse," in Smitherman-Donaldson and van Dijk, eds., *Discourse and Discrimination*, (Wayne State University Press, 1988).

NO: Michael Dyson, from "Bill Cosby and the Politics of Race," *Z Magazine*, (September 1989)

ISSUE SUMMARY

YES: Professor John Downing states that "The Cosby Show" allows for the analysis of discourse about race in a racist society, particularly because this show is atypical and highly popular, and he concludes that its treatment of sexism, the family, and social class has enabled it to convey positive messages to multiple audiences.
NO: Philosopher and media critic Michael Dyson argues that "The Cosby Show" has been successful in addressing major social problems, such as sexism, and so should not ignore in the way it does the problems of racism. He feels that the juxtaposition of comedy and conscience is not impossible and that this show has the moral authority to show that concern for issues of race should be the concern of all human beings.

Few shows in the history of television programming have been as universally loved and applauded as "The Cosby Show," which revived the situation comedy—a genre that some media critics had declared moribund—as the smash hit of the 1984 season. Since then "Cosby" has been hailed as a breakthrough in the portrayal of black families.

Throughout the history of television programming, portrayals of black family units were, for the most part, absent from television. Premiering in 1968, "Julia" was the first program starring a black person to do well in the ratings since the infamous "Amos 'n' Andy." Diahann Carrol starred as a widow and nurse raising her young son. Although it was popular, many blacks found Julia too assimilated into the white middle class. Despite the rarity of programs with black lead characters, viewers saw frequent coverage of the civil rights movement during that era. The 1970s saw the introduction of a number of shows focusing on black families. In 1971, Norman Lear introduced "Sanford and Son," a situation comedy starring Redd Foxx as a junk dealer in business with his son in Watts in Los Angeles. In 1972, Lear introduced "Good Times," a portrayal of a ghetto family with particular attention to their problem son, J. J.—comedian Jimmy Walker. Finally, in 1975, Lear introduced "The Jeffersons." These financially successful shows paved the way for programs that highlighted black characters and families. Yet these shows have all been criticized for flaws such as falling back on racial stereotypes for their comedic effect, failing to portray strong black fathers, and not providing professional role models. The 1980s brought an end to these criticisms with "The Cosby Show," a portrayal of an upper-middle-class family in which Dr. Heathcliff Huxtable and his lawyer wife, Claire, humorously and competently deal with the domestic issues involved in raising five children.

There are many reasons to like the Huxtables. As John Downing notes, "Cosby" is a show that is out of the ordinary in many ways. This is a show with wide appeal to black and white audiences—necessary for survival in today's media marketplace. Downing reviews its treatment of social class, the family, sexism and racism as essential to appreciation of the full character of the show and especially to aid in accurately evaluating "Cosby" as a discourse within a racist society. "Cosby," he concludes, has not ignored racism; it has worked within the confines of a commercial system to erode it.

Michael Dyson argues that such a powerful figure as Bill Cosby should do more to combat racism in American society. The portrayal of an affluent black family on television is in jarring contrast to the social status of black Americans. The underclass is ignored, as are the limited opportunities that many blacks face, for the social and economic prospects of many black Americans are bleak. Although "Cosby" admirably succeeds in depicting the everyday concerns of black people (and all people in general) while avoiding a preoccupation with race, it does so at the cost of ignoring the barriers that racism has imposed.

YES

John D. H. Downing

"THE COSBY SHOW" AND AMERICAN RACIAL DISCOURSE

INTRODUCTION

"The Cosby Show" is a key case for the analysis of discourse and discrimination, precisely because on so many levels it is atypical of American television fare. Media images of Americans of African descent have usually varied from the blatantly to the latently racist. This portrayal has often been challenged by black protest, from those against *The Birth of a Nation* in 1915 to those against "Amos 'n Andy," to *Fort Apache—The Bronx* in the early 1980s. It has also been challenged by black independent film-makers.

However, in academic literature, the roles and images of black people in television, in particular, have been woefully understudied and undercritiqued. A recent bibliography on black involvement in television was compelled to devote most of its pages, not to books or journal articles, but to magazine and newspaper commentary. From one angle, then, a critique of black images in the media has many potential targets, not least including their backdrop, the abysmal representation of black people in professional and management positions in the media. In such a situation, it might seem a little odd to analyze a television show that has had excellent ratings from the general public, from television critics, and—most significantly—from within black communities. Why not analyze instead a program like "The Jeffersons," another all-black comedy running for many years, which was widely felt to convey a farcical, lampooning depiction of black people? And if not "The Jeffersons," there were other possibilities; indeed the fall of 1985 saw the emergence of two new all-black comedies, "227" and "Charlie & Co.," modeled on the success of "The Cosby Show." Besides these there were shows such as "Benson," "The A-Team," and "Miami Vice" with black actors in leading roles, not to mention the many shows in which a black face was never to be seen at all.

It is, however, relatively easy to go into the fray with fists and feet flying if standard network television fare such as "The Jeffersons" is the target. In my view it is more demanding and more constructive to focus on a positive achievement, a show out of the ordinary in many respects. First, though, "The Cosby Show" must be contextualized. . . .

In 1986, then, despite appearances and despite some real victories, the black struggle for justice and equality in the United States still confronted a mountain of obstacles. "The Cosby Show" must be read in that context. In no way was it an index of problems solved. . . .

SOCIAL CLASS DISCOURSE

The Huxtable family is patently upper middle class, yet class is always assumed rather than affirmed. The father (Cliff) is a gynecologist and obstetrician, the wife (Clair) a lawyer. Their oldest daughter (Sondra) is at Princeton University, and their second (Denise) is expecting to go away to a university, the third generation of the family to attend college. They live in a very sizable brownstone on a leafy Brooklyn street. . . . Cliff and Clair pay for his parents to go on a European cruise . . . to celebrate their forty-ninth wedding anniversary. The house furnishings, the children's clothes, all bespeak a very comfortable life-style.

There is no specific discourse naming "class" as there might be in some academic treatise, but class perspectives are evident at a series of points. Cliff is confronted in one episode with a friend of Denise's who has a urinary infection, but has not told her parents because it might mean admitting she was sexually active. He remarks to Clair afterward: "[She is] a lovely girl, intelligent, beauti-

ful—could've been one of *our* children." (On one level, this is simply a statement of opinion and of enlightened sexual ethics, but implicit is also a class judgment: Denise's friend is not a run-of-the-mill, sexually precocious, irresponsible child.) When seventeen-year-old Denise buys her first secondhand car, Clair says, "she has passed the Huxtable driving text; now she must pass the Huxtable quiz" (meaning a series of do's and don't's about letting friends drive the car and so on). This implies a structure of expectations not characteristic of "lesser" families. . . .

These . . . instances also serve as a useful introduction to the general discursive style of "The Cosby Show." Crass, crude statements of the kind that abound in American television are rare indeed. Humor, adroit verbal fencing, and quiet suggestions for daily living are frequently in evidence. Yet the difference between "our" type of children and others, between "our" family and others, the ethic of individual responsibility, are all implicit expressions of upper-middle-class codes. They are emphasized lightly, but, we may surmise, all the more effectively for that very lightness of touch. I am not implying that working class codes, with their greater emphasis on commonality, exclude these emphases. I am suggesting that "The Cosby Show" evokes its response on the twin bases of "race" and social class.

Social class values are at their clearest in the repetitive emphasis given to the importance of doing schoolwork. In general, there is a closure at the end of each episode; this topic was the only major developing theme across episodes. Theo, the fifteen-year-old only son, is in some sense a muted echo of the high school dropout and his/her alienation. He does as little homework as possible, complains bitterly about his math teacher (nicknamed "dragon lady"), and wants no more than to be left alone to hang out with his friend Walter (nicknamed "Cockroach") and to impress his charms on the opposite sex (clumsily). His room normally looks as though a bomb had hit it. His friend "Cockroach" has even less time for schoolwork and is reckoned to be the least interested student in Theo's class.

In a number of episodes, the question of Theo's attitude to education is a major topic. Mrs. Westlake, a Brazilian woman married to an American citizen, is his math teacher. The very first day he is in her class, Theo is grousing to Cliff about her practice of giving out lots of homework and of calling on students who do not have their hands raised. Cliff listens attentively and then says, deadpan, he is going to phone the school about it in the morning. "What are you going to do?" asks Theo, interested. "I am going to ask if she will come to live here!" says Cliff. Again, a strong message, tempered by humor. . . .

In a [later] episode, Mrs. Westlake is forced to stay away from giving a major test to Theo's and Cockroach's class because she has given birth the day before. In her absence, her substitute teacher is faced with advanced classroom disorder, one pupil even playing a radio. Cockroach then leaps to his feet and reads the class the riot act:

> You guys are making me sick! We are Mrs. Westlake's class and look how we are behaving! Now this woman has worked hard all year to try to teach us something and we are not going to let her down. To show her how much we care, I want each and every one of you to go home tonight and study. Study

like you've never studied before. And get the best grades we've ever gotten. So she will be proud she was our teacher. And if I find out that any one of you did not give your hundred percent, you're going to have to answer to me!

The rebel unexpectedly turns missionary, the strongest tribute, the most effective voice. The class, or part of it, goes to visit Mrs. Westlake in the hospital to give her a congratulatory signed card in the shape of a huge parallelogram. She especially thanks Cockroach, asking him to stay behind a moment so she can speak with him. "Why?" she asks. "It—I don't know. It just wasn't your class." In a gesture of friendliness she says to him as he leaves: "Good-bye—Cockroach!"

This episode seemed to be communicating several things: first, that adolescent resistance is often aware that it is taking self-destructive forms, and may suddenly crack open like a chrysalis at quite unexpected moments; second, that dedicated teachers can achieve a great deal with what first seem to be unpromising students, especially in conjunction with the students' parents; and third, that a mixture of firmness in the classroom and friendliness outside it is a winner. All these messages are rolled together in the basic message, however, which is that a positive attitude to education is essential and that teenagers must be persisted with if they display a negative attitude toward it. And sparkling around the edges of the message is the power of human energy and warmth.

Not only does the discourse reflect a class experience—and so a view—of education, it effectively offers a series of recipes whereby resistance to that view may be whittled away, and one or two beacons to encourage the weary and fainthearted to persist. In some ways

"The Cosby Show" presents what seems a *realizable utopia*, with hints and suggestions, not for gardening or cooking, but for solving life's problems. The prescriptions offered are not conveyed like commandments, but emerge from the action like a contemporary morality play. When Theo gets 89 for his math test, Cliff tells him: "You studied. You studied for a whole week. *That's* why you got the 89." In a different episode we have seen Theo's preferred, minimalist mode of studying, as we have also Vanessa's, his twelve-year-old sister. The practical contrast is there for anyone with eyes; insistent, but not pious.

THE FAMILY DISCOURSE

The family in its nuclear form—the Huxtable version—has often been the site of both intense affection and deep hatreds. It has, particularly, been the location in which the mother either works in isolation or works her second shift, and in which her children have learned that that is normal, even acceptable, even god-willed. Both the warmest of human emotions and the perpetuation of sexism have been nurtured within the selfsame structure. The public discourse about the family in the United States in the mid-1980s, by and large defining it as a perfect institution under threat. . . .

Apart from nuclear, what kind of family is the Huxtables'? A little larger than the average (five children, ranging from six to nineteen). There are four daughters and one son, and so a family in which women dominate. Its social class we know already. The show strongly emphasized their individuality: in the opening credits of each episode, they were shown dancing, each one of them with a clearly identifiable personal style. The

three major young actors in the episodes studied were Denise, Theo, and Vanessa, respectively presented as a little kooky; as an awkward teenager; and as a nice but empty-headed, dress-conscious twelve-year-old striving hard to seem older than she really was. (The youngest member of the family, Rudy, was really there as a clown-figure, though it has to be said that her performance, timing, and delivery were exemplary.) But what was the dynamic of their interactions? First let us look at parent-child relationships, then at sibling relationships.

Cliff and Clair are a mixture of firmness and a readiness to talk matters through with their children. They have family conferences, for example, on Sondra's wish to spend her first summer vacation from Princeton with a girlfriend in a Paris apartment, or when Cliff becomes anxious that the children will conceal problems from them, as Denise's friend did with her parents about her urinary infection. In the first of these conferences there was a vote, in which Cliff found himself a minority of one. The children dispute with their parents, though never rudely and never whining.

At the same time, there is considerable structure in the form of clearly stated rules. Vanessa is not allowed to make or receive telephone calls after ten at night. . . . When Theo has striven to get by with the bare bones of homework for a test on Macbeth, Clair tells him he will have to do her test on the play as well. . . .

There are other detailed statements of parental understanding, very much in the implicit prescriptive mode for viewers. On one occasion Clair complains to Cliff that Theo and Cockroach are tearing the place apart. Cliff says, in terms that adeptly combine insight and humor:

"They're boys, dear, fifteen-year-old boys. Fifteen-year-old boys get together and the first thing they do is talk about girls. See, that then gets them all excited. Then they don't know what to do with each other, so they start throwing each other up against the wall." . . .

The parents always seem to be able to set aside time immediately for the children when they need it—a circumstance made much easier by the routines of the comedy than by the pressures of everyday life. It is another important prescriptive "message" from the show, underlined in one scene by the camera panning slowly across the children's intently listening faces as Cliff speaks to them in deliberate tones of the unique love he and Clair have for them. At the same time, the parents exhibit no saccharine piety about the children. On Rudy's first day at school, Cliff wakes Clair up:

> "Clair, Clair, it's the first day of school."
>
> "The first day of school?"
>
> "The first day of school."
>
> "We get the house back?"

Sibling conflicts, which often seem to be the very warp and woof of family life, are also given space in the show. [A] clash between Denise and Vanessa about [a] sweater . . . ends with the two physically fighting each other with such passion that Cliff, off balance as he tries to separate them, topples over on to the floor. Similarly, when Denise's attractive girlfriend comes over to do a high school sociology project on the Huxtable family, Theo is all over her, unable to let her hand go when he meets her, tidying his room, saying all the "proper," mature things that he thinks will impress her, appearing apparently casual with his shirt open to the waist, to the point where Denise is trembling with fury at his antics.

Yet they are shown to be prepared to help each other too. Denise . . . stays up all night to help Theo with a history test. They all support Sondra in her conflict with Cliff about spending the summer in Paris. There is a careful balance between realism and positive prescription here, of a kind that mirrors the frequent reality of sibling conflict/comradeship.

It is hard, though, completely to credit the muted level of the conflicts expressed. Theo is the furthest "out," but even he never expresses any of the snarling truculence so often encountered in adolescent rages. No one sinks into catatonia, no one stays out all night without permission or letting the parents know where they are, no one even hints at drugs or alcohol (the nearest is a friend of the parents who is dependent on cocaine). Denise's friend is sexually active but not pregnant, and in every other respect a model daughter. Middle-class families are in no way exempt from these traumas, and to some extent the Huxtable family seems never to have been tested beyond a moderate point for its resourcefulness in dealing with real crisis.

THE DISCOURSE OF SEXISM

Curiously, the only form of discrimination named as such in "The Cosby Show" is sexism. Neither class nor racism is specified in this way. Yet sexism is often on the agenda.

On one occasion, Theo and Cockroach are shown in the corridor of their high school, together spotting a new, attractive female student. Their private code for such a person is "burger." "Burger alert!" says Theo. Cockroach comments: "De-luxe burger! With the works!"

Later, at home, they are trying to work out a fast way to find out about Macbeth, which they have not read, for a test the next day. Denise suggests they get some study notes from the bookstore near Brooklyn College.

THEO: Oh, Cockroach, I bet some great burgers hang out there.

COCKROACH: (*enthusiastically*): Yeah.

DENISE: What's a burger?

THEO: It's a good-looking girl.

DENISE: (*scandalized*): You call them 'burgers'?

THEO: (*grinning*): Yeah.

DENISE: A burger is a piece of *meat*.

THEO: We don't mean it that way.

DENISE: I don't care. It has to be one of the most sexist, degrading remarks I ever heard. You don't call a woman a "burger" or any other object. We're people. I ought to call you a—a "Clydesdale." You know, "Look at that Clydesdale, he's a twelve-wagon puller."

VANESSA (*entering*): You guys off the phone yet?

DENISE: Hey, d'you know what these guys call a good-looking girl?

VANESSA: You mean "burgers"?

DENISE: You *know*?

VANESSA: I thought it was kind of cute.

DENISE: Vanessa, it's wrong. As a woman you should be insulted. A burger is a piece of meat.

VANESSA: I never thought about it that way. You guys are *disgusting*!

THEO: We're sorry.

COCKROACH: We won't do it again, we promise.

THEO: Hey Denise, how do we get to the bookstore?

DENISE: If you want to know, ask *another* "burger"—Clydesdale!

This lengthy quotation underlines two things: the extent to which sexism is on the explicit agenda of "The Cosby Show" and the comparative silence about class or racism as such. How this contrast should be interpreted will be discussed in the conclusions.

On another occasion, Sondra's Princeton boyfriend Elvin is in the Cosby home. They are noted to have broken up on a previous occasion because of his tasteless, patronizing attitude toward women. He is given a series of gauche lines, putting his foot ever further in it, and visibly straining the patience of both Cliff and Clair. Another time, when the family is preparing to celebrate the grandparents' forty-ninth anniversary, Sondra and the other daughters have offered to cook the meal:

SONDRA: We thought it would be nice if we cooked the meal for grandpa and grandma's anniversary.

THEO: And I'm sure you girls will do a great job.

SONDRA: Theo, I mean all of us.

THEO: I don't cook.

CLAIR: Maybe you should learn.

THEO: Why?

CLAIR: Theo, you're going to leave this house one day, and you're going to want to eat.

THEO: I'll have my girlfriend cook.

CLAIR (*angrily*): Now where are you getting this attitude from?

THEO: Cockroach. You see we decided we're only going to date girls who cook.

SONDRA (*with a little Princeton hauteur*): Women of today have better things to do than stay in the kitchen.

THEO (*smirks and thumps his chest*): Women of today haven't met the man of tomorrow!

This exchange is also indicative of "The Cosby Show" 's discursive style. Theo is barraged by the women's irritated responses, but is allowed the last, jokey word—which nonetheless underlines his callowness. Similarly, when mightily trying to impress Denise's friend as she does her sociology project, he says: "Now some guys might find it hard—living with four sisters. But it's made *me* more sensitive to the wants and needs of women." By this time, Denise is nearly ready to kill him, especially as her friend appears impressed by this hyperbole. The audience, however, is heavily prompted to see Theo's behavior largely through Denise's eyes, to the point where her friend appears naive in continuing to take Theo seriously.

Thus the program is thorough in its identification of sexism as a force to be denounced and resisted. Sexism is, though, a phenomenon basically exemplified by callow youths. This makes for a good scoring point, but does not penetrate very far into the heart of the problem. In the fifteen episodes studied, too, only one briefly showed Clair at her lawyer's office.

The relation between Cliff and Clair is basically portrayed as one of great mutual respect and love. . . . Cliff can be outvoted, pressured to change his mind, teased, fenced with, mildly ridiculed, told off. Their sexual relationship is handled with grace, the viewer left in no doubt that that component of their marriage is very much alive, but without any of the lumpen soft pornography of the "steamy" soaps. Yet Cliff is a (benevolent) paterfamilias, a strong father not in the sense of harshness or rigidity for its own sake, but representing the personification of what fatherhood is supposed to mean at its conventional best. He is the one who ceremonially hands over the carving set to Theo at the outset of the Thanksgiving dinner, because Theo has been asking him if he could carve, and it is, is it not, the role of the man of the house. He is the one who restrains Clair from her instant impulse to scream at Theo for his crashing about in his bedroom and over her garden. . . . He always has the effective last word in any situation, even if he rides with the punches along the way (see the dialogues reproduced in the section below on humor). He is patriarchy with a human face.

Yet his condemnation of everyday sexism perhaps communicates itself all the more powerfully to male viewers precisely because he cannot be written off as a henpecked wimp. . . . His behavior could equally reasonably be interpreted as the assertiveness of a strong but considerate human being, maybe wrong on occasion, but not oppressive, because always open to discussion, to reason, to change. His posture is about as fair as could be demanded . . . though we may still question how common his stance is in families up and down the land.

THE DISCOURSE OF RACISM

By contrast with sexism, racism was never once mentioned in the fifteen episodes I analyzed. The discourse was *always* indirect, allusive. There was exactly one moment when it seemed as though racism was about to figure directly in the action, when Rudy announced she was not going back to school after her first day there, because she hated it. Asked why, she says a boy had called her names. Asked what, she said "Rudy Huckleberry." Cliff advises her how to respond to childish pranks of this sort, and the trivial matter disappears.

Yet there is an abundance of black culture in the series, expressed without fanfare, but with constant dignity. The picture Clair buys for eleven thousand dollars is by Ellis Wilson (said to be Clair's great-uncle) and formerly in the family. Elvin, Sondra's Princeton boyfriend, knows Wilson's work. . . . There are other paintings with black subjects hanging on the walls of the Huxtable home. Theo has . . . an "Abolish Apartheid" sticker [in his bedroom], which apparently NBC fought unsuccessfully to have removed. Denise has pictures of Frederick Douglass and Martin Luther King hanging in her bedroom.

African-American music is also often an element in the show, whether in Cliff's reminding Clair that Ray Charles's "I Can't Stop Loving You" was playing when he proposed to her . . ., or in the entire family entertaining the grandparents with a hilarious mime to Ray Charles and the Raelettes' "Night Time Is the Right Time." One episode centered on Denise having a slight accident with Stevie Wonder's car, which ends with Stevie Wonder inviting the entire family to spend some time in his recording studio. Stevie Wonder's consistent commitment to black causes . . . made his presence on the show at least as much symbol as entertainment.

In the episode in which Denise and Vanessa have their fracas about the sweater, presented in mid-January 1986, the style of handling these subjects was well illustrated. At the close of the episode, Cliff and Clair move from the kitchen into the living room to find Rudy all by herself watching television with great attention. A newsreel of Martin Luther King's "I have a dream" speech at the 1963 March on Washington is playing, in commemoration of his birthday, being observed for the very first time as a federal holiday. They sit and watch, and all the other children come to watch as well. Vanessa steals a glance at Denise, catches her eye, and mouths "Sorry"; Denise's face melts into a smile. The scene closes on King speaking. His message, its implications for relationships within a black family and within the black community as well as the relations between black and white are not enunciated—but they *are* communicated. The absolute respect that his presence and his speech command, the honor this remarkable twentieth-century leader from their country and community evidently enjoys in the Huxtable family speak volumes without words.

The very solidity of the family itself . . . is an assertion of black dignity. The painting that had been in Clair's family and now was returned to it, the carving set that had been in Cliff's family for generations, the grandparents' forty-ninth anniversary, their obvious devotion to each other were all indexes of family strength. The Huxtable family stood as both model and rebuttal.

Similarly, their relations with the relatively few white characters were typified by relaxed good humor, with none of the false friendliness or the eye-avoiding tension that normally pass for race "relations" in the United States. Whether Rudy's pudgy, comically tongue-tied playmate Peter . . . or the delightful Danny Kaye playing the family dentist, the white characters are themselves, the Huxtables are themselves, and there is neither reticence nor apology nor caution nor awkwardness. When Mrs. Westlake is lying in her hospital bed waiting to be trundled down to the delivery room, Cliff asks her if she is nervous. "Now that you are here, I feel totally confident," she replies. The prospect of having a black male obstetrician is one that would still haunt the racist sensibilities of many white American women. Again, it is a brief exchange, with no meaningful pauses or looks or camera flicking from face to face to batter the presumed semi-conscious viewer over the head with the fact that SOMETHING SIGNIFICANT IS BEING SAID. The relation between them is personal, totally transcending "race." So are Cliff's relations with his prenatal class in the clinic, a group of women of many nationalities and skin colors, with whom he clearly has a wonderful rapport. . . .

In other words, a set of relationships is portrayed at length and in detail in which racism and the response to racism have been definitively transcended, and yet not simply glossed over in the spurious ways common to American television. There is no black character resembling the semimute, totally loyal assistant to Raymond Burr in "Ironside"; no comic relief jackass of the Huggy Bear type in "Starsky and Hutch"; no childlike gorilla like Mr. T in "The A-Team"; no super-cool cop like Philip Michael Thomas (Tubbs) in "Miami Vice." Judged in this context, "The Cosby Show" is simply light-years ahead of most American television. Yet given the strengths of the series, the viewer might wonder whether this sleeping giant might not have powerful resources with which to tackle the enduring menace of racism head on. This will be discussed in the conclusions. . . .

HUMOR IN THE DISCOURSE

One of the problems in analysis of creative works is that the butterfly's wings are often destroyed by the analyst's leaden tread. It would be a travesty if "The Cosby Show" 's discourse were to be examined without reference to its frequently sparkling wit, which is an integral element of its style. Not merely is it funny, however; not merely do Cliff and Rudy clown around. Its humor is often offered as a sweetened prescription to couples and families in dispute.

One example is when the children, rather than going to find one another to speak to each other, yell for each other through the house (a familiar familial scenario). Cliff and Clair decide to bellow a series of questions and answers at each other, standing almost eyeball to eyeball, to give the children some idea of what their noise sounds like. The children are totally nonplussed, because no one explains to them what is going on, but the audience, having seen the total sequence, might be thought to have ingested a point through its laughter.

Especially in the relationship between Cliff and Clair, after more than twenty years of marriage, humor is a method of defusing minor tensions. In one episode Cliff has just said that at least Theo has good taste in the opposite sex, alluding to his instant infatuation with Denise's attractive classmate.

CLAIR: Better than yours. I saved you. . . . You were chasing a girl of eighteen who was still in the ninth grade. I saved you, you poor thing.

CLIFF: I still wonder about her sometimes.

CLAIR (*taking him by the throat*): And *what* do you still wonder?

CLIFF: Uh-u-u-uh—I wonder if she's still in the ninth grade.

On another occasion, there is a brilliant example of verbal fencing. When Rudy has broken the juicer, it turns out that Cliff had left it plugged in and so bears some share of the blame. His wife puts on her lawyer's tone and air:

CLAIR: May I ask you a question, Dr. Huxtable? Who left the juicer plugged in to the electrical socket with the top off?

CLIFF (*pauses for reflection; deadpan*): Theo.

CLAIR: Perhaps I should remind you of the penalty for perjury in this state. Let me rephrase the question, Dr. Huxtable: Did *you* leave the juicer plugged into the socket with the top off?

CLIFF (*reluctantly*): See I don't think that—

CLAIR: Just answer the question, please. Yes or no?

CLIFF: What I'm trying to—

CLAIR: Yes? Or no?

CLIFF: Yes but—

CLAIR: Then you admit it! You are guilty! You are guilty of contributing to the delinquency of a six-year-old!

CLIFF (*brainwave*): I object.

CLAIR (*sitting down in a large chair, and dropping her voice an octave*): Overruled.

CLIFF (*moving toward her on his knees and taking her hand*): Well then I throw myself on the mercy of the court.

CLAIR: The court has *no* mercy in this case. You are hereby sentenced to five years of appliance probation, which means you may not buy, look at, or touch an appliance. (*Cliff kisses her hand, very deliberately.*) You're trying to influence the judge. That's ten more years! (*Cliff fondles her hand and kisses it again.*) I find you in contempt of court. That's

fifteen more years. (*Clair strains back as Cliff leans over and tries to kiss her neck.*) Dr. Huxtable, what *are* you *doing*?

CLIFF: I'm going for life. (*Clair cracks up, and Cliff kisses her.*)

This playacting, with its ambivalent messages, its tension, and its final resolution through Cliff's superior verbal wit—his habit of winning in the end was noted above—is absolutely characteristic of the depiction of their relationship, and of the timbre of the series in general. Humor is used as a method of distancing from conflict, to give more perspective on it. Cliff's parents, for instance, are seen reminiscing with each other about his years as a teenager. His mother says: "Did you ever think he would wind up with such a fine family?" Her husband replies, "I had my doubts. When you have a boy that clowns around in school, never cleans his room, and tries to parachute off a garage—it's hard to say, 'Well, there's someone who should raise children'!" Their comments are intercut with Cliff and Clair as they talk about their own children, and the editing underlines the importance of not getting too distraught about teenage behavior.

On another occasion, Denise and Clair have had a particularly rambunctious run-in with each other. Denise, her voice cracking with anger, has attacked her parents for refusing to let her use her $1600 savings on buying a secondhand car. "Are we still in America or what?" she snaps. Clair has read her the riot act in return: "If you *ever* take *this* attitude with *us* again, you can take whatever is in that bank account of yours and go *discover* America!" Cliff acts as rational defuser of the row, and, the temperature lowered, just after Denise has gone out of the door, he quips to Clair: "That's *your* child!" Clair's emotions are still riding high, but she is spurred to a moment's self-reflection and does not make a further rejoinder.

The humor in the show is never of the "laughometer" variety, never cheap. Perhaps being taped before a live studio audience helps a great deal, insofar as it obviates the wooden pauses for canned mirth that punctuate so many other comedies. But the scriptwriting, in which Cosby himself plays a major role, and the general acting are of a much higher order than the general run, and these elements are integral to the program's success.

Compared with the use of humor in programs such as "Till Death Us Do Part" and its clones (not only "All in the Family," but also a West German and a short-run Dutch series), humor in "The Cosby Show" is a different commodity. In those, humor was claimed by the scriptwriters and the broadcasting authorities to be a safety valve for racist tensions, in that audiences were invited to laugh at the absurd, ranting prejudices of the male lead, and so to distance themselves from their own identification with those prejudices. In the event, many people found their prejudices confirmed and solidified by their canonization in a public medium. In his excellent analysis, Charles Husband has drawn attention to the multiple dimensions of humor in society, especially its destructive potential in the relaying of racist "jokes" which—precisely because they are deemed harmless—all people who choose to think of themselves as somehow postracist to connive in the perpetuation of racism. The humor of "The Cosby Show" has different functions, as indicated already. In the context of American culture, especially in the context of the family debates, the Huxtable family's humor, especially Cliff's and Clair's, would perhaps mark them out as something akin to magicians for being able to respond to teenage mayhem with such artistry. In this sense, their wit may suggest to white audiences that there are indeed enormous but untapped resources within the black community, that it is indeed highly racist when the black minority in the United States is categorized, as it is so often by liberals and conservatives alike, as a series of problem-creating people. . . . Cosby's wit, often unscripted, which is reputed to make him hard to work with for less experienced screen professionals, if fundamentally a healing wit, directed always to the construction or reconstruction or reaffirmation of caring human relationships, to the encouragement of imaginative ways of interacting with other human beings during difficulties. He and the show remind us that conflicts with people close to us need not be permanently rending, yet without glibly preaching at us. But if not glib, is the series not all the same a little creamy? This question, which has surfaced several times, will be addressed in the conclusions.

CONCLUSIONS

On one level "The Cosby Show" may function as a kind of televisual Doctor Benjamin Spock manual on family interaction: detailed, humane, rational, helpful, enjoyable, insightful. For families suffering from tortured, tense teenage relationships, that can be a contribution. On another level, "The Cosby Show" may operate as a reinstatement of black dignity and culture in a racist society where television culture has generally failed to communicate these realities, and has often flatly negated them. On another level, it may celebrate the virtues of upper-middle-class existence as the most desirable way of life to which the vast mass of citizens can reasonably aspire (indeed "Dallas," "Dynasty," "Knots Landing," basically suggest that ruling class life is very little fun at all). We might further consider that the first and third of these aspects, combined with the program's notable dramatic qualities, may well be the factors that allowed the second message to be communicated at all, given the conventional processes at work in decision making about prime-time television.

Certainly the audience for "The Cosby Show" is multiple, as already emphasized, so that a variety of messages must be being communicated, though many of them simultaneously rather than separately. The suggestion that the attack on sexism might be all the more effective because Cliff comes across as a strong individual is an instance of the potential complexity of the text.

The only dimension of this multiple communication in the discourse that can be examined at this time is the one central to this essay: the question of racism and the closely connected issue of whether life is not too easy in the series. What follows is in the form of statements, but each one would require further detailed analysis to be considered as fully grounded.

Does "The Cosby Show" let the ever present problem of racism off the hook? If the question requires that the issue be addressed head-on, as I put it earlier, the answer would have to be affirmative. However, I am going to suggest that that would be a misconceived question in most respects. First and foremost, let us look at the practicalities of getting a prime-time series on the air, over an extended period of time, which did indeed deal frontally with the question of racism: neither the numerous layers of network executives whose vetoes have to be evaded, nor the advertising executives whose views of programs are also influential either directly or by experienced anticipation, would exactly leap to embrace such a show. When I described "The Cosby Show" as a sleeping giant earlier, perhaps I should have altered the image a little. The series might better be seen as Gulliver, ensnared and helpless through the myriad webs tied by the busy Lilliputians swarming around his frame, each one, in the case of television decision makers, acting (as always) as the exquisitely tuned measure of the public's sensibilities.

There is still another dimension to this question though, which is that on one level, the public is inured to a type of gritty, "let's eat these indigestible facts" program, which is often couched in a format that seems designed to tickle the masochistic palate, for which a ration of gloom and degradation is an acquired by academically essential taste. If "The Cosby Show" had been cast in that mold, it is uncertain that its effect would be so strong, however many critical plaudits it might have earned. Lastly, in terms of television practices, it is pointless to expect a particular product somehow to carry the weight of the failures of all the others, and single-handedly to compensate for them. If then "The Cosby Show" were to be urged to realize its full potential, the targets of public demand would have to be the networks and the advertisers, not the people who create the show. The former are the forces with which "The Cosby Show" has had to negotiate its existence; indeed, ABC turned the series proposal down. To be as good as it is *and* to have gotten past these barriers is a major achievement in itself.

However, some components of this achievement, in moving the culture forward a little from its racist roots, are worthy of reemphasis. First, the attack on sexism. By implication, if this is identified and denounced in a household where major black political leaders are clearly honored, then racism is also discountenanced. Sojourner Truth's picture is not in evidence in the Huxtable residence, but her presence is. Without beating an antiracist gong, this stance and commitment, combined with the fact the Huxtables are black, make the antiracist message potent and assimilable at the same time.

Second, social class. Because social class mobility and success are important components of dignity in cultural perception in the United States, the class position of the Huxtable family is likely to convey a positive message about black dignity. . . .

[F]or the white audience, the Huxtables' class position may help negate the dismissal of black people as insignificant, unachieving members of society, for the black audience it may additionally suggest an insulation against the sharpest effect of a racist society. . . .

Herman Gray has argued,[1] based on his analysis of black male roles in "Benson," "Webster," "Different Strokes," and "The Jeffersons" (all comedies with a regular or entire black cast), that American television comedies "[idealize] racial harmony, affluence, and individual mobility" and notes that these options are "simply not within the reach of millions of black Americans. . . . The major impact . . . is to deflect attention from the persistence of racism, inequality, and differential power" (p. 239).

The force of this argument is indisputable, and "The Cosby Show" is not exempt from its strictures. Yet the *full* effect of "The Cosby Show" cannot be so defined. Frederic Jameson has argued that mass culture contains "utopian" as well as manipulative components: "works of mass culture . . . cannot manipulate unless they offer some genuine shred of content as a fantasy bribe to the public about to be manipulated . . . cannot do their job without deflecting . . . the deepest and most fundamental hopes and fantasies. . . ."[2]

Insofar as this position is valid, the treatment of social class in "The Cosby Show" is not simply a matter of blanking out the ugly realities of continuing oppression, but also of offering some sense of resolution to the grinding everyday realities of racial tension and mistrust in the United States, as well as some vision of what a financially secure family life might be like. The hopes and fantasies nurtured a little in this communication are *also* the stuff of continuing resistance to a harsh reality, not simply its denial.

Finally, one more comment on the family itself. It presents in microcosm the importance of black unity—between genders and generations—without any sloganizing about the necessity of holding together for survival in a hostile environment. Nor is any child in the family favored for her or his lighter skin shade, historically one of the most insidious penetrations of the majority's racism into the minority's everyday life. The family's assured dignity and fundamental cohesion offer a powerful communication on several levels, countering the "shambles" image of black family life referred to above.

Thus, addressed to the American public in its mid-1980s condition, "The Cosby Show" 's treatment of sexism, the family, and social class actually enabled it to convey positive messages to multiple audiences. These messages addressed the problem of racism, not by focusing directly upon it, but rather upon three of its many "correlates," if the term may be so employed. Sexism, social class, and the family were used as key points of access from which to erode racism, still the most glaring division in the daily culture of the United States. The implications may be considerable for future strategies to this end.

NOTES

1. Herman Gray, "Television and the New Black Man: Black Male Images in Prime-time Situation Comedy," *Media, Culture, and Society* 8 (1986), 223–42. My thanks are due to Professor Gray for sending me an early copy of his article.

2. Frederic Jameson, "Reification and Utopia in Mass Culture," *Social Text* 1 (1979), 130–48. The quotation in the text is taken from p. 144.

NO
Michael Dyson

BILL COSBY AND THE POLITICS OF RACE

Bill Cosby is, arguably, the reigning national icon. He is a powerful symbol of the graceful confluence of talent, wealth, and industry that are the American Dream. His television series, "The Cosby Show," has singlehandedly revived the situation comedy, spawning numerous imitations, surely the sincerest form of media flattery. His show has even spun off the highly successful "A Different World," a sitcom about contemporary black college life, second only to "The Cosby Show" in rating a popularity. As if that weren't enough, "The Cosby Show" is now in syndication, with the prospect of generating almost a billion dollars in revenue.

Cosby's philanthropic gestures, too, have matched his larger than life television persona. He and Camille Cosby's recent gifts to black colleges and universities, totaling almost $25 million, have both aided the beleaguered black academy and generated renewed interest in black charitable activity. At Harlem's famed Apollo Theatre, Cosby raised more than $100,000 for Jesse Jackson's presidential campaign. And at the beginning of the Tawana Brawley case, Cosby and Essence Communications Chief Executive Ed Lewis offered a $25,000 reward, in part to signal their disdain for all forms of violence.

It is somewhat ironic, then, that as "The Cosby Show" enters this month, its sixth season, there is continuing controversy about its treatment of the issue of race. From the very beginning, the Cosby series has been shadowed by persistent questions growing out of the politics of racial definition, such as: Is "The Cosby Show" really black enough? Does "The Cosby Show" accurately reflect most African-American families, or should it attempt to do so? Shouldn't "The Cosby Show" confront the menacing specter of the black underclass, and address a few of its attendant problems, such as poverty and unemployment?

The answers to these questions are not so simple, because they involve larger issues of how one defines racial identity and the role of television in catalyzing, or anesthetizing, social conscience. Needless to say "The Cosby Show" does not exist in a socio-historical vacuum, in film and television history, or the larger history of American culture.

From Michael Dyson, "Bill Cosby and the Politics of Race," Z *Magazine* (September 1989). Reprinted by permission of Z *Magazine*.

Part of the pressure on Cosby results from the paucity of positive mass media images of African-Americans. Most black American characters in early film were celluloid enfleshments of stereotypes that reinforced prevailing notions of black character and culture. Whole categories of black personality were socially constructed and then visually depicted, including the coon, the buck, the clown, the mammy, the darky, the spook, the shiftless shine, and the shuffling Negro.

The history of television has not improved much on this sad state of affairs. In most cases, TV has merely updated conventional film practices with new fangled glosses on old character types, such as Amos 'n' Andy and Rochester, (Jack Benny's valet, played by Eddie Anderson). Even when there has been growth in representing black characters, television has often presented problematical versions of racial progress. With the likes of George Jefferson, J.J. "Kid Dyn-o-mite," and Arnold or Webster, blacks were either high class variations on the theme of clown, filing another social slot as a stereotypical slum dweller, or beneficiaries of white patrons-cum-adoptive parents, whose largess brought domestic stability and upward mobility to chosen black children. Each of these options reinforced the narrow range of options open to black actors, reinscribed the stereotype-creating practices of white directors and writers in the construction of black characters on television, and downplayed the increasing diversity and robust complexity of African-American culture.

Cosby's series is a marked departure from racial stereotyping, a leap made possible in large part by the social transformation of race relations under the aegis of the civil rights movement. The role of innovator is not alien to Cosby, who was the first black to appear in a regular role in a television series, starring opposite Robert Culp for three years in "I Spy." "The Cosby Show" has shattered narrow conceptions of African-American identity and culture, presenting an intact, two-parent upper middle class black family. Indeed, Cosby's show has assumed authoritative status in popular culture, establishing the Cosby viewpoint as an authentic lens on the American worldview. Cosby's television brood, the Huxtables, now occupy privileged territory in the folklore of American family relations. The show, in many respects, is a televisual compendium of received wisdom about adults and adolescents where Spock and McLuhan easily embrace. Cliff, an obstetrician, and Claire, a lawyer, are an exemplary dual career couple. They smoothly meld tradition and change into a formula of tender devotion and tough love, blending parental authority and adolescent autonomy in perfect measure.

Despite all of this, or perhaps because of it, the question persists: is the Huxtable family "authentically black?" Such a question raises the ire of Cosby and his show's consultant, well known Harvard Psychiatrist Alvin Poussaint. First of all, such a question presumes a monolithic conception of racial identity, and a narrow view of the diversity of black culture. Poussaint, in an October 1988 issue of *Ebony Magazine*, comments: "As opportunities for Blacks expand, it is reasonable to expect that certain styles and actions, which might have typified past Black behavior, will change and vary widely in the future. . . . The Huxtable family is helping to dispel old stereotypes and to move its audience toward more realistic perceptions. Like Whites,

Blacks on television should be portrayed in a full spectrum of roles and cultural styles, and no one should challenge the existence of such as array of styles within a pluralistic society."

Both Cosby and Poussaint have argued that no other sitcom is expected to address the issue of racism, and that it is unfair to hold "The Cosby Show" responsible for such racial and cultural didacticism. "No one asks whether 'Three's Company' is going to deal with racism," Cosby has remarked. Furthermore, they argue that the sitcom, designed to entertain, is not well suited to handle such weighty matters as racism, and their attempt to do so would only compromise the possible impact of addressing such an important social issue in a more responsible fashion. Poussaint writes: "The sitcom formula also limits the range of what are considered appropriate story lines; audiences tune in to be entertained, not to be confronted with social problems. Critical social disorders, like racism, violence, and drug abuse, rarely lend themselves to comic treatment; trying to deal with them on a sitcom could trivialize issues that deserve serious, thoughtful treatment."

Cosby and Poussaint's arguments are certainly on target when they suggest the difficulty of addressing (especially with integrity) social problems such as racism. But it is certainly not impossible. In fact, one encouraging sign derives from the very success of "The Cosby Show" in addressing other tough social issues. For instance, "The Cosby Show" has consistently addressed the issue of sexism, creatively and comically showing how it should be debunked and resisted. There have been many insightful encounters between Claire and her Princeton educated son-in-law Elvin, a bona

fide chauvinist. Cliff and Claire have continually attempted to counsel Elvin away from his anachronistic patriarchal proclivities, cajoling him, for example, about the folly of a gender division of domestic labor.

Also, Cliff has occasionally confronted the issue of misdirected machismo, promoting a fuller meaning of manhood and a richer understanding of fatherhood. He has influenced the husbands of clients who thought the responsibility of child rearing was "woman's work." Cosby has said that in deciding to make his character an obstetrician, besides wanting to make women feel comfortable about giving birth, he wanted "to talk to their husbands and put a few messages out every now and then. . . . That fathering a child isn't about being a macho man, and if you think it is, you're making a terrible mistake. It's about becoming a parent. . . . In one episode last season, a new husband comes into Cliff's office and says, 'I'm the man, the head of the household. Women should be kept barefoot and pregnant.' Cliff tells the guy that being a parent has nothing to do with that kind of concept of manhood. And he really straightens him out by telling him that neither he nor his wife will be in charge of he house—their children will." And Cliff is often seen in the kitchen preparing meals for the family.

Such positive images of responsible male participation in all aspects of life on Cosby's show reflect a real life concern, and no mean influence on such matters, as attested to by his best-selling book, *Fatherhood*, and his new book on marriage. Thus, "The Cosby Show" has shown how a complex social issue such as sexism can be addressed humorously, producing socially responsible entertainment. The juxtaposition of comedy and conscience is not impossible, nor does it necessarily cost ratings.

Of course, as Cosby and Poussaint maintain, other sitcoms are not pressed about addressing issues of race. One implication of their point suggests that other shows should shoulder responsibility for addressing crucial social concerns. And that is right. Similar to what occurs in American culture, real progress in race relations is not made until white persons introduce norms of social equality within their own communities, workplaces, and homes, not simply waiting for a black spokesperson to deliver that message. Other sitcoms and dramatic series, therefore, must reflect a heightened degree of social awareness in regard to many issues, including race, sex, and class.

But that doesn't mean that "The Cosby Show" shouldn't touch such issues, even within the context of a half-hour sitcom. One of the most useful aspects of Cosby's dismantling of racial mythology and stereotyping is that it has permitted America to view black folk as *human beings*. "The Cosby Show" has shown that much of what concerns human beings transcends race, such as issues of parenting, family relations, work, play, and love. This does not, however, negate that some issues and concerns affect particular groups in more harmful ways than other groups. That black people continue to be burdened with racial stereotyping in the workplace, for example, cannot be avoided, even as Cosby clarifies the ways in which black folk are just human beings. The two insights must not be considered mutually exclusive.

Cosby has amassed a good deal of moral authority and cultural capital, and has captured the attention of millions of Americans who may have otherwise not tuned in or who would have categorized "The Cosby Show" as "just another black sitcom." Thus, he is in a unique position to show that concern for issues of race need not be merely the concerns of *black folk*, but can, and should, be the concern of *human beings*. To the degree, then, that his show is about an upper middle class family that "happens to be black," his show, as do others, bears part of the responsibility for dealing with social issues, which he has proven can be effectively done without sacrificing his large viewing audience or humorous effect. "The Cosby Show" can also indicate that being concerned about issues of race as black American human beings is legitimate and healthy, and should not be avoided. It must communicate that despite the upward social mobility experienced by an increasing number of black people, racism continues though in new and different ways. For instance, while the architecture of legal segregation has been largely dismantled, the persistence of inequitable socioeconomic conditions limits the range of opportunities to the educated upper and middle classes. And even among those blacks who make substantial economic and social progress, the subtlety of racist ideologies, social practices, and cultural expressions means that racism's hibernation in slippery presuppositions, ambiguous attitudes, and equivocal behavior (which have the benefit of appearing neutral, but which actually endorse racist thought or deed), must be exposed and repudiated. To a captive white audience, Cosby's message could create useful awareness about the subversive shift in the ways racism persists and continues to manifest itself.

It is certainly healthy for Cosby not to be obsessed with race consciousness, which would indicate that black life is lived only in response to white racism, that black culture is merely reactive and incapable of forming visions of life beyond the reach of race. That is not the same, however, as acknowledging that race continues to determine social relations and influence employment opportunities. Even obstetricians, lawyers, and upper middle class black children are not exempt from the prospect of racial tensions of some sort.

More pointedly, issues of race, sex, and class could be handled in a way that avoids the banal stereotyping that prevails elsewhere on television. Cosby's show has a responsibility to address these issues precisely because he has created cultural space for the legitimate existence of upper middle class blacks on television. The progressive vision of his show as exhibited in its insightful handling of the issue of sexism, then, creates the reasonable expectation of addressing such matters. Thus, the very skillful debunking of racial stereotypes that is generated by his show, and not the insistence that "black shows should do black stuff," is the reason Cosby's show must at least in some form address the problems of race and class.

"The Cosby Show" reflects the increasing diversity of African-American life, including the continuous upward social mobility by blacks, which provides access to new employment opportunities and expands the black middle class. Such mobility and expansion ensure the development of new styles for blacks that radically alter and impact African-American culture. Cosby's show is a legitimate expression of one aspect of that diversity. Another aspect is the intraracial class division and differentiation introduced as a result of this diversification of African-American life.

"The Cosby Show" is, therefore, also emblematic of the developing gulfs between black Americans who occupy varying social and class slots in American life, a symbol of the gap between the upper and under classes. As I have argued before, black track from the ghetto, which mimicked earlier patterns of white flight from the inner city, has resulted in severe class changes in many black communities. A sense of social isolation has also resulted as upper middle class blacks leave, and those left behind experience loss of economic support, role models, and social continuity, and cultural contact with more well-to-do blacks.

Cosby is certainly not expected to answer the enormously complex problem of the underclass and its relationship to the black middle and upper middle classes, a problem that social scientists continue to debate. But what is certain is that the silence and invisibility of the underclass in American life and television, except in threatening, stereotypical or negative ways, continues to reinforce the belief that *all* occupants of the underclass are black, and are active participants in illegal criminal behavior. Cosby's silence on the underclass, and their complete invisibility on his show is therefore troubling. Cosby could go a ways toward helping America to see that many occupants of the underclass are conscientious people who are victimized, often by socioeconomic forces beyond their immediate control. "The Cosby Show" could certainly brush the fringes of the problem, and at least give acknowledgment to the crisis that so many Americans who are black live with.

Some indication of the existence of less fortunate blacks, some visiting relative whose situation is desperate; some deserving youth whose intellectual brilliance is not matched by material resources could *both* alert America to the vicious effects of poverty on well meaning people, and send the message that the other side of the American Dream for many is the American Nightmare.

It is perhaps this lack of acknowledgment of the underside of the American Dream that is the most unfortunate feature of the Huxtable opulence. Cosby defends against linking the authenticity of the Huxtable representation of black life to the apparently contradictory luxury the family lives in when he says: "To say that they are not black enough is a denial of the American dream and the American way of life. My point is that this is an American family—an *American* family—and if you want to live like they do, and you're willing to work, the opportunity is there."

But surely Cosby knows better than this. Such a statement leads us to believe that Cosby is unaware that there are millions of people, the so-called working poor, who work hard but nonetheless fall beneath the poverty level. Surely Cosby understands that Martin Luther King indicated in 1967, less than a year before his death, that he had lived long enough to see his American Dream turn into an American Nightmare on the streets of too many northern cities, and that King died in the midst of a campaign . . . for the poor *across* racial and ethnic lines.

Cosby's statement about opportunity provokes even closer scrutiny of Cosby's career. He has risen to such phenomenal cultural stature precisely because he embodies so much of the power of the ideology of Americanism: an individual who, despite a poor beginning, overcame problems of race and class in order become a great stand-up comedian, actor, and spokesperson for several companies, including Jell-O, E. F. Hutton, Ford, and Coke. Cosby's career, too, is a lesson about how the management and commodification of staggering talent lead to even more staggering success, which is then recycled in the production of American fantasies about duplicating or somehow participating in that success.

Cosby's career also reveals the consolidation of the relationship between television, the shaping of consumptive desires and appetites for material goods, and the dissemination and perpetuation of the myths of universal access to the American dream. Inevitably, too, his career entails some contradictions which attest to the powerful ability of that success to transform, for good and ill, one's perspective. In his dissertation, as cited by Daniel Okrent in the February 1987 *New England Monthly*, Cosby stated: "Each day advertisers bombard millions of viewers with their products to satisfy all the sensory needs, both internal and external. This mesmerized audience chases one fad after one another in the effort to 'build a more healthier, happier, beautiful you.' " Cosby's subsequent endorsements as the most highly esteemed pitchman in American culture speaks volumes about the price of progress.

We must certainly celebrate material progress, social advancement, educational attainment, and professional development, but not at the expense of remembering that for too long access to the higher reaches of the American Dream has been based on structural factors like race, class, and gender. This awareness, then, must inform the African-American construction of television images, characters, and families. Black folk like Cosby, who are influential in television, must, like the rest of us, scrutinize the values and visions that contribute to the development of lifestyles, the adoption of beliefs, or the formation of social conscience, especially as they are represented on TV.

Perhaps the greatest lesson from "The Cosby Show" is that being concerned about issues which transcend race and therefore display our humanity is fine; but that does not mean we should buy into a vacuous, bland universality that stigmatizes diversity, punishes difference, and destroys dissimilarities. As we painfully learned in the past, we cannot be thrown into the pot and melted down into one phenomenon called The American Experience. Though Cosby unquestionably runs up against the limits of the televisual medium, which seeks the lowest common denominator in human experience as a basis for blurring the differences between peoples and cultures, and which seeks to maintain present power relations, systems of distributing wealth, and ways of assigning cultural authority, his show should teach us how to display the diversity of African-American life without compromising conscience, or consciousness about those closed out of the American dream.

Similar to Spike Lee, but with a much different aesthetic feel, Cosby presents a black universe as the norm, feeling no need to announce the imposition of African-American perspectives, since they are assumed. But it is probably the case that many upper middle class black folk continue to talk about the racism of American culture, whether discussing its diminishing impact, its paralyzing persistence, or its prayed for demise. Cosby has shown us that we need not construct the whole house of our life experience from the raw material of our racial identity, and that black folk are interested in issues which transcend race. However, such coming-of-age progress should not lead to zero sum social concern, so that to be aware of race-transcending issues *replaces* or cancels out concern about the black poor or issues which generate intraracial conflict. "The Cosby Show" is an important advance in the fight to portray the profound complexity and rich diversity of black life on the small screen, because it shows a side of African-American life that is rarely seen on television. But "The Cosby Show" (and other TV sitcoms and drama series), must be pushed to encompass and attend to other parts of that diversity within the worldview that Cosby has the power and talent to present.

POSTSCRIPT

Media Images of Blacks: Does "The Cosby Show" Adequately Address Issues of Race?

In this set of readings as in the upcoming set on the portrayal of women, one important question arises concerning the consequences of long-term exposure to media messages. This is, of course, an essential question about the unintended consequences of television viewing. It is generally assumed that television has an effect on people's conception of the world around them; that is, their "social reality"—how they think about the world, their cognitive system, their frame of reference. If television does influence how people think about the world, it has far-reaching implications for culture and communication.

Although race portrayals may be changing, a number of studies over the years have demonstrated negative and/or limited portrayals of blacks and other minorities.

Clint Wilson and Felix Gutierrez in *Minorities and the Media: Diversity and the End of Mass Communication* (Sage, 1985) examine portrayals of blacks, American Indians, Latinos, and Asians. Carolyn Martindale in *The White Press and Black America* (Greenwood, 1986) examines newspaper coverage of racial news and analyzes its deficiencies. Nancy Signorielli in *Role Portrayal and Stereotyping on Television: An Annotated Bibliography of Studies Relating to Women, Minorities, Aging, Sexual Behavior, Health, and Handicaps* (Greenwood, 1985) annotates articles from journals, books, and government reports on role portrayal and stereotyping. F. Earle Barcus analyzes children's programs in *Images of Life on Children's Television: Sex Roles, Minorities, and Families* (Praeger, 1983).

ISSUE 3

Is Television Harmful for Children?

YES: Marie Winn, from *Unplugging the Plug-In Drug* (Penguin Books, 1987)

NO: Daniel R. Anderson, from "How TV Influences Your Kids," *TV Guide,* (March 3, 1990)

ISSUE SUMMARY

YES: Author and children's advocate Marie Winn argues that television has a negative influence on children and their families and worries that time spent with television displaces other activities such as family time, reading, and play.
NO: Dan Anderson, a professor of psychology, does not find evidence that television turns children into "zombies." He believes that television, used properly, can be a source of positive education and entertainment and that many negative consequences attributed to television seem to be symptoms of larger social problems than effects of the medium itself.

From the earliest years of television broadcasting, parents and educators have expressed concerns that television is harmful, particularly to a vulnerable population such as children. These concerns have become important public policy issues. Groups such as Action for Children's Television have lobbied the Federal Communications Commission (FCC) for guidelines on host selling, program-commercial separators, limiting the number of advertising minutes during children's shows, and expanding the hours of children's programs. Networks have responded in some cases by arguing that the concerns are unfounded and by placing the responsibility for viewing control within the family. Has television become a convenient scapegoat for the ills of society, or is it guilty as charged?

Researchers began to study the impact of television on children by asking who watches television, how much and why, what children see on television, and what influence that has on their cognitive development, school achievement, family interaction, prosocial and antisocial behaviors, and general attitudes and opinions.

Their attempts to answer these questions could and do fill several volumes. However, because we are dealing with such a large and complex social issue, even that amount of research has not provided final answers to all the questions that concerned parents, educators, professional mass communicators, and legislators have raised.

Is television a powerful force that can no longer be considered innocuous entertainment? Many would answer affirmatively and would point to the content of children's viewing, arguing that the incidental learning it promotes is a significant part of the socialization process and decrying the stereotypes, violence, and mindlessness of much of television fare. Others point to the negative influence of television viewing per se: passive children who stare at the screen for hours, shortened attention span, and the displacement of other activities, all resulting in a host of negative consequences.

Television is a large part of daily life. Yet the amount of time spent in this activity is the primary concern of Marie Winn. She specifically recommends that parents try a TV-Turn Off, recounting examples of children's personal, educational, and social development when involved in such programs. She feels that children are too important to leave their education and socialization to the television set.

Television is, indeed, an important part of a child's environment, and consequently, children and adults should use it for the positive benefits it can promote. Daniel Anderson reviewed more than 100 research studies to conclude that "there is no consistent evidence that TV makes children mentally passive, impairs their attention span, reduces their interest in education or otherwise impairs their ability to think." Children actively process television, as demonstrated by their learning from it. It is their ability to learn from television that prompts Anderson to warn that negative consequences can and do occur but are unlikely if parents are involved and loving. Parental mediation—through establishing content and time restrictions as well as co-viewing and discussing media messages—establishes the family context within which the messages of television are interpreted. Anderson argues that for children who view within such a family context, television can provide a rich source of entertainment and information.

YES   Marie Winn

THE TROUBLE WITH TELEVISION

Of all the wonders of modern technology that have transformed family life during the last century, television stands alone as a universal source of parental anxiety. Few parents worry about how the electric light or the automobile or the telephone might alter their children's development. But most parents do worry about TV.

Parents worry most of all about the programs their children watch. If only these weren't so violent, so sexually explicit, so cynical, so *unsuitable*, if only they were more innocent, more educational, more *worthwhile*.

Imagine what would happen if suddenly, by some miracle, the only programs available on all channels at all hours of day and night were delightful, worthwhile shows that children love and parents wholeheartedly approve. Would this eliminate the nagging anxiety about television that troubles so many parents today?

For most families, the answer is no. After all, if programs were the only problem, there would be an obvious solution: turn the set off. The fact that parents leave the sets on even when they are distressed about programs reveals that television serves a number of purposes that have nothing to do with the programs on the screen.

Great numbers of parents today see television as a way to make child-rearing less burdensome. In the absence of Mother's Helper (a widely used nineteenth-century patent medicine that contained a hefty dose of the narcotic laudanum), there is nothing that keeps children out of trouble as reliably as "plugging them in."

Television serves families in other ways: as a time-filler ("You have nothing to do? Go watch TV"), a tranquilizer ("When the kids come home from school they're so keyed up that they need to watch for a while to simmer down"), a problem solver ("Kids, stop fighting. It's time for your program"), a procrastination device ("I'll just watch one more program before I do my homework"), a punishment ("If you don't stop teasing your little sister, no TV for a week"), and a reward ("If you get an A on your composition you can watch an extra hour of TV"). For parents and children alike it serves as an avoidance mechanism ("I can't discuss that now—I'm watching my program"), a substitute friend ("I need the TV on for company"), and an escape mechanism ("I'll turn on the TV and try to forget my worries").

Most families recognize the wonderful services that television has to offer. Few, however, are aware that there is a heavy price to pay. Here are eight significant ways television wields a negative influence on children and family life:

1. TV Keeps Families from Doing Other Things

> The primary danger of the television screen lies not so much in the behavior it produces—although there is danger there—as in the behavior it prevents: the talks, the games, the family festivities and arguments through which much of the child's learning takes place and through which his character is formed. Turning on the television set can turn off the process that transforms children into people.[1]

Urie Bronfenbrenner's words to a conference of educators almost two decades ago focus on what sociologists call the "reduction effects" of television—its power to preempt and often eliminate a whole range of other activities and experiences. While it is easy to see that for a child who watches 32 hours of television each week, the reduction effects are significant—obviously that child would be spending 32 hours doing *something* else if there were no television available—Bronfenbrenner's view remains an uncommon and even an eccentric one.

Today the prevailing focus remains on improving programs rather than on reducing the amount of time children view. Perhaps parents have come to depend so deeply on television that they are afraid even to contemplate the idea that something might be wrong with their use of television, not merely with the programs on the air.

2. TV Is a Hidden Competitor for All Other Activities

. . . Almost everybody knows that there are better, more fulfilling things for a family to do than watch television. And yet, if viewing statistics are to be believed, most families spend most of their family time together in front of the flickering screen.

Some social critics believe that television has come to dominate family life because today's parents are too selfish and narcissistic to put in the effort that reading aloud or playing games or even just talking to each other would require. But this harsh judgment doesn't take into consideration the extraordinary power of television. In reality, many parents crave a richer family life and are eager to work at achieving this goal. The trouble is that their children seem to reject all those fine family alternatives in favor of television.

To be sure, the fact that children are likely to choose watching television over having a story read aloud to them, or playing with the stamp collection, or going out for a walk in the park does not mean that watching television is actually more entertaining or gratifying than any of these activities. It does mean, however, that watching television is easier.

In most families, television is always there as an easy and safe competitor. When another activity is proposed, it had better be *really special;* otherwise it is in danger of being rejected. The parents who have unsuccessfully proposed a game or a story end up feeling rejected as well. They are unaware that television is still affecting their children's enjoyment of other activities, even when the set is off.

Reading aloud is a good example of how this competition factor works. Virtually every child expert hails reading aloud as a delightful family pastime. Educators encourage it as an important way for parents to help their children develop a love for reading and improve their reading skills. Too often, however, the fantasy of the happy family gathered around to listen to a story is replaced by a different reality: "Hey kids, I've got a great book to read aloud. How about it?" says the parent. "Not now, Dad, we want to watch 'The Cosby Show,' " say the kids.

It is for this reason that one of the most important *Don'ts* suggested by Jim Trelease in his valuable guide *The Read-Aloud Handbook* is the following:

> Don't try to compete with television. If you say, "Which do you want, a story or TV?" they will usually choose the latter. That is like saying to a 9-year-old, "Which do you want, vegetables or a donut?" Since *you* are the adult, *you* choose. "The television goes off at eight-thirty in this house. If you want a story before bed, that's fine. If not, that's fine too. But no television after eight-thirty." But don't let books appear to be responsible for depriving children of viewing time.[2]

3. TV Allows Kids to Grow Up Less Civilized

. . . It would be a mistake to assume that the basic child-rearing philosophy of parents of the past was stricter than that of parents today. American parents, in fact, have always had a tendency to be more egalitarian in their family life than, say, European parents. For confirmation, one has only to read the accounts of eighteenth- or nineteenth-century European travelers who comment on the freedom and audacity of American children as compared to their European counterparts. Why then do parents today seem far less in control of their children than parents not only of the distant past but even of a mere generation ago? Television has surely played a part in this change.

Today's parents universally use television to keep their children occupied when they have work to do or when they need a break from child care. They can hardly imagine how parents survived before television. Yet parents *did* survive in the years before TV. Without television, they simply had to use different survival strategies to be able to cook dinner, talk on the telephone, clean house, or do whatever work needed to be done in peace.

Most of these strategies fell into the category social scientists refer to as "socialization"—the civilizing process that transforms small creatures intent upon the speedy gratification of their own instinctive needs and desires into successful members of a society in which those individual needs and desires must often be left ungratified, at least temporarily, for the good of the group.

What were these "socialization" strategies parents used to use? Generally, they went something like this: "Mommy's got to cook dinner now (make a phone call, talk to Mrs. Jones, etc.). Here are some blocks (some clay, a pair of blunt scissors and a magazine, etc.). Now you have to be a good girl and play by yourself for a while and not interrupt Mommy." Nothing very complicated.

But in order to succeed, a certain firmness was absolutely necessary, and parents knew it, even if asserting authority was not their preferred way of dealing with children. They knew they had to work steadily at "training" their child to behave in ways that allowed them to do those normal things that needed to be done. Actually, achieving this goal was not terribly difficult. It took a little effort to set up certain patterns—perhaps a few days or a week of patient but firm insistence that the child behave in certain ways at certain times. But parents of the past didn't agonize about whether this was going to be psychologically damaging. They simply had no choice. Certain things simply *had to be done*, and so parents stood their ground against children's natural struggle to gain attention and have their own way.

Obviously it is easier to get a break from child care by setting the child in front of the television set than to teach the child to play alone for certain periods of time. In the first case, the child is immediately amused (or hypnotized) by the program, and the parent has time to pursue other activities. Accustoming children to play alone, on the other hand, requires day-after-day perseverance, and neither parent nor child enjoys the process very much.

But there is an inevitable price to pay when a parent never has to be firm and authoritative, never has to use that "I mean business" tone of voice: socialization, that crucial process so necessary for the child's future as a successful member of a family, a school, a community, and a nation is accomplished less completely. A very different kind of relationship between parent and child is established, one in which the parent has little control over the child's behavior.

The consequences of a large-scale reduction in child socialization are not hard to see in contemporary society: an increased number of parents who feel helpless and out of control of their children's lives and behavior, who haven't established the parental authority that might protect their children from involvement in such dangerous activities as drug experimentation, or from the physical and emotional consequences of precocious sexual relationships.

4. Television Takes the Place of Play

. . . Once small children become able to concentrate on television and make some sense of it—usually around the end of their second year of life—it's not hard to understand why parents eagerly set their children before the flickering screen: taking care of toddlers is hard! The desperate and tired parent can't imagine *not* taking advantage of this marvelous new way to get a break. In consequence, before they are three years old, the opportunities of active play and exploration are hugely diminished for a great number of children—to be replaced by the hypnotic gratification of television viewing.

Yet many parents overlook an important fact: children who are suddenly able to sustain attention for more than a few minutes on the TV screen have clearly moved into a new stage of cognitive development—their ability to concentrate on TV is a sign of it. There are therefore many other new activities, far more developmentally valuable, that the child is now ready for. These are the simple forms of play that most small children enjoyed in the pre-television era: cutting and pasting, coloring and drawing, building with blocks, playing games of make-believe with toy soldiers or animals or dolls. But the parent who begins to fill in the child's time with television at this point is unlikely to discover these other potential capabilities.

It requires a bit of effort to establish new play routines—more effort, certainly, than plunking a child in front of a television screen, but not really a great deal. It requires a bit of patience to get the child accustomed to a new kind of play—play on his own—but again, not a very great deal. It also demands some firmness and perseverance. And a small amount of equipment (art materials, blocks, etc.), most of it cheap, if not free, and easily available.

But the benefits for both parent and child of *not* taking the easiest way out at this point by using television to ease the inevitable child-care burdens will vastly outweigh the temporary difficulties parents face in filling children's time with less passive activities. For the parent, the need for a bit more firmness leads to an easier, more controlled parent-child relationship. For the child, those play routines established in early childhood will develop into lifelong interests and hobbies, while the skills acquired in the course of play lead to a sense of accomplishment that could never have been achieved if the child had spent those hours "watching" instead of "doing."

5. TV Makes Children Less Resourceful

. . . Many parents who welcome the idea of turning off the TV and spending more time with the family are still worried that without TV they would constantly be on call as entertainers for their children. Though they *want* to play games and read aloud to their children, the idea of having to replace television minute-for-minute with worthwhile family activities is daunting. They remember thinking up all sorts of things to do when they were kids. But their own kids seem different, less resourceful, somehow. When there's nothing to do, these parents observe regretfully, their kids seem unable to come up with anything to do besides turning on the TV.

One father, for example, says, "When I was a kid, we were always thinking up things to do, projects and games. We certainly never whined to our parents, 'I have nothing to do!'" He compares this with his own children today: "They're simply lazy. If someone doesn't entertain them, they'll happily sit there watching TV all day."

There is one word for this father's disappointment: unfair. It is as if he were disappointed in them for not reading Greek though they have never studied the language. He deplores his children's lack of inventiveness, as if the ability to play were something innate that his children are missing. In fact, while the *tendency* to play is built into the human species, the actual *ability* to play—to imagine, to invent, to elaborate on reality in a playful way—and the ability to gain fulfillment from it, these are skills that have to be learned and developed.

Such disappointment, however, is not only unjust, it is also destructive. Sensing their parents' disappointment, children come to believe that they are, indeed, lacking something, and that this makes them less worthy of admiration and respect. Giving children the opportunity to develop new resources, to enlarge their horizons and discover the pleasures of doing things on their own is, on the other hand, a way to help children develop a confident feeling about themselves as capable and interesting people.

It is, of course, ironic that many parents avoid a TV Turn-Off out of fear that their children won't know what to do with themselves in the absence of television. It is television watching itself that has allowed them to grow up without learning how to be resourceful and television watching that keeps them from developing those skills that would enable them to fill in their empty time enjoyably.

6. TV Has a Negative Effect on Children's Physical Fitness

. . . Not long ago a study that attracted wide notice in the popular press found a direct relationship between the incidence of obesity in children and time spent viewing television. For the 6–11 age group, "children who watched more television experienced a greater prevalence of obesity, or superobesity, than children watching less television. No significant differences existed between obese, superobese, and nonobese children with respect to the number of friends, their ability to get alone with friends, or time spent with friends, alone, listening to the radio, reading, or in leisure time activities," wrote the researchers. As for teenagers, only 10 percent of those teenagers who watched TV an hour or less a day were obese as compared to 20 percent of those who watched more than five hours daily. With most other variables eliminated, why should this be? The researchers provided a commonsense explanation: Dedicated TV watchers are fatter because they eat more and exercise less while glued to the tube.[3]

7. TV Has a Negative Effect on Children's School Achievement

. . . It is difficult if not impossible to prove that excessive television viewing has a direct negative effect on young children's cognitive development, though by using cautionary phrases such as "TV will turn your brain to mush" parents often express an instinctive belief that this is true.

Nevertheless an impressive number of research studies demonstrate beyond any reasonable doubt that excessive television viewing has an adverse effect on children's achievement in school. One study, for instance, shows that younger children who watch more TV have lower scores in reading and overall achievement tests than those who watch less TV.[4]

Another large-scale study, conducted when television was first introduced as a mass medium in Japan, found that as families acquired television sets children showed a decline in both reading skills and homework time.

But it does not require costly research projects to demonstrate that television viewing affects children's school work adversely. Interviews with teachers who have participated in TV Turn-Offs provide confirmation as well.

Almost without exception, these teachers testify that the quality of homework brought into class during the No-TV period was substantially better. As a fifth grade teacher noted: "There was a real difference in the homework I was getting during No-TV Week. Kids who usually do a good job on homework did a terrific job. Some kids who rarely hand in assignments on time now brought in surprisingly good and thorough work. When I brought this to the class's attention during discussion time they said, 'Well, there was nothing else to do!' "

8. Television Watching May Be a Serious Addiction

. . . A lot of people who have nothing but bad things to say about TV, calling it the "idiot box" and the "boob tube," nevertheless spend quite a lot of their free time watching television. People are often apologetic, even shamefaced about their television viewing, saying things like, "I only watch the news," or "I only turn the set on for company," or "I only watch when I'm too tired to do anything else" to explain the sizable number of hours they devote to TV.

In addition to anxiety about their own viewing patterns, many parents recognize that their children watch too much television and that it is having an adverse effect on their development and yet they don't take any effective action to change the situation.

Why is there so much confusion, ambivalence, and self-deception connected with television viewing? One explanation is that great numbers of television viewers are to some degree addicted to the *experience* of watching television. The confusion and ambivalence they reveal about television may then be recognized as typical reactions of an addict unwilling to face an addiction or unable to get rid of it.

Most people find it hard to consider television viewing a serious addiction. Addictions to tobacco or alcohol, after all, are known to cause life-threatening diseases—lung cancer or cirrhosis of the liver. Drug addiction leads to dangerous behavioral aberrations—violence and crime. Meanwhile, the worst physiological consequences of television addiction seem to be a possible decline in overall physical fitness, and an increased incidence of obesity.

It is in its psychosocial consequences, especially its effects on relationships and family life, that television watching may be as damaging as chemical addiction. We all know the terrible toll alcoholism or drug addiction takes on the families of addicts. Is it possible that television watching has a similarly destructive potential for family life?

Most of us are at least dimly aware of the addictive power of television through our own experiences with the medium: our compulsive involvement with the tube too often keeps us from talking to each other, from doing things together, from working and learning and getting involved in community affairs. The hours we spend viewing prove to be curiously unfulfilling. We end up feeling depressed, though the program we've been watching was a comedy. And yet we cannot seem to turn the set off, or even *not* turn it on in the first place. Doesn't this sound like an addiction?

NOTES

1. Urie Bronfenbrenner, "Who Cares for America's Children?" Address presented at the Conference of the National Association for the Education of Young Children, 1970.

2. Jim Trelease, *The Read-Aloud Handbook*. Penguin, 1985.

3. W. H. Dietz and S. L. Gortmaker, "Do We Fatten Our Children at the Television Set? Obesity and Television Viewing in Children and Adolescents." *Pediatrics* 75 (1985).

4. S. G. Burton, J. M. Calonico, and D. R. McSeveney, "Effects of Preschool Watching on First-Grade Children." *Journal of Communications* 29:3 (1979).

NO   Daniel R. Anderson

HOW TV INFLUENCES YOUR KIDS

A few months ago, when she was 23 months old, Sarah started to watch TV. "She *cries* when *Mister Rogers' Neighborhood* goes off the air," her mother wrote me. "The first time she saw it, she sat quietly with me and watched the whole show. She talked about it for the rest of the day."

Children typically begin paying consistent attention to a few television programs at about age 2. If Sarah continues to be a typical American child, she will spend about 30 percent of her waking hours in front of a TV, watching a wider range of programs as she matures. In terms of sheer exposure, television has the potential to be a major influence on Sarah's, and most children's, development. In recent years, researchers have begun to clarify the nature of that influence. The news is both good and bad.

The good news is that, contrary to a widespread theory, TV doesn't transform children into mindless "vidiots." The theory first gained popularity in the 1970s when social critics began to write that television mesmerizes young children by its rapid scene changes. A consequence, so these critics believe, is that children watch TV mindlessly and passively, with little thought and reflection. And they believe the long-term effects are worse: a short attention span and a diminished intellect.

But the theory has a flaw. It's been based mostly on anecdotes, never convincingly proved. And more than 100 studies on TV and children's attention span, comprehension and intellectual development have largely discredited it. In other words, there is no consistent evidence that TV makes children mentally passive, shortens their attention span, reduces their interest in education or otherwise impairs their ability to think. In fact, researchers are finding that young children aren't mesmerized by TV. Children seem to pay the greatest attention when they are most mentally involved with the program. The studies also show that young children tend to ignore or reject programs that they don't understand.

From Daniel R. Anderson, "How TV Influences Your Kids," *TV Guide* (March 3, 1990). Copyright © 1990 by Daniel R. Anderson. Reprinted by permission.

Sarah's TV viewing illustrates this. She now enjoys watching many children's TV shows, her mother reports, but not all. When a science program directed at older kids comes on, Sarah asks her mother, " 'Change? Change TV?' She doesn't just turn away," her mother wrote. "She's insistent we get rid of that program."

The fact that children actively think about television indicates that television can be an effective tool for education, an idea supported by a great deal of research. For 20 years PBS's *Sesame Street* has helped preschoolers learn elementary reading and arithmetic, and *Mister Rogers' Neighborhood*, also on public TV, has helped them deal with emotions and self-control. The potential of television for teaching children is beginning to be demonstrated with such science programs as *3-2-1 Contact* and the math program *Square One TV,* both on PBS.

Despite the lack of evidence that TV impairs intellectual development, many educators blamed TV when national achievement-test scores declined. While it is true that heavy viewers have lower achievement scores, studies suggest that heavy TV viewing is more a symptom of poor achievement than a cause. Poor achievers tend to come from disrupted families or have parents who fail to provide intellectually stimulating activities. Such families tend to be heavy TV viewers.

Unfortunately, much of what kids watch is intended for adults and may not be limited or interpreted by their parents. When it comes to adult-oriented TV, young children take in the information but jumble up the meaning. Consider my conversation with 6-year-old Sebastian. He had just seen a commercial in which a young couple sitting on the grass share a sumptuous lunch in front of their new Mercedes. When asked what the ad meant, Sebastian answered unhesitatingly, "They want you to buy picnics!"

Sebastian's misunderstanding was benign and amusing. Less amusing is the realization that uncontrolled TV viewing can expose a child to large doses of violence, antisocial values and sexual imagery. To the adult, this fare may have entertainment value. A given violent program may even deliver the implicit message that criminals get punished, so crime doesn't pay. The problem is that the child may see the violence of the crime and the criminal's glamorous lifestyle but not make the connection between those things and the criminal's subsequent downfall.

We know a lot about the effects of television violence. Studies suggest that TV has a role in producing aggressive play and real-life violence. Children who watch a lot of TV violence are described by other children as more aggressive. And some long-term studies find that viewing violent programming contributes to later aggressive behavior. Some of the most disturbing incidents occurred in 1973 after the movie "Fuzz" was aired. Apparently reenacting scenes in which youths set homeless people on fire, teenagers in Boston and Miami fatally burned two people.

Most researchers who study the effects of TV violence suggest that children are not equally susceptible to its influence. If parents are loving and discourage aggressive behavior, their children are unlikely to be influenced. But if parents are unavailable or permissive of violence, children are more likely to be influenced.

For many children from broken homes and poor neighborhoods, television may be the only window to the world outside.

At its worst, television provides these children images of violence and crime associated with wealth and glamour. At its best, television provides these children with knowledge of positive alternatives in life and gives them hope.

Sarah, who just began watching TV, has loving parents who will monitor and limit her viewing. They will discuss programs with her and instill social values that will enable her to evaluate the things she experiences from TV. TV won't be her only entertainment and learning resource. For Sarah, TV will provide positive education and wholesome entertainment.

POSTSCRIPT

Is Television Harmful for Children?

The prospect of government intervention in children's programming seems unlikely, particularly given the deregulation movement that began in the 1980s during the Reagan administration and which continues today. (See Issue 7 for more on the topic of government regulation of commercial broadcasting.) Therefore, the family must decide how to regulate a child's exposure. With the advent of cable, particularly children's channels such as Nickelodeon, and the availability of the VCR, control of program content is greater than it has ever been before. Yet a warning note is sounded by Winn: It is the act of viewing that should concern us. A similar warning would be sounded by Anderson: Mediation is essential, good content does not repeal the need for co-viewing.

Although there is great debate over precisely how television influences attitudes and behavior and little agreement on whether or not its influence is for good or bad, there is no doubt that television has become very influential as an agent of socialization—that is, as a means by which young people come to understand their world. (See also Issue 8 on the censorship of records, which deals with many of the same concerns about the socialization process as are raised in this debate over the effects of television on children.)

Marie Winn is best known for her book, *Unplugging the Plug-In Drug*, rev. edition, (Penguin Books, 1987). Neil Postman in his *The Disappearance of Childhood* (Delacorte, 1982) argues that media affect the socialization of a child, in many cases causing the premature departure of childhood inno-cence. Shearon Lowery and Melvin DeFleur in their book *Milestones in Mass Communication Research,* 2nd edition, (Longman, 1988), describe the results of a number of studies of the influence of television on children. Aimee Dorr in *Children and Television: A Special Medium for a Special Audience* (Sage, 1986) emphasizes the active role of children in interpreting television and the implications that has for determining the effects of the medium and its content on children.

ISSUE 4

Are Media Messages About Women Improving?

YES: Diana M. Meehan, from "The Strong-Soft Woman: Manifestations of the Androgyne in Popular Media," in Stuart Oskamp, ed., *Television as a Social Issue* (Sage, 1988)

NO: Elayne Rapping, "Liberation in Chains: 'The Woman Question' in Hollywood," *Cineaste*, vol. 17 (1989)

ISSUE SUMMARY

YES: Diana Meehan, an author and communications professor, notes that in the past few decades there have been some changes in the portrayal of female characters in the popular media. The image of a strong, autonomous female that combines aspects of "masculine" strength with "feminine" caring and warmth has emerged and is an encouraging sign for those who advocate more varied gender portrayals.

NO: Elayne Rapping, media critic and professor of communication, contends that, in recent films, traditional marriage and family norms are the standard for women's personal happiness, and she sees in Hollywood a reactionary backlash against feminist ideals that has resulted in portrayals of career women as mostly unhappy and neurotic, or even insane.

Television shows us a male-dominated world. On prime time television, males outnumber females about 3 to 1. Females tend to be portrayed in more limited, stereotyped occupations and in domestic roles. Indeed, women's marital status is much more likely than men's to be revealed in the program content. Diana Meehan comments in her 1983 book *Ladies of the Evening* (Scarecrow) that "American viewers have spent more than three decades watching male heroes and their adventures, muddied visions of boyhood adolescence replete with illusions of women as witches, bitches, mothers, and imps. Television has ignored the most important part of women's lives—their concepts, sensations, aspirations, desires, and dreams. It's time to tell the stories of female heroes—heading families, heading corporations, conquering fears, and coping with change. Good models are needed to connect women to each other and to their society."

Yet women's roles in U.S. society have changed dramatically in the past 30 years. Have the media *portrayals* of women really not improved even though the status of women has changed in society?

Meehan has become more hopeful about the portrayal of women on television. In this article, published in 1988, she has seen an important addition to the traditionally limited role portrayals of female characters: the androgynous female.

Elayne Rapping is less convinced that improvements have occurred and bases her analysis on the symbol systems inherent in several contemporary films. Symbol systems, particularly those of film and television, must be analyzed to understand how it is that we learn to be what our culture calls "women" as against what are called "men." According to her analysis, current films present a kind of warning to real women: Women are incapable of living up to the demands of liberation; straying from traditional roles and life-styles disrupts society and is personally self-destructive; having a career poses a threat to the stabililty of the individual and to institutions like the family.

Both these authors present analyses of gender in media content. Concern with women directors and images of women emerged strongly in the 1960s and has enabled the development of feminist criticism in film studies. A similar set of approaches to television is now emerging. H. Leslie Steeves in an article in *Critical Studies in Mass Communication* (June 1987) provides an extensive analysis of the varieties of feminist media research that are emerging in the the field of communication.

It is one thing to establish that media portrayals are limited or stereotyped, but what is the influence of these portrayals on audiences? How much do we rely on the picture presented in the media as guides for the construction of social realities? Strong influence is implied in the above articles and research into the influence of gender portrayals on children has established that children are more likely to pay attention to, learn from, and identify with same-sex role models. Television is a guide for appropriate sex-role behaviors and can effectively change sex-role expectations of children. Are we, as adults, immune from these influences?

YES

Diana M. Meehan

THE STRONG-SOFT WOMAN: MANIFESTATIONS OF THE ANDROGYNE IN POPULAR MEDIA

One clue regarding what it means to be a female in our society is provided by popular media. The behaviors, attitudes, and options permissible for women in our society are presented in the soaps and sitcoms, comic strips, and who-done-its of the popular media. Although the context is fanciful and exaggerated, these portrayals present the parameters of femaleness in our society, an index to acceptable womanhood.

Traditionally we've watered down the model passed to us from contributing cultures. In America, women characters have been weakened, the villains defanged, female heroes made to resemble damsels in distress. Cinderella in old-world versions of the tale is strong and clever; in America she has been translated as helpless and distraught (Yolen, 1983). Snow White is here represented as Disney's passive innocent; in European tales she represents "life-asserting qualities" (Kolbenschlag, 1979, p. 31). Moreover, Snow White has a sister in some versions, a foil, Rose Red, who is extroverted and active. She is missing in American stories.

Media analysts have noticed some change in female characters in the last decade. Daytime soap operas of the 1980s are less sex-typed than those of the previous decade (Cantor & Pingree, 1983). Radway (1984) found that recent romance novels represent female characters in male-dominated jobs, exhibiting behavior that is typically masculine, impelled by a desire for individuation and autonomy. These two genres are enormously popular and have been stereotypically "feminine" in appeal and approach. Their presentation of stronger, more autonomous females than in the past augurs well if it represents a trend in the media. I suggest that it does.

My analysis of various genres in several popular media has yielded a number of categories or types, one of which, the androgyne, is a strong, autonomous female image. It is a character who combines masculine-instrumental and feminine-expressive traits and behaviors, representing the full range of human potential (Bem, 1974; Heilbrun, 1973). Physically, she is frankly female—but is athletic, assertive, dominant, independent, and strong (masculine traits) and is also empathic, affectionate, gentle, nurturant, tender, and warm (feminine traits). This is a positive, balanced image of womanhood (Bem, 1975). Furthermore, it appears to be more popular than ever.[1]

PRINT MEDIA

Print media offer some early examples of the type. In 1930 a pair of writers, Harriet S. Adams and Andrew Svenson, using the pseudonym Carolyn Keene, created a detective for the juvenile market, androgyne Nancy Drew. The female hero of this series of novels, still selling after more than 50 years, more than 50 volumes, and more than 50 million in sales, is a girl from River Heights in heartland America. Nancy is technically a teenager, 18 years old, but with abilities and circumstances a middle-aged hero could envy. Her lawyer, mentor, and male role model is her father; he treats her as an equal, inviting her advice on some of his law cases, providing emotional and financial support. Female support is provided by housekeeper Hannah Gruen, who worries about Nancy, cooks and cares for her "like a second mother," Nancy's biological mother being dead. Thus both male and female figures advise her and provide balance for Nancy.

A male-female balance is embodied in Nancy herself. Male characteristics include her work outside the home, where she has a reputation among professional criminologists as a good sleuth. Sleuthing itself would seem to be a masculine occupation the way she does it, since it is dominant (order-giving and judging) and rational rather than emotional. Another masculine attribute that Nancy possesses is independence; her financial status is moderate wealth, which provides her with clothes, car, free time, and a certain autonomy. She is also emotionally independent, linked to a boyfriend who is undemanding and occasionally helpful, an outside pillar to augment the support at home. Nancy is also athletic (without being obvious), able to swim, run, and mountain-climb; and she is active, dashing about in her own blue roadster, tracking clues, interviewing police.

Nancy's female characteristics are underscored by her physical form and hairstyle, which are feminine and conservative (and apparently timeless, as they've been serving her since 1930 without signs of age). She has shoulder-length, titian-colored hair and a large wardrobe including sports clothes and evening attire to cloak her trim figure. That she has a boyfriend reminds the reader she isn't gay, although her primary allegiance and time commitment is to her two female friends. She is loyal to her father, friends, and boyfriend, gentle with children and the elderly, and she does the dishes after dinner. She is also expressive, appreciating dainty cakes and tea, beautiful objects, comfort, and good manners. Manners are an important value in the novels, and their absence is a clue to criminal identity. Nancy asks politely, shows sympathy, avoids slang, uses titles, and displays the cues of feminine nonverbal behavior (Lakoff, 1975). By contrast, criminal suspects speak harshly and quickly, make noise, don't make eye contact. As a sleuth, her work may be as covert as theirs, but Nancy does it like a lady.

Whereas Nancy is a combination of masculine-feminine associations, her female friends are cousins who are polar opposites. One is fretful, decorative, comfort-loving; the other is impatient, impassive, forceful, and has a boy's name. Examples are evident in every novel:

> Bess and George were cousins but there any likeness ended. Bess, blond and pretty, had a penchant for second desserts and frilly dresses. She shared Nancy's adventure out of a deep loyalty to her but was constantly fearful of the dangers involved. George was as boyish as her name. Her hair was dark, her face handsomely pert. (Keene, 1967, p. 20)
> "I never turn down an invitation to anything exciting," George answered. (Keene, 1936, p. 81)
> "Here's his razor," said George, rushing in. Bess admitted that she was frightened. "The intruder certainly has a key to this house," she declared. (Keene, 1939, pp. 47-48)
> Suddenly one of Bess' turquoise earrings fell into her lap. "Oh this old earring makes me so mad. It's always falling off." "Why don't you tighten it?" George asked. She was apt to be impatient with her feminine cousin. (Keene, 1934, p. 5)

The cousins don't always get along with each other, but they both care very much for Nancy, endorsing her behavior with approval from both poles of masculinity and femininity. They provide a context within which to view the style and acts of the androgyne, a repeated motif in media representations of the androgyne. In the case of Nancy Drew, her positive traits are further emphasized by the support of the two adults, her father who praises and encourages her, and Hannah who nurtures her and serves her, making no demands (more in the manner of a godmother than a real mother). Thus Nancy has the blessings of both worlds.

Another androgyne was popular among readers of serial comic strips in the 1940s—the beautiful redhead, Brenda Starr. She is a newspaper reporter, flying to far lands to cover world events, ever stylishly coiffed and garbed. She has a beau, an elusive, romantic figure who is only occasionally met; but her primary supporters are two female friends—a mannish-looking colleague, Hank O'Hair, and her "pleasantly plump" cousin, Abretha Breeze, as round as Hank is angular.

As an androgyne, Brenda combines the ruthless pursuit of a rational order with a fabulous fashion sense. In comic strip simplicity, she has it all, the best of both dimensions. As with Nancy Drew and her cousins, Brenda Starr's appeal as a paragon is enhanced by the presence of her two friends, one somewhat masculine in dress and demeanor, the other overly feminine. Their portrayal of negative masculine and negative feminine features (O'Hair's aggressive and Breeze's weakness, for example) contrast with Brenda's positive portrayal.

TELEVISION

Television has had few androgyne characters in prime time until recently (Meehan, 1983). Then in 1970 the season opened with a series built around androgyne hero Mary Richards, named for its star "The Mary Tyler Moore Show." Mary Richards, in her early 30s, is older than Brenda Starr or Nancy Drew and more realistically and fully drawn as a character.

In many ways Mary is atypical of the television characterization of women. For example, Tedesco (1974) found that male TV characters generally surpass female characters in activity, independence, maturity, seriousness, power, and intelligence. Mary Richards, however, is more independent, emotionally and intellectually, than the male characters in her series. She possesses more power (by personality as well as position) than all but one of the male characters, and she is mature, serious, and intelligent. Her high activity level is evident in typical episodes of the 1974 season: Mary attends a broadcast convention (Lloyd, 1974a); Mary becomes the producer of the news (Lloyd, 1974b); Mary accepts a Teddy award for executive producer Lou Grant, who is too emotionally paralyzed to make the acceptance speech (Lloyd, 1974c). Except for male mentor Lou Grant (who she calls "Mr. Grant"), Mary surpasses the men in positive male attributes.

Positive female attributes are also well represented, as Mary counsels, consoles, supports Lou in areas where he is weak, and encourages and cares for her co-workers, yet without acting the mother. She isn't one who pushes advice on friends, but one who expects friends to behave well:

Murray: I thought I'd stop over at Judith's and look at that piano on the way home . . . So what do you think:
Mary: Murray, don't do this to me . . . I think you want some sort of permission from me and you're not going to get it. (Silverman, 1974, p. 34)

With woman friends, Mary is affectionate and gentle; she is fond of Phyllis, her landlady, and warmly supportive of Rhoda, her closest friend. Without overmuch fanfare, Mary is supportive of women in general, sympathetic to the female condition.[2] In one episode she explains to Murray, "It's not fair to ask Marie [his wife] to have another child if she doesn't want one. Sometimes I think men have no idea of what's involved in caring for a baby, how much time it takes out of a woman's life" (Weinberger & Daniels, 1974, p. 24).

Mary's feminine attributes are shown physically by her slim woman's body, set off by stylish attire, earrings, shoulder-length hair. As with androgynes before her, all this is contrasted with the extreme attributes of her two female friends: Phyllis, the bony, angular apartment owner who is critical of others, argumentative, bold, and bossy; Rhoda, somewhat plump, artistic, insecure about men, whose work is nurturing plants. These two do not get along, but both admire Mary.

At work there are other female characters to contrast with Mary: Georgette, the news anchor's wife, a curly-haired waif with a little-girl voice; and Sue Ann, Mary's antagonist. Sue Ann is the reverse of the androgyne, a combination of the worst of masculine and feminine traits—overly sweet yet aggressive, dependent yet competitive. Sue Ann is a television chef, a job that combines domesticity and the spotlight in an ill-suited match, one that fosters a hearts-and-lace exterior and barely disguises the power-hungry businesswoman behind the scene. She sees Mary as competition for Lou and any available male in sight, but even with Sue Ann, Mary remains even-tempered, balanced, intrepid:

Sue Ann: Competing with a man is both aggressive and unfeminine. I don't know what you hope to achieve, but your ambition is certainly obvious.
Mary: Sue Ann, Mr. Grant has to stay here. (Lloyd, 1974a, p. 15)

When Mary went off the airwaves in 1977, the prime-time landscape emptied of strong adult women (with few exceptions). Mary was gone, Maude was gone, bionic Jamie Sommers was gone. The most popular female-prominent shows were "Laverne and Shirley," "Charlie's Angels," "Alice," and "One Day at a Time," all of which showed female bondings, but none of which portrayed the strong-soft androgyne. Three of them were set in domestic or food environs, traditional female territory, while the characters on "Charlie's Angels" were sexual decoys or imp types whose forays into the violent world of men required constant rescues, if only by each other. The situation temporarily looked bleak.

Then in the early 1980s there came a corps of interesting television women who countered the drudges and decoys of the late 1970s. Many of the new characters were the creations of former or current writers from MTM, the production company that had invented Mary Richards: Elaine Nardo, the single, working mother of "Taxi"; Joyce Davenport, "Hill Street Blues" sassy, sexy lawyer; Dr. Annie Cavanero and female nurses, administrators, and resident physicians of "St. Elsewhere"; Laura Holt, detective-businesswoman of "Remington Steele"; and, finally, the androgyne Elyse Keaton of "Family Ties."

In the 1984 season chosen for review, Elyse Keaton is an architect (a field dominated by men), and Steven Keaton's wife, and the mother of their four children. The duality of her full existence is exemplified by this exchange:

Steven: So, how was your day?
Elyse: Well, let's see. First the Esposito's decided that instead of a guest house they want a greenhouse. It seems they have more plants than friends. Then, when I got home Mallory and Alex were still arguing about the shirt and Jennifer was in the sixth straight hour of her phone-a-thon with Chrissy. I'd

say the highlight of my day came when Andrew spit up his lunch.
Steven: I miss so much when I'm not here. (Reinhart, 1984, p. 21)

Elyse Keaton is a sexually mature, socially responsible adult woman whose life is characterized by a balance between masculine and feminine, between the outside world and the world of the family. She possesses all the androgyne attributes and, as two female foils, she has daughters Mallory and Jennifer.

Mallory is sensitive, socially active, obsessed with cashmere sweaters and clothing sales; her primary concern is matching her eyeliner with her outfit. Jennifer is the athlete, the good student, who punches the school bully for teasing her friend Adam. As their mother, Elyse participates in both worlds, advising Mallory on outfits and secretly enjoying Jennifer's victory over the bully. The ages of the other two females in the family serve to remind us that extremes in behavior are phases of growing up and that both dimensions are represented in the healthy adult. The aesthetic side of Elyse is expressed in her architecture career; the roles of tomboy and athlete have matured into a mate with a playful sense of fun:

Steven: (throwing a football underhand lightly as Elyse enters)—Yo, Elyse, look alive!
Elyse: (dropping a suit case and packages to make the catch)—Steven.
Steven: And they say that pregnant women can't catch.
Elyse: That's just an old wive's tale. (She throws the ball back to him.) (Weithorn & Bennett, 1984, pp. 1-2)

Androgyne Elyse Keaton appears on the second most popular television show in the country. The number one series, "The Bill Cosby Show," also has an androgyne lead in character Clair Huxtable, lawyer, doctor's wife, mother of five children. It is interesting to note that Clair Huxtable and Elyse Keaton between them mother nine children; it is as if their femininity is exaggerated to compensate for their success in masculine-identified professions.

By the mid-1980s, there are other androgynes, all in the most popular series on the airwaves: Maddie Hayes of "Moonlighting," a former fashion-model, owner of a detective agency, yet gentle, sensitive, and non-violent; Jessica Fletcher, the post-prime-aged writer of murder mysteries, who is rational, independent, empathic, and nurturing in "Murder, She Wrote"; Amanda King, the housewife-spy whose mother and whose coworker Francine provide the polar opposites for her to play against in "Scarecrow and Mrs. King."

FILMS

Added to television's crop of androgyne heroines are those of the cinema. Joan Wilder is an adventurer and writer of romance novels in two recent releases, *Romancing the Stone* and *Jewel of the Nile*; she has a boyfriend who is a somewhat unreliable partner, a female literary agent who is brassy and supportive, and a sister who is more dependent than Joan and requires rescuing in the first film. In addition to having the positive attributes of the androgyne, she is occasionally defensive and demanding, indicating that she is still evolving.

Just Between Friends, a movie by writer-director Allan Burns (co-creator of "The Mary Tyler Moore Show" of the 1970s), has two female characters who are also evolving into androgyne women: Sandy Dunlap, assertive newscaster, and Holly Davis, an ex-dancer housewife. The film

is about female bonding and becoming whole and balanced; each woman is incomplete as a solo operator but helps the other to fulfill her potential, even as they face the disturbing discovery that they've both loved the same man, Holly's husband. The two complement each other and contrast with other female types in the film: the sexpot at Sandy's station; the coach-owner of the exercise spa, who has little subtlety or sensitivity and the manner of a drill sergeant; and Holly's accommodating, dependent mother who discourages her daughter's attempts at autonomy. In spite of the obstacles, each principal finds strength to strive for autonomy, and the empathy and generosity to forgive the other.

CONCLUSION

At this stage we can only speculate as to what effects the androgynes have as role models on their audiences. On one hand, the positive images that androgynes portray may be largely offset by the crime-filled alleys and creaky elevators of the all-male spy-detective novels, the crime shows on television, and exploitative films in which women appear as cheerleaders or, worse, as victims.

Another drawback may be that the androgynes who do appear in popular media have always been of the fantasy variety: Clair Huxtable and Elyse Keaton with successful careers, happy husbands, and 4 or 5 children are clearly superwomen; Maddy Hayes is poor but fabulously chic; Jessica Fletcher has no dirty dishes, dust balls, or writer's deadlines to keep her from her avocation; and Amanda King has an obliging mother to do the chores. These are fantasy creatures removed from the struggles and difficulties of real life.

And yet their good points may still serve us well. They invite us to dream—which is at least 50% of role-playing. If they ignore the drudgery and the doubt of real women's lives, perhaps they may be forgiven in light of the aspirations, the desires, and dreams that they inspire. A plethora of strong-soft, assertive-affectionate women on small screen and large cannot be a bad thing. It may encourage real women and girls to be heroes in their own lives—heading families, heading corporations, conquering fears, and coping with change. Personally, I think we could not have had Geraldine Ferraro without Nancy Drew and Brenda Starr, and I expect Madam President of the future will be beholden to Mary Richards and Elyse Keaton.

NOTES

1. In a book entitled *Ladies of the Evening: Women Characters of Prime Time Television*, Meehan (1983) described and analyzed popular female characters who peopled evening episodic television from 1950 until 1983. She found 10 types: *Imp* (rebellious and rowdy), *Goodwife* (beneficent but banal), *Harpy* (aggressive single woman), *Bitch* (strong-willed, selfish, and destructive), *Victim* (one who suffered pain, disease, imprisonment, or death), *Decoy* (bait in chic clothing), *Siren* insidiously sexy), *Courtesan* (an entrepreneur in painted face and peacock feathers), *Witch* (woman with special power), and *Matriarch* (prominent, competent, courageous older woman). The *Androgyne* appeared on television in the late 1960s in the short-lived "Ghost and Mrs. Muir" and then as the lead character in "The Mary Tyler Moore Show" discussed here. The type was relatively rare on popular prime-time programs until the 1980s, when such women appeared in major roles on "Taxi," "Hill Street Blues," "Cagney and Lacey," "Remington Steele," "St. Elsewhere," "Cheers," "Family Ties," "Kate and Allie," "The Bill Cosby Show," and "Golden Girls," among television's most popular, honored episodic programs.
2. "The Mary Tyler Moore Show" is pro-woman, but not necessarily pro women's movement. Mary seldom endorses movement goals, other than equal employment, and the show steers a wide berth around issues such as abor-

tion, lesbianism, and child care. The premise seems to be that women as individuals can fight for their rights and make great gains. The women's movement, however, specifically advocates group support for group gain. Mary may be liberated but she's no "women's libber."

REFERENCES

Bem, S. L. (1974). The measurement of psychological androgyny. *Journal of Consulting and Clinical Psychology, 42,* 155-162.

Bem, S. L. (1975). Sex role adaptability: One consequence of psychological androgyny. *Journal of Personality and Social Psychology, 31,* 634–643.

Cantor, M. G., & Pingree, S. (1983). *The soap opera.* Newbury Park, CA: Sage.

Heilbrun, L. G. (1973). *Toward a recognition of androgyny.* New York: W. W. Norton.

Keene, C. (1934). *The clue in the broken locket.* New York: Grosett & Dunlap.

Keene, C. (1936). *The mystery of the ivory charm.* New York: Grosett & Dunlap.

Keene, C. (1939). *The clue of the tapping heels.* New York: Grosett & Dunlap.

Keene, C. (1967). *Secret of the wooden lady.* New York: Grosett & Dunlap.

Kolbenschlag, M. (1979). Breaking the spell of feminine myths and models. In *Kiss Sleeping Beauty good-bye.* New York: Bantam.

Lakoff, R. (1975). *Language and woman's place.* New York: Harper & Row.

Lloyd, D. (1974a). Anybody who hates kids and dogs. *The Mary Tyler Moore show,* No. 7400.

Lloyd, D. (1974b). Mary the producer. *The Mary Tyler Moore show,* No. 7422.

Lloyd, D. (1974c). What are friends for? *The Mary Tyler Moore show,* No. 7425.

Meehan, D. (1983). *Ladies of the evening: Women characters of prime time television.* Metuchen, NJ: Scarecrow.

Radway, J. A. (1984). *Reading the romance: Women, patriarchy, and popular literature.* Chapel Hill: University of North Carolina Press.

Reinhart, R. (1984). Bringing up baby. *Family ties,* No. 60584-067.

Silverman, T. (1974). The affair. *The Mary Tyler Moore show,* No. 7401.

Tedesco, N. (1974). Patterns in prime time. *Journal of Communication, 24,* 119–124.

Weinberger, E., & Daniels, S. (1974). Baby, baby. *The Mary Tyler Moore show,* No. 7419.

Weithorn, M. & Bennett, R. (1984). Lost weekend. *Family ties,* No. 60584-049.

Yolen, J. (1983). America's Cinderella. In A. Dundes (Ed.), *Cinderella: A casebook.* New York: Wildman.

NO

Elayne Rapping

LIBERATION IN CHAINS: 'THE WOMAN QUESTION' IN HOLLYWOOD

Since the 1960s, 'The Woman Question' has, arguably, become more important to Hollywood filmmakers than it ever was to the Marxists who coined the phrase. Where do women fit into the social and political spectrum of American life? What happens to marriage and kids in a society where traditional roles and lifestyles are in mindboggling disarray? Perhaps most urgently, what do we, as a society, do about feminism and its often disruptive goals and values?

Its easy to chart the dominant Hollywood approach to these matters. The Woman's Film or—perhaps more accurately—The Family Film is by now a genre unto itself, with its own thematic and stylistic conventions and its own periodic trends. First came the *Alice Doesn't Live Here Anymore* phase in which liberal Hollywood gave its assent to the most basic feminist principles. Women like Jill Clayburgh in *An Unmarried Woman* and Ellen Burstyn in *Alice* were portrayed as triumphantly leaving bad relationships to go off into the sunset in pursuit of their own goals.

Not surprisingly, the mostly male moguls—like the rest of the powerful males in this country—weren't comfortable with that approach for very long. What, after all, was to become of the family—of men and their children—if women just went off to find themselves and never came back? That vision was too simplistic, anyway. Women generally did come back, for reasons economic and political. The work world was not ready to pay them much. The government was not about to provide child care and other social services necessary for working single mothers. The retreat, by many, from feminism to traditional family patterns says more about the failure of society to pay other than lip service to feminists' most important demands than about women themselves.

Hollywood, however, has chosen to see it differently. Its version of the decline and fall of the feminist vision has gone through a few clear phases by now. Not surprisingly, none has addressed the matters of money and human needs. Instead, movies have increasingly portrayed women themselves as

From Elayne Rapping, "Liberation in Chains: 'The Woman Question' in Hollywood," *Cineaste*, vol. 17, no. 1 (1989). Reprinted by permission of the publisher.

responsible for the retreat from, and backlash against, feminist ideals. First, 'liberation' was depicted as not all it was cracked up to be. Then, women themselves were portrayed as not emotionally capable of living up to their own ideal self images. Finally, having buried women alive in these negative portraits, there came a virtual avalanche of films that simply restated the old 1950s truisms: what real women really want and all they really need to be fulfilled is a good man, a good roll in the hay, and a baby.

In the early 1980s we got the first version: In two typical films, *Violets Are Blue* (1986) and *Just Between Friends* (1982), Sissy Spacek and Christine Lahti, respectively, play successful career women whose loneliness and despair, and gut envy for the traditional little housewives preferred by the male principals, were extreme to the point of bathos. To hear Spacek, as a world famous photojournalist, whine about her lonely Paris apartment which lacked even such signs of life as a cat or houseplant, was to hear the first bell of serious backlash begin to toll.

With the re-affirmation in mid-decade of the Reagan 'revolution' and its reactionary sexual and family values, however, Hollywood let us have it. Neurotic, incompetent women were all over the screen. From Meryl Streep's pathetic husband destroyer in *Plenty* to Glenn Close's emotionally weak, easily exploitable attorney in *Jagged Edge* (both 1987), women were portrayed as responsible for their own failures and miseries in a male-dominated world. Strong women were no longer just lonely, they were, depressingly often, downright looney—clearly in need of a good man and some old fashioned institutional structures to

hold them up and keep them from self-destructing.

It is only in the most recent women's films, however, that women have been portrayed not simply as failures and malcontents in a man's world, but as openly in retreat to pre-*Feminine Mystique* lifestyles and values. Women are once again appearing frequently in major roles. But what a bunch they are. They resemble *The Stepford Wives* without the tongue-in-cheek humor or science fiction weirdness. These films, in more or less interesting ways, are sheer propaganda for the return to hearth and home. Starting with the more interesting, we have Woody Allen, the chronicler of relationship failures as a feature of the modern condition, doing an about-face and ending *Hannah and her Sisters* (1987) with the soppiest of connubial happily-ever-afters for all his angst-ridden, neurotic principals.

From there it's pretty much downhill. In the screwball comedy *Overboard*, for example, Goldie Hawn plays a wealthy, bitchy woman who suffers a bout of amnesia that turns her into a nauseatingly happy wife/mother/slave to a macho carpenter and his messy brood. She chooses to stay that way. In the *noire*sque romantic thriller *Someone to Watch Over Me* a wealthy career woman loses her policeman lover to his infinitely less interesting homebody wife. This one ends with a tableau of nuclear family solidarity with the 'other woman' watching from the sidelines, that would make Jerry Falwell smile.

Can we get any more schmaltzy or explicit than that? Actually, yes. Three box office smashes of the last year are overwhelmingly heavy-handed in their portrayals of the misery of independence and the sheer bliss of matrimony. The astonishingly popular *Moonstruck* has Cher playing a gutsy independent woman who is literally swept off her feet by sexual passion. This theme—á la *A Midsummer Night's Dream*—doesn't stop with one blissfully love-smitten woman but has its entire cast, all members of an extended Italian working class family, succumb to the lure of romance, candlelight, and roses.

Baby Boom is almost as distasteful in its view of the good female life. It tells the silly tale of a hotshot financial consultant who inherits a baby and chucks everything to live in Vermont on the income she gets from making baby food in her own little kitchen with her own little hands and the support—both physical and emotional—of Sam Shepard as a good simple country vet.

The all time misogynist blockbuster, of course, was *Fatal Attraction*. Not content to make its heroine the purest incarnation of the blissful fulltime wife and mother, it created a horror film monster version of the successful but discontented career woman. This creature, a sexy, smart, publishing executive, seduces the Decent Family Man and turns, before our eyes, into a sexually-obsessed psychopath. The script even saddles her with an eating disorder, lest we miss the point that such women are unfulfilled and compulsively needy. When, finally, the Good Woman kills off the Bad Woman in a finale of carnage and cruelty, the oft-cited audience response—pure bloodlust—is as upsetting as the text itself.

Moving from the ridiculous to the merely perplexing, we can't overlook *Crossing Delancey*, Joan Micklin Silver's very hip New York version of the trend, all the sadder because it's made by a woman herself associated with the progressive values she proceeds to trounce. This time our heroine is an Upper West Side career woman whose work, at a bookstore, involves setting up readings for local artists, one of whom, a manipulative phony, nearly seduces her. In the nick of time, she's saved by a good man, a Lower East Side pickle salesman selected for her by her grandmother and an old-fashioned matchmaker.

What's most offensive about this film is its anti-intellectualism. What, after all, is wrong with a woman wanting to live a life of the mind? Not all writers, after all, are misogynist bastards. Nor, certainly, are most pickle salesmen as bright, sexy, and together as this one. No matter. Our hip heroine, like all the sillier versions, heads for the altar and permanent bliss as though lobotomized.

There is no doubt that these films, by virtue of their frequency (more titles could be mentioned) and blatant anti-feminism, constitute a dangerous trend. Still, they are so easy to read, so transparent, that they are less disturbing in many ways than another set of current films which seem, only on the surface, to be ambiguous about the Woman Question or downright profeminist.

Let's examine *Broadcast News, Running on Empty* . . . and *The Good Mother* as works that deal with the lives of women torn, in one way or another, between a desire for family life, for marriage and babies, and some other set of values which is, or seems to be, taken unusually seriously. In all of them, the heroine ends up far short of 'having it all.' That particular message is less blatant in its anti-feminism or misogyny than in films like *Fatal Attraction*. They submerge reactionary attitudes toward women in narratives that hang on the resolution of some other matter entirely, one posed as more weighty than mere matters of wedding and bedding.

Their stories do not focus on feminism, certainly. In fact, these films present themselves as, shall we say, past all that. Yes, yes, yes, they mutter around the edges of the frame; we have no argument with feminism, with women's right to any number of good and important things. Having established that as an assumption, however, they proceed to undermine their heroines' rights to equality, dignity, justice, meaningful work, and sexual fulfillment anyway, and to imply, yet again, that marriage and family are women's best hopes. This might be called post-feminist filmmaking. It might also be considered more demeaning and dangerous than the more blatant anti-feminism of the day.

Broadcast News may be the first of the clearly post-feminist films. It takes for granted what earlier women's films did not: that women can and should be doing the same important work as men. Its heroine, Jane, is a classic post-feminist woman, a daughter of the Second Wave of feminists, the generation—rooted in 1960s politics—that fought for and won personal and professional victories for generations to come. From the start, as a little girl, Jane is ambitious, determined, and quite certain of her ability and right to succeed in what used to be a male world. The film's subtle subtext, however, insists that she is also obsessive, compulsive, and driven.

As an adult in her early thirties, Jane has made it. She's a big-time television news producer on her way to the top. The narrative revolves around two themes. As the film's title suggests, it presents itself, mostly, as a critique of television journalism. Yet its more basic theme concerns the problems that arise when men and women work together as equals, the sexual tensions between colleagues and their effects on work and private lives. Jane is desired by two men—the bright, serious, klutzy Aaron who is her intellectual and professional soulmate, and the hunky, not too bright anchorman Tom, who represents everything she hates professionally, but for whom she has a serious case of the hots.

The film, directed in high sitcom style by James L. Brooks, a co-creator of "The Mary Tyler Moore Show," pretends to be a serious critique of 'Happy News' as an affront to the hallowed Walter Cronkite tradition of 'serious journalism.' In fact, it's a glorified sitcom itself, centering on personal relations at the workplace with a similar kind of wit, razzle dazzle, and superficiality.

The central drama revolves around, shall we say, Jane's Choice. Will she stick to her principles or succumb to a guy she doesn't respect? She sticks to her principles. The hunk gets his walking papers because, in Jane's view, he committed a cardinal ethical sin. In making this choice, Jane also chooses a lifestyle which is, to say the least, unattractive and undesirable. Likewise, Jane herself, when you get past the lofty but disingenuous presentation of the media issue, is presented as rather unattractive and unenviable. She bites her nails, worries compulsively, has regular crying jags, and is often obnoxious. She takes no pleasure in life. She dresses dowdily, eats on the run, and has no social life, much less sex life, whatsoever.

What becomes of women like Jane? The coda shows all three characters several years later, unveiling the grim news. Aaron has a wife and kids. Tom has a gorgeous, apparently loving wife. And Jane? She has a long-distance relationship which is relatively new and inherently a minor aspect of her life.

Many people can relate to Jane's character, claim to know women like her; but no one would want to be her. Far better, the film subtly suggests, to be Aaron or Tom and really 'have it all.' Under the guise of showing a complex, interesting, true-to-life 'New Woman,' *Broadcast News* subtly undermines feminists' demands for wholeness, for work as well as joy, and it paints career women so distastefully that few would want to pursue that course. The implication is clearly there: Maybe marriage and babies should be reconsidered.

The Good Mother makes a similar point, in a similar way. Based on Sue Miller's bestseller about a woman who leaves a repressive conventional marriage and then loses custody of her daughter when her ex-husband charges her and her artist lover with 'sexual irregularities,' the film seems to be about a woman's right to sexual fulfillment and the evils of a court system that presumes to judge private morality. Here too, the apparently serious issue works to obfuscate and submerge what ends up as a very reactionary message to women.

Like Brooks, director Leonard Nimoy seems to be on the side of women. Anna is presented sympathetically; so is her lover Leo. All the male authority figures are depicted negatively. Like Jane's Choice in *Broadcast News*, Anna's Choice—to give up her lover in a futile effort to keep her child—is politically loaded in its implications about what women can and cannot expect in this post-feminist age. Anna never defends her lifestyle. On the contrary, she caves in immediately to the men who dictate social policy and virtually throws Leo to the lions, letting him take the rap for what is presented, in court, as "her mistake."

Her obsessive desire to remain Molly's fulltime mother is understandable. But what about her rights as a woman to sexual and emotional joy? Unlike its far more complex and sophisticated source, the film jettisons these ideals with little sense of the tragic costs to women implicit in this either/or system. The sex scenes themselves—and here is where the film fails most miserably—are not only lukewarm, they lack the thematic power and centrality they are given in the novel. Audiences will feel the tragic loss of Molly far more than that of Leo, because the relationship seems to be little more than a post-divorce fling.

Most disturbing, as in *Broadcast News*, is the ending. Anna and Molly romp on the beach as Anna smiles to herself in happiness that Molly is now "in a real family," and dreams, moonily, of someday being in that blissful state herself. Again, we have a film that pretends feminism is a settled, agreed-upon matter and then proceeds, sneakily, to subvert some of its major tenets and restate the old ideal: marriage and motherhood are the only roads to fulfillment, and being single, for whatever reason, is a grim, deprived state.

Running on Empty is politically the most disturbing of the three films, both generally and in its portrayal of a serious woman. Ostensibly about a 1960s radical couple forced underground for 15 years after bombing a military center, it's more basically, like the others, about the superiority for women of family life over a life of work based on commitment and principle.

Having raised two children while moving from town to town, changing identities and jobs at the drop of a headline, Annie and Artie Pope face the dissolution of their family structure—all they have in the world—when their 17-year-old son wants to go away to college and become a musician. Like the other two films, this one undermines feminist principles while pretending to be about loftier issues. In this case, the feminist principles also happen to be broader political principles. The Popes, after all, had devoted their lives to political change. Fifteen years later, they can barely remember why.

Annie, the stronger and more interesting of the two, is the one who quite explicitly denounces her earlier 'mistakes.' "We didn't accomplish anything," she says at one point. At another, like Anna in *The Good Mother*, she tearfully apologizes to her ruling class father for her past and begs him to take her son in and send him to Juilliard. In a year of nostalgia for the New Left, this film sets up a quite atypical couple of college activists (after all, bombing buildings wasn't what the Sixties were about, except in the media's view), and trounces political activism. It inveigles us into a false dichotomy between being a good parent and being an activist. Once more, women can't have it all. Annie chooses motherhood over politics in a way that a 1970s heroine like Norma Rae, for example, certainly did not.

That Annie does not espouse feminism, in any sense, only further muddies the political waters. It's as though feminist principles are beside the point in films about strong women. A woman's right and ability to be a mother while doing political work are implicitly denied here. Only traditional marriage and family norms set the standard for women's personal happiness. Most depressingly, the idea that political activities and values might actually enrich one's ability to mother and give children more, not less, of ourselves and the world is simply ignored and thus denied.

The Eighties have generally been bad years for feminism. What women have actually achieved—an amazing amount in twenty years—is everywhere being undermined, distorted, co-opted. Women executives have more magazines and advertisements geared to them than almost any other group. There's a myth that we really can have it all, but its subtext says: Only if we play by corporate rules and make enough money to pay for all the things—childcare, housekeepers, car service—that make it possible to live with some element of dignity and leisure. The problem is not just that few women can do that. It's that even if we could, we would have abandoned most of what feminism was about, and it was not about becoming a Joan Crawford character.

These films are signs of the times. They're on the money about what's at stake, honest about dominant attitudes toward sex and family issues these days. They're also seductive in their retronightmares—of losing a child, living alone or in limbo—and therefore, much more scary.

POSTSCRIPT

Are Media Messages About Women Improving?

There are a number of books and articles that describe past and current images of women. One that has become a classic is Gaye Tuchman, Arlene Kaplan Daniels, and James Benet's *Hearth and Home: Images of Women in the Mass Media* (Oxford, 1978) for its analysis of the treatment of women on television and in newspapers and magazines. Katherine Fishburn in *Women in Popular Culture: A Reference Guide* (Greenwood, 1982) offers a historical treatment of women in America as portrayed in the media and in popular culture. Erving Goffman in *Gender Advertisement* (Harvard University Press, 1979) analyzes the symbols and rituals concerning gender in television advertisements.

Useful bibliographies are provided by Leslie Friedman in *Sex Role Stereotyping in the Mass Media: An Annotated Bibliography* (Garland, 1977) and by Nancy Signorielli in *Role Portrayal and Stereotyping on Television: An Annotated Bibliography of Studies Relating to Women, Minorities, Aging, Sexual Behavior, Health, and Handicaps* (Greenwood, 1985).

Barrie Gunter in *Television and Sex Role Stereotyping* (John Libbey, 1986) critiques research in the area of sex role stereotyping. Mary Ellen Brown, editor of *Television and Women's Culture: The Politics of the Popular* (Sage, 1990), examines the place of popular media in the diffusion of women's culture. E. Ann Kaplan writes in *Channels of Discourse: Television and Contemporary Criticism*, Robert Allen, editor (University of North Carolina Press, 1987), about feminist criticism of television. An influential book on women's use of "women's media" written from a feminist perspective is Janice Radway's *Reading the Romance: Women, Patriarchy, and Popular Literature* (University of North Carolina Press, 1984).

71

Photo courtesy of the IBM Corporation

PART 2

Media Ethics

Media ethics concerns the delicate balance between society's interests and the interests of individuals, groups, and institutions such as the press and government. Questions of ethics are, by definition, issues of right and wrong. But they are among the most difficult issues we face because they require decisions of us, even in the face of articulate and intelligent opposition. What is the appropriate balance between liberty and responsibility? Who should decide where the lines between right and wrong are drawn, and on what values should these decisions be made? Are all decisions relative to the individual case, or are there larger, overriding principles to which we should all pledge our allegiance? Finally, to whom do we entrust the power to make and implement ethical choices?

Do Journalists Routinely Deceive Their Subjects?

Can Privacy Be Protected in the Information Age?

73

ISSUE 5

Do Journalists Routinely Deceive Their Subjects?

YES: Janet Malcolm, from "Reflections: The Journalist and the Murderer," *The New Yorker* (March 13, 1989)

NO: Martin Gottlieb, from "Dangerous Liaisons: Journalists and Their Sources," *Columbia Journalism Review* (July/August 1989)

ISSUE SUMMARY

YES: *New Yorker* staff writer and journalist Janet Malcolm investigates the relationship between Joe McGinniss, author of the nonfiction best-seller *Fatal Vision*, and his subject, Jeffrey MacDonald, and maintains that all journalists betray and manipulate their subjects.
NO: Journalist and professor Martin Gottlieb argues against this claim by presenting his own interviews with prominent journalists who have read the Malcolm article; each explores how he or she maintains professional distance from a subject.

The scope of journalism has grown over the years due to alternative forms of broadcast and narrowcast media. The print media has also undergone a revolution that began in the 1960s with the introduction of advocacy, alternative, and muckraking styles, to name but a few. When a journalist writes an information piece for a newspaper one day and has a nonfiction best-seller on the charts the next day, is that person still acting as a journalist?

Author Joe McGinniss met Dr. Jeffrey MacDonald in 1979, nine years after MacDonald's wife and two daughters had been murdered. Although Mac-Donald had been arrested for the murder and found innocent by an Army tribunal (MacDonald was a captain in the Army living on an Army base at the time of the murders), his dead wife's stepfather convinced the Justice Department to investigate, and eight years after the murder, MacDonald was tried for the crime. MacDonald asked McGinness to attend the trial and write a book about the case, and in return, MacDonald would share in the book's profits.

When McGinniss's book, *Fatal Vision*, was published, it overwhelmingly supported the idea that MacDonald was guilty of the triple murder even though the court case ended in a hung jury and no verdict was given. MacDonald subsequently sued McGinniss, and in the legal battle that followed, McGinniss was questioned as to whether it was the outcome of the trial that convinced him of MacDonald's guilt or whether he had betrayed MacDonald's confidence by writing something that MacDonald had not agreed to.

In her initial article on the McGinniss/MacDonald case, Janet Malcolm wrote that every journalist is a con man who preys on the willingness of subjects to be interviewed and betrays them in the end. Her position and provocative remarks created a controversy over ethics and has prodded many authors to examine their own relationships with their subjects.

Martin Gottlieb interviewed many journalists to assess their impressions of Malcolm's assertions and to explore with them the relationship they have with their sources. While some of those interviewed agreed with Malcolm's position, those included in this selection are the ones who felt that if anyone is being manipulated, it is the *journalist* who is manipulated by the *source.*

The NO selection also provides some interesting information on how some of the journalists have developed tactics to get information from their sources. Some of these behaviors may seem ethical, while others do not. The end result, then, is a question of whether journalists report facts or construct stories.

In addition, the positions articulated in these two selections lead us away from traditional textbook definitions of journalistic practices and ask us to explore the field of journalism from a different angle: Do we expect too much from a journalist? How important is a good story? Does a good story take precedence over truth? How much investigating should a writer do to explore the issue adequately enough to begin writing? Have journalists crossed a special boundary when they practice their trade by writing books, screenplays, or the like that exceed the journalist category and label them as critics? Or perhaps as evidenced by the McGinniss-MacDonald case, is it ethical for an author to enter into a business partnership with his subject?

YES

Janet Malcolm

REFLECTIONS: THE JOURNALIST
AND THE MURDERER

I—THE JOURNALIST

Every journalist who is not too stupid or too full of himself to notice what is going on knows that what he does is morally indefensible. He is a kind of confidence man, preying on people's vanity, ignorance, or loneliness, gaining their trust and betraying them without remorse. Like the credulous widow who wakes up one day to find the charming young man and all her savings gone, so the consenting subject of a piece of nonfiction writing learns—when the article or book appears—*his* hard lesson. Journalists justify their treachery in various ways according to their temperaments. The more pompous talk about freedom of speech and "the public's right to know"; the least talented talk about Art; the seemliest murmur about earning a living.

The catastrophe suffered by the subject is no simple matter of an unflattering likeness or a misrepresentation of his views; what pains him, what rankles and sometimes drives him to extremes of vengefulness, is the deception that has been practiced on him. On reading the article or book in question, he has to face the fact that the journalist—who seemed so friendly and sympathetic, so keen to understand him fully, so remarkably attuned to his vision of things—never had the slightest intention of collaborating with him on his story but always intended to write a story of his own. The disparity between what seems to be the intention of an interview as it is taking place and what it actually turns out to have been in aid of always come as a shock to the subject. His situation resembles that of the subject of Stanley Milgram's famous psychological experiment (conducted at Yale in the early sixties), who was tricked into believing that he was participating in a study of the effect of punishment on learning and memory when in fact what was being studied was his own capacity for cruelty under the pressure of authority. In an ingenious fake laboratory setup, the "naïve subject"—a volunteer who had answered an advertisement in a New Haven news-

From Janet Malcolm, *The Journalist and the Murderer* (Alfred A. Knopf, 1990). Copyright © 1990 by Janet Malcolm. Reprinted by permission of Alfred A. Knopf, Inc. Originally appeared in *The New Yorker*, vol. 65 (March 13, 1989).

paper—was told to give an increasingly painful electric shock to a person, presumably another volunteer, in response to every wrong answer to a test question. In "Obedience to Authority," his book about the experiment, Milgram writes of his surprise at the large number of subjects who obeyed the experimenter, and kept on pulling the lever even though the receiver of the shocks was screaming with pain—or, rather, with simulated pain, since the whole thing was rigged: the electrical apparatus to which the victim was strapped was a stage prop, and the victim himself was an actor. Milgram's idea had been to see how ordinary Americans would behave when put in a situation roughly comparable to that of the ordinary Germans who were ordered to participate actively in the destruction of the Jews of Europe. The results were not encouraging. Although a few subject refused to go on with the experiment at the first sign of distress from the victim, most subjects docilely continued giving shock after shock. However, Milgram's chilling findings are not the point. The point lies in the *structure* of the situation: the deliberately induced delusion, followed by a moment of shattering revelation. The dizzying shift of perspective experienced by the subject of the Milgram experiment when he was "debriefed," or "dehoaxed," as Milgram calls it, is comparable to the dislocation felt by the subject of a book or article when he first reads it. The subject of the piece of writing has not suffered the tension and anxiety endured by the subject of the "Eichmann experiment" (as it has been called)—on the contrary, he has been on a sort of narcissist's holiday during the period of interviews—but when the moment of peripetia comes, he is confronted with the same mortifying spectacle of himself flunking a test of character he did not know he was taking.

However, unlike the reader of "Obedience to Authority," with whom Milgram shares the technical details of the deception, the reader of a work of journalism can only imagine how the writer got the subject to make such a spectacle of himself. The subject, for his part, is not likely to supply the answer. After his dehoaxing, he tends to pick himself up and walk away from the debacle, relegating his relationship with the journalist to the rubbish heap of love affairs that ended badly and are best pushed out of consciousness. Occasionally, a subject will have become so enmeshed with the journalist that he cannot let go of him, and long after the galling book has been remaindered the relationship is maintained through the interminable lawsuit that the subject launches to keep the writer bound to him. Yet even here the journalist's perfidy is not exposed, for the lawyer who takes the subject's case translates his story of seduction and betrayal into one or several of the conventional narratives of libel law, such as defamation of character or false statement of facts or reckless disregard of the truth.

IN THE SUMMER OF 1984, A LAWSUIT WAS filed by a subject against a writer in which, remarkably, the underlying narrative of betrayed love was not translated into any of those conventional narratives but, rather, was told straight—and, moreover, told so compellingly that at trial five of the six jurors were persuaded that a man who was serving three consecutive life sentences for the murder of his wife and two small children was deserving of more sympathy than the writer who had deceived him.

I learned of the case only after the trial had ended, when I received a letter, dated September 1, 1987, from a certain Daniel Kornstein. The letter—which had been sent to some thirty-odd journalists throughout the country—began:

> I am the lawyer who defended Joe McGinniss, author of "Fatal Vision," in a six-week jury trial recently concluded in Los Angeles. As you may know, the suit was filed by convicted triple murderer Jeffrey MacDonald, the subject of McGinniss's book.
>
> The trial ended in a hung jury. Although the plaintiff recovered nothing, the possibility of a retrial means that in a very real sense the issues raised by the trial are still alive, open, and undecided. Indeed, one of the jurors—who admitted she had not read a book since high school—was reported to have said afterwards that she would have awarded "millions and millions of dollars to set an example for all authors to show they can't tell an untruth" to their subjects.

Kornstein went on to characterize the suit as an attempt "to set a new precedent whereby a reporter or author would be legally obligated to disclose his state of mind and attitude toward his subject during the process of writing and research," and to speak of the "grave threat to established journalistic freedoms" that such a precedent would pose:

> For the first time, a disgruntled subject has been permitted to sue a writer on grounds that render irrelevant the truth or falsity of what was published. . . . Now, for the first time, a journalist's demeanor and point of view throughout the entire creative process have become an issue to be resolved by jury trial. . . . The MacDonald claim suggests that newspaper and magazine reporters, as well as authors, can and will be sued for writing truthful but unflattering articles should they ever have acted in a fashion that indicated a sympathetic attitude toward their interview subject.

With his letter Kornstein enclosed transcripts of the testimony of William F. Buckley, Jr., and Joseph Wambaugh, who had appeared as expert witnesses for the defense, and excerpts from his own closing statement, "in which I tried to stress the gravity and scope of this new threat to freedom of expression." He concluded, "Joe McGinniss and I both feel that the danger is sufficiently clear and present as to warrant your close attention and concern." . . .

McGinniss IS FORTY-SIX YEARS OLD AND has published six books, the most recent being "Blind Faith," of earlier this year [in 1989]. The first, "The Selling of the President, 1968," written when he was twenty-six, brought him immediate fame and acclaim. In the 1968 Nixon-Humphrey campaign, he had penetrated the inner councils of the advertising agency hired by Nixon, and in his book he revealed the techniques by which Nixon had been made to appear less awful on television. This was in the early days of television's use in politics, and McGinniss's revelations (today very tame) seemed startling and ominous. The defeated Humphrey was quoted on the book jacket as saying, "The biggest mistake in my political life was not to learn how to use television," and "I'm fighting packaged politics. It's an abomination for a man to place himself completely in the hands of the technicians, the ghost writers, the experts, the pollsters and come out only as an attractive package."

During our talk, McGinniss spoke of how he had come to write "The Selling of the President," and surprised me when he said that he had first taken his idea of reporting a Presidential-advertising campaign to the Humphrey camp. "Humphrey's people said, 'Are you crazy? This is all secret. The public shouldn't know about this. No way.' Humphrey's advertising agency was Doyle Dane Bernback, a very sophisticated group who recognized right up front that a book calling attention to the process would not be in their best interest, so they wouldn't give me any access at all. Nixon's people were almost touchingly naïve. They said, 'Oh, gosh, really—a book? Yeah, sure.' These were people who had had very little experience of being written about." Then, as if the ghost of Bostwick had just appeared at his side, McGinniss added, "But I hardly felt the obligation to say when I arrived at their offices every morning, 'Gentlemen, I must again remind you that I'm a registered Democrat who plans to vote against Mr. Nixon, and that I think what you're doing—which is trying to fool the American people—is sinister and malevolent, and that I intend to portray you in terms that you are not going to find flattering.' I felt no obligation to make that statement." . . .

McGinniss met MacDonald in June, 1979, in Huntington Beach, California. McGinniss had just finished "Going to Extremes," a work of reportage about Alaska that was to restore to him the reputation he had lost with "The Dream Team" and "Heroes," and establish him as a humorist of no inconsiderable gifts. He was in California as a visiting columnist for the Los Angeles *Herald Examiner,* writing a column of light, sharp commentary. However, the meeting with MacDonald put a halt to McGinniss's traffic with comedy, and brought him to a genre—the "true-crime novel"—in which he had never worked. Fortunately for him, the books of this genre published in America today apparently need to fulfill only one requirement—that they be interminably long—and when "Fatal Vision," the true-crime novel McGinniss eventually wrote, weighed in at six hundred and sixty-three pages it insured for itself the place on the best-seller list that its publishers had anticipated when they gave him a three-hundred-thousand-dollar advance.

McGinniss was led to his subject by an item he read while scanning the Los Angeles newspapers for topics for his column: the Long Beach Police Officers Association was sponsoring a dinner dance to raise funds for the legal defense of Jeffrey MacDonald, a local physician, who was about to be tried for murder. McGinniss remembered the crime, which had occurred nine years earlier. On February 17, 1970, MacDonald's pregnant wife, Colette, aged twenty-six, and his two daughters, Kimberly and Kristen, aged five and two and a half, were bludgeoned and stabbed to death in the family's apartment at Fort Bragg, North Carolina, where MacDonald was serving as a doctor in a Green Beret unit. MacDonald was charged with the murders and then cleared by an Army tribunal. But his story about waking up to the screams of his wife and older daughter and about seeing four intruders—three men holding clubs and knives and a woman with long hair holding a candle and chanting "Acid is groovy" and "Kill the pigs"—led to no arrests, and continued to raise the question of why no traces of the intruders were found in the apartment, and why MacDonald was merely knocked unconscious and slightly cut up when his wife and children were savagely done to death. In response to pressure from Alfred Kassab, the stepfather of the murdered woman, the Justice Department revived the investigation in 1971 and, over a period of years, built up a compelling enough case against MacDonald to bring him to trial. In the intervening eight years, MacDonald had moved to California, and had made a life for himself that appeared to be shadowed neither by the loss of his family nor by the cloud of suspicion that had hung over him from the day of the murders. He had not remarried and was leading a pleasant, blameless life in the California style. He was a hard-working, successful physician—he had become director of emergency medicine at St. Mary's Hospital, in Long Beach—and he lived in a small, attractive condominium apartment on the water, to which he liked to bring friends and girlfriends, often entertaining them with rides in his thirty-four-foot boat named (what else?) the Recovery Room. He was a handsome, tall, blond, athletic man of thirty-five, who had grown up in a lower-middle-class household in Patchogue, Long Island, the second of three children, and had always had about him a kind of preternatural equipoise, an atmosphere of being at home in the world.

MacDonald went to Princeton on a scholarship in 1961 (he was apparently the first student from Patchogue High School to go to an Ivy League college), then to Northwestern University Medical School, and then to Columbia-Presbyterian Medical Center, in New York, for his internship. In the summer following his sophomore year at Princeton and her sophomore year at Skidmore, Mac-Donald's girlfriend Colette Stevenson became pregnant. The couple decided against abortion and were married in the fall of 1963. Colette left Skidmore, and Kimberly was born in Princeton; Kristen was born in Illinois. Photographs show Colette to have been a pretty, blond girl with a soft, rounded face; all accounts of her stress her reserve, her quietness, her kindliness, and her conventional femininity. At the time of her death, she was taking an evening course in psychology at the North Carolina State University extension at Fort Bragg.

A few days before the fund-raising dinner dance, McGinniss went to see MacDonald at his apartment and interviewed him for his column. Near the end of the interview, MacDonald asked McGinniss if he would like to attend the murder trial—in Raleigh, North Carolina—and write a book about the case from the perspective of the defense team, with whom he would live, and to all of whose plans, strategies, and deliberations he would be privy. This proposal had a special appeal for McGinniss. The situation that MacDonald outlined resembled McGinniss's situation with the Nixon advertising people, which had had such a successful result. Although none of us ever completely outgrows the voyeurism of childhood, in some of us it lives on more strongly than in others—thus the avid interest of some of us in being "insiders" or in getting the "inside" view of things. In my talk with McGinniss in Williamstown, he used an arresting image: "MacDonald was clearly trying to manipulate me, and I was aware of it from the beginning. But did I have an obligation to say, 'Wait a minute. I think you are manipulating me, and I have to call your attention to the fact that I'm aware of this, just so you'll understand you are not succeeding'? Do little bells have to go off at a certain point? This has never been the case before. This could inhibit any but the most superficial reporting. We could all be reduced to standing in the street interviewing the survivors of fires."

McGinniss, of course, wanted to be in the burning house itself, and when MacDonald presented his proposition the allure of the flames was strong enough to cause him to accept a condition that another writer might have found unacceptable—namely, that he give MacDonald a share of the book's proceeds. McGinniss was not the first writer MacDonald had approached. For many years, at the prodding of his lawyer, Bernard Segal (who had defended him before the Army tribunal, and who remained his lawyer until 1982), MacDonald had been offering himself as a subject to writers. It had been Segal's idea—fantasy, as it proved—that a book would bring in a sizable portion of the money needed to pay for MacDonald's defense. "We were running into the red substantially," Segal testified at the McGinniss trial. "People were working without salaries . . . and I thought a book with an advance that was substantial and fair would help out." Two writers who had nibbled at the bait but had not been netted were Edward Keyes and Joseph Wambaugh; Keyes couldn't get the necessary advance, and Wambaugh couldn't come to the trial, because he was making a film. The hope of finding a writer had been pretty much abandoned, and when McGinniss turned up on the eve of the trial he was like the answer to a prayer one had no longer thought worth uttering. The dovetailing of desires was remarkable: McGinniss would get his insider's spot ("I wouldn't have wanted to just go to the trial and sit out there with the other reporters," he told me. "I wanted to do it from the inside looking out, and I wanted total access to MacDonald and his lawyers"), and MacDonald would get his money. In the deal that was presently struck—presided over by Segal and Sterling Lord, McGinniss's agent, who had got McGinniss a contract with the Dell/Delacorte publishing company and his three-hundred-thousand-dollar advance—McGinniss would receive not only total access but also a written promise of exclusivity and a release from all legal liability: MacDonald would lend himself to no other writer and would not sue McGinniss for libel if he didn't like what was written. For his part, MacDonald would receive twenty-six and a half per cent of the advance and thirty-three per cent of the royalties. The arrangement was a kind of reification of the hopes and good intentions that writers and subjects normally exchange at the beginning of their enterprise. The money that MacDonald was to get was simply a more tangible manifestation of the reward that every subject expects to receive at the end of the project—why else would he lend himself to it? And, similarly, the written assurances that McGinniss received from MacDonald were no different from the tacit ones that writers normally receive from subjects: It is *understood* that the subject will not sue, and that he will not faithlessly go to another writer. . . .

In the MacDonald-McGinniss encounter—the encounter of a man accused of a terrible crime with a journalist whom he tries to keep listening to his tale of innocence—we have a grotesquely magnified version of the normal journalistic encounter. Even though the crimes to which the normal subject pleads innocent—vanity, hypocrisy, pomposity, inanity, mediocrity—are less serious than those of which MacDonald stood accused, the outcome tends to be the same: as MacDonald's tale ultimately failed to hold McGinniss—whose attention soon shifted to the rhetorically superior story of the prosecution—so do the majority of stories told to journalists fail of their object. The writer ultimately tires of the subject's self-serving story, and substitutes a story of his own. The story of subject and writer is the Scheherazade story with a bad ending: in almost no case does the subject manage to, as it were, save himself. . . .

In the summer of 1979, MacDonald and McGinniss were Damon and Pythias. In common with many other subjects and writers, they clothed their complicated business together in the mantle of friendship—in this case, friendship of a particularly American cast, whose emblems of intimacy are watching sports on television, drinking beer, running, and classifying women according to looks. A few weeks after writing about MacDonald for the *Herald Examiner*, McGinniss gave up his guest column and flew to Raleigh to take up his insider's post with the MacDonald defense; he moved into the Kappa Alpha fraternity house on the North Carolina State University campus, which Segal had rented for the summer, and there joined MacDonald, his mother, Segal, and the various lawyers, paralegals, law students, and volunteers of the defense group. One member of the this group was Michael Malley, a lawyer, who had been MacDonald's roommate at Princeton and had taken part in MacDonald's defense at the Army hearing that dismissed the charges against him in 1970. Now, on leave from his law firm in Phoenix, Malley had once again put himself at

the service of his friend, and, alone of the group, was not happy about the insertion of McGinniss into its midst. As Malley was to testify later, he had nothing against McGinniss personally—indeed, he liked him, the way everyone else did—but he felt there was something fundamentally risky about letting a writer into the inner councils of the defense. . . .

The criminal trial in Raleigh lasted seven weeks and ended, on August 29th, with MacDonald's conviction—to the shock and horror of the defense. McGinniss, on hearing the verdict, cried, as did everyone else in the defense group. MacDonald was put in handcuffs and taken to a federal prison in Butner, North Carolina. The next day, he wrote a letter to McGinniss—the first letter in a correspondence that was to last almost four years. "I've got to write to you so I won't go crazy," he began. His letter ended with this emotional paragraph:

I want to see Bernie [Segal], because I love him & he is probably hurting beyond belief & wants to know he is not to blame. I want to see my Mom, because no matter how I look, by seeing me she will be better (and I probably will be, too). I would also love to see my best friends—including (I hope) you. But in all honesty, I'm crying too much today, and do cry whenever I think of my close friends. I feel dirty & soiled by the decision & can't tell you why, and am ashamed. I somehow don't feel that way with Bernie & Mom but think today it would be difficult to look at you or shake your hand—I know I'll cry and want to hug you—and yet the verdict stands there, screaming, "You are guilty of the murder of your family!!" And I don't know what to say to you except it is not true, and I hope you know that and feel it and that you are my friend.

McGinniss did not "know that." In the course of the trial, he had become persuaded of MacDonald's guilt and had found himself once again in the position—the one he had held with the Nixon advertising group—of enemy infiltrator. In July, 1983, two months before the publication of "Fatal Vision," Bob Keeler, a reporter from *Newsday*, who had also attended the criminal trial, interviewed McGinniss for an article he was writing for *The Newsday Magazine* and question him closely about the uncomfortableness of his situation in Raleigh. "There was nobody to talk to," McGinniss told Keeler. "I couldn't react. I couldn't say to someone sitting next to me in the courtroom, 'Hey, this doesn't sound good.' "

"What was your anticipation of the result when the jury went out to deliberate?" Keeler asked.

"I was not convinced they were going to convict him. At the same time, I said to myself, 'If I were a juror I would vote to convict.' But I didn't think that those twelve people were all going to come to the same conclusion I had come to. I didn't know if it was going to be a hung jury or an acquittal. But I think I would have predicted either of those two results ahead of the conviction."

"O.K. So the day after the conviction you went down to Butner, and Jeff hugs you and says he hopes you're going to be his friend forever. What were your feelings at the moment? Obviously, by that time you must have known the book was going to come out showing him to be a guilty guy. How did you feel at that moment?"

"I felt terribly conflicted. I knew he had done it—no question—but I had just

spent the summer with the guy, who on one level is a terribly easy person to like. But how can you like a guy who has killed his wife and kids? It was a very complex set of emotions I felt, and I was very happy to leave him behind in prison."

Later in the interview, Keeler asked McGinniss this blunt question: "One of the theories among the reporters at the trial was that you were going to write this Jeffrey MacDonald-the-tortured-innocent book. Another theory was that you were going to do to Jeffrey MacDonald what you'd done to Richard M. Nixon—that is to say, to be in his presence and in his confidence for a number of months and then run it up his butt sideways. And I'm wondering, since the latter has turned out to be the case, whether that's going to provide a problem for you in the future. That is to say, is anybody ever going to trust you again?"

"Well, they can trust me if they're innocent," McGinniss retorted.

"You don't feel that you in any sense betrayed Jeffrey or did him dirt or anything?"

"My only obligation from the beginning was to the truth."

"How would you describe your feelings about Jeffrey MacDonald now? This is a complex question, obviously, but obviously you're going to be asked this on talk shows, and you're going to have thirty seconds or ten seconds to think about it. How would you describe it?"

"Right now, I have a strange absence of feeling toward him. He has occupied so much of my consciousness and subconscious for so long that, with the book finally done, I find myself kind of numb in regard to him. I don't have a feeling except the feeling that has been with me, which isn't focussed so specifically on him but on the whole thing—a sadness that just doesn't go away. It's just sadness, sadness, sadness. Such a tragic, terrible waste, and such a dark and internally persecuted human being he is. He is so different from what he appears to be. I feel very sad that he didn't turn out to be who he wanted me to think he was. Because that would have been a lot easier to handle."

NO

Martin Gottlieb

DANGEROUS LIAISONS: JOURNALISTS AND THEIR SOURCES

Few articles on the subject of journalism have triggered more newsroom and cocktail-party debate, more belligerent editorializing, and more honest soul-searching than Janet Malcolm's New Yorker *series called "Reflections: The Journalist and The Murderer." The articles, appearing last March 13 and 20, focused on the relationship between Joe McGinniss, author of the nonfiction bestseller* Fatal Vision, *and his subject and business partner, Jeffrey MacDonald, an ex-Green Beret who was convicted of murdering his wife and two daughters.*

But Malcolm went beyond the particulars to make the case that all journalism, by its nature, is "morally indefensible." In her memorable lead she describes the journalist as "a kind of confidence man, preying on people's vanity, ignorance, or loneliness, gaining their trust and betraying them without remorse."

To many journalists, these assertions seemed simply ridiculous. Yet it seems unlikely that they would have reacted as they did—often furiously—had there not been some truth in what Malcolm wrote.

No hard and fast rules define the relationship that should, ideally, be maintained between a journalist and a source. Most journalists have, accordingly, worked out their own rules. Over the years, writers like James Agee, Tom Wolfe, and Joan Didion have provided impetus for journalistic self-questioning; none of these writers, however, attacked the craft of journalism in such a vigorous and sweeping—and, in the view of many, overly broad—fashion as Malcolm.

Malcolm's articles, and also the unusual nature of the McGinniss-MacDonald relationship, raise some specific questions: Should McGinniss have entered into a business partnership with a controversial figure whose story he sought to tell—and, indeed, should any journalist enter into such a relationship? Did MacDonald's subsequent lawsuit against McGinniss, by compelling the author to reveal his state of mind while writing, constitute a dangerous new threat to First Amendment rights? Was McGinniss's behavior in writing sympathetic letters to MacDonald while preparing a devastating book about him morally defensible? . . .

In an attempt to focus on Malcolm's essential charge the [Columbia Journalism] Review asked a number of prominent journalists—including Malcolm and McGin-

From Martin Gottlieb, "Dangerous Liaisons: Journalists and Their Sources," *Columbia Journalism Review* (July/August 1989). Reprinted by permission of *Columbia Journalism Review*.

niss, who declined to be interviewed—
whether they had qualms about their work,
whether they thought their attempts to elicit
information from subjects and sources could
fairly be called "seduction," and whether
Malcolm's charge that journalists betray
their subjects was legitimate. . . .

J. ANTHONY LUKAS

There can scarcely be a reporter, a writer, an editor, or, for that matter, a reader, in America who is not arrested by Malcolm's startling opening sentence. I must say, however, that the beginning seems to me a profoundly silly one.

I am certainly not denying that reporters do their share of manipulation. Of course they do. But the relationship is *mutually* manipulative. And that's because human relationships are mutually manipulative. We all manipulate each other: husbands manipulate wives, wives manipulate husbands, friends manipulate friends. I mean life is complicated, after all. And therefore the relationship between a source and reporter is complicated and Malcolm thunderously oversimplifies it.

In my experience, the relationship between reporter and source, particularly one of long term, is filled with collaboration and manipulation, with affection and distrust, with a yearning for communion and a yearning to flee.

Malcolm's opening sentence, arresting though it may be, is utterly without necessary distinctions. Many newspaper reporters spend their lives largely reporting the doings of more or less public figures who are quite sophisticated about the press—and who manipulate the press as much as they are in turn manipulated.

The road to advancement in American journalism is, it seems to me, inexorably a road that involves covering politics. You may start covering city hall and crown your career by covering the White House. Well, in that world I think Malcolm's sweeping statement is utterly *not* true. It is very much more likely to be the man in power who is manipulating the reporter.

Some years ago when I was doing two full issues of *The New York Times Magazine* on Watergate, I got an interview with Elliot Richardson. He was out of office at the time, so he received me, very shrewdly, at his northern Virginia home—a lovely, rambling old farmhouse—and it was winter, as I recall, and he seated us in front of a roaring fire. There were beautiful prints on the wall and it was, oh, just very cozy and pleasant. And seated across from me was this enormously handsome, articulate man who had recently come through the "Saturday night massacre" looking very heroic indeed. And about halfway through this interview I remember thinking to myself, He likes me. Elliot Richardson likes me. And he trusts me and he is speaking to me not as a subordinate, not as a mere reporter, but as a literate and perceptive man who can understand. He probably can't talk this way to most Washington reporters. He is really opening up to me.

It wasn't until I was in the cab on my way back to Washington that I thought, Schmuck, you've been had. You've just been treated to the treatment that this guy is exceptionally good at, and you fell for it—and may have taken a little sting off some of your questions in return.

This isn't to say that I wasn't trying to manipulate Elliot Richardson; I was. I was trying to get information out of him which he didn't want to give me.

I think that one would certainly have to say that, when one moves on to the nonpublic person, Malcolm's opening assertion is somewhat more on target. There are subjects/sources who know very little about the way the press works and they are therefore subject to a kind of seduction.

But, by and large, in the seven and a half years I spent writing *Common Ground* [a book about three Boston families and the ways they were affected by Boston's school desegregation plan], I did not have to use my seducer's skills to get my subjects to talk to me. They wanted to talk to me for reasons of their own, often very complex.

I devised with them, and with Knopf, a technique which I freely admit is unorthodox and which may strike some reporters or some editors as not justified. I devised releases in which they promised not to sue me for invasion of privacy and, in a couple of cases, not to sue me for libel, and, in the cases where they wouldn't agree not to sue for libel, they agreed not to sue me for libel except on specific items which were identified prior to publication. They were given the right to read the chapters about themselves, not the entire book, prior to publication. Further, they were invited to identify not only those points they felt were libelous but any verifiable matter of fact they thought was inaccurate.

With regard to matters of interpretation, the release said, You may argue with me and I will listen—as long as you fully understand that I make no promise to make changes. And, finally, there was a paragraph that explicitly said, You are going to have all these interviews with me, most of them are going to be on tape,

you can withdraw nothing. One family did urge me to withdraw material and, on reflection, I declined to do so.

But the fact of the matter is that the three families did not feel I seduced and betrayed them. On my birthday following the publication of the book they gave me a party.

Although this was *my* story, *my* vision of what happened in Boston, I think I went to considerable lengths to make sure that the members of these three families were treated in such a way that they would recognize themselves. And I think that Malcolm does me and many of my colleagues a great disservice to suggest that we are cynical and manipulative.

There is one rather important point I wish Malcolm had explored at greater length, which is that a source has to face up to the fact that the journalist who seemed so friendly and sympathetic, so remarkably attuned to the source's vision of things, never had the slightest intention of collaborating with him; that the journalist always intended to write a story of his own. I think that is true.

When I went to Boston I set out to in effect cast my book as if I were a theatrical director. I was looking for a black family, an Irish family, and a Yankee family who would play almost theatrical roles in my drama—and it was *my* drama. Are we, to use Malcolm's words, appropriating their lives for our stories? Yes, we are. And does that raise problems? Yes, it does. And does the craft of literary nonfiction, with all its excitement and the wonderful books that it has produced, create problems? Yes, it does.

But I would say, with due respect to Malcolm, that we ought not to be turning this into a question of moral culpability. We are, I think, honest craftsmen by and large, working at an evolving craft, trying to tell our stories, and if we make mistakes it is not moral culpability we are talking about, but mistakes—sometimes serious ones—that are the mistakes of craftsmen.

J. Anthony Lukas is the author of Common Ground: A Turbulent Decade in the Lives of Three American Families, *and has won two Pulitzer Prizes.*

JOSEPH WAMBAUGH

Those ivory-tower arguments of Malcolm's were just so much crap to me. That opening sentence just blew me away. If anything, I think many of the people I have interviewed as a policeman and as a journalist were trying to con *me* all the time. I never felt that I was conning anybody.

It is hard to con a con, you know, and the folks I dealt with as a cop were cons themselves. So I felt it was my job to keep from getting conned. And I think reporters feel the same way. I mean, after all, when they write about people aren't those people trying to be seen in their best light? Don't they want reporters to love them? Don't they want reporters to report them in a way that they see themselves?

So I think that the seducer is the one who is doing the talking. In testifying on journalistic procedure at the McGinniss-MacDonald trial, my point was that there is something between truth and lie, as we all know. I don't think Malcolm quoted me fairly. I think that because large portions of my testimony were not quoted, she didn't fairly convey my meaning or what I was talking about.

As a journalist, I would say you don't lie to anybody. You don't lie to anybody in life, why would you lie to people you

are interviewing? But are there times in life when I don't tell the exact truth? If my wife comes home and says, "How do you like my new dress that just cost five-hundred dollars?"—that sort of thing. As I said in my testimony, you go to a thirty-year reunion and everybody is saying things that aren't true. But nobody is lying. There is a hell of a difference. My idea of a lie is an untruth that is told with ill will, malice, or bad intent, or that is uttered with knowledge that it could harm the person.

Another thing absent from her article: I was limiting my testimony as an expert witness to my dealings in life as a policeman and as an author with sociopathic killers, who will manipulate you. I was trained as an investigator to interview this kind of person—the most heinous kind of horrendous person. And when one of these people who has just raped a defenseless woman says to the investigator, "You know what you feel like sometimes, you get this urge and they ask for it, don't they?" you react a certain way. You are trying to get this guy to confess so you can put the bastard behind bars so he can't rape anybody else. I was trained that you are supposed to say something like, "Oh sure, Charlie, I know how you feel. Jesus, I mean I can't quit smoking and drinking. How can I criticize you?"

Malcolm quoted me as testifying that even though I didn't believe one of the murderers in *The Onion Field*, I said I did when he asked me if I agreed that he didn't shoot the police officer. I don't know if I said the word "said" or if a court reporter wrote down "said" or if Malcolm misquoted me. But if I had to be precisely correct now as a result of this debate I would say I would *imply* understanding. I would say to the guy something noncommittal, something like, "Well, I haven't really thought it all out completely." That is no more true than it is not true because obviously I had come to a conclusion.

But is it a lie? If it's a lie, tell me where there is malice, ill will, or bad intent.

I am limiting this to dealing with sociopathic murderers. I am not talking about my interviews with victims, witnesses, or ordinary people. I am talking specifically about a Jeffrey MacDonald who must manipulate his interviewer as he must manipulate everyone in his life. At those precise moments I think it is fair play to give him a vague and noncommittal answer which is not exactly the truth.

I think Joe McGinniss's behavior was very unusual. It was very unusual to have that sort of an arrangement with MacDonald. I would never give anyone a percentage of my royalties, I don't care who it was. To me that sort of taints a relationship to begin with. But, on the other hand, Joe was very naive about sociopaths. I, on the other hand, am not naive about people like that and I know how their m.o. works, and I would never ever get involved in a relationship with one of them or one who could be such a person by the very nature of what he is being accused of.

Joseph Wambaugh is the author of novels and nonfiction books.

WENDELL RAWLS, JR.

As reporters, we generally deal with adults, grown people, who should understand that we are seeking what we hope is the truth. To call this process indefensible is ludicrous. Without sounding too high-minded about it, we are in the business of informing the public, and

that's more important than the feelings of the person being interviewed.

Yes, there are times when I feel uncomfortable reporting facts that I imagine will cause a source some pain. I deal with it by calling up the source and telling him what I'm going to do. I don't let the source get ambushed.

But what concerns me most is sloppy reporting. Having been an editor for two and a half years and also having been the subject of several interviews by supposedly first-rate journalists, I am very concerned at how inaccurate the reporting is. I've found that reporters are very selective about which quotes they're going to use and also rearrange quotes to prove a point. And too many reporters play fairly fast and loose with what somebody said. They don't take good notes. They are listening to only half the quote, then get back to the office and can't remember what the other half was and are embarrassed to call the person back to ask for a clarification. I think that's a much more severe problem in American journalism and a severe test of our credibility. It has nothing to do with betraying anybody; it's simply a matter of craftsmanship.

One more point: I think Malcolm is a little off base in the way she uses the term "journalist." To me a journalist is a person who writes for newspapers and magazines and when he starts writing books he's an author, not a journalist. I know it's convenient to talk about book-length journalism but that's really just general nonfiction. A newspaper or magazine reporter generally doesn't spend enough time with a source to develop an emotional relationship that can lead to betrayal. The reporter is seeking information and moving on. Book writers come to a subject with a point of view. As an author you sell that point of view in order to make money. You sell access, you sell insider information, you sell, sell, sell. The journalist doesn't do that. He puts together facts for a story on a given day and his salary doesn't change. To me there's a big difference between an author telling a publisher how this or that is going to improve his book and a reporter telling his editor, "This is the truth."

Wendell Rawls, Jr. is assistant managing editor of The Atlanta Journal *and* Constitution.

BARBARA WALTERS

I think most of the time reporters come in and say, "Look, I want to do a piece on you and I believe that I will be fair and that it will be a balanced piece. Do you want to do it?" Still, there is a kernel of truth in what Malcolm says. It's not that the reporter comes on and lies; it's that there is a tendency in doing articles, especially magazine profiles, to look for what's sensational.

At the moment two different authors whom I don't know are writing books about me. From what comes back to me from the people they have called, the intent of one of them clearly seems to be to write something critical, derogatory, scathing, because that's what sells. Scathing profiles seem to sell more than flattering ones. I myself don't like to be interviewed for a magazine article. I feel much more comfortable being interviewed by television people because even if the interview is edited, some of what you said gets on. And there isn't the same opportunity to work in things like "she said sarcastically" or "she said, with a grin" or "with a smirk." I think

everyone worries about being the victim of a hatchet job.

One of the reasons my specials with celebrities have been a success as long as they have been is that these people know that after I've talked to them I'm not going to go behind their back and talk to their ex-husband or the manager they fired or whatever. I mean, what you see is what you get. And that's one of the reasons they do these interviews. Nobody has been tricked, nobody has been deceived.

There are times when you're editing an interview when you think, Oh, I know he's not going to like this, but I'm going to leave it in. I *have* to leave it in. That's why you try not to do interviews with friends. But this just isn't the same as what Malcolm is talking about. I mean I never lead someone to think I'm going to do a flattering piece and then do something very different. For example, I was invited to do an interview with the Duvaliers. My feeling is that they probably thought they were going to come out very well. But I had a lot of cancelled checks that showed thousands of dollars on their government expense accounts for personal jewelry, for example.

Now the interview did the Duvaliers absolutely no good; if anything, it did them harm. But I didn't come on and say to the Duvaliers, "Look, I'm your greatest admirer. I promise you, you're going to look good."

There was something Mrs. Duvalier said. She's very articulate, very attractive, but she came on and she said—you know, you just can't live in Port au Prince without air conditioning, which in that poverty-stricken country certainly didn't make her look very good. Well, so do you cut that out? Of course you don't. You don't even have to make a comment.

Barbara Walters is co-host of ABC News's 20/20 *and host of* The Barbara Walters Specials.

THOMAS B. MORGAN

When I have defended McGinniss, because I basically feel McGinniss has won this argument, a lot of people say, "Oh, you're one of those people who believes the end justifies the means," and I say, "No, I believe some ends justify some means. He wrote an honest book, he got his story." I think the means were justified by the end. Because to me the whole issue of integrity centers on what a journalist puts on paper, what he publishes in a magazine or a book.

As for my own journalistic means—and I don't say this with any pride—I have many times pretended to be amused by people who are not amusing, have nodded in agreement when I do not really agree, have asked ten irrelevant questions, knowing that the eleventh question is going to be kárate chop. I feel that morally defensible journalism is rarely, to paraphrase Hemingway, what you feel good about afterward; it is only that which makes you feel better than you would otherwise.

As a rule, the people I wrote about—and I must have written some forty or fifty profiles—were all in the public eye. Now people who present themselves to the public consciously project a certain image, and I always felt it was my job to deconstruct that image, so to speak. The whole thrust of most of my articles was: now we will test this or that person's image against reality. That's really what the New Journalism was all about.

The older form was typified by one of my favorite profiles, the one Lillian Ross did of Hemingway in *The New Yorker.* You don't feel her presence in that article. Then in the late fifties we nobodies, representing all the other nobodies, got access to the great, the famous, and the beautiful, and, as I say, we went into the business of deconstruction. The people we were writing about were people of power, people of substance, people of great fame, and some of them turned out to be, *in our opinion*—and it was always just our opinion—quite unworthy of it.

There were limits, self-imposed limits. For instance, I never wrote about a subject's sex life. As a matter of fact, I usually didn't write about a subject's married life at all. I felt that was private. I had a strong sense of what was private and what was public in a public person.

Thomas B. Morgan is a novelist and journalist whose profiles written in the late 1950s and early '60s are considered precursors of the New Journalism.

BARRY MICHAEL COOPER

There is a bit of the con man in the journalist. You have to console, you have to empathize, you have to plead, to get to the truth. And if you don't, if you are just blunt, you can say something that totally turns your subject off and he won't talk to you again. It's happened to me.

But I don't consider that malicious lying. I'd call it slanted empathy—empathy with a purpose. And that purpose is that you are trying to get to a larger truth. You are trying to establish what the real story is.

A lot of times reporting is war; you have to do what you have to do to get a truth. Once you are adept at getting someone off guard, I think you become a good interviewer.

Because I am always open to having my mind changed, I am not being two-faced. Essentially, what I am trying to do is to gather information. I will give you a case in point. In my interview with Larry Davis [who was charged with injuring six police officers in a shootout in the Bronx, but acquitted of the most serious charges], I knew I wasn't betraying him, even though my story was very critical in the end. I didn't know what I was going to write when I spoke with him. And he was spinning *me* around. I was just trying to get information from the guy. And I empathized with him in a few instances and in others I came right out and said, "I don't believe you."

I think a lot of times when you are honest with your subject you can get a reaction that tells the truth about him. Davis got impatient with me because I kept saying, "Tell me details you haven't told anybody else. Tell me the real truth." He got mad at first and then he started laughing and he said, "Wait for the movie." And that was a telling remark and an important part of the story because it was Davis seeing himself as what he had become: a media image.

This doesn't mean that I will print anything—particularly when the subject might not realize what he's saying. Sometimes, whether with Arsenio Hall or with Latinos who lived near the kids accused of raping the jogger in Central Park, I'll shut off the tape when I think they could be hurting themselves inadvertently. I'll say something like, "I want you to understand that this tape isn't running. What was recorded is on the record, as we agreed, but are you sure you want to continue with this conversation?"

In almost every case they say yes. In black and Latino neighborhoods in particular, I feel I have to do this. I hate to say it, but to be very honest, a lot of white journalists and reporters come to the black neighborhoods and never explain these things to people and the people wind up getting hurt. I find that when you are very honest with your subject—about what you know and what you think you are going to do—nine times out of ten people in the inner city are very honest in response and they respect you in the end.

Barry Michael Cooper is a staff writer for The Village Voice *who has written about teenage drug gangs in Detroit and Baltimore and about the youths accused of the gang rape of a jogger in New York's Central Park this spring.*

DAVID HALBERSTAM

Malcolm really hit on something germane, but she has gone after it with a sledgehammer. I think "betrayal" is a very, very strong and ugly word. And to say that journalists, as a matter of course, do this is particularly offensive to anybody who was a reporter in the South, where many sources were very vulnerable to the white power structure, and reporters kept their trust; to anyone who was a reporter in Vietnam, where we often had sources who were enormously vulnerable to a powerful military machine, and where we kept the trust; or to colleagues of mine who worked with dissidents in the Soviet Union and kept the trust.

Now I think you can practice journalism well and do your job and be straight. But I also think there is the potential for an imbalance here. The reporter has dealt with hundreds of people in all kinds of situations. And reporters by dint of their training have a considerable amount of charm and grace and the ability to get people to talk—to project a kind of pseudo-intimacy. By contrast, in many cases far from public-domain journalism they are dealing with ordinary people who have never dealt with a reporter before. Perhaps the way to confront this is to think of members of your own family: How would you want them to be treated?

When I was in Vietnam, Horst Faas of the AP and I got these little name tags that we sewed on our fatigue jackets that said "Halberstam, New York Times," and "Faas, AP." Most of the reporters began to do this. We didn't want anyone to speak to us with any misimpression of who we were.

I think the relationship is much easier with sources in the traditional public domain. Both sides tend to know the rules of the game and how to play it. Neil Sheehan tells a very accurate story in *A Bright Shining Lie* about John Vann, the lieutenant colonel who was certainly in the great tradition of sources in that he was using us to disseminate information and we were relying on him for what we believed was his realistic appraisal of what was happening.

There was a moment when he virtually got court martialed because of his relationship with me. He was being sent home and we gave him a small silver cigarette box at the airport and he and I walked across the tarmac to his plane and I said, "You know, I was always scared that when I was writing about you I would hurt you."

He gave me a quite cold, steely look and said, "You never hurt me any more than I wanted to be hurt."

I think Malcolm is writing about a new and important and contemporary phenomenon, a change in nonfiction letters,

where the book is show-business driven and the reporter is not so much a reporter in the classic sense but an agent of Hollywood. I would call this mini-series journalism, where the journalist covers a murder in no small part because it has a potential mini-series in it.

The networks like these mini-series done off real life stories. And, of course, they want releases from the subjects. In this area Malcolm is quite right: the writer wants to ingratiate himself or herself with X or Y in order to get not just the story, but the release.

I think this leads to all kinds of abuses. Instead of normal access you need a new level of intimacy and a legal relationship. The murderer may be your literary partner.

McGinniss's relationship with MacDonald was bizarre, and I think it was unnecessary. Joe McGinniss is so talented he could have written a wonderful book without MacDonald being his best pal, roommate, and literary partner. Whether he could have gotten a legal agreement which released the mini-series is another thing. I am terribly bothered by a contract that gives a man like MacDonald 30 or 35 percent. I think Joe should be ashamed of himself.

David Halberstam, who won a Pulitzer Prize for his reporting from Vietnam in 1964 for The New York Times, *is the author of several books of nonfiction.*

JOHN TAYLOR

Malcolm's main assertion is so overly broad as to be ridiculous. But there are aspects of what she says that are worth considering seriously.

I think the journalist has a responsibility not to take advantage, for the sake of his own article, of the kind of human, weak, foolish things that we all do and say in the course of our lives. To make merciless fun of someone who has agreed to be profiled is, I think, very unfair. To me that is like breaching the sort of social contract you have entered into.

It's a different matter if you are doing a story about a person who hasn't cooperated; the same sort of social contract doesn't exist. This doesn't mean, however, that you are required to be totally ruthless and exploit every weakness and slip up on the part of your subject. After all, the point of writing a profile is to capture the spirit of the person and what that person is all about in unguarded moments. We are all vain and pompous and ridiculous and a portrait could be done of us that is nothing more than an accumulation of our failings. But that isn't what we are all about; there is more to all of us than the sum of our flaws.

John Taylor writes for New York *magazine; his article "Holier Than Thou," published in* New York *in March, [1989], explored Jeffrey Masson's libel suit against Janet Malcolm.*

MARK SINGER

The thing I most resent about this whole controversy is that, by forcing us to defend ourselves against the charge that journalism is morally indefensible, it makes those of us who practice journalism sound like self-righteous jerks. And that's regrettable, because the issue in the abstract is really important and it is not one that I had ever seen discussed.

Here is how I relate to it. I get an actual, physical symptom when I go out to do reporting—a kind of butterflies-in-the-stomach feeling. And that's because I have to sort of barge in on somebody's life. Why I do it? Because, for me, it's fun

to find something out. I don't see the process as heartless or cold-blooded but as an act of discovery. Whenever I write about someone at length, something approximating friendship arises. I get to know them, and I have learned things about them. I happen to be the sort of person who feels compelled—and I hope not in a narcissistic way but out of a sense of fairness—to reveal part of myself to the person I am writing about. This comes in part from a genuine feeling that I am an invader, an intruder. Ultimately, with most of my subjects I come to feel that they have revealed too much of themselves. Let's say a person reveals that he or she is having an extramarital affair, and adds, "But please don't print that." What happens with me is that I wouldn't print it anyway. It bothers me that the subject even raises the issue.

My point is that, as a journalist, you're given a lot of responsibility. I'm aware that there are some people out there who abuse it. But I just don't believe that it is done universally. That notion is ridiculous.

As for myself, I am more bothered by my own peculiar need to omit and I struggle with that more than I do with the idea that I could mug somebody. Perhaps I could be accused of betraying the truth by protecting the subject, but as far as I'm concerned the word "betrayal" isn't relevant to what most journalists do.

Mark Singer is a staff writer at The New Yorker *and the author of* Funny Money *and* Mr. Personality.

POSTSCRIPT

Do Journalists Routinely Deceive Their Subjects?

The history of journalism has borne witness to many styles of writing and approaches to a story. In his book *Goodbye Gutenberg: The Newspaper Revolution of the 1980s*, Anthony Smith says that "investigation has become the most highly praised and highly prized form of journalism, taking the place of opinion leadership, the historic purpose of the press." The investigative reporter finds him- or herself in the position of both judge and jury—the authority to whom we turn to get the whole story. In many ways, McGinniss was asked to be an investigative journalist in this very manner—even using the original material of the courtroom drama to tell his story.

While it is sometimes easy to think of people in any profession by lumping them together with a few descriptive terms, this issue outlines the importance of the journalist as a human being, with very real emotions and biases that may well affect their work. The nature of ethical issues should not be easily resolved: We should always struggle to discuss them, think about them, and let them guide our consciences. Only when we cease thinking about them is it too late to do anything about them.

There are many books on different styles of journalism, and it is often interesting to read biographies of such people as Greeley, Hearst, Pulitzer, and even Murdoch to see how each individual shaped a special time in journalism history. In addition to the Smith book mentioned above, other sources that describe journalistic themes and public reaction include Ben H. Bagdikian's *The Information Machines: Their Impact on Men and the Media* (Harper & Row, 1971); The Roper Organization's *Trends in Public Attitudes Toward Television and Other Media, 1969–1974* (Television Information Office, 1975); and John P. Robinson's, *Daily News Habits of the American Public*, ANPA News Research Center Study No. 15 (September 22, 1978).

There are also several periodicals that cover journalistic styles and practices. Among them are *Columbia Journalism Review, Editor and Publisher*, and the *American Society of Newspaper Editors (ASNE) Newsletter*.

ISSUE 6

Can Privacy Be Protected in the Information Age?

YES: James B. Rule, from "Data Wars: Privacy Protection in Federal Policy," in Paula R. Newburg, ed., *New Directions in Telecommunications Policy* (Duke University Press, 1989)

NO: David H. Flaherty, from *Protecting Privacy in Two-Way Electronic Services* (Knowledge Industry Press, 1985)

ISSUE SUMMARY

YES: Sociologist James Rule argues that a legal infrastructure for privacy protection currently exists within this country and he calls for adherence to both the spirit and the letter of the Privacy Act.
NO: David Flaherty, a Canadian professor of history and law, warns that the preponderance of new technologies and the individuals or corporations who are responsible for their use do little to consider privacy of the individual as a primary goal to be maintained.

Our personal lives in the home as well as our professional lives in the workplace have been subject to possible invasions of privacy through the collection of data about ourselves and the use or abuse of controls placed upon that information. Every time we subscribe to a cable television system, order telephone service, apply for a credit card, or even request a check-cashing card at a local grocery store, data files about us are compiled. Today, with the use of vast computer data bases, information may be compiled and processed without our knowing it. Normally, for most people, this may not be a problem—until we find that some of the information in the data bank may be incorrect.

Consider the case of Frank G. Palermo, who was one of the unfortunate subjects described in Clark Norton's article "Threats to Privacy: Is There No Confidentiality?" (*Comment*, January 1990). When Palermo broke his thumb in a skiing accident, the hospital summoned his medical records from his family physician. The file indicated that Palermo had had his kidney stones removed; had broken his nose and recently a leg; and that he had had his gall bladder removed at the age of two. As it turned out, the family physician had mistakenly compiled the medical records of three Frank G. Palermos—the subject of the study, his cousin, and a grandfather, who all had the same name.

Other breaches of security that invade privacy have included the misuse of personal information about individuals. For example, a company in Pittsfield, Massachusetts, worked with the local cable company to feed certain commercials to some homes. When the homeowner went to the local grocery store and paid by check, the check number and products purchased were measured against the commercials the individual had seen, thereby testing the effectiveness of those commercials on purchasing behavior. While these two examples may not seem like serious invasions of privacy, they do illustrate how information about us can be collected, sold, and used without our knowledge or consent.

Many companies routinely sell individuals' names, addresses, telephone numbers, and occasionally demographic data to companies who wish to market products to specific target audiences. In making a profit on information about us, do these companies violate our privacy? When a telemarketer wakes us up and tries to sell us a new product or service, is that a violation of our privacy? In many ways, both actions do abuse our right as private citizens to live within the "security of [our] person."

As we subscribe to new technological services, furnish private information about our consumption habits, and create paper-trails through paying by check or credit card, we willingly, even if unknowingly, give up personal information about ourselves. All too often, the people processing this information have no security clearances. One student in class told us of her experiences working as a bank teller near an Army base: when she was asked for a date by a serviceman, and she was often asked, she would routinely look up his bank balance before deciding on whether or not to go out with him!

The answer to ensuring privacy is to create sophisticated encoding devices that make sure that unauthorized individuals do not misuse the information that has been stored, but we know that no computer system is infallible. It has been said that computer crime is the number-one crime in America today—but the problem is often detecting *when* information has been abused. All too often we only find out about incorrect personal information when we are denied a loan, turned down for a job, or denied access to services or organizations based upon incorrect information in a data base. Untangling the web of inaccurate or misleading data can be troublesome and costly.

Most states have their own specific laws or guidelines concerning the privacy of their residents, and the federal government has 14 different agencies dealing with aspects of personal privacy. As the two selections that follow indicate, legislating for privacy is indeed a difficult matter.

YES   James B. Rule

DATA WARS: PRIVACY PROTECTION
IN FEDERAL POLICY

In 1966 federal officials and private users of government information had an
historic inspiration. The federal government, they noted, possessed rich
repositories of information on private citizens, ranging from census data to
Internal Revenue Service (IRS) files to Social Security data. The trouble was
that these data were dispersed; even where regulations permitted it, the
costs of locating and assembling them were prohibitive. What was needed
was a National Data Center to collate and centralize such information and
make them quickly and economically available.

The Data Center, as then conceived, was to provide aggregate information
to researchers, rather than data on identifiable individuals to administrative
or enforcement agencies. Still, the idea tapped a sensitive nerve among
elected officials concerned about their constituents' privacy. As Congressman Frank Horton stated, "Good computermen know that one of the most
practical of our present safeguards of privacy is the fragmented nature of
present information. It is scattered in little bits and pieces across the
geography and years of our life. Retrieval is impractical and often impossible.
A central data bank removes completely this safeguard." The administration
of President Lyndon Johnson got the message, Plans for the National Data
Center, though originally backed by powerful interests within the executive
branch, were shelved without legislation ever being submitted to Congress.

The brief controversy over the National Data Center idea might be taken to
mark the beginning of federal controversies over what has come to be called
"privacy protection." Ironically, the groundswell of suspicion of that project,
and the diffident response of the Johnson administration, were little indication of the pattern of events to ensue.

Privacy protection debates show remarkable parallels to other policy
controversies. . . . All turn on disputes over creation, maintenance, and use
of various forms of information; all take on special intensity in the context of
sale or appropriation of data against the will of those who consider it "their
own." Such questions arise in policy disputes over automatic identification

of callers' phone numbers in telephone communications; over copyright disputes concerning software and computer chip design; over licensing of radio and television stations; and in a host of other contexts. In the privacy issue these themes follow certain familiar lines. When may personal information be collected for filing and use by government and private organizations? When *must* such collection be done? Who may use the data, what decisions may be based on it, how are those decisions to be made, and with whom may the data be shared? When do those depicted in such data files have the right to shape the uses of "their" information, and what should the specifics of such rights be? Controversies on these themes have generated an extensive but ambiguous legacy of federal "privacy protection" principles, which now have their parallels both in the fifty states and abroad. . . .

"Privacy" is in fact a curious name for these issues. When we use the term in ordinary English, we usually refer to withholding certain forms of information, disclosure of which might be embarrassing or otherwise uncomfortable; maintaining privacy is to defend boundaries across which certain forms of personal information may not pass. Yet in privacy controversies of the sort considered here, the passage of personal data is often taken for granted. The record systems—computerized or otherwise—that have been at the center of these controversies have been created in the expectation, both by the organizations that create them and by the people to whom they refer, that the flow of such data is essential for specific purposes. The difficult political and ethical questions that they raise have to do not so much with the possibility of absolute concealment, but with questions of controlling the flow of personal information and the uses made of it.

ORIGINS OF THE ISSUE

There can be no doubt that the American public perceives life in the United States as marked by increasing pressures on privacy. Public opinion polls show consistently rising concern over these issues since at least the 1970s. These anxious attitudes have ample basis in actual social practice. Consider the points in the life of a typical American where a particular relationship or transaction is shaped by the content of a written or computerized "record" on the person concerned. Early this century one might well have expected to go through life untouched by such encounters; the great "trunk lines" of personal information flow—in consumer credit, Social Security, income taxation, insurance, and banking—had yet to arise. In the late twentieth century, in contrast, an enormous variety of life junctures require recourse to one's "record" before they can be successfully completed. Not only income taxation, consumer credit and Social Security, but also access to insurance and medical care, treatment by law enforcement agencies, international travel, purchases made by credit and debit cards, and a wide variety of other life junctures are dominated by the content of one's "file."

How is one to account for these growing demands by organizations for personal information? For most people, one suspects, the origin of these trends is in the rise of computing. But this explanation is incorrect, at least in this simple form.

In fact, many key forms of personal record-keeping, now thoroughly computerized, were already well instated before the computer. Consumer credit records, now held and transmitted through sophisticated computerized systems, existed in the tens if not scores of millions before computerization. Social security, income taxation, passport, insurance and a variety of other record systems served many of the same purposes under conventional technologies. Some of these systems, including welfare-state benefit systems abroad, go back as far as the early decades of this century. Computing has undoubtedly streamlined the growth and impact of these systems, but it has hardly created them de novo.

For many organizations, both public and private, an essential "product" or output is some form of treatment of people. Such organizations use personal information to shape these treatments. This statement holds true for the widest variety of data-using organizations— from law enforcement systems to consumer credit, from schools and hospitals to tax collection bureaucracies. For all such bodies a key task is to administer precisely the "correct" action to each of what may be millions of individuals, in light of the full detail of relevant facts on each separate case. Thus a constant flow of decisions: for merchants and financial institutions, to deny or grant consumer credit—and if to grant, to what extent; for law enforcement agencies, to arrest, to monitor, or to ignore a particular individual—and if he or she is arrested, what sanctions to apply; for insurance firms, to deny insurance or to offer it—and if the latter, at what rates; for tax collection agencies, who is liable to pay—and how much. Such examples could extend end-

lessly. The contents of these actions may be welcome or unwelcome to the individual; they may be benign or coercive. But in all such cases the quest for discrimination in treatment requires development of, and attention to, written or computerized records.

Thus, it is easy to understand why large-scale systems of personal records compiled and used by organizations have attracted so much controversy. They matter enormously in what happens to individuals. They govern whether someone will be promoted or dismissed, accorded welfare payments or denied them, kept under surveillance or favored with benign neglect. We should hardly be surprised at the breadth and intensity of disputes that have grown up over the workings of these systems. . . .

What does it mean to "protect privacy" from the abuses of large-scale personal record systems? What constitute reasonable legal and institutional strategies for supporting both individual rights and the abstract values, such as freedom of expression, affected by such systems? A variety of approaches have been entertained. . . .

The United States is virtually unique among countries with significant privacy protection legislation in lacking a permanent national institution responsible for monitoring personal data systems and defending privacy interests in the workings of these systems. Such a body was envisaged in the legislation that was to become the Privacy Act of 1974. But strong opposition from the Ford administration resulted in its removal from the final version.

Canada and most Western European countries now have such boards. Their responsibilities vary by country, but in general they are charged with investigating and publicizing personal data systems and defending individuals in some way aggrieved by the systems. In some countries the boards also license systems in the private sector. Typically the boards have little peremptory power to force keepers of data systems to change their practices, but they do have power to attract public attention and to recommend that other public agencies consider forceful action.

In the United States the Privacy Act of 1974, like most other privacy legislation, normally requires individual action by an interested party to set its provisions in motion. In the words of the Report of the Privacy Protection Study Commission, there is an effort to create an "assertable interest" on the part of individuals to act in their own behalf. Such powers of oversight over compliance with the Privacy Act as exist within the executive branch are lodged with the Office of Management and Budget. . . .

Until the late 1960s the American public seems to have been largely unaware of the existence of the credit reporting industry. Credit reporting bureaus, then just beginning to computerize, devote themselves to collecting, storing, and selling data on "private" consumer creditworthiness. These data included—and still include—information on income, performance in paying past credit accounts, history of bankruptcies, litigation, liens and the like, along with address, family status and similar data. The contents of such reports did, and do, have major influence on applications for credit and, sometimes, employment and other opportunities. But Americans in the late 1960s were shocked to find that the industry responsible for generating such reports was virtually free of legal obligations to ensure accuracy of records or to open credit records to the people depicted in them.

The Fair Credit Reporting Act of 1970 established such a legal framework. It authorized reporting for virtually all purposes for which firms had been accustomed to doing so—including credit, employment, insurance, licensing, and to any buyer who "otherwise has a legitimate business need for the information in connection with a business transaction involving the customer." It authorized provision of data without subpoena from credit files to police and other investigators. It limited the age of information that can be reported in credit reports, though the limits (normally seven years) are beyond what most agencies would find it profitable to report.

Perhaps most importantly, the act requires that credit reporting agencies disclose to people the contents of their own records and to correct inaccuracies in such records when they are pointed out. Buyers of credit reports who decline applications as the result of such reports are required to refer the applicants to the bureau.

The Fair Credit Reporting Act is noteworthy both for the changes it dictates in record-keeping practice and in the limits it sets for itself. In the terms used above the thrust of the act is overwhelmingly procedural, rather than substantive. Its provisions make the information processes it addresses more open, less mysterious and more subject to influence by the persons concerned. To this extent it has undoubtedly smoothed the flow of credit transactions and avoided certain injustices and inconveniences, especially those stemming from mistaken identity.

At the same time virtually nothing in the law restricts access of the industry to its key sources of personal data, nor does it interfere with other entrenched practices that many would consider invasive of privacy. The Fair Credit Reporting Act creates "rules of the game" in which both institutions and individuals can pursue their interests, on the assumption that nothing must be allowed to interfere with the flow of data "needed" for the smooth processing of credit transactions.

The principles underlying the Fair Credit Reporting Act became the basis for key pronouncements and legislation in the years to follow. The year 1973 saw publication of *Records, Computers and Rights of Citizens* by the Department of Health, Education and Welfare (HEW); this influential document took stock of privacy controversies and proposed a core of principles for dealing with them. As summarized by Priscilla Regan of the Office of Technology Assessment, these are as follows:

—There must be no personal data record-keeping system whose very existence is secret.
—There must be a way for an individual to find out what information about him or her is in a record and how it is used.
—There must be a way for an individual to prevent information about him or her that was obtained for one purpose from being used for other purposes without his or her consent.
—There must be a way for an individual to correct or amend a record of identifiable information about him or her.
—Any organization creating, maintaining, using or disseminating records of identifiable personal data must assure the reliability of the data for their intended use and must take precautions to prevent misuse of the data.

While an unexpected manifesto for privacy protection, these precepts were not intended to apply to all record systems, even in principle; records maintained for investigation or espionage purposes were exempted from consideration ab initio.

The Privacy Act of 1974 took its inspiration directly from the principles enunciated in the HEW study. The act remains the most fundamental and far-reaching of federal privacy legislation. Passed at the height of impact of Watergate on American opinion, it clearly represented the effort of Congress to respond vigorously to public indignation at government data-gathering. The Privacy Act deals with record systems maintained by government institutions; it excludes the Central Intelligence Agency and most law enforcement bodies from most of its provisions.

With some exceptions the act requires that creation of new personal record systems be acknowledged in a Federal Register notice. It requires that federal agencies covered by the act maintain only such records as are "relevant and necessary to accomplish" their missions; they are to collect data "to the greatest extent practicable from the subject individual," and to inform persons of the authority on which information is demanded on them.

In a particularly significant provision the act limits disclosure from agency files to other agencies having "routine uses" of the record for purposes "compatible with the purposes for which it was collected"—and to law enforcement agencies. This provision has been subject to some remarkable interpretations over the ensuing years.

Finally, like the Fair Credit Reporting Act, the Privacy Act provides for access to files by their subjects and makes provision for subjects to dispute contents and make changes. Individuals dissatisfied with the content of their files are, as in the credit legislation, entitled to add a statement of their own to the files, to be disseminated with the files themselves.

Like the Fair Credit Report Act, then, the Privacy Act is far more procedural than substantive. The great emphasis is on opening up record keeping procedures and creating protections against inaccurate or incomplete information. The act recognizes no conflict between expansion of record-keeping and protection of individual privacy interests.

One exception is the "routine uses" provision. This provision presupposes that more comprehensive, more thoroughgoing, more efficient uses by government of information on individuals may not always be a good thing. Instead, it implies the wisdom of artificial barriers, such that information available to one government agency should not flow automatically elsewhere. The fact that data of one kind are made available for medicare transactions, for example, should not necessarily mean that these same data are to be used for tax collection purposes or security checks. Such assumptions turn out to be important in the elaboration of legislation and policy during the years since 1974.

In lieu of creating a permanent privacy protection agency within the federal government, the Privacy Act provided for creation of the Privacy Protection Study Commission (PPSC). This temporary body was to recommend further legislation extending the act to organizations in the private sector. The commission mounted a significant research effort into personal data practices in such diverse areas as direct mail, credit card companies, and insurance, including both many documentary searches and public

hearings. Its ensuing report contained some 162 recommendations for further legislation.

Continuity with the principles underlying earlier official thinking and legislation is evident in these recommendations. The Privacy Commission authors state their guiding aims as follows:

—to create a proper balance between what an individual is expected to divulge to a record-keeping organization and what he seeks in return (*to minimize intrusiveness*);
—to open up record-keeping operations in ways that will minimize the extent to which recorded information about an individual is itself a source of unfairness in any decision about him made on the basis of it (*to maximize fairness*); and
—to create and define obligations with respect to the uses and disclosures that will be made of recorded information about an individual (*to create legitimate, enforceable, expectations of confidentiality*).

True to the tradition of which it is part, the Privacy Commission proposed few recommendations that would block major established record-keeping practices. Most of its recommendations aim at making existing procedures more accessible to the individuals concerned and more subject to due-process rules.

Here and there, however, commission recommendations did call into question the efficiency of record-using organizations as the unique value at stake in personal data management. For example, they recommend restrictions on access of investigative agencies to "personal papers" of private individuals held by third parties—for example, bank account records and credit files—access which is certainly efficient from the standpoint of the agencies involved.

Similarly, they recommend against use of the polygraph by employers. These recommendations are important, for they point to some serious issues not often acknowledged in writing and legislation on privacy protection: substantive issues of how much information should be collected and used, or of what organizational purposes are important enough to warrant such collection and use. Compared to the goals of making existing or prospective data systems more open to scrutiny and participation by those affected and more just, these substantive questions are considerably more nettlesome. . . .

The simplest and most direct step toward asserting strong privacy interests would be to enforce the Privacy Act of 1974, in both letter and spirit. Initiatives could come either from the Congress or the executive branch.

NO
David H. Flaherty

THE PROTECTION OF PRIVACY

THE NATURE OF PRIVACY

In simple terms, concern for personal privacy involves an individual's basic desire to be left alone to enjoy a private life. People want to choose freely under what circumstances, and to what extent, they will reveal their attitudes and their behavior to others.

Alan F. Westin, in *Privacy and Freedom* (1967), identified four integral states of privacy which, when taken together, add focus to the definition of the term. These are the concerns of an individual to enjoy solitude, intimacy, anonymity and reserve. Solitude, the most pristine form of privacy, refers to the individual's desire to be let alone without outside interference. Intimacy refers to the state of privacy that two friends, a husband and wife, or a family might want to enjoy together away from the outside world. Anonymity refers to a person's wish to be free of external surveillance. Finally, reserve refers specifically to an individual's desire to control the flow of information about himself or herself. All of these concerns have some relevance to the privacy interests at stake in using two-way services.

Arnold Simmel, in the *International Encyclopedia of the Social Sciences* (1968), ties together several of Westin's states of privacy in the following useful comment: "Privacy is a concept related to solitude, secrecy and autonomy, but it is not synonymous with these terms; for beyond the purely descriptive aspects of privacy as isolation from the company, the curiosity and the influence of others, privacy implies a normative element: the right to exclusive control to access to private realms." This last phrase has particular relevance to any household's right to regulate all forms of outside intrusion into the activities carried out and opinions expressed within strictly private domain. . . .

Public Concern About Privacy
While some individuals may place more value on privacy than others, recent studies have indicated that, on the whole, privacy is an issue of significant

concern to the general public. Indeed, according to a May 1982 survey conducted by Bell Canada ("Public Attitudes Toward the New Micro-Electronic Technologies"), "privacy and confidentiality of personal information is the key public issue surrounding the spread of new technologies."

A Louis Harris survey, commissioned by the Southern New England Telephone Co. and reported in the December 8, 1983 *New York Times* found that the percentage of the general public "very concerned" about privacy threats had grown from 31% in 1978 to 48% by September 1983, when the telephone poll of 1256 persons was undertaken. In addition, some 84% of respondents believed that it would be easy for someone to assemble a master profile about them that would invade their privacy. A similar percentage favored criminal sanctions against data-collecting businesses that violated an individual's privacy.

The findings of the London Privacy Survey, which polled a random sample of 210 households in London, Ontario in 1982, also confirm the extent to which the general public is concerned about the preservation of its privacy; 90% of respondents cited the protection of privacy as important or very important. When compared to other major social and economic issues, the protection of privacy was rated as only slightly less important than controlling inflation, unemployment and crime, yet it was deemed more important than stopping the spread of nuclear weapons and ending strikes. Sixty-two percent of those polled were very concerned or somewhat concerned about the threats to their personal privacy in Canada today. Eighty-four percent agreed wholly or partially that storage of personal information on computers poses a danger to personal privacy, and 80% agreed or somewhat agreed that cable companies offering two-way services would have access to too much information about their personal lives. Survey results also indicate that people do not trust governments and the private sector to use personal information properly; 62% of the London respondents were concerned about how businesses used personal information solicited from them, while 49% expressed distrust about the federal and provincial governments' use of information.

It should be mentioned here that individuals residing in different countries or even different regions of the same country have diverse opinions both as to the importance of privacy and about what personal information is regarded as sensitive. For the most part, Canadians and residents of the United Kingdom have been much less openly concerned to date about the protection of personal privacy than citizens in the United States, Sweden and West Germany.

When abuses of personal privacy are brought to public attention by newspapers or commissions of inquiry in Canada, for example, the degree of public outrage seems to be very muted or at best, short-lived. One result is that Canadian politicians have felt very little pressure to strengthen legislation for the protection of privacy, especially at the provincial level. However, there have been signs that this situation in Canada is changing. In the spring of 1982 the Quebec government passed legislation creating a data protection commission along European lines to regulate the public sector. In addition, in July 1982 the federal government passed a new and reinvigorated federal Privacy Act. In May 1984 the Ontario government hosted a symposium and interprovincial meeting, which concluded that the protection of personal information in both the public and private sectors has become an important issue.

Privacy, Voluntariness and Informed Consent

To date, there has been only limited recognition, especially under Canadian and English law, of the individual's *legal* right to privacy. Such non-legal status seems appropriate considering that the enjoyment of privacy will always be governed by personal preferences and the balancing of conflicting interests by each individual. While governments, law enforcers and courts may establish the limits of an individual's claim to privacy, the search for privacy should also touch on various non-legal concerns, such as the character of family, neighborhood and community life; communications and correspondence; and the effects of institutional life on individuals. Because privacy is such a broad and general concept and one defined on a personal, individualized basis, it is unlikely that it will achieve complete recognition as a legal and constitutional right, no matter how desirable that goal might seem to be.

Since under Canadian and American law people are for the most part left to their own devices when it comes to protecting their privacy, the issues of voluntariness and informed consent become essential elements in understanding and dealing with the potential dangers to privacy posed by the use of two-way services. A person can, for example, voluntarily choose whether to subscribe to two-way services, whether to limit the specific interactive services that are brought into the home, and whether to-

restrict the use of the system to what the individual regards as nonsensitive matters. If a person were to choose freely to subscribe to every available two-way service, with reasonable awareness of its implications for his or her personal privacy, one might question the person's judgment but could not claim that invasion of the person's privacy was occurring. There are, no doubt, some individuals who would have no objection to having their opinions on particular issues continually recorded or their TV viewing habits identified in detail. But individuals should be fully informed of the information being collected by companies offering two-way services and what is being done with it. With this end in mind, companies must adopt a standard code of fair information practices, which includes controls on the collection and transfer of personal information, and terms and conditions for the maintenance of data and the preservation of their security.

Because interactive cable services can collect information about individuals and their behavior within the confines of their own homes and often without their knowledge—e.g., the data available to cable company computers as a result of channel-monitoring capacity—they represent a heretofore unprecedented potential for violation of personal privacy and challenge the traditional concept that "a man's house is his castle."

As stated in a 1981 Collingwood Associates study for the U.S. Federal Trade Commission, "it is difficult for consumers to ever learn that their privacy has been breached. Again, consumers may not even know about the privacy implications of the services in the first place." The study added that "even if consumers had such information, they could do little as individuals to protect their privacy."[1]

Both the Collingwood Associates study and a 1982 Gardner and White study for the New York State Consumer Protection Board suggest that governments and companies have an obligation to educate consumers about the privacy risks of interactive services. There is, of course, a difference between educating and protecting consumers. In Canada, some consumer protection has generally been accepted as the responsibility of one level of government or another. Yet, except in the credit information field, few government initiatives have been taken with respect to the private sector protection of privacy. Gardner and White note that consumers become part of the problem because of their orientation to convenience and general insensitivity to privacy issues: "the privacy-convenience trade-off is a silent, invisible one. . . ."[2]

GOVERNMENT INITIATIVES IN DATA PROCESSING

The buildup of automated personal information systems has clearly made the protection of private life very difficult. The new media, which include everything from interactive cable television and telephone services to electronic newspapers and videotex services, and the accompanying use of computers, microchip technology, and satellite and microwave communications are making possible the continued accumulation, storage, use and transfer of massive amounts of personal information on every aspect of life in model industrial societies. This information about individuals must be kept appropriately confidential so that their personal privacy is upheld. The preservation of the confidentiality and security of personal information is called data protection; at present, it is the most pressing area of concern for the protection of privacy. . . .

CABLE INDUSTRY RESISTANCE TO PRIVACY REGULATION

There is some tendency in the cable industry to regard privacy as an issue of concern only for extremists, faddists and civil libertarians. The heavy involvement of cable companies in the capital-intensive phase of building and rebuilding their systems tends to relegate concern for social issues such as privacy to the back burner. In addition, under one-way cable systems privacy was not a problem industry participants had to confront. Because of the proliferation of two-way services, however, cable companies now need to bring the same level of sophisticated consideration to privacy issues as they have to their technical and financial needs.

Among the arguments put forth by some cable company spokesmen denying the need for privacy protection are the ideas that subscribers have to trust the companies, that no privacy problems currently exist, that privacy is not a pressing issue for subscribers, that subscribing to cable is a voluntary act and that cable companies are just common carriers.

In general, cable companies are resistant to any further regulation by government authorities and therefore shun government intervention on behalf of privacy protection. Cable companies in Canada believe they are already operating under a substantial regulatory burden, especially in comparison to their American counterparts. A number of cable industry participants also feel that there is no need to legislate morality when it comes to such issues as the protection of privacy. (The contrasting opinion, held by radical sociologists, for example, is that the private sector will never decide "to do good," unless forced to do so.)

Reliance on the Marketplace
A popular viewpoint is that because cable companies have to rely on the goodwill of subscribers to stay in business, they would not want to jeopardize consumer trust by misuse of personal information. But this assertion does not deal with the economically motivated possibility that at some point a cable company may decide to sell personal information for profit. Indeed, cable companies, currently under considerable pressure to improve their marketing functions, are recruiting marketing and advertising specialists who may quite soon become aware of the monetary value of identifiable data on consumers collected from subscribers to two-way cable services. It therefore becomes easy to believe that, as suggested by a recent report to the New York State Consumer Protection Board, reliance on the marketplace as a form of privacy protection is an obsolete and simplistic notion.

In addition, almost no legal restrictions exist at present to prevent a cable company from selling personal information in its possession, since the general view in North America is that such data belong to the company itself. In Canada, however, the CRTC regulates all aspects of a "broadcasting receiving undertaking" (the legal term for a local cable company), and it could therefore interfere with any attempt to sell subscriber data to generate income. Since the U.S. does not regulate cable in the same way,

there are no legal prohibitions on a local cable company selling personal data, unless there is a municipal ordinance or a cable privacy statute to the contrary. . . .

Similarities to Other Industries
Cable companies content that they are no different from other private businesses that collect personal information, such as credit card and telephone companies, who face similar problems with respect to confidentiality. This is a valid argument, to some extent, and one which serves as a useful reminder that all two-way services pose significant privacy problems, whether delivered over coaxial cable, telephone wires, or via fiber optics. It is therefore quite appropriate to take an integrated approach to solving the problems of protecting privacy, confidentiality and security in all forms of interactive services. But . . . the privacy problems inherent in interactive services are much greater than any previously encountered in the use of traditional telephone or cable services.

It is nevertheless helpful to examine the potential threats to privacy posed by the use of telephone services, as many of these are similar to those encountered in the use of interactive cable. The telephone is a two-way system that enters almost every North American home. Transmissions that occur on the telephone are subject to legal and illegal wiretaps. Eavesdropping is also possible by third parties, including company personnel. Long-distance calls via satellites can be readily intercepted, especially by national security agencies. In addition, the telephone company may monitor conversations as part of its regular work and it maintains long-distance billing records, which specify numbers called.

Moreoever, the existence of the telephone in the home makes possible intrusive and unwanted telephone calls.

Fortunately, telephone companies have taken a number of steps toward the protection of privacy . . . and their efforts at self-regulation can serve as a model for cable companies. But in spite of these measures, the degree to which privacy can be violated provides compelling arguments for external regulation of both cable and telephone companies for the protection of confidentiality.

Credit card companies also possess a great deal of personal information about cardholders. The record of a credit card purchase can in fact establish the presence and activities of a given consumer at a particular place on a particular date, and such data may be recorded in a computerized cardholder file shortly after the transaction has been completed. Current billing processes are being handled with ever greater frequency in an online mode, so that a company like American Express, for example, is immediately notified about a credit charge through an automated point-of-sale device that also authorizes the transaction, or receives the charge data at the end of a business day through direct links between the computers of a retail operation and those of the credit card company. Thus, existing credit card systems also have considerable unregulated capacity for invading the privacy of individuals.

It must be kept in mind that, along with the similarities we have just examined, there are some substantial differences between the cable industry and other industries. The most significant of these for our purposes is that, because it is financially less secure than telephone and credit card companies, the cable industry may find itself under more economic pressure to sell information about subscribers.

NOTES

1. Deanna Collingwood Nash and John B. Smith, *Interactive Home Media and Privacy.* Prepared for the Office of Policy Planning, U.S. Federal Trade Commission (Washington, DC: Collingwood Associates, Inc., January 1981), pp. 12, 14.

2. *Ibid.*, p. 17. Sidney L. Gardner and Robin White, *New Technology and the Right to Privacy: State Responses to Federal Inaction. A Report to the New York State Consumer Protection Board.* (Unpublished draft, August 1982), pp. 6-8.

POSTSCRIPT

Can Privacy Be Protected in the Information Age?

Because privacy issues are often treated ad hoc or as a secondary area of inquiry for new technologies and services, abuses may occur. Unfortunately, the only way we find out about abuses is after they have taken place. Federal initiatives are lauditory, but unless they can be enforced, abuses may still complicate the lives of those individuals who suffer needlessly.

Many countries around the world have entered into their own legislation to protect the privacy of their citizens and to suggest guidelines for businesses operating within their borders. As the computer networks often used for the storage and transmission of personal data become increasingly large depositories for information, and those repositories are locating in other countries, issues of privacy may become even more important for local, regional, and governmental control. Could this lead to a type of "Big Brother" environment, where everyone's actions are watched? Perhaps the efficacy of the guidelines will tell the story.

For further reading in this interesting, yet complicated, issue, consult the U.S. government's *Privacy Journal* newsletter or the *Privacy Times*. Many government reports also address the complexities of privacy and interactive systems, such as *Interactive Home Media and Privacy* by Deanna Collingwood Nash and John B. Smith, prepared for the Office of Policy Planning, U.S. Federal Trade Commission (Washington, DC: January 1981), or the *Minutes of Proceedings and Evidence of the Subcommittee on Computer Crime*, Issue 5 (Ottawa: Canadian Government Publishing Centre, May 1983).

Worth reviewing also is the U.S. government's Freedom of Information Act of 1966, which provides for making information held by federal agencies available to the public unless the information falls within one of the specific categories exempt from public disclosure. Exempt records are those whose disclosure would impair rights of privacy or national security. Virtually all agencies of the executive branch of the federal government have issued regulations to implement the Freedom of Information Act. These regulations inform the public where certain types of information may be obtained, how other information may be obtained on request, and what internal agency appeals are available if the request for information is refused. For a comparative perspective, see Donald C. Rowat, ed., *Administrative Secrecy in Developed Countries* (Columbia University Press, 1979).

PART 3

Regulation

The issues in this section deal with concepts of who should be responsible for media content and the protection of the rights guaranteed to individuals in American society by the Constitution. We interpret policies and laws by reflecting on specific precedents, and these selections focus on perennial questions of interpretation.

Should the Federal Government
   Continue to Deregulate Commercial
   Broadcasting?
   _____

Should the Content of Records Be
   Censored?
   _____

Should Pornography Be Protected as
   Free Speech?

ISSUE 7

Should the Federal Government Continue to Deregulate Commercial Broadcasting?

YES: Mark S. Fowler and Daniel L. Brenner, from "A Marketplace Approach to Broadcast Regulation," *Texas Law Review* 60 (February 1982)

NO: Timothy E. Wirth, "The Television Environment: Cultivating the Wasteland," in Stuart Oskamp, ed., *Television as a Social Issue* (Sage, 1988)

ISSUE SUMMARY

YES: Former FCC chairman Mark Fowler and his legal assistant, Daniel Brenner, here articulate the most complete rationale for the deregulation of the communications industries. Their efforts on behalf of the Reagan administration did eventually bring about a lifting of all government broadcasting regulations.
NO: Senator Tim Wirth (D-Colorado), views deregulation as "not a goal" but a "means to an end" and therefore calls for greater governmental responsibility toward broadcast media.

In the two articles that follow, the authors discuss the relationship of government and broadcasters and the concurrent effect on broadcast content. Both selections acknowledge that the proliferation of new technologies and distribution systems call for a change in traditional practices, but the authors differ on what changes would better serve the public interest.

The Fowler and Brenner selection argues that the traditional "trusteeship model" of broadcast regulation, which called for ambiguous interpretation of the "public interest, convenience, and necessity," was impractical and has infringed upon the First Amendment rights of broadcasters. Calling attention to the founding philosophy of broadcast regulation, which deemed the airwaves as the property of the people, the authors state that airwave *scarcity* is no longer an issue with the multiplicity of channels and distribution forms, and therefore, a marketplace model would better serve the broadcaster and the listener/viewer's interests.

Indeed, during Fowler's tenure as FCC chairman, radio and television were both deregulated, thereby changing ownership rules, content restrictions, and extending the licensing period, having the effect of eliminating ascertainment and changing the interpretation of "public interest, convenience, and necessity." The determination of the Supreme Court's ruling on the famed *Red Lion* case, which found that the rights of the public were more important than the rights of the broadcasters, has been reinterpreted by Fowler's deregulatory position.

While the purpose of deregulation is to open the market to create more competition for business, there can often be several side effects that result in less maintenance and control of content. Tim Wirth sees the value of deregulation as an opening of the market for competition in new technologies and distribution but warns that content may suffer if deregulation proceeds unchecked.

Wirth argues that the most important need for society is to be responsive to the deregulation of television aimed at children. In this case, deregulation and market forces have lifted restrictions on children's television, creating half-hour-long ads for products and exposing children to life-styles that elevate consumption of goods as the most important aspect of the televised experience.

While noting the importance of diversity in the marketplace, he cautions that just as the government should not dictate what is "good" information, private entities or monopolies should also never have that power. A diversity of viewpoints, then, could be accomplished by greater numbers of people programming channels and experimenting with new content rather than large-scale operations that cater to traditional tastes.

Wirth calls for legislative steps to be taken that would not return the government to the days of broadcast regulation but would encourage broadcasters to seek excellence in programming and require a greater component of responsibility to the public. Recalling the words of former FCC chairman Newton Minnow, who called television "the vast wasteland," Wirth believes that the "wasteland can be cultivated" with proper government, industry, and public response.

It is interesting to note that two attempts to rewrite the Communication Act of 1934 have failed in Congress, largely due to the difficulties in separating technical, content, and ownership issues. The first attempt at a rewrite suggested the disbanding of the FCC and the establishment of a new organization that would be responsible for drafting a new Telecommunications Act. Discussions of this possibility were halted during the change of presidential administration in 1988, although George Bush was strongly in favor of pursuing this option. Whether this possibility becomes a reality during the Bush presidency still remains to be seen.

YES

**Mark S. Fowler
and Daniel L. Brenner**

A MARKET APPROACH
TO BROADCAST REGULATION

This article proposes a new direction for governmental regulation of broadcasting in the United States. The ideas raised are not entirely new, but they have been ignored by those who have been busy raising and lowering the drawbridge of licensing. Our thesis is that the perception of broadcasters as community trustees should be replaced by a view of broadcasters as marketplace participants. Communications policy should be directed toward maximizing the services the public desires. Instead of defining public demand and specifying categories of programming to serve this demand, the Commission [FCC] should rely on the broadcasters' ability to determine the wants of their audiences through the normal mechanisms of the marketplace. The public's interest, then, defines the public interest. And in light of the first amendment's heavy presumption against content control, the Commission should refrain from insinuating itself into program decisions made by licensees. . . .

THE TRUSTEESHIP MODEL

Instead of being exchanged as a property right, exclusivity to a radio frequency has been assigned by the Commission on the amorphous "public interest" standard. Broadcaster responsibility officially runs to the viewing public as defined by the Commission, not to shareholders, sponsors, or even the users of the sponsors' products or services who indirectly finance the stations. Two considerable evils have come from this arrangement: "broadcasters take advantage of the public-interest myth to promote a variety of protectionist policies, motivated in fact by economic self-interest . . . [and] . . . the public at large is misled in its perception of the role and function of broadcasting in America. In short, by abandoning a marketplace

From Mark S. Fowler and Daniel L. Brenner, "A Marketplace Approach to Broadcast Regulation," *Texas Law Review*, vol. 60, no. 2 (February 1988), pp. 209-210, 213-218, 221-222, 236-247, 256-257. Copyright © 1988 by the Texas Law Review Association. Reprinted by permission. Notes omitted.

approach in the determination of spectrum utilization, the government created a tension, in both first amendment and economic terms, that haunts communications policy to this day.

The trusteeship model of broadcast regulation can be traced to the beginning of radio regulation in the United States in the early part of the twentieth century. Federal regulation of radio broadcasting emerged in the early part of the century out of the congestion in ship-to-shore and ship-to-ship communications, which the Department of the Navy described as an "etheric bedlam produced by numerous stations all trying to communicate at once." Congress perceived spectrum scarcity to be a significant enough problem to justify federal oversight and abandonment of market techniques in spectrum management, and enacted the Radio Act of 1912, which forbade operation of a radio apparatus without a license from the Secretary of Commerce and Labor. The limited regulatory power of the Commerce Department, however, did not extend beyond the role of nondiscriminating registrar, and the result was a frequency free-for-all in the mid-1920's, that doomed the 1912 scheme. . . .

Over the years the Commission has gradually developed the trusteeship approach, fleshing out the programming obligations of broadcasters under the "public convenience, interest, or necessity" standard. In 1946 the Commission published the so-called "Blue Book," named after the hue of its cover, entitled *Public Service Responsibility of Broadcast Licensees*. Although never actively enforced, the Blue Book stated that the Commission "proposes to give particular consideration" to four types of programming: (1) local and network programs that were carried on a sustaining (i.e., noncommercial) basis; (2) local live programs; (3) programs devoted to discussion of public issues; and (4) station efforts to limit the amount of time it devoted to hourly advertising.

The Commission's next major effort to influence broadcaster service appeared in the *Report and Statement of Policy* in its *En Banc Programming Inquiry*, which it issued in 1960 in the wake of the quiz show scandals on network television. The 1960 *Statement* emphasized the importance of broadcaster service to the community: "The principal ingredient of such obligation consists of a diligent, positive and continuing effort by the licensee to discover and fulfill the tastes, needs and desires of his service area. If he has accomplished this he has met his public responsibility." The *Statement* recognized that the Commission "may not condition the grant, denial or revocation of a broadcast license upon its own subjective determination of what is or is not a good program." Yet, because the broadcaster is required to act in the public interest, the Commission did not view itself as "barred by the Constitution or by statute from exercising any responsibility with respect to programming."

The *Statement* articulates fourteen "major elements [of programming] usually necessary to meet the public interest, needs and desires of the community. . . . The major change established by the *Statement* was the insertion of the ascertainment exercise into the application process. Ascertainment was supposed to be the way for a station to factor the fourteen major elements into its program service. In order to enable broadcasters and their lawyers to prepare initial and renewal applications with adequate specificity, the Commission has issued a series of primers that articulate an acceptable scheme for determining community needs. Since 1960, the Commission has adopted percentage guidelines for news and public affairs programs, which were eliminated for radio but remain in effect for television.

The Commission thus has not hesitated to consider program content and prescribe categories of desirable programming when defining the duties of licensees. Governmental guidance in broadcast decision-making, the fundamental characteristic of the trusteeship model, sets it apart from a marketplace approach.

The first amendment to the Constitution and section 326 of the Communications Act both forbid censorship of broadcasters. There is a tension between these prohibitions and the Commission's examination of past or proposed programming to determine which of several competing applicants should receive a license. The Commission does employ noncontent criteria to distinguish among applicants, e.g., in considering whether an applicant already has media properties in the community, whether station owners will be involved in the daily management of the station, and whether the applicant's record in providing equal employment opportunity is adequate. But if all other criteria are equal, the Commission looks at the content of proposed programs. Historically, the Commission has attempted to avoid content criteria. Nevertheless, because these criteria most directly predict what service to expect from an applicant, the Commission cannot avoid considering such criteria under the judgmental directive of the "public interest." . . .

The Flawed Rationales Supporting the [Trusteeship] Model [and an Argument for the Marketplace Approach]

. . .Spectrum scarcity always has been the cornerstone of the justification for abandoning the marketplace approach and reducing first amendment protection for broadcasters. . . . Scarcity is a relative concept even when applied to the limited spectrum earmarked for broadcast use. Additional channels can be added, without increasing the portion reserved for broadcast, by decreasing the bandwidth of each channel. Technology is an independent variable that makes scarcity a relative concept. At some point, quality becomes so reduced or costs so great that new channels should not be added. But until that point is reached, saturation of the spectrum has not occurred. The continued evolution of spectrum efficiency techniques makes it difficult to say with certainty that saturation of channels will ever be permanent in any market. . . .

The reasons articulated by the Commission and the courts for the trusteeship model are hardly convincing, let alone compelling, when poised in a constitutional balance against the rights of broadcasters. Scarcity analysis is theoretically misguided and, in many cases, factually erroneous. Other facets of broadcasting, such as intrusiveness, failure to segregate child and adult audiences, and "captiveness," do not call for government involvement. There is reason to believe that marketplace forces can, and indeed do, affect the success or failure of television programming, just as they affect the content of nonbroadcast media. . . . A marketplace approach to broadcast regulation . . . emphasizes the role of new competitors, and new competition among existing firms, to ensure service in the public interest. . . .

1. The First Amendment Rights of Listeners and Viewers Under the Speech Clause.—The Supreme Court's recently repeated formulation of the hierarchy of values in broadcasting—that "the right of the viewers and listeners, not the right of the broadcasters . . .is *paramount*"—is central to a first amendment analysis of broadcast regulation. Under this hierarchy, initially set forth in *Red Lion*, the rights of listeners "to receive suitable access to social, political, esthetic, moral and other ideas and experiences" outweigh the first amendment claims of broadcasters when the two conflict. This ranking does not, however, create an individual right of access to broadcast time in any single listener or viewer.

Even before *Red Lion*, the Court had subordinated broadcaster claims of first amendment rights to the public's interest in access to ideas and information and to rules designed to enhance that interest. In *NBC*, where the issue was the independence of station owners from network control, the Court rejected the broadcasters' claim that the licensing criteria established in the chain broadcasting rules offended their freedom of speech.

The *Red Lion* decision addressed the first amendment question more directly. The Court endorsed a right of access to ideas and upheld the Commission's requirement that a radio or television station give an individual time to reply to personal attacks and political editorials. Five years later, in *Miami Herald Publishing Co. v. Tornillo*, the Supreme Court unanimously rejected a similar regulation when applied to a daily newspaper. But the Court in *Tornillo* did not attempt to harmonize the disparate holdings of the two cases.

In *CBS v. FCC*, the Court, relying on *Red Lion*, again concluded that the public interest in access to particular communications outweighed the impact on editorial functions of the broadcaster. The Court faced a conflict between the broadcaster's first amendment claim and a Commission interpretation concerning presentation of the viewpoints of candidates for federal office under a congressionally created right of "reasonable" paid access. The Court noted that a statutory right of access did not preclude broadcasters from presenting any particular viewpoint or program and sustained the Commission's mandate of air time for the Carter-Mondale reelection committee under the reasonable access provisions.

A divided Supreme Court subordinated the broadcaster's constitutional rights in a different manner in *FCC v. Pacifica Foundation. Pacifica* has little to commend its constitutional analysis. The majority lacked support both for its claim that broadcasting "has received the most limited first amendment protection," and also for maintaining that a sound basis for more regulation is the pervasive "power" of the electronic media. Yet like the other broadcasting cases, *Pacifica* indicated that the Commission can, indeed should, subordinate a broadcaster's claim to editorial freedom to the perceived needs of the general public for access to expression over the airwaves or (as in *Pacifica*) for protection against harm from such expression.

What do the Supreme Court's repeated holdings on the hierarchy of first amendment interests tell us about a marketplace approach to broadcasting? First, it should be noted that the language of the first amendment protects the right of speech, not the right of access to ideas or even the right to listen. The direct concern of the first amendment is with the active speaker, not the passive receiver. The listener's interest is certainly enhanced by the exercise of the right of free speech, especially where the first amendment is viewed as a tool for self-governance. But listener rights are not the same as the individual's right to speak, and no such rights exist in broadcasting. Thus, it remains unclear exactly what listener interests are protected under the first amendment, aside from the "values" spilling over from the exercise of free speech.

Even assuming the existence of a protected right of access to ideas under the first amendment, it is illogical to assume that broadcasting, and broadcasting alone, is the exclusive arena for the exercise of this right, as the language in *Red Lion* might suggest. "Crucial" access to ideas pertinent to self-governance or self-fulfillment can be provided by many sources other than the airwaves. Furthermore, broadcasters should not shoulder a broader responsibility for providing important information than other media. The argument that listener access to broadcasting is crucial may prove too much. For if listener rights are deemed "paramount" to broadcaster rights, so the rights of newspaper readers should be paramount to the rights of the publishers and editors and the rights of movie patrons superior to those of exhibitors, distributors, and producers. This is the logical result once one stops analyzing the issue in terms of the rights of individuals under the first amendment.

Finally, even assuming that the interest in access to ideas is more pronounced in radio and television than in other media, it does not follow that only governmental regulations can ensure this access. . . .

WNCN provides the most instructive precedent, since in *WNCN* the Court confronted the free market approach and the *Red Lion* hierarchy for the first time. The Court rejected the claim that the Commission's laissez-faire policy toward radio format changes conflicted with the first amendment rights of listeners under *Red Lion*. It recognized that *Red Lion* provided individual listeners with no right to control the abandonment of a format and concluded that the Commission's reliance on market forces did not violate listeners' first amendment rights. Rather, the Court found that a station's format generally would reflect listener interests and therefore be consistent with the first amendment hierarchy in broadcasting.

The Court did more than avoid a potential conflict between the rights of listeners and broadcasters in dismissing the *Red Lion* claim. It affirmed the importance of listener rights, regardless of broadcaster rights. But the Court agreed with the Commission that this "paramount" interest is best served when a broadcaster in the marketplace is free to respond to perceived listener demand. In this marketplace approach, the interests of listeners and broadcasters, in the past sometimes in conflict (such as over a right of individual access to the media) converge. The commercial broadcaster maximizes profits by providing the service it believes consumers most desire. In choosing a service that maximizes profit, the licensee serves listener interests because the choice of service is geared to attracting the most listeners. The market approach is superior to the alternatives because it does not put the government between the licensee and the listener it is wooing.

Thus, a Commission policy that equates the functions of the marketplace in commercial broadcasting with satisfaction of listener interests finds support in the Court's analysis of the first amendment rights of listeners. Once the Commission concludes that market forces, rather than its own judgments, are most likely to produce programming that best serves the people, the paramount claims set forth in *Red Lion* are satisfied.

Admittedly, this conclusion reads much from the *WNCN* result, for the *Red Lion* claim is not analyzed at length in the decision. And one can characterize the recent *CBS* case, announced shortly after *WNCN*, as reducing the scope of licensee editorial discretion. But the 1981 *CBS* case dealt with a narrow access statute, itself an exception to the result in the Supreme Court's 1973 decision in *CBS v. Democratic National Committee*. In denying a general right of individual access in the 1981 case, the Commission did not allow licensee discretion to override its own interpretation of the statute's purpose. Absent an express Commission finding that it cannot rely on licensee discretion to carry out its congressional mandate, however, *WNCN* suggests the compatibility of a marketplace approach and *Red Lion*'s emphasis on listeners' rights.

2. The First Amendment Rights of Broadcasters Under the Press Clause.—The marketplace approach emphasizes broadcaster discretion as a way to maximize listener welfare. An independent first amendment interest also protects broadcaster discretion from the dictates of the government. As Professor Kalven has sentiently observed.

> We have been beginning, so to speak, in the wrong corner. The question is not what does the need for licensing permit the Commission to do in the public interest; rather it is what does the man-

date of the First Amendment inhibit the Commission from doing even though it is to license.

Application of the first amendment to broadcasting largely dates from dictum in *United States v. Paramount Pictures, Inc.* Justice Frankfurter's analysis in the 1943 *NBC* case, however, suggests that the Court already had recognized that broadcasters have a constitutional basis for objecting to overly intrusive regulation. Despite later dictum in *Pacifica* devaluing the first amendment interests of broadcasters, the Court in *CBS v. Democratic National Committee* championed the editorial freedom of broadcasters. It rejected a claim that the first amendment and the "public interest" standard required licensees to sell time for editorial advertisements. "For better or worse," the Court stated, "editing is what editors are for; and editing is selection and choice of material."

The belated recognition of the first amendment rights of broadcasters may be due to the relatively late development of broadcast journalism as a serious professional calling. News and interpretation have always been part of radio programming, but both radio and television have remained primarily entertainment media. Until recently, investigative broadcast journalism was scheduled sporadically, and it remains the exception to the rule despite its sometimes significant impact. Questions of entertainment program selection and scheduling, not newsroom judgments, dominate the broadcaster's first amendment activity. . . .

In light of the fifty-five years of spectrum regulation under the trusteeship model, the problems of applying market techniques to spectrum use are more practical than theoretical. One approach would be to require all spectrum users to retire their licenses. The Commission would hold an auction to select new users and frequency rights would go to the highest bidders, who under a market theory should put the frequencies to their best use. If a higher use for a frequency later emerged, the holder could resell the frequency rights.

Although a good way to have started in the 1920's, an auction would substantially disrupt current service and frustrate the expectations of those who have long held spectrum rights and of their customers. Another way to encourage optimum frequency use would be to allow licenses to be bought and sold freely after the initial grant, regardless of whether the initial grant is determined by auction, lottery, or under the old trusteeship approach. On resale, the seller, rather than the government, would capture the higher value of the frequency, but the allocation of resale profit would not prevent the frequency from reaching its highest use, thereby achieving the market objective.

To some, the major objection to free resale would be the windfall to incumbent licensees. The windfall, to the extent that it actually occurred, would consist of the increased value of a deregulated license created by its release from content and ownership restrictions and its new, freely transferable character. The problem presented by the windfall of free transferability is not entirely novel. Except for distressed properties or those that have never been transferred, the price paid to a transferor under existing assignment rules already reflects the steadily increasing value of the exclusivity. It is almost always greater than the value of the nonlicense assets being transferred. Restricted resales under section 310(d) of the 1934 Act have already

occurred several times with respect to many licenses, so that the windfall has been captured. . . .

More generally, the marketplace approach could be most expeditiously introduced to broadcasting by granting existing licensees "squatter's rights" to their frequencies. These rights embody the reasonable expectation of renewal that licensees presently enjoy for satisfactory past performance. The critical next step, from a market viewpoint, would be to deregulate fully the sale of licenses.

This approach to resale need not preclude the use of lotteries or auctions for new assignments to broadcasters or other spectrum users. Consider the Commission's handling of low-power television service. Announcement of this new service led to the submission of thousands of applications, many mutually exclusive, so that the Commission is faced with choosing among competing applicants. Although the Commission has approved a comparative process to license this new service, initial grants using either a lottery and resale or an auction could inject market incentives into the distribution of this service. Either technique would be likely to raise the frequency exclusivity to its highest use as a broadcast frequency.

In addition to promoting resale, the marketplace approach requires an end to program regulation. Government oversight of broadcast content arrogates editorial responsibilities protected by the first amendment and interferes with the functioning of market forces as well. The agenda for restoring competition to the television market should include scrapping the content-oriented regulations that prescribe minimum amounts of nonentertainment programs and limit advertising. Their elimination would allow broadcasters to satisfy consumer desires based on their reading of what viewers want, from all-news to all-entertainment programming. The Commission also should seek repeal of other content regulations, such as the fairness doctrine and the political speech rules, although it might assign access obligations for political candidates and referenda to public broadcasters.

Restrictions that impede resale should be the first barriers abandoned in the move to a market environment. The rule on "trafficking" licenses, which require applications for license assignment or transfer of stock control to be designated for hearing unless the license has been held for at least three years, are particularly perverse. The rule condemns licensees who acquire a station and dispose of it in less than three years. Yet such behavior is not restricted in other segments of the economy. To the contrary, we generally reward those who buy an ailing company and, having turned its fortunes around, sell it. Under a trusteeship approach it is conduct unbecoming a public steward; under a market approach it is conduct rewarded by profit on resale.

The Commission should also consider abolishing rules that restrict growth by existing players or limit entry of new players in any of the competitive video fields. It should place particular attention on its restrictions on ownership of media facilities. For example, the Commission has long enforced a "7-7-7" rule, which restricts one licensee to seven AM, seven FM, and seven television outlets, no more than five of which can be VHF stations. The rule stems from the Commission's desire to establish some limit on the number of stations a single licensee can operate. This arbitrary rule has almost certainly promoted inefficiency, for it does not measure a licensee's share of the homes using television nationwide. An operator with twenty-one stations in the bottom twenty-one markets possesses far less market control than the owner of three stations in the top three markets. If national concentration is a concern, the Commission could limit station ownership by the percentage of homes reached rather than by an arbitrary number of stations. But even a percentage approach should have to demonstrate that a limit on ownership bears a close relationship to preventing an identifiable harm.

In revising the 7-7-7 rule, the Commission should consider whether express limitations on concentration are warranted or whether they create undesirable barriers to entry in programming or distribution. Concentration of media outlets, particularly in a local market, can pose special problems. But this fact alone should not subject the media industries to limitations on the ownership rights freely permitted in other concentrated industries.

A less restrictive policy toward group ownership would also aid program diversity. The 1952 allocation scheme led to the development of only three full-time television networks. Significant group ownership in broadcasting exists outside of stations licensed to the networks, but the Commission's regulations have prevented these groups from gaining access to important markets and establishing alternatives to the traditional three-network structure. In its review of the 7-7-7 rule and other ownership limits, the Commission should be aware that the right of group owners to acquire additional stations might make alternative networks viable. It should also consider anew the scrutiny it gives to financial and character qualifications in transfers and at renewals. The governing principle in this hard look is whether any Commission rule fosters or undermines market forces, forces designed to discover and meet the public's interest. . . .

The Communications Act provides the Commission with discretion to translate consumer wants into the programming decisions of broadcasters by invoking marketplace principles. The need for a fresh approach to broadcasting, now spurred by competitive challenges from cable and other video providers, is long overdue. This new approach concludes that broadcasters best serve the public by responding to market forces rather than governmental directives. It restores the broadcasting business to the unregulated status of American enterprise generally. In doing so, it also recognizes that content regulation of commercial radio and television is fundamentally at odds with the first amendment status of broadcasting.

The time has come for Congress and the Commission to recognize the role of broadcasting within overall spectrum usage and adopt a more rational approach to broadcast regulation. One possible, though inessential, approach would be to charge for the exclusivity provided by a government license. Congress must also clarify the purpose of the noncommercial licensing function. Congress should either ratify the mission of public broadcasting in the overall scheme for the reserved broadcast spectrum or instruct the Commission to return its frequencies for reassignment to face the rigors of the marketplace. The end result should be a commercial broadcasting system in which market forces rather than trustee duties govern as far as possible the provision of broadcast service to the American people.

NO

Timothy E. Wirth

THE TELEVISION ENVIRONMENT: CULTIVATING THE WASTELAND

Television is one part of a vast telecommunications revolution, sweeping the country and the globe. For the last 6 years I've watched this revolution from a special vantage point—the chairmanship of the House Subcommittee on Telecommunications, Consumer Protection and Finance. As earlier legislators oversaw the building of our canals and railroads and superhighways—the opening of America and the connecting of a continent—I have seen our newest infrastructure for commerce and ideas take form.

In telecommunications policy, the challenge of change is equally profound and revolutionary. No longer are we dealing with the rules of the past: scarce spectrum; monopoly; pervasive government regulation; national isolation. Today we are dealing with potential abundance of spectrum; competition and increasing entrepreneurial activity; much less regulation; and an intertwined international economy and communications structure. Public policy cannot remain static, and the challenge that we face is to adapt our policy, laws, and regulations to a rapidly changing environment.

GOALS OF TELECOMMUNICATIONS POLICY

To make the necessary changes, we first had to settle on the basic goals that we believed our society's telecommunications policy ought to achieve. Presumably form follows function—but unhappily too little public policy is made with a national set of goals in mind.

In early 1981, we embarked on an extensive set of hearings, designed to solicit views from all quarters on what the goals should be, and then to try to develop a political consensus around our central goals. The hearings were broadly criticized as being too academic, too abstract, and too comprehensive. But out of them a consensus slowly emerged on what our communications goals ought to be—and I think these goals characterize much of our policy today. Throughout the industry, I think most people are agreed that, first, all citizens of the United States should have access to communications at a reasonable price. Second, a *diversity* of information, program, and technology supply should be encouraged. And third, wherever possible, the telecommunications market should be managed by *competition*, not by monopoly and government regulation. Further, these three goals of access, diversity, and competition should be nurtured by government action where necessary.

Now I should not suggest that we reached this consensus and started to act on it without considerable resistance. In this industry, as in others in our national experience, those who become established or entrenched work hard to keep out the newcomers: AM radio broadcasters sought protection against the challenge of FM; VHF television stations lobbied the government not to allocate UHF spectrum; over-the-air broadcasters tried desperately to restrain the cable industry; and now the cable industry is having its problems adjusting to the competitive threat of the backyard satellite dish.

Resisting change brought about by technological developments is nothing new. I recently came across a letter purportedly sent in 1829 by Martin Van Buren, then the Governor of New York, to President Andrew Jackson:

Dear Mr. President:

The canal system of this country is being threatened by the spread of a new form of transportation known as "railroads." The federal government must preserve the canals for the following reasons:

One. If canal boats are supplanted by "railroads" serious unemployment will result. Captains, cooks, drivers, hostlers, repairmen and lock tenders will be left without means of livelihoods, not to mention the numerous farmers now employed in growing hay for horses.

. . .

As you may well know, Mr. President, "railroad" carriages are pulled at the enormous speed of 15 miles per hour by "engines" which, in addition to endangering life and limb of passengers, roar and snort their way through the countryside, setting fire to crops, scaring the livestock and frightening women and children. The Almighty certainly never intended that people should travel at such breakneck speed.

Signed,

Martin Van Buren, Governor of New York

Resistance to change is nothing new. Remarkably, in the field of telecommunications, the industry and public policy underlying it have done a pretty good job of encouraging innovation.

ACCESS TO COMMUNICATIONS

Concerning access, we have been very successful. Television reaches 98.2% of all U.S. households. More of us own TV sets than have indoor plumbing, telephones, or clothes washers. Indeed, the average American household contains 1.78 televisions. And we have the sets on for an average of seven hours a day—or 2,555 hours a year—25% more than the average American works. We are almost 13 times more likely to be watching the tube than reading a newspaper or a magazine, activities that each take up an average of 200 hours annually. And while Americans in general give only about 10 hours a year to books, our children—by the time they finish high school—have spent more time watching television than in the classroom.

DIVERSITY

Diversity is a second goal—to encourage more video outlets in the marketplace, to bring greater program and viewpoint diversity so that we may have an electronic media market "with many tongues, speaking many voices." That was the marketplace of political ideas envisioned in the Federalist Papers. Government should encourage information to flow from as many sources as possible, carrying many messages and views to animate, to inform, and to engage democracy's decision makers—our citizens. As the Supreme Court, in discussing the First Amendment in its landmark *Red Lion* ruling, clearly stated: "It is the right of the viewers and listeners, not the right of the broadcasters, which is paramount."

Just as government should never determine what information is "good," neither should a handful of *private* entities monopolize such decisions. In our information age, the survival of our democracy depends on an electorate choosing from a broad menu of diverse views.

The Fairness Doctrine ensures that all sides of important public controversies are aired. This Doctrine is not a government regulation to chill or inhibit speech as the Federal Communications Commission (FCC) has suggested in seeking its repeal. It is simply a statement by the government saying let there be more speech—let's make sure that a broadcaster who is licensed to serve the public transmits not only his own views, but other sides as well. And in cable television, the Cable Communications Policy Act requires cable operators to set aside 10–15% of their channels for programming by independent third parties. The public policy goal: More people programming channels bring more diversity of viewpoints.

COMPETITION

We also continue to strive to reach our third goal—to govern through marketplace forces wherever possible.

While the three major networks still dominate the video marketplace, a vast array of outlets now offer viewers choices as never before. Streams of alternative programming flow through electronic media outlets such as cable television, LPTV (low power television), MMDS (multichannel multipoint distribution service), SMATV (satellite master-antenna television), STV (subscription television), ITFS (instructional television fixed service), Videotext, optical discs, DBS (direct broadcast satellites), VCRs (video cassette recorders), and the latest video technology to sweep America, backyard satellite dishes. We now have an all-news channel, a 24-hour public affairs channel, an all-music channel, a financial-news channel, and even an all-weather channel. Programming tastes that traditional broadcasters barely sampled can now be widely satisfied.

THE GOVERNMENT'S ROLE

I assumed the Chairmanship of the Telecommunications Subcommittee just as the Reagan administration came to town. To head the regulatory agencies that my subcommittee oversees, the administration appointed officials who felt government should not govern, but should get out of the way. For example, the Chairman of the FCC, Mark Fowler, assumed his position espousing not deregulation, but "unregulation." These consensus goals—access, diversity, and competition—have not been shared by all.

I have no gripe with deregulating markets—but the administration and Chairman Fowler pursue deregulation solely for its own sake. Deregulation is not a goal. It is a means to an end.

The canals that opened up the way West, and the railroads that Leland Stanford and others built to link the continent, embodied the traditional American partnership of public investment in private vision. The land-grant universities, the G.I. Bill, and the National Defense Education Act committed community resources to developing individual skills. Federal water projects brought electric power and irrigation to desert land; government financing breathed life into public television.

Over and over Americans have seen that such teamwork works. Government serves, as Lincoln imagined it, "to do for a community of people whatever they need to have done, but cannot do at all, or cannot do so well for themselves, in their separate and individual capacities." That definition sets both a positive and a negative agenda for government. It pools our strength to spur progress. And it safeguards our freedoms against the excesses or excessive power of special interests in society. Those are the legitimate purposes of democratic government. They do not assure government a role in every endeavor or make it the answer to every problem. They define its necessary functions and leave each generation of Americans to find the correct balance of power, the right strategy for partnership.

If we have done well in achieving our three goals of access, diversity, and competition; and if most of us agree that government is an important partner in helping to achieve these goals, it then remains to ask the deeper questions:

How are we using television's potential for teaching our young, informing our citizens, enriching our lives, and thereby strengthening self-government and democratic society? Twenty-five years ago, Newton Minow, former Chairman of the FCC, described television as a "vast wasteland." Is that description accurate today? And what steps should be taken to cultivate the wasteland? We should take an especially careful look at (1) the impact of television on children, (2) the involvement of television in the political process, and (3) how we might strengthen public television.

CHILDREN'S TELEVISION

Historically, three great institutions have educated and socialized our young—family, church, and school. Now there is a fourth—television—with extraordinary potential.

Unhappily, most of commercial television today treats children—our most precious natural resource—as consumers of products and entertainment, not of useful knowledge. The marketplace provides a special niche for them on Saturday mornings and fills it with such enduring classics as "Snorks," "Gummie Bears," "Smurfs," "Alvin and the Chipmunks," "Kidd Video," "Mr. T.," "Spider Man," "13 Ghosts of Scooby," "The Super Powers Team," and "Hulk Hogan's Rock 'N' Wrestling." The gap between what television could deliver, and what it does provide, is deepest in the field of children's programs.

We have learned what a positive influence educational programming can have on our young. We know that television can teach a wide range of skills and behavior. We know that television can motivate and interest children in what they need to know and learn. We know that TV can simultaneously entertain and educate.

Ignoring these lessons, the FCC has recently lifted the restrictions on commercial minutes allowed, and refused even to consider the issue of increased commercializing of children's programs. The marketplace responded accordingly. It gave us a new phenomenon—the program-length commercial, a vast array of animated shows—not developed to enlighten, teach, or enrich the nation's children, but developed instead to enrich the toy makers who turn their products into cartoon characters.

That, of course, is just what cartoon shows like "G.I. Joe," "He-Man and Masters of the Universe," and "Transformers" now do. They don't advertise toys directly. They just animate them as the centerpieces of the entertainment, but the effect is a protracted, effective sell. If it weren't working, producers would not now be investing $21 million to develop an animated series called "Galaxy Rangers" and planning a line of toys to go on sale when the programs go on the air.

A commercial by any other name is still a commercial.

In contrast, two-thirds of the "Sesame Street" schedule is reruns. The "Electric Company" programs on the air now include no show that is less than 10 years old. And except for 40 half-hours of "3-2-1 Contact" made in 1983, that science series is limited to its original 65 episodes.

In addition, we have explored and documented the effect of televised violence on children. In 1972, the United States Surgeon General issued a report that concluded that there was a short-run causal relationship between viewing of televised violence and aggressive behavior in children. Ten years later, the National Institute of Mental Health released a follow-up study. The conclusion: Televised violence also caused *long-term* aggressive behavior in children, and if you had not already guessed it, you will not be surprised to learn that weekend cartoons have dished up the heaviest frequency of violent acts per hour.

We are aware of what television provides young viewers, and we should also acknowledge what is left out. Why are the comics so accessible, and the classics of children's literature almost impossible to find? With science so vital to our children now and our growth tomorrow, why can children not explore its wonders more fully on television after school? We don't have to teach Latin on television, but we do have to know our history, know the best of our culture—and we *can* teach those lessons on television. We can. But we don't. I would cite here Wirth's paradox: The more we know about the power of television in educating our young, the less we use this powerful medium.

Whether we are parents, educators, public policymakers, or students, we should be fed up with the failure to make television the positive force that it could be for our young. How we have treated children's television in this country is, plain and simple, a national disgrace.

TELEVISION AND THE POLITICAL PROCESS

As to TV's influence on the political process, we know that the early projection of election returns by the networks depresses voter turnout. Congress, with the backing of both national political parties and the League of Women Voters, called for voluntary restraint by the networks. We did not want to *mandate* network silence until the polls closed in the West; we simply asked the networks to voluntarily restrain themselves and their desire to be "first" regardless of the consequences. Unfortunately, the response was limited: The network news executives claimed that exit polling results were news, and had to be reported right away. But why don't you exercise judgment, we asked, as you do all the time with news? The networks hold back news shows for three hours every evening between air time on the East and West coasts. Why can't they exercise the same voluntary restraint to protect the most important of all democratic processes, the election of our president?

There is another serious threat to the political process—negative political advertising by independent political action groups with the funds to lay down a barrage of ads against opponents without the resources for adequate response. It creates an imbalance in the political process that gives well-financed special interest groups power beyond their numbers, the power to control political debate. We must ask what these practices are doing to our democratic processes. We can't afford to let the poison spread and seek no antidote.

These problems remain in an industry that has made extraordinary strides, from its introduction of more quality entertainment programming to the stimulating presentation of news and analysis. C-SPAN brings debates live from the House floor and from congressional committees into the voters' living rooms. The legislative process has been put on public display, and we are all the better for it.

It is now time for the legislative and public process to mobilize itself and help to cultivate the wasteland. And I have a number of proposals to share with you. Adlai Stevenson once said, "Your public servants serve you right." So do our public communications. If we don't demand excellence, we won't get it. We will get—we do get—what we appear to want. We must demand excellence in television, just as we pursue it in all our other quests.

SOME PROPOSALS

There are some legislative steps that we can take to encourage excellence. For example, to ensure that commercial broadcasters meet the needs of children whom they are licensed to serve, we could require broadcasters to program 1 hour a day intended to enhance the education of children. Until recently, broadcasters were required to pay particular attention to the special population of children, but that preference was dropped by this FCC. I have introduced this legislation for the last 4 years; Senator Lautenberg has introduced identical legislation last session in the Senate. We should open the debate and get going on this legislation.

Turning to commercial TV, how can we treat commercial broadcasting in a deregulatory political climate and simultaneously strengthen public broadcasting. I have proposed the initiation of a "free market" spectrum fee as a way to ensure that the public is compensated for the use the broadcaster gets of a valuable resource. If we treated the airwaves as though they were public lands, we would be charging fees for broadcast licenses as we do for timber, grazing, or mineral rights. The "rents" that would come in from such fees could then be used, instead of general revenues, to underwrite educational, children's, community affairs, and minority programming.

We can exploit the vast number of unused cable access channels to increase public affairs and local programming. I have proposed setting aside a portion of the franchise fee that cable operators pay to the cities where they operate. Rather than putting this money into filling potholes, why not pour a portion of it back into enriching the video marketplace in ways that the market, on its own, will starve?

In the 1950s citizens' groups sprang up all over America to influence neighborhood zoning decisions. In the 1960s, citizens recognized the tremendous problem of air and water pollution and fought it by forming hundreds of environmental groups. In the 1970s came Crime Watch, local citizens' groups to help police their own streets, to make their homes safe. During the rest of this century, why don't we create a new environmental movement—one focused on the television environment? A citizen movement dedicated to establishing grass-roots community organizations to engage in active dialogue with broadcasters, cable operators, and programmers. A citizens' movement overseeing our passive role in our media environment. A citizens' movement serving as a constructive partner with the media in attempting to tackle many of the challenges that regulatory solutions cannot now meet.

The national Parent-Teacher Association (PTA)—with 27,000 local chapters—and the American Academy of Pediatrics have tried to open the dialogue on the impact of children's television. Why not expand their efforts? Broadcasters, cable operators, and programmers should welcome such audience activism and invite criticism, analysis, and questioning.

Recent strides in this area give me hope. For example, when some citizen groups organized to fight drunk driving and alcohol abuse, and called for banning beer and wine advertising on television, broadcasters and community groups got together all across the country. The result has been a veritable blitz of public service TV announcements forcefully making the case against drunk driving and alcohol abuse.

The National Association of Broadcasters (NAB) deserves much credit for helping steer such a constructive course. This broadcast group has undertaken another voluntary initiative—a national telethon or other fund-raising event to support public broadcasting. The NAB is also aggressively pursuing a campaign geared toward making broadcast stations think long and hard before accepting negative political advertising. This is a good beginning—a new beginning—that gives us all hope that a future television environment shaped by a voluntary partnership between mobilized citizens and media managers can be a reality.

No change comes about without leadership. The Carnegie Foundation took the lead 20 years ago, and again in the late 1970s, in laying down a blueprint for what has become the nation's Public Broadcasting System (PBS). Today, public broadcasting is fighting to continue its long-term commitment to excellence. We must do more to encourage this and other sources of alternative programming, such as cable access channels. Why not call once again on the Carnegie Foundation, for a third Carnegie Commission to study and recommend how we might enhance and enrich programming? We have a multitude of outlets but a poverty of programs—how can we combine resources and better reach the potential of television?

We should stir up trouble over the quality of "kid vid" and the poverty of public TV finances. We should explore the international frontier of telecommunications—TV's role in covering international terrorist incidents, and TV satellites as export earners, carrying our television programming to consumers abroad. Television can bring the peoples of the world closer; it can cut tension and reduce conflict. Telecommunications may even be a major route to economic growth for new generations around the world.

This job of cultivating our electronic resources, however, cannot be left to educational institutions alone. This challenge requires true national leadership at the highest levels. We have held White House conferences on the aging, White House conferences on children, and now it is time for a White House conference on television. Only if we elevate these concerns to such a level of national priority can we realistically expect to raise the public consciousness sufficiently to begin to make our television all it can be.

We must move to make the most of this medium. We must act to get the best of the television environment, the best of ourselves. The wasteland can be cultivated; the spectrum belongs to all of us and we should use it for the excellent, the noble, and the future.

POSTSCRIPT

Should the Federal Government Continue to Deregulate Commercial Broadcasting?

Although the rights of the public to hear and see alternative viewpoints will continue to be a major issue for the government and broadcasters in the future, Mark Fowler's commitment to market forces dominating the broadcast environment have significantly changed many important principles of broadcasting, such as the interpretation of "public interest, convenience, and necessity," the *Red Lion* case, and both the Fairness Doctrine and Section 315, which called for a diversity of political views to be a part of responsible broadcasting. There has been a concentrated effort on the part of many legislators to have the Supreme Court overturn *Red Lion* and rule that the Fairness Doctrine and Section 315 are unconstitutional.

Fowler is no longer with the FCC, but the current commissioners share his dedication to market forces. Alternatives are being kept alive by legislators like Tim Wirth and citizen groups such as Action for Children's Television (ACT) as well as other interest groups.

Media policies and regulations generally reflect two factors: precedent and president. Throughout the Reagan years and with the help of his FCC appointee, Mark Fowler, the president successfully overturned many precedents. Whether Bush continues in this manner still remains to be seen, but the political influence on media policy, regulation, and the relationship of the various players in the broadcast environment could also be changed in the future by other presidents.

Although somewhat dated now, Barry Cole and Mal Oettinger's *The Reluctant Regulators: The FCC and the Broadcast Audience* (Addison-Wesley, 1978) provides an informative history of the relationship among the FCC, government, and public. Don R. LeDuc's *Beyond Broadcasting: Patterns in Policy and Law* (Longman, 1987) compares the similarities and differences between policy and practice and provides a social assessment of what legal changes have affected our media marketplace.

More speculative assessments of what may happen in the field of telecommunications may be found in *Future Competition in Telecommunications*, edited by Stephen P. Bradley and Jerry A. Housman (Harvard Business School Press, 1989), and the international scene is discussed in *Marketplace for Telecommunications: Regulation & Deregulation in Industrialized Democracies*, edited by Marcellus S. Snow (Longman, 1986).

Finally, the most recent government perspective can be found in publications of the U.S. Department of Commerce, such as the *NTIA Telecom 2000: Charting the Course for a New Century*, National Telecommunications and Information Administration (U.S. GPO, October 1988).

ISSUE 8

Should the Content of Records Be Censored?

YES: Parents Resource Music Center, from a Hearing before the Committee on Commerce, Science, and Transportation, U.S. Senate, 99th Congress (September 19, 1985)

NO: Frank Zappa, from a Hearing before the Committee on Commerce, Science, and Transportation, U.S. Senate, 99th Congress (September 19, 1985)

ISSUE SUMMARY

YES: The Parents Music Resource Center (PMRC) requests in congressional testimony that Congress encourage the manufacturers of record albums, cassette tapes, and compact discs to establish a rating system for their music. **NO:** Musician Frank Zappa advocates protecting the musician's First Amendment right to free speech and endorses the use of printed texts of music lyrics rather than a labeling system.

Often issues of censorship are pitted against the Constitutional guarantee of "freedom of speech." In 1985 a group of concerned parents in the Washington, D.C., area organized the Parents Music Resource Center (PMRC) with the expressed goal of making parents aware of the contents of recorded material, particularly rock music and more specifically, "heavy metal" music. In their congressional testimony, PMRC indicates that music lyrics, record covers, rock videos, and live concerts promote a potential hazard to very young children, who might be confused and harmed by repeated references to sex, violence, drugs, and satanic practices. While the PMRC originally called for a categorized rating system that would have provided ratings for all recorded music, they had modified their position by the time they testified to the Senate Committee. In speaking to the Committee, Tipper Gore (wife of Senator Albert Gore, member of the Committee) clarifies that the PMRC is not asking for censorship but rather for labeling that would provide "truth in packaging."

Musician Frank Zappa, speaking as a private citizen, claims that the proposals offered by the PMRC would lead to censorship of other forms of media and calls attention to the difficulties in policing the PMRC proposals, which would not only stigmatize artists but would also restrict the sale of records that the PMRC found unsuitable, thereby inhibiting the musician's First Amendment right to freedom of speech.

What complicates this matter is the problem of who should be responsible for questionable content. If parents are monitoring their children's media habits, is there any need for the government to step in? If the government does step in, does it make it easier for parents to avoid the issue?

The PMRC has become known as the "Washington Wives" because many of its participants are married to representatives in Congress, and that added to the controversy.

The traditional problem with any form of censorship has to do with the rights of the individual in society (to decide what he or she might like to see or hear) and the responsibility of the government to protect those who might not be able to make decisions for themselves (such as children). The issue of when censorship can be legally invoked is problematic. The U.S. Constitution provides for the protection of freedom of speech but does not provide for definitions of obscenity, pornography, or "prurient interest." As a result, most cases dealing with issues of restriction of content are considered issues of censorship, or the restriction of speech.

YES   Parents Music Resource Center

STATEMENT OF THE PARENTS MUSIC RESOURCE CENTER

STATEMENT OF THE PMRC

Mrs. BAKER. The Parents Music Resource Center was organized in May of this year [1985] by mothers of young children who are very concerned by the growing trend in music toward lyrics that are sexually explicit, excessively violent, or glorify the use of drugs and alcohol.

Our primary purpose is to educate and inform parents about this alarming trend as well as to ask the industry to exercise self-restraint.

It is no secret that today's rock music is a very important part of adolescence and teenagers' lives. It always has been, and we don't question their right to have their own music. We think that is important. They use it to identify and give expression to their feelings, their problems, their joys, sorrows, loves, and values. It wakes them up in the morning and it is in the background as they get dressed for school. It is played on the bus. It is listened to in the cafeteria during lunch. It is played as they do their homework. They even watch it on MTV now. It is danced to at parties, and puts them to sleep at night.

Because anything that we are exposed to that much has some influence on us, we believe that the music industry has a special responsibility as the message of songs goes from the suggestive to the blatantly explicit.

As Ellen Goodman stated in a recent column, rock ratings:

> The outrageous edge of rock and roll has shifted its focus from Elvis's pelvis to the saw protruding from Blackie Lawless's codpiece on a WASP album. Rock lyrics have turned from "I can't get no satisfaction" to "I am going to force you at gunpoint to eat me alive."

The material we are concerned about cannot be compared with Louie Louie, Cole Porter, Billie Holliday, et cetera. . . . There is a new element of vulgarity and violence toward women that is unprecedented.

From U.S. Senate. 99th Congress, 1st Session. Committee on Commerce, Science, and Transportation. *Record Labeling.* Hearing, September 19, 1985. Washington, D.C.: Government Printing Office, 1985. (S.Hrg. 99/529)

While a few outrageous recordings have always existed in the past, the proliferation of songs glorifying rape, sadomasochism, incest, the occult, and suicide by a growing number of bands illustrates this escalating trend that is alarming.

Some have suggested that the records in question are only a minute element in this music. However, these records are not few, and have sold millions of copies, like Prince's "Darling Nikki," about masturbation, sold over 10 million copies. Judas Priest, the one about forced oral sex at gunpoint, has sold over 2 million copies. Quiet Riot, "Metal Health," has songs about explicit sex, over 5 million copies. Motley Crue, "Shout at the Devil," which contains violence and brutality to women, over 2 million copies.

Some say there is no cause for concern. We believe there is. Teen pregnancies and teenage suicide rates are at epidemic proportions today. The Noedecker Report states that in the United States of America we have the highest teen pregnancy rate of any developed country: 96 out of 1,000 teenage girls become pregnant.

Rape is up 7 percent in the latest statistics, and the suicide rates of youth between 16 and 24 has gone up 300 percent in the last three decades while the adult level has remained the same.

There certainly are many causes for these ills in our society, but it is our contention that the pervasive messages aimed at children which promote and glorify suicide, rape, sadomasochism, and so on, have to be numbered among the contributing factors.

Some rock artists actually seem to encourage teen suicide. Ozzie Osbourne sings "Suicide Solution." Blue Oyster Cult sings "Don't Fear the Reaper." AC/DC sings "Shoot to Thrill." Just last week in Centerpoint, a small Texas town, a young man took his life while listening to the music of AC/DC. He was not the first.

Now that more and more elementary school children are becoming consumers of rock music, we think it is imperative to discuss this question. What can be done to help parents who want to protect their children from these messages if they want to?

Today parents have no way of knowing the content of music products that their children are buying. While some album covers are sexually explicit or depict violence, many others give no clue as to the content. One of the top 10 today is Morris Day and the Time, "Jungle Love." If you go to buy the album "Ice Cream Castles" to get "Jungle Love," you also get, "If the Kid Can't Make You Come, Nobody Can," a sexually explicit song.

The pleasant cover picture of the members of the band gives no hint that it contains material that is not appropriate for young consumers.

Our children are faced with so many choices today. What is available to them through the media is historically unique. The Robert Johnson study on teen environment states that young people themselves often feel that they have: One, too many choices to make: two, too few structured means for arriving at decisions: and three, too little help to get there.

We believe something can be done, and Tipper Gore will discuss the possible solution. Thank you.

Mrs. GORE. Thank you, Mr. Chairman.

We are asking the recording industry to voluntarily assist parents who are concerned by placing a warning label on music products inappropriate for younger children due to explicit sexual or violent lyrics.

The Parents Music Resource Center originally proposed a categorical rating system for explicit material. After many discussions with the record industry, we recognize some of the logistical and economic problems, and have adjusted our original suggestions accordingly. We now propose one generic warning label to inform consumers in the marketplace about lyric content. The labels would apply to all music.

We have asked the record companies to voluntarily label their own products and assume responsibility for making those judgments. We ask the record industry to appoint a one-time panel to recommend a uniform set of criteria which could serve as a policy guide for the individual companies. Those individual recording companies would then in good faith agree to adhere to this standard, and make decisions internally about which records should be labeled according to the industry criteria.

We have also asked that lyrics for labeled music products be available to the consumer before purchase in the marketplace. Now, it is important to clearly state what our proposal is not.

A voluntary labeling is not censorship. Censorship implies restricting access or suppressing content. This proposal does neither. Moreover, it involves no Government action. Voluntary labeling in no way infringes upon first amendment rights. Labeling is little more than truth in packaging, by now, a time honored principle in our free enterprise system, and without labeling, parental guidance is virtually impossible.

Most importantly, the committee should understand the Parents Music Resource Center is not advocating any Federal intervention or legislation whatsoever. The excesses that we are discussing were allowed to develop in the marketplace, and we believe the solutions to these excesses should come from the industry who has allowed them to develop and not from the Government.

The issue here is larger than violent and sexually explicit lyrics. It is one of ideas and ideal freedoms and responsibility in our society. Clearly, there is a tension here, and in a free society there always will be. We are simply asking that these corporate and artistic rights be exercised with responsibility, with sensitivity, and some measure of self-restraint, especially since young minds are at stake. We are talking about preteenagers and young teenagers having access to this material. That is our point of departure and our concern.

Now, Mr. Chairman, one point we have already made, that the material that has caused the concern is new and different. It is not just a continuation of controversies of past generations. To illustrate this point, we would like to show a slide presentation, and to this end I turn the microphone over to Jeff Ling, who is a consultant to our group, and he will show you some of the material that we are talking about.

Thank you.

Mr. LING. Mr. Chairman, if we could have the lights turned down.

[Slides were then shown.]

Mr. LING. Mr. Chairman and distinguished members of the committee, thank you for allowing me to speak to you today. The purpose of this presentation is to acquaint you with the type of material that is in question.

I will be covering the themes of violence and sexuality. Bear in mind that what you are about to see and hear is a small sample of the abundant material available today. Today the element of violent, brutal erotica has exploded in rock music in an unprecedented way. Many albums today include songs that encourage suicide, violent revenge, sexual violence, and violence just for violence's sake.

This is Steve Boucher. Steve died while listening to AC/DC's "Shoot to Thrill." Steve fired his father's gun into his mouth.

A few days ago I was speaking in San Antonio. The day before I arrived, they buried a young high school student. This young man had taken his tape deck to the football field.

He hung himself while listening to AC/DC's "Shoot to Thrill." Suicide has become epidemic in our country among teenagers.

Some 6,000 will take their lives this year. Many of these young people find encouragement from some rock stars who present death as a positive, almost attractive alternative.

The album I am holding up in front of you is by the band Metalica. It is on Electra Asylum records. A song on this album is called "Faith in Black." It says the following. " I have lost the will to live. Simply nothing more to give. There is nothing more for me. I need the end to set me free."

"Death greets me warm. I will just say good-bye."

Consider the self-destructive violence that is encouraged in their song "Whiplash." "Bang your head against the stage like you never have before. Make it rain, make it bleed, make it really sore. In a frenzied madness, now is the time to let it rip, to let it . . . loose. We are gathered here to maim and kill, for this is what we choose."

Ozzie Osbourne on his first solo album, shown here, sings a song called "Suicide Solution." Ozzie insists that he in no way encourages suicidal behavior in young people, and yet he appears in photographs such as these in periodicals that are geared toward the young teenage audience.

For those of you who cannot make that out because of the lights, it is a picture of Ozzie with a gun barrel stuck into his mouth.

This is the cover of Twisted Sister's high selling LP for Atlantic Records called "Stay Hungry." An example of Twisted Sister's appeal to young people is evident in the back to school contest being run by MTV. First prize is a get together with Twisted Sister. The first prize is a meeting with Twisted Sister.

The hit song from the album, "We're Not Going to Take It," was released as a video, which you saw just a moment ago, a video in which the band members proceed to beat up daddy, who will not let them rock. Their first album, which has been released by Atlantic Records, is called "Under the Blade." . . .

This is the cover of the new album by the band Abattoir.

The title song is about a homocidal maniac, and notice on the cover the arms of the man wrapped around the woman. In one hand is a long knife. The other hand holds a hook being pressed against the woman's breast.

This is the cover of an album entitled "Rise of the Mutants" by the band Impaler.

Notice the man with the bloody meat in his mouth and hand. He is kneeling over the bloody arm of a woman.

The back cover shows a woman with a bloody face at the feet of the drummer.

While both of these albums were released on independent labels as opposed to major labels, they are reviewed and featured in teen rock magazines and are available in local record stores.

This band, WASP, recently signed a $1.5 million contract with Capital Records. This is their first release. The capital item is entitled "The Torture Never Stops." Violence permeates the album as well as their stage show, which has included chopping up and throwing raw meat into the audience.

Drinking blood from a skull.

And until recently the simulated rape and murder of a half-nude woman. . . .

While we will not consider the subject in depth at this time, it should be noted that occultic themes, primarily Satanism, is prevalent among such bands as Slayer, Venom, and Merciful Fate, one of whose albums is shown in this picture.

Let us move on to sexuality, a theme which has been part of rock music since its beginning. Today's rock artists are describing sexual activity and practice in terms more graphic than ever before. Many of you are aware of Purple Rain, the multimillion seller by Prince. Much has been said about the song "Darling Nikki" from the album. "I met a girl named Nikki. I guess you could say she was a sex fiend. I met her in a hotel lobby masturbating with magazines.". . . .

This is Betsy. She is the lead singer of a band called Bitch. The album is called "Be My Slave." It is available in record stores. One of the songs is called "Give Me a Kiss." "The way you grab me makes my knees shake. The way you pull my arms makes my body quake. The way you yank my hair, it just makes me want to kill you. I will take off my clothes. Kick me in the shins. Come on and slap me in the face, and I will get down on my knees and move you like this."

And the song "Leatherbound." "The whip is my toy. Handcuffs are your joy. You hold me down, and I am screaming for more. When you tie me up and gag me, the way you give me pain, come on, give me lashes." . . .

Mr. Chairman, that concludes my remarks. I thank you. . . .

The CHAIRMAN. Thank you very much for being here. I know that for all of you it was not the most pleasant of experiences to read some of the lyrics in public. But it was very helpful and we appreciate your attendance.

NO

Frank Zappa

STATEMENT OF FRANK ZAPPA

Mr. ZAPPA. My name is Frank Zappa. . . .

The first thing I would like to do, because I know there is some foreign press involved here and they might not understand what the issue is about, one of the things the issue is about is the First Amendment to the Constitution, and it is short and I would like to read it so they will understand. It says:

> Congress shall make no law respecting an establishment of religion or prohibiting the free exercise thereof, or abridging the freedom of speech or of the press, or the right of the people peaceably to assemble and to petition the government for a redress of grievances.

That is for reference.

These are my personal observations and opinions. I speak on behalf of no group or professional organization.

The PMRC proposal is an ill-conceived piece of nonsense which fails to deliver any real benefits to children, infringes the civil liberties of people who are not children, and promises to keep the courts busy for years dealing with the interpretational and enforcemental problems inherent in the proposal's design.

It is my understanding that in law First Amendment issues are decided with a preference for the least restrictive alternative. In this context, the PMRC demands are the equivalent of treating dandruff by decapitation.

No one has forced Mrs. Baker or Mrs. Gore to bring Prince or Sheena Easton into their homes. Thanks to the Constitution, they are free to buy other forms of music for their children. Apparently, they insist on purchasing the works of contemporary recording artists in order to support a personal illusion of aerobic sophistication. Ladies, please be advised: The $8.98 purchase price does not entitle you to a kiss on the foot from the composer or performer in exchange for the family Victrola.

Taken as a whole, the complete list of PMRC demands reads like an instruction manual for some sinister kind of toilet training program to house-

From U.S. Senate. 99th Congress, 1st Session. Committee on Commerce, Science, and Transportation. *Record Labeling.* Hearing, September 19, 1985. Washington, D.C.: Government Printing Office, 1985. (S.Hrg. 99/529)

break all composers and performers because of the lyrics of a few. Ladies, how dare you?

The ladies' shame must be shared by the bosses at the major labels who, through the RIAA, chose to bargain away the rights of composers, performers, and retailers in order to pass H.R. 2911, The Blank Tape Tax, a private tax levied by an industry on consumers for the benefit of a select group within that industry.

Is this a consumer issue? You bet it is. The major record labels need to have H.R. 2911 whiz through a few committees before anybody smells a rat. One of them is chaired by Senator Thurmond. Is it a coincidence that Mrs. Thurmond is affiliated with the PMRC?

I cannot say she is a member, because the PMRC has no members. Their secretary told me on the phone last Friday that the PMRC has no members, only founders. I asked how many other District of Columbia wives are nonmembers of an organization that raises money by mail, has a tax-exempt status, and seems intent on running the Constitution of the United States through the family paper-shredder. I asked her if it was a cult. Finally, she said she could not give me an answer and that she had to call their lawyer.

While the wife of the Secretary of the Treasury recites "Gonna drive my love inside you" and Senator Gore's wife talks about "bondage" and "oral sex at gunpoint" on the CBS Evening News, people in high places work on a tax bill that is so ridiculous, the only way to sneak it through is to keep the public's mind on something else: Porn rock.

Is the basic issue morality? It is mental health? Is it an issue at all? The PMRC has created a lot of confusion with improper comparisons between song lyrics, videos, record packaging, radio broadcasting, and live performances. These are all different mediums, and the people who work in them have the right to conduct their business without trade-restraining legislation, whipped up like an instant pudding by "The wives of Big Brother."

Is it proper that the husband of a PMRC nonmember/founder/person sits on any committee considering business pertaining to the blank tape tax or his wife's lobbying organization? Can any committee thus constituted find facts in a fair and unbiased manner? This committee has three that we know about: Senator Danforth, Senator Packwood, and Senator Gore. For some reason, they seem to feel there is no conflict of interest involved.

Children in the vulnerable age bracket have a natural love for music. If as a parent you believe they should be exposed to something more uplifting than "Sugar Walls," support music appreciation programs in schools. Why have you not considered your child's need for consumer information? Music appreciation costs very little compared to sports expenditures. Your children have a right to know that something besides pop music exists.

It is unfortunate that the PMRC would rather dispense governmentally sanitized heavy metal music than something more uplifting. Is this an indication of PMRC's personal taste or just another manifestation of the low priority this administration has placed on education for the arts in America?

The answer, of course, is neither. You cannot distract people from thinking about an unfair tax by talking about music appreciation. For that you need sex, and lots of it.

The establishment of a rating system, voluntary or otherwise, opens the door to an endless parade of moral quality control programs based on things certain Christians do not like. What if the next bunch of Washington wives demands a large yellow "J" on all material written or performed by Jews, in order to save helpless children from exposure to concealed Zionist doctrine?

Record ratings are frequently compared to film ratings. Apart from the quantitative difference, there is another that is more important: People who act in films are hired to pretend. No matter how the film is rated, it will not hurt them personally.

Since many musicians write and perform their own material and stand by it as their art, whether you like it or not, an imposed rating will stigmatize them as individuals. How long before composers and performers are told to wear a festive little PMRC arm band with their scarlet letter on it?

Bad facts make bad law, and people who write bad laws are in my opinion more dangerous than songwriters who celebrate sexuality. Freedom of speech, freedom of religious thought, and the right to due process for composers, performers and retailers are imperiled if the PMRC and the major labels consummate this nasty bargain.

Are we expected to give up article 1 so the big guys can collect an extra dollar on every blank tape and 10 to 25 percent on tape recorders? What is going on here? Do we get to vote on this tax?

I think that this whole matter has gotten completely blown out of proportion, and I agree with Senator Exon that there is a very dubious reason for having this event. I also agree with Senator Exon that you should not be wasting time on stuff like this, because from the beginning I have sensed that it is somebody's hobby project.

Now, I have done a number of interviews on television. People keep saying, can you not take a few steps in their direction, can you not sympathize, can you not empathize? I do more than that at this point. I have got an idea for a way to stop all this stuff and a way to give parents what they really want, which is information, accurate information as to what is inside the album, without providing a stigma for the musicians who have played on the album or the people who sing it or the people who wrote it. And I think that if you listen carefully to this idea that it might just get by all of the constitutional problems and everything else.

As far as I am concerned, I have no objection to having all of the lyrics placed on the album routinely, all the time. But there is a little problem. Record companies do not own the right automatically to take these lyrics, because they are owned by a publishing company.

So, just as all the rest of the PMRC proposals would cost money, this would cost money, too, because the record companies would need—they should not be forced to bear the cost, the extra expenditure to the publisher, to print those lyrics.

If you consider that the public needs to be warned about the contents of the records, what better way than to let them see exactly what the songs say? That way you do not have to put any kind of subjective rating on the record. You do not have to call it R, X, D/A, or anything. You can read it for yourself.

But in order for it to work properly, the lyrics should be on a uniform kind of a sheet. Maybe even the Government could print those sheets. Maybe it should even be paid for by the Government, if the Government is interested in making sure that people have consumer information in this regard.

And you also have to realize that if a person buys the record and takes it out of the store, once it is out of the store you can't return it if you read the lyrics at home and decide that little Johnny is not supposed to have it.

I think that that should at least be considered, and the idea of imposing these ratings on live concerts, on the albums, asking record companies to reevaluate or drop or violate contracts that they already have with artists should be thrown out.

That is all I have to say.

The CHAIRMAN. Thank you very much, Mr. Zappa. You understand that the previous witnesses were not asking for legislation. And I do not know, I cannot speak for Senator Hollings, but I think the prevailing view here is that nobody is asking for legislation.

The question is just focusing on what a lot of people perceive to be a problem, and you have indicated that you at least understand that there is another point of view. But there are people that think that parents should have some knowledge of what goes into their home.

Mr. ZAPPA. All along my objection has been with the tactics used by these people in order to achieve the goal. I just think the tactics have been really bad, and the whole premise of their proposal—they were badly advised in terms of record business law, they were badly advised in terms of practicality, or they would have known that certain things do not work mechanically with what they suggest.

The CHAIRMAN. Senator Gore.

Senator GORE. Thank you very much, Mr. Chairman.

I found your statement very interesting and, although I disagree with some of the statements that you make and have made on other occasions, I have been a fan of your music, believe it or not. I respect you as a true original and a tremendously talented musician.

Your suggestion of printing the lyrics on the album is a very interesting one. The PMRC at one point said they would propose either a rating or warning, or printing all the lyrics on the album. The record companies came back and said they did not want to do that.

I think a lot of people agree with your suggestion that one easy way to solve this problem for parents would be to put the actual words there, so that parents could see them. In fact, the National Association of Broadcasters made exactly the same request of the record companies.

I think your suggestion is an intriguing one and might really be a solution for the problem.

Mr. ZAPPA. You have to understand that it does cost money, because you cannot expect publishers to automatically give up that right, which is a right for them. Somebody is going to have to reimburse the publishers, the record industry.

Without trying to mess up the album jacket art, it should be a sheet of paper that is slipped inside the shrink-wrap, so that when you take it out you can still have a complete album package. So there is going to be some extra cost for printing it.

But as long as people realize-that for this kind of consumer safety you are going to spend some money and as long as you can find a way to pay for it, I think that would be the best way to let people know.

Senator GORE. I do not disagree with that at all. And the separate sheet would also solve the problem with cassettes as well, because you do not have the space for words on the cassette packs.

Mr. ZAPPA. There would have to be a little accordion-fold.

Senator GORE. I have listened to you a number of times on this issue, and I guess the statement that I want to get from you is whether or not you feel this concern is legitimate.

You feel very strongly about your position, and I understand that. You are very articulate and forceful.

But occasionally you give the impression that you think parents are just silly to be concerned at all.

Mr. ZAPPA. No; that is not an accurate impression.

Senator GORE. Well, please clarify it, then.

Mr. ZAPPA. First of all, I think it is the parents' concern; it is not the Government's concern.

Senator GORE. PMRC agrees with you on that.

Mr. ZAPPA. Well, that does not come across in the way they have been speaking. The whole drift that I have gotten, based upon the media blitz that has attended the PMRC and its rise to infamy, is that they have a special plan, and it has smelled like legislation up until now.

There are too many things that look like hidden agendas involved with this. And I am a parent. I have got four children. Two of them are here. I want them to grow up in a country where they can think what they want to think, be what they want to be, and not what some-

body's wife or somebody in Government makes them be.

I do not want to have that and I do not think you do either.

Senator GORE. OK. But now you are back on the issue of Government involvement. Let me say briefly on this point that the PMRC says repeatedly no legislation, no regulation, no Government action. It certainly sounded clear to me.

And as far as hidden agenda, I do not see one, hear one, or know of one.

Mr. ZAPPA. OK, let me tell you why I have drawn these conclusions. First of all, they may say, we are not interested in legislation. But there are others who do, and because of their project bad things have happened in this country in the industry.

I believe there is actually some liability. Look at this. You have a situation where, even if you go for the lyric printed thin in the record, because of the tendency among Americans to be copycats—one guy commits a murder, you get a copycat murder—now you've got copycat censors.

You get a very bad situation in San Antonio, TX, right now where they are try to pass PMRC-type individual ratings and attach them to live concerts, with the mayor down there trying to make a national reputation by putting San Antonio on the map as the first city in the United States to have these regulations, against the suggestion of the city attorney, who says, I do not think this is constitutional.

But you know, there is this fervor to get in and do even more and even more.

And the other thing, the PMRC starts off talking about lyrics, but when they take it over into other realms they start talking about the videos. In fact, you misspoke yourself at the beginning in your introduction when you were talking about the music does this, the music does that. There is a distinct difference between those notes and chords and the baseline and the rhythm that support the words and the lyrics.

I do not know whether you really are talking about controlling the type of music.

The CHAIRMAN. The lyrics.

Mr. ZAPPA. So specifically we are talking about lyrics. It began with lyrics. But even looking at the PMRC fundraising letter, in the last paragraph at the bottom of the page it starts looking like it is branching into area areas, when it says: "We realize that this material has pervaded other aspects of society." And it is like what, you are going to fix it all for me?

Senator GORE. No. I think the PMRC's acknowledging come of the statements by some of their critics who say: Well, why single out the music industry.

Do I understand that you believe there is a legitimate concern here?

Mr. ZAPPA. But the legitimate concern is a matter of taste for the individual parent and how much sexual information that parents wants to give their child, at what age, at what time, in what quantity, OK. And I think that, because there is a tendency in the United States to hide sex, which I think is an unhealthy thing to do, and many parents do not give their children good sexual education, in spite of the fact that little books for kids are available, and other parents demand that sexual education be taken out of school, it makes the child vulnerable, because if you do not have something rational to compare it to when you see or hear about something that is aberrated you do not perceive it as an aberration.

Senator GORE. OK, I have run out of time. . . .

Senator EXON. . . . Let us try and get down to a fundamental question here that I would like to ask you, Mr. Zappa. Do you believe that parents have the right and the obligation to mold the psychological development of their children?

Mr. ZAPPA. Yes, I think they have that right, and I also think they have that obligation.

Senator EXON. Do you see any extreme difficulty in carrying out those obligations for a parent by material falling into the hands of their children over which they have little or no control?

Mr. ZAPPA. Well, one of the things that has been brought up before is talking about very young children getting access to the material that they have been showing here today. And what I have said to that in the past is a teenager may go into a record store unescorted with $8.98 in his pocket, but very young children do not.

If they go into a record store, the $8.98 is in mom or dad's pocket, and they can always say, Johnny, buy a book. They can say, Johnny, buy instrumental music; there is some nice classical music for you here; why do you not listen to that.

The parent can ask or guide the child in another direction, away from Sheena Easton, Prince, or whoever else you have been complaining about. There is always that possibility.

Senator EXON. As I understand it from your testimony—and once again, I want to emphasize that I see nothing wrong whatsoever; in fact, I salute the ladies for bringing this to the attention of the public as best they see fit. I think you could tell from my testimony that I agree with them.

I want to be very careful that we do not overstep our bounds and try and—and I emphasize once again—tell somebody else what they should see. I am primarily worried about children.

It seems to me from your statement that you have no obligation—or no objection whatsoever to printing lyrics, if that would be legally possible, or from a standpoint of having the room to do that, on records or tapes. Is that not what you said?

Mr. ZAPPA. I think it would be advisable for two reasons. One, it gives people one of the things they have been asking for. It gives them that type of consumer protection because, if you can read the English language and you can see the lyrics on the back, you have no excuse for complaining if you take the record out of the store.

And also, I think that the record industry has been damaged and it has been given a very bad rap by this whole situation because it has been indicated, or people have attempted to indicate, that there is so much of this kind of material that people object to in the industry, that that is what the industry is.

It is not bad at all. Some of the albums that have been selected for abuse here are obscure. Some of them are already several years old. And I think that a lot of deep digging was done in order to come up with the songs . . . they were talking about before.

Senator EXON. If I understand you, you would be in support of printing the lyrics, but you are adamantly opposed to any kind of a rating system?

Mr. ZAPPA. I am opposed to the rating system because, as I said, if you put a rating on the record it goes directly to the character of the person who made the record, whereas if you rate a film, a guy who is in the film has been hired as an actor. He is pretending. You rate the film, whatever it is, it does not hurt him.

But whether you like what is on the record or not, the guy who made it, that is his art and to stigmatize him is unfair.

Senator EXON. Well, likewise, if you are primarily concerned about the artists, is it not true that for many many years, we have had ratings of movies with indications as to the sexual content of movies and that has been, as near as I can tell, a voluntary action on the part of the actors in the movies and the producers of the movies and the distributors?

That seems to have worked reasonably well. What is wrong with that?

Mr. ZAPPA. Well, first of all, it replaced something that was far more restrictive, which was the Hayes Office. And as far as that being voluntary, there are people who wish they did not have to rate their films. They still object to rating their films, but the reason the ratings go on is because if they are not rated they will not get distributed or shown in theaters. So there is a little bit of pressure involved, but still there is no stigma. . . .

Senator HOLLINGS. . . . Now, it is not considered unfair in the movie industry, and I want you to elaborate. I do not want to belabor you, but why is it unfair? I mean, it is accurate, is it not?

Mr. ZAPPA. Well, I do not know whether it is accurate, because sometimes they have trouble deciding how a film gets to be an X or an R or whatever. And you have two problems. One is the quantity of the material, 325 films per year versus 25,000 4-minute songs per year, OK.

You also have a problem that an album is a compilation of different types of cuts. If one song on the album is sexually explicit and all the rest of it sounds like

Pat Boone, what do you get on the album? How are you going to rate it?

There are little technical difficulties here, and also you have the problem of having somebody in the position of deciding what's good, what's bad, what's talking about the devil, what is too violent, and the rest of that stuff.

But the point I made before is that when you rate the album you are rating the individual, because he takes personal responsibility for the music; and in the movies, the actors who are performing in the movies, it does not hurt them.

Senator HOLLINGS. Well, very good. I think the actual printing of the content itself is perhaps even better than the rating. Let everyone else decide.

Mr. ZAPPA. I think you should leave it up to the parents, because not all parents want to keep their children totally ignorant.

POSTSCRIPT

Should the Content of Records Be Censored?

The PMRC's testimony suggests many "direct effects" associated with listening to lyrics, viewing videos, album covers, or live performances. Does exposure to sexually suggestive or violent and abusive lyrics influence behavior? Is so, how much? The assumptions of the PMRC make us question the "magic bullet theory" (explained in this volume's Introduction) and causes us to consider the broader issue of social responsibility. As Frank Zappa indicates, there are no easy answers to these questions, and the problems associated with them involve issues of civil liberties, interpretation, and enforcement.

After several years of debate, the National Association of Recording Merchandisers announced in May 1990 that it would comply with a voluntary labeling plan that would caution parents about albums that could be objectionable based upon explicit lyrics dealing with sex, violence, suicide, or substance abuse. The black and white labels would appear on the lower right-hand corner of records, cassettes, and compact discs that might be objectionable.

Industries responding voluntarily to efforts for some type of labeling procedure usually do so in response to a fear that greater government regulation could follow. One such example is the voluntary rating of movies by the Motion Picture Association of America (MPAA). In September of 1990, as we go to press with this book, the MPAA announced a major revision of its movie ratings system, a system that was first introduced in 1968. *The New York Times* reported in a front page story on September 27, 1990, by Larry Rohter, that the "MPAA has created a new 'No Children' category for adult films to replace the 'X' rating that has become synonymous with pornography and a focus of bitter dispute. The new 'NC-17' category will be applied to movies that include adult themes or content and is intended to deny admittance to such films to all viewers under 17 years of age. . . . [A]ssociation officials said the new NC rating would be trademarked to prevent its unauthorized use by others. The association's failure to obtain a trademark for the X category allowed the makers of pornographic films to appropriate that rating as a promotional lure, which in turn forced the makers and marketers of serious films to avoid an X rating at all costs."

In the case of record ratings or labeling, 19 states had begun to propose legislation that would require warning labels, but 16 of them gave up their plans when the industry promised to institute a uniform label. Even though the labeling controversy has subsided, we are certain to see future debate over what constitutes censorship as well as whether the government or parents have the right to determine what their children see or hear.

ISSUE 9

Should Pornography Be Protected as Free Speech?

YES: Frank Easterbrook, from *American Booksellers Association, Inc. vs. Hudnut,* U.S. Court of Appeals for the Seventh Circuit (1984)

NO: James C. Dobson, from *Final Report of the U.S. Attorney General's Commission on Pornography* (June 1986)

ISSUE SUMMARY

YES: Judge Frank Easterbrook holds that an ordinance regulating pornography is an unconstitutional infringement on freedom of speech and press.
NO: Psychologist James Dobson, a member of the 1985 U.S. government commission that investigated pornography, is convinced of the devastation inflicted on victims of pornography. He describes how the Meese commission came to their decision and lists nine ways in which pornography does harm.

Opinion is divided on the pornography debate between those who worry on the one hand that pornography is being used to torture and murder women and on the other hand that the antipornography movement is a conservative backlash that will ultimately threaten freedom of speech and press.

Antipornography advocates agree that violent pornography teaches people to connect sex with violence and fuels discrimination against women. They believe that the proliferation of these materials harms society in general and children in particular. This has led to an unusual political alliance between conservatives and some feminists, both of whom agree that pornography should be banned because it is destructive, abusive, and detrimental to society. In 1985 the government Commission on Pornography, appointed by then-attorney general Edwin Meese, came to the controversial conclusion that empirical evidence exists that links pornography with antisocial behavior. Violent pornography, they concluded, is harmful and should not be decriminalized; child pornography should be prosecuted more vigorously. James Dobson, a psychologist who served on the Meese commission, clearly supports this conclusion. He describes the process whereby the commission arrived at its decision and responds to some of the graphic evidence that was reviewed.

To some, these conclusions are not clear-cut. Critics of the Meese Commission Final Report argue that scientific studies have revealed no causal connection between pornography and violence against women and that, furthermore, the possible therapeutic uses of pornography were overlooked as was evidence that showed that rape has not increased in nations that have removed restrictions on pornography. The Meese commission, they conclude, was biased.

To still others, the criminalization of pornography is an infringement on their rights under the First Amendment—the rights of free speech and free press. This is a significant debate which positions freedoms that have long been important to those who study or work with communication in the United States against the social harm that may emerge when those freedoms are exercised by pornographers. From a legal point of view, the question is whether or not pornography should be protected under the First Amendment. Obscenity, for example, is not protected. Does pornography, like obscenity, contribute so little to society that the protection of the First Amendment is irrelevant? Frank Easterbrook argues that pornography should be protected in the following U. S. Court of Appeals decision concerning an Indianapolis ordinance. The city had passed an ordinance banning the distribution of pornography within its city limits. Several groups went to court arguing that this law interfered with their First Amendment rights. Federal District Court and, on appeal, the Federal Court of Appeals ruled that the law was indeed a violation of the Constitution.

YES

Frank Easterbrook

PORNOGRAPHY AND
THE FIRST AMENDMENT

Indianapolis enacted an ordinance defining "pornography" as a practice that discriminates against women. "Pornography" is to be redressed through the administrative and judicial methods used for other discrimination. The City's definition of "pornography" is considerably different from "obscenity," which the Supreme Court has held is not protected by the First Amendment.

To be "obscene" under *Miller v. California*, 413 U.S. 15, S.Ct. 2607, 37 L.Ed.2d 419 (1973), "a publication must, taken as a whole, appeal to the prurient interest, must contain patently offensive depictions or descriptions of specified sexual conduct, and on the whole have no serious literary, artistic, political, or scientific value." *Brockett v. Spokane Arcades, Inc.,*—— U.S.——, 105 S.Ct. 2794, 2800, 86 L.Ed.2d 394 (1985). Offensiveness must be assessed under the standards of the community. Both offensiveness and an appeal to something other than "normal, healthy sexual desires" (*Brockett, supra*, 105 S.Ct. at 2799) are essential elements of "obscenity."

"Pornography" under the ordinance is "the graphic sexually explicit subordination of women, whether in pictures or in words, that also includes one or more of the following:

(1) Women are presented as sexual objects who enjoy pain or humiliation; or
(2) Women are presented as sexual objects who experience sexual pleasure in being raped; or
(3) Women are presented as sexual objects tied up or cut up or mutilated or bruised or physically hurt, or as dismembered or truncated or fragmented or severed into body parts; or
(4) Women are presented as being penetrated by objects or animals; or
(5) Women are presented in scenarios of degradation, injury, abasement, torture, shown as filthy or inferior, bleeding, bruised, or hurt in a context that makes these conditions sexual; or
(6) Women are presented as sexual objects for domination, conquest, violation,

From U.S. Court of Appeals for the Seventh Circuit, *American Booksellers Association, Inc. v. William H. Hudnut III*, November 19, 1984. (598 F.Supp 1316, 106 S.Ct. 1172) exploitation, possession, or use, or through postures or positions of servility or submission or display."

Indianapolis Code § 16–3(q). The statute provides that the "use of men, children, or transsexuals in the place of women in paragraphs (1) through (6) above shall also constitute pornography under this section." The ordinance as passed in April 1984 defined "sexually explicit" to mean actual or simulated intercourse or the uncovered exhibition of the genitals, buttocks or anus. An amendment in June 1984 deleted this provision, leaving the term undefined.

The Indianapolis ordinance does not refer to the prurient interest, to offensiveness, or to the standards of the community. It demands attention to particular depictions, not to the work judged as a whole. It is irrelevant under the ordinance whether the work has literary, artistic, political, or scientific value. The City and many amici point to these omissions as virtues. They maintain that pornography influences attitudes, and the statute is a way to alter the socialization of men and women rather than to vindicate community standards of offensiveness. And as one of the principal drafters of the ordinance has asserted, "if a woman is subjected, why should it matter that the work has other value?" Catharine A. MacKinnon, *Pornography, Civil Rights, and Speech*, 20 Harv.Civ.Rts.—Civ.Lib.L.Rev. 1, 21 (1985).

Civil rights groups and feminists have entered this case as amici on both sides. Those supporting the ordinance say that it will play an important role in reducing the tendency of men to view women as sexual objects, a tendency that leads to both unacceptable attitudes and discrimination in the workplace and violence away from it. Those opposing the ordinance point out that much radical feminist literature is explicit and depicts women in ways forbidden by the ordinance and that the ordinance would reopen old battles. It is unclear how Indianapolis would treat works from James Joyce's *Ulysses* to Homer's *Iliad*; both depict women as submissive objects for conquest and domination.

We do not try to balance the arguments for and against an ordinance such as this. The ordinance discriminates on the ground of the content of the speech. Speech treating women in the approved way—in sexual encounters "premised on equality" (MacKinnon, *supra*, at 22)—is lawful no matter how sexually explicit. Speech treating women in the disapproved way—as submissive in matters sexual or as enjoying humiliation—is unlawful no matter how significant the literary, artistic, or political qualities of the work taken as a whole. The state may not ordain preferred viewpoints in this way. The Constitution forbids the state to declare one perspective right and silence opponents.

I

The ordinance contains four prohibitions. People may not "traffic" in pornography, "coerce" others into performing in pornographic works, or "force" pornography on anyone. Anyone injured by someone who has seen or read pornography has a right of action against the maker or seller.

Trafficking is defined in § 16–3(g)(4) as the "production, sale, exhibition, or distribution of pornography." The offense excludes exhibition in a public or educational library, but a "special display" in a library may be sex discrimination. Section 16-3(g)(4)© provides that the trafficking paragraph "shall not be construed to make isolated passages or isolated parts actionable."

"Coercion into pornographic performance" is defined in § 16-3(g)(5) as "[c]oercing, intimidating or fraudulently inducing any person . . . into performing for pornography. . . . " The ordinance specifies that proof of any of the following "shall not constitute a defense: I. That the person is a woman; . . . VI. that the person has previously posed for sexually explicit pictures . . . with anyone . . . ; . . . VIII. That the person actually consented to a use of the performance that is changed into pornography; . . . IX. That the person knew that the purpose of the acts or events in question was to make pornography; . . . XI. That the person signed a contract, or made statements affirming a willingness to cooperate in the production of pornography; XII. That no physical force, threats, or weapons were used in the making of the pornography; or XIII. That the person was paid or otherwise compensated."

"Forcing pornography on a person," according to § 16-3(g)(5), is the "forcing of pornography on any woman, man, child, or transsexual in any place of employment, in education, in a home, or in any public place." The statute does not define forcing, but one of its authors states that the definition reaches pornography shown to medical students as part of their education or given to language students for translation. MacKinnon, *supra*, at 40-41.

Section 16-3(g)(7) defines as a prohibited practice the "assault, physical attack, or injury of any woman, man, child, or transsexual in a way that is directly caused by specific pornography."

For purposes of all four offenses, it is generally "not . . . a defense that the respondent did not know or intend that the materials were pornography. . . . " Section 16-3(g)(8). But the ordinance provides that damages are unavailable in trafficking cases unless the complainant proves "that the respondent knew or had reason to know that the materials were pornography." It is a complete defense to a trafficking case that all of the materials in question were pornography only by virtue of category (6) of the definition of pornography. In cases of assault caused by pornography, those who seek damages from "a seller, exhibitor or distributor" must show that the defendant knew or had reason to know of the material's status as pornography. By implication, those who seek damages from an author need not show this. . . .

The district court held the ordinance unconstitutional. 598 F.Supp. 1316 (S.D. Ind. 1984). The court concluded that the ordinance regulates speech rather than the conduct involved in making pornography. The regulation of speech could be justified, the court thought, only by a compelling interest in reducing sex discrimination, an interest Indianapolis had not established. The ordinance is also vague and overbroad, the court believed, and establishes a prior restraint of speech.

II

The plaintiffs are a congeries of distributors and readers of books, magazines, and films. The American Booksellers Association comprises about 5,200 bookstores and chains. The Association for American Publishers includes most of the country's publishers. Video Shack, Inc., sells and rents video cassettes in

Indianapolis. Kelly Bentley, a resident of Indianapolis, reads books and watches films. There are many more plaintiffs. Collectively the plaintiffs (or their members, whose interests they represent) make, sell, or read just about every kind of material that could be affected by the ordinance, from hard-core films to W. B. Yeats's poem "Leda and the Swan" (from the myth of Zeus in the form of a swan impregnating an apparently subordinate Leda), to the collected works of James Joyce, D. H. Lawrence, and John Cleland. . . .

III

"If there is any fixed star in our constitutional constellation, it is that no official, high or petty, can prescribe what shall be orthodox in politics, nationalism, religion, or other matters of opinion or force citizens to confess by word or act their faith therein." *West Virginia State Board of Education v. Barnette,* 319 U.S. 624, 642, 63 S.Ct. 1178, 1187, 87 L.Ed. 1628 (1943). Under the First Amendment the government must leave to the people the evaluation of ideas. Bold or subtle, an idea is as powerful as the audience allows it to be. A belief may be pernicious—the beliefs of Nazis led to the death of millions, those of the Klan to the repression of millions. A pernicious belief may prevail. Totalitarian governments today rule much of the planet, practicing suppression of billions and spreading dogma that may enslave others. One of the things that separates our society from theirs is our absolute right to propagate opinions that the government finds wrong or even hateful.

The ideas of the Klan may be propagated. *Brandenburg v. Ohio,* 395 U.S. 444, 89 S.Ct. 1827, 23 L.Ed.2d. 430 (1969).

Communists may speak freely and run for office. *DeJonge v. Oregon,* 299 U.S. 353, 57 S.Ct. 255, 81 L.Ed 278 (1937). The Nazi party may march through a city with a large Jewish population. *Collin v. Smith,* 578 F.2d 1197 (7th Cir.), *cert. denied,* 439 U.S. 916, 99 S.Ct. 291, 58 L.Ed.2d 264 (1978). People may criticize the President by misrepresenting his positions, and they have a right to post their misrepresentations on public property. *Lebron v. Washington Metropolitan Area Transit Authority,* 749 F.2d 893 (D.C.Cir. 1984) (Bork, J.). People may teach religions that others despise. People may seek to repeal laws guaranteeing equal opportunity in employment or to revoke the constitutional amendments granting the vote to blacks and women. They may do this because "above all else, the First Amendment means that government has no power to restrict expression because of its message [or] its ideas. . . . " *Police Department v. Mosley,* 408 U.S. 92, 95, 92 S.Ct. 2286, 2290, 33 L.Ed.2d 212 (1972). See also Geoffrey R. Stone, *Content Regulation and the First Amendment,* 25 William & Mary L.Rev. 189 (1983). . . .

Under the ordinance graphic sexually explicit speech is "pornography" or not depending on the perspective the author adopts. Speech that "subordinates" women and also, for example, presents women as enjoying pain, humiliation, or rape, or even simply presents women in "positions of servility or submission or display" is forbidden, no matter how great the literary or political value of the work taken as a whole. Speech that portrays women in positions of equality is lawful, no matter how graphic the sexual content. This is thought control. It establishes an "approved" view of women, of how they may react to sexual encounters, of how the sexes may relate to each other. Those who espouse the approved view may use sexual images; those who do not, may not.

Indianapolis justifies the ordinance on the ground that pornography affects thoughts. Men who see women depicted as subordinate are more likely to treat them so. Pornography is an aspect of dominance.[1] It does not persuade people so much as change them. It works by socializing, by establishing the expected and the permissible. In this view pornography is not an idea; pornography is the injury.

There is much to this perspective. Beliefs are also facts. People often act in accordance with the images and patterns they find around them. People raised in a religion tend to accept the tenets of that religion, often without independent examination. People taught from birth that black people are fit only for slavery rarely rebelled against that creed; beliefs coupled with the self-interest of the masters established a social structure that inflicted great harm while enduring for centuries. Words and images act at the level of the subconscious before they persuade at the level of the conscious. Even the truth has little chance unless a statement fits within the framework of beliefs that may never have been subjected to rational study.

Therefore we accept the premises of this legislation. Depictions of subordination tend to perpetuate subordination. The subordinate status of women in turn leads to affront and lower pay at work, insult and injury at home, battery and rape on the streets. In the language of the legislature, "[p]ornography is central in creating and maintaining sex as a basis of discrimination. Pornography is a systematic practice of exploitation and subordination based on sex which differentially harms women. The bigotry and contempt it produces, with the acts of aggression it fosters, harm women's opportunities for equality and rights [of all kinds]." Indianapolis Code § 16-1(a)(2).

Yet this simply demonstrates the power of pornography as speech. All of these unhappy effects depend on mental intermediation. Pornography affects how people see the world, their fellows, and social relations. If pornography is what pornography does, so is other speech. Hitler's orations affected how some Germans saw Jews. Communism is a world view, not simply a *Manifesto* by Marx and Engels or a set of speeches. Efforts to suppress communist speech in the United States were based on the belief that the public acceptability of such ideas would increase the likelihood of totalitarian government. Religions affect socialization in the most pervasive way. The opinion in *Wisconsin v. Yoder*, 406 U.S. 205, 92 S.Ct 1526, 32 L.Ed.2d 15 (1972), shows how a religion can dominate an entire approach to life, governing much more than the relation between the sexes. Many people believe that the existence of television, apart from the content of specific programs, leads to intellectual laziness, to a penchant for violence, to many other ills. The Alien and Sedition Acts passed during the administration of John Adams rested on a sincerely held belief that disrespect for the government leads to social collapse and revolution—a belief with support in the history of many nations. Most governments of the world act on this empirical regularity, suppressing critical speech. In the United States, however, the strength of the support for this belief is irrelevant. Seditious libel is protected speech unless the danger is not only grave but also imminent. See *New York*

Times Co. v. Sullivan, 376 U.S. 254, 84 S.Ct. 710, 11 L.Ed.2d 686 (1964). . . .

Racial bigotry, anti-semitism, violence on television, reporters' biases—these and many more influence the culture and shape our socialization. None is directly answerable by more speech, unless that speech too finds its place in the popular culture. Yet all is protected as speech, however insidious. Any other answer leaves the government in control of all of the institutions of culture, the great censor and director of which thoughts are good for us.

Sexual responses often are unthinking responses, and the association of sexual arousal with the subordination of women therefore may have a substantial effect. But almost all cultural stimuli provoke unconscious responses. Religious ceremonies condition their participants. Teachers convey messages by selecting what not to cover; the implicit message about what is off limits or unthinkable may be more powerful than the messages for which they present rational argument. Television scripts contain unarticulated assumptions. People may be conditioned in subtle ways. If the fact that speech plays a role in a process of conditioning were enough to permit governmental regulation, that would be the end of freedom of speech.

It is possible to interpret the claim that the pornography is the harm in a different way. Indianapolis emphasizes the injury that models in pornographic films and pictures may suffer. The record contains materials depicting sexual torture, penetration of women by red-hot irons and the like. These concerns have nothing to do with written materials subject to the statute, and physical injury can occur with or without the "subordination" of women. As we discuss in Part IV, a state may make injury in the course of producing a film unlawful independent of the viewpoint expressed in the film.

The more immediate point, however, is that the image of pain is not necessarily pain. In *Body Double*, a suspense film directed by Brian DePalma, a woman who has disrobed and presented a sexually explicit display is murdered by an intruder with a drill. The drill runs through the woman's body. The film is sexually explicit and a murder occurs—yet no one believes that the actress suffered pain or died. In *Barbarella* a character played by Jane Fonda is at times displayed in sexually explicit ways and at times shown "bleeding, bruised, [and] hurt in a context that makes these conditions sexual"—and again no one believes that Fonda was actually tortured to make the film. In *Carnal Knowledge* a woman grovels to please the sexual whims of a character played by Jack Nicholson; no one believes that there was a real sexual submission, and the Supreme Court held the film protected by the First Amendment. *Jenkins v. Georgia*, 418 U.S. 153, 94 S.Ct. 2750, 41 L.Ed.2d 642 (1974). And this works both ways. The description of women's sexual domination of men in *Lysistrata* was not real dominance. Depictions may affect slavery, war, or sexual roles, but a book about slavery is not itself slavery, or a book about death by poison a murder.

Much of Indianapolis's argument rests on the belief that when speech is "unanswerable," and the metaphor that there is a "marketplace of ideas" does not apply, the First Amendment does not apply either. The metaphor is honored; Milton's *Aeropagitica* and John Stewart Mill's *On Liberty* defend freedom of speech on the ground that the truth will prevail, and many of the most important cases under the First Amendment recite this position. The Framers undoubtedly believed it. As a general matter it is true. But the Constitution does not make the dominance of truth a necessary condition of freedom of speech. To say that it does would be to confuse an outcome of free speech with a necessary condition for the application of the amendment.

A power to limit speech on the ground that truth has not yet prevailed and is not likely to prevail implies the power to declare truth. At some point the government must be able to say (as Indianapolis has said): "We know what the truth is, yet a free exchange of speech has not driven out falsity, so that we must now prohibit falsity." If the government may declare the truth, why wait for the failure of speech? Under the First Amendment, however, there is no such thing as a false idea, *Gertz v. Robert Welch, Inc.*, 418 U.S. 323, 339, 94 S.Ct. 2997, 3006, 41 L.Ed.2d 789 (1974), so the government may not restrict speech on the ground that in a free exchange truth is not yet dominant.

At any time, some speech is ahead in the game; the more numerous speakers prevail. Supporters of minority candidates may be forever "excluded" from the political process because their candidates never win, because few people believe their positions. This does not mean that freedom of speech has failed.

The Supreme Court has rejected the position that speech must be "effectively answerable" to be protected by the Constitution. For example, in *Buckley v. Valeo*, *supra*, 424 U.S. at 39–54, 96 S.Ct. at 644–51, the Court held unconstitutional limitations on expenditures that were neutral with regard to the speakers' opinions and designed to make it easier for one person to answer another's

speech. . . . In *Mills v. Alabama*, 384 U.S. 214, 86 S.Ct. 1434, 16 L.Ed.2d 484 (1966), the Court held unconstitutional a statute prohibiting editorials on election day—a statute the state had designed to prevent speech that came too late for answer. In cases from *Eastern Railroad Presidents Conference v. Noerr Motor Freight, Inc.*, 365 U.S. 127, 81 S.Ct. 523, 5 L.Ed.2d 464 (1961), through *NAACP v. Claiborne Hardware Co.*, 458 U.S. 886, 102 S.Ct. 3409, 73 L.Ed.2d 1215 (1982), the Court has held that the First Amendment protects political stratagems—obtaining legislation through underhanded ploys and outright fraud in *Noerr*, obtaining political and economic ends through boycotts in *Clairborne Hardware*—that may be beyond effective correction through more speech.

We come, finally, to the argument that pornography is "low value" speech, that it is enough like obscenity that Indianapolis may prohibit it. Some cases hold that speech far removed from politics and other subjects at the core of the Framers' concerns may be subjected to special regulation. E.g., *FCC v. Pacifica Foundation*, 438 U.S. 726, 98 S.Ct. 3026, 57 L.Ed.2d 1073 (1978). . . . These cases do not sustain statutes that select among viewpoints, however. In *Pacifica* the FCC sought to keep vile language off the air during certain times. The Court held that it may; but the Court would not have sustained a regulation prohibiting scatological descriptions of Republicans but not scatological descriptions of Democrats, or any other form of selection among viewpoints. . . .

At all events, "pornography" is not low value speech within the meaning of these cases. In Indianapolis seeks to prohibit certain speech because it believes this speech influences social relations and politics on a grand scale, that it controls attitudes at home and in the legislature. This precludes a characterization of the speech as low value. True, pornography and obscenity have sex in common. But Indianapolis left out of its definition any reference to literary, artistic, political, or scientific value. The ordinance applies to graphic sexually explicit subordination in works great and small. The Court sometimes balances the value of speech against the costs of its restriction, but it does this by category of speech and not by the content of particular works. See John Hart Ely, *Flag Desecration: A Case Study in the Roles of Categorization and Balancing in First Amendment Analysis*, 88 Harv.L.Rev. 1482 (1975). . . . Indianapolis has created an approved point of view and so loses the support of these cases.

Any rationale we could imagine in support of this ordinance could not be limited to sex discrimination. Free speech has been on balance an ally of those seeking change. Governments that want stasis start by restricting speech. Culture is a powerful force of continuity; Indianapolis paints pornography as part of the culture of power. Change in any complex system ultimately depends on the ability of outsiders to challenge accepted views and the reigning institutions. Without a strong guarantee of freedom of speech, there is no effective right to challenge what is.

NOTES

1. Pornography constructs what a woman is in terms of its view of what men want sexually. . . . Pornography's world of equality is a harmonious and balanced place. Men and women are perfectly complementary and perfectly bipolar. . . . All the ways men love to take and violate women, women love to be taken and violated. . . . What pornography *does* goes be-yond its content: It eroticizes hierarchy, it sexualizes inequality. It makes dominance and submission sex. Inequality is its central dynamic; the illusion of freedom coming together with the reality of force is central to its working. . . . [P]ornography is neither harmless fantasy nor a corrupt and confused misrepresentation of an otherwise neutral and healthy sexual situation. It institutionalizes the sexuality of male supremacy, fusing the erotization of dominance and submission with the social construction of male and female. . . . Men treat women as who they see women as being. Pornography constructs who that is. Men's power over women means that the way men see women defines who women can be. Pornography . . . is a sexual reality." MacKinnon, *supra*, at 17–18 (note omitted, emphasis in original). See also Andrea Dworkin, *Pornography: Men Possessing Women* (1981). A national commission in Canada recently adopted a similar rationale for controlling pornography. Special Commission on Pornography and Prostitution, 1 *Pornography and Prostitution in Canada* 49–59 (Canadian Government Publishing Centre 1985).

NO

James C. Dobson

PORNOGRAPHY HARMS SOCIETY

Now that the work of the Attorney General's Commission on Pornography has come to an end, I look back on this fourteen-month project as one of the most difficult . . . and gratifying . . . responsibilities of my life. On the down side, the task of sifting through huge volumes of offensive and legally obscene materials has not been a pleasant experience. Under other circumstances one would not willingly devote a year of his life to depictions of rape, incest, masturbation, mutilation, defecation, urination, child molestation, and sadomasochistic activity. Nor have the lengthy and difficult deliberations in Commission meetings been without stress. But on the other hand, there is a distinct satisfaction in knowing that we gave ourselves unreservedly to this governmental assignment and, I believe, served our country well.

I now understand how mountain climbers must feel when they finally stand atop the highest peak. They overcome insurmountable obstacles to reach the rim of the world and announce proudly to one another, "we made it!" In a similar context, I feel a sense of accomplishment as the Commission releases its final report to the President, the Attorney General and the people. For a brief moment in Scottsdale last month, it appeared that our differing philosophies would strand us on the lower slopes. And of course, we were monitored daily by the ACLU, the pornographers, and the press, who huddled together and murmured with one voice, "they are doomed!" But now as we sign the final document and fling it about to the public, it does not seem pretentious to indulge ourselves in the satisfaction of having accomplished our goals. By George, I think we made it!

Let me indicate now, from the viewpoint of this one commissioner, what the final report *is* and *is not*. First, it is not the work of a biased Commission which merely rubber stamped the conservative agenda of the Reagan administration. A quick analysis of our proceedings will reveal the painstaking process by which our conclusions were reached. If the deck were stacked, as some have suggested, we would not have invested such long, arduous hours in debate and compromise. Serving on the Commission were three attorneys, two psychologists, one psychiatrist, one social worker, one

From *Final Report of the Attorney General's Commission on Pornography.* Washington, D.C.: U.S. Government Printing Office, June 1986, pp. 71-87.

city council member, one Catholic priest, one federal judge, and one magazine editor. Some were Christians, some Jewish, and some atheists. Some were Democrats and some Republicans. All were independent, conscientious citizens who took their responsibility very seriously. Our diversity was also evident on strategic issues about which society itself is divided. Our voting on these more troublesome matters often split 6–5, being decided by a swing member or two. Some whitewash! So the characterization of this seven-man, four-woman panel as an ultraconservative hit squad is simply poppycock. Read the transcripts. You will see.

Second, the final report does not do violence to the First Amendment to the Constitution. The *Miller* standard,* by which the Supreme Court clearly reaffirmed the illegality of obscene matter in 1973, was not assaulted during any of our deliberations. No suggestion was made that the Court had been too lenient... or that a constitutional Amendment should lower the threshold of obscenity . . . or that the Justices should reconsider their position. No. The *Miller* standard was accepted and even defended as the law of the land. What *was* recommended, to the consternation of pornographers, was that government should begin enforcing the obscenity laws that are already on the books . . . criminal laws that have stood constitutional muster! Considering the unwillingness of our elected representatives to deal with this issue, that would be novel, indeed.

Third, the hearings on which this report was based were not manipulated to produce an anti-pornography slant. *Every*

* Dobson refers to the case of *Miller v. California* (1973).—Eds.

qualified libertarian and First Amendment advocate properly requesting the right to testify was granted a place on the agenda, limited only by the constraints of time. A few individuals and organizations on *both* sides of the issue were unable to testify because the demand far exceeded available opportunities. However, objective procedures were established to deal fairly with those wishing to be heard, and complaints alleging bias were, I believe, unfounded. In fact, several organizations were asked to speak on behalf of sexually explicit materials but either declined or failed to appear. It *is* true that more witnesses testified against pornography than those who favored it, but that was a function of the disproportionate requests that were received by the executive director. Furthermore, I think it also reflects a disproportionate number of American citizens who oppose the proliferation of obscenity.

Looking now at the other side of the coin, let me express what the final report is and what I believe its impact is likely to be. First, the Commission expressed an unmistakable condemnation of sexually explicit material that is violent in nature. We were unanimous in that position throughout our deliberations. There is no place in this culture for material deemed legally obscene by the courts which depicts the dismemberment, burning, whipping, hanging, torturing, or raping of women. The time has come to eradicate such materials and prosecute those who produce it. There was no disagreement on that point.

Second, we were also unanimous in our condemnation of sexually explicit materials which depict women in situations that are humiliating, demeaning, and subjugating. I can still recall photographs of nude young women being penetrated by broom handles, smeared with feces, urinated upon, covered in blood or kneeling submissively in the act of fellatio. Most American citizens have no idea that such gruesome scenes are common in the world of obscene publications today. When asked to describe pornography currently on the market, they think in terms of airbrushed centerfolds in the popular "men's magazines." But steady customers of pornography have long since grown tired of simple heterosexual nudity. Indeed, a visit to an adult bookstore quickly reveals the absence of so-called "normal" sexuality. The offerings today feature beribboned 18- to 20-year-old women whose genitalia have been shaved to make them look like little girls, and men giving enemas or whippings to one another, and metal bars to hold a woman's legs apart, and 3-foot rubber penises, and photographs of women sipping ejaculate from champagne glasses. In one shop which our staff visited on Times Square, there were 46 films for sale which depicted women having intercourse or performing oral sex with different animals . . . pigs, dogs, donkeys, and horses. This is the world of pornography today, and I believe the public would rise up in wrath to condemn it if they knew of its prominence.

Finally, our Commission was unanimously opposed to child pornography in any form. Though categorically illegal since 1983, a thriving cottage industry still exists in this country. Fathers, step-fathers, uncles, teachers, and neighbors find ways to secure photographs of the children in their care. They then sell or trade the pictures to fellow pedophiles. I will never forget a particular set of photographs shown to us at our first hearing in Washington, D.C. It focused on a cute,

nine-year-old boy who had fallen into the hands of a molester. In the first picture, the blond lad was fully clothed and smiling at the camera. But in the second, he was nude, dead, and had a butcher knife protruding from his chest. I served for 14 years as a member of a medical school faculty and thought I had seen it all. But my knees buckled and tears came to my eyes as these and hundreds of other photographs of children were presented . . . showing pitiful boys and girls with their rectums enlarged to accommodate adult males and their vaginas penetrated with pencils, toothbrushes, and guns. Perhaps the reader can understand my anger and disbelief when a representative for the American Civil Liberties Union testified a few minutes later. He advocated the free exchange of pornography, *all* pornography, in the marketplace. He was promptly asked about material depicting children such as those we had seen. This man said, with a straight face, that it is the ACLU's position that child pornography should not be produced, but once it is in existence, there should be no restriction on its sale and distribution. In other words, the photographic record of a child's molestation and abuse should be a legal source of profit for those who wish to reproduce, sell, print, and distribute it for the world to see. And that, he said, was the intent of the First Amendment to the Constitution!

Speaking personally, I now passionately support the control of sexually explicit material that is legally obscene, whether it relates to children or adults. Though the Commission has dealt at some length in its report with specific "harms" associated with pornography, I would like to list the dangers here from my own point of view. Our critics have alleged that the Commission wishes to usher in a new era of sexual repression . . . that we favor governmental interference in America's bedrooms and even in our thoughts. That is nonsense. On the other hand, I have seen enough evidence in the past year to convince me of the devastation inflicted on victims of pornography. It is on their behalf that we must intervene. Here, then, are the harms as I perceive them.

(1) Depictions of violence against women are related to violence against women everywhere. Though social research on this subject has been difficult to conduct, the totality of evidence supports the linkage between illustration and imitation. Furthermore, pornography perpetrates the so-called "rape myth" whereby women are consistently depicted as wanting to be assaulted even when they deny it. They are shown as terrified victims in the beginnings of rape scenes, but conclude by begging for more. Men who want to believe that women crave violent sex can find plenty of pornographic evidence to support their predilections.

(2) For a certain percentage of men, the use of pornographic material is addictive and progressive. Like the addiction to drugs, alcohol, or food, those who are hooked on sex become obsessed by their need. It fills their world, night and day. And too often, their families are destroyed in the process.

(3) Pornography is degrading to women. How could any of us, having heard Andrea Dworkin's moving testimony, turn a deaf ear to her protest? The pornographic depictions she described are an affront to an entire gender, and I would take that case to any jury in the land. Remember that men are the purchasers of pornography. Many witnesses testified that women are typically repulsed by visual depictions of the type therein described. It is provided primarily for the lustful pleasure of men and boys who use it to generate excitation. And it is my belief, though evidence is not easily obtained, that a small but dangerous minority will then choose to act aggressively against the nearest available females. Pornography is the theory; rape is the practice.

(4) It appears extremely naive to assume that the river of obscenity which has inundated the American landscape has not invaded the world of children. This seven-billion-dollar industry pervades every dimension of our lives. There are more stores selling pornographic videos than there are McDonald hamburger stands. More than 800,000 phone calls are made each day to dial-a-porn companies in New York (180,000,000 in 1984), many placed by boys and girls still in elementary school. Furthermore, recent clinical observations by Dr. Victor Cline and others have indicated that a growing number of children are finding their parents' sexually explicit videos and magazines, and are experimenting with what they have learned on younger children. The problem is spreading rapidly. Obviously, obscenity cannot be permitted to flow freely through the veins of society without reaching the eyes and ears of our children. Latchkey kids by the millions are watching porn on Cable TV and reading their parents' adult magazines. For 50 cents, they can purchase their own pornographic tabloids from vendor machines on the street. Or they can hear shocking vulgarities for free on their heavy metal radio stations. At an age when elementary school children should be reading Tom Sawyer and viewing traditional entertainment in the spirit of Walt Disney, they are learning perverted

facts which neither their minds nor bodies are equipped to handle. It is my belief, accordingly, that the behavior of an entire generation of teenagers is being adversely affected by the current emphasis on premarital sexuality and general eroticism seen nightly on television, in the movies, and in the other sources of pornography I have mentioned. It is not surprising that the incidence of unwed pregnancy and abortions has skyrocketed since 1970. Teens are merely doing what they've been taught, that they should get into bed, early and often. And to a large degree, pornography has done this to them.

(5) Organized crime controls more than 85 percent of all commercially produced pornography in America. The sale and distribution of these materials produces huge profits for the crime lords who also sell illegal drugs to our kids and engage in murder, fraud, bribery, and every vice known to man. Are we to conclude that the 7 billion (or more) tax-free dollars that they receive each year from the pornography industry is not harmful to society? Is malignant melanoma harmful to the human body?

(6) Pornography is often used by pedophiles to soften children's defenses against sexual exploitation. They are shown nude pictures of adults, for example, and are told, "See. This is what mommies and daddies do." They are then stripped of innocence and subjected to brutalities that they will remember for a lifetime.

(7) Outlets for obscenity are magnets for sex-related crimes. When a thriving adult bookstore moves into a neighborhood, an array of "support-services" typically develops around it. Prostitution, narcotics, and street crime proliferate. From this perspective, it is interesting that

law enforcement officials often claim they do not investigate or attempt to control the flow of obscenity because they lack the resources to combat it. In reality, their resources will extend farther if they first enforce the laws relating to pornography. The consequent reduction in crime makes this a cost-effective use of taxpayer's funds.

The City of Cincinnati, Ohio, has demonstrated how a community can rid itself of obscenity without inordinate expenditures of personnel and money.

(8) So-called adult bookstores are often centers of disease and homosexual activity. Again, the average citizen is not aware that the primary source of revenue in adult bookstores is derived from video and film booths. Patrons enter these 3-by-3 foot cubicles and deposit a coin in the slot. They are then treated to about 90 seconds of a pornographic movie. If they want to see more, they must continue to pump coins (usually quarters) in the machine. The booths I witnessed on New York's Times Square were even more graphic. Upon depositing the coin, a screen was raised, revealing two or more women and men who performed live sex acts upon one another on a small stage. Everything that is possible for heterosexuals, homosexuals, or lesbians to do was demonstrated a few feet from the viewers. The booths from which these videos or live performers are viewed become filthy beyond description as the day progresses. Police investigators testified before our Commission that the stench is unbearable and that the floor becomes sticky with semen, urine, and saliva. Holes in the walls between the booths are often provided to permit male homosexuals to service one another. Given the current concern over sexually transmitted diseases and especially Ac-

quired Immune Deficiency Syndrome (AIDS), it is incredible that health departments have not attempted to regulate such businesses. States that will not allow restaurant owners or hairdressers or counselors or acupuncturists to operate without licenses have permitted these wretched cesspools to escape governmental scrutiny. To every public health officer in the country I would ask, "Why?"

(9) Finally, pornography is a source of significant harm to the institution of the family and to society at large. Can anything which devastates vulnerable little children, as we have seen, be considered innocuous to the parents who produced them? Raising healthy children is the primary occupation of families, and anything which invades the childhoods and twists the minds of boys and girls must be seen as abhorrent to the mothers and fathers who gave them birth. Furthermore, what is at stake here is the future of the family itself. We are sexual creatures, and the physical attraction between males and females provides the basis for every dimension of marriage and parenthood. Thus, *anything* that interjects itself into that relationship must be embraced with great caution. Until we *know* that pornography is not addictive and progressive . . . until we are *certain* that the passion of fantasy does not destroy the passion of reality . . . until we are *sure* that obsessive use of obscene materials will not lead to perversions and conflict between husbands and wives... then we dare not adorn them with the crown of respectability. Society has an absolute obligation to protect itself from material which crosses the line established objectively by its legislators and court system. That is not sexual repression. That is self-preservation.

If not limited by time and space, I could describe dozens of other harms associated with exposure to pornography. Presumably, members of Congress were also cognizant of these dangers when they drafted legislation to control sexually explicit material. The President and his predecessors would not have signed those bills into criminal laws if they had not agreed. The Supreme Court must have shared the same concerns when it ruled that obscenity is not protected by the First Amendment—reaffirming the validity and constitutionality of current laws. How can it be, then, that these carefully crafted laws are not being enforced? Good question! The refusal of federal and local officials to check the rising tide of obscenity is a disgrace and an outrage. It is said that the production and distribution of pornography is the only unregulated industry remaining today . . . the last vestige of "free enterprise" in America. Indeed, the *salient* finding emerging from 12 months of testimony before our commission reflected this utter paralysis of government in response to the pornographic plague. As citizens of a democratic society, we have surrendered our right to protect ourselves in return for protection by the State. Thus, our governmental representatives have a constitutional mandate to shield us from harm and criminal activity . . . including that associated with obscenity. It is time that our leaders were held accountable for their obvious malfeasance. Attorney General Meese, who has courageously supported other unpopular causes, has been reluctant to tackle this one. He is reportedly awaiting the final report from the Commission before mobilizing the Department of Justice. We will see what happens now. . . .

[It] is my hope that the effort we invested will provide the basis for a new public policy. But that will occur only if American citizens demand action from their government. Nothing short of a public outcry will motivate our slumbering representatives to defend community standards of decency. It is that public statement that the pornographers fear most, and for very good reason. The people possess the power in this wonderful democracy to override apathetic judges, disinterested police chiefs, unmotivated U.S. Attorneys, and unwilling federal officials. I pray that they will do so. If they do not, then we have labored in vain.

POSTSCRIPT

Should Pornography Be Protected as Free Speech?

Pornography is one of several social issues that have split the nation, social issues in which individual freedom is pitted against other individual freedoms or general social good. Abortion, gun control, or affirmative action are only a few of the complex social issues that our society is trying to resolve. The debate over pornography contrasts individual freedom against perceived social harm. What is the influence of pornography on readers and viewers? Even if we cannot be sure of the effects, should pornography be protected?

The reading list on pornography is vast. A quick scan of the *Readers' Guide to Periodical Literature* will provide extensive material on this issue. Specialized indexes such as the *Education Index, Humanities Index,* and *Social Sciences Index* will provide information on writings in academically oriented journals. A recent book entitled *Pornography: Research Advances and Policy Considerations* by Jennings Bryant and Dolf Zillmann, eds. (Erlbaum, 1989), would be a good beginning point, as it covers a variety of concerns including content analysis of pornography, effects of consumption, and legal and regulatory policy issues. Another comprehensive book is Frank Osauka and Sara Lee Johann's *Sourcebook on Pornography* (Lexington Books, 1989).

Whatever your conclusion about this debate, it is certain that others will disagree. Clearly, this is a debate in which the importance of the evidence is subordinate to the ethical and/or civil rights beliefs of the advocates.

PART 4

Mass Media and Politics

The relationship of government, politics, and the media has a long, interesting history. The presence of the media has certainly changed past democratic practices such as voting, debating, and influencing personal choice. The selections here focus on the overt practices of political campaigns and the influence of messages about political issues. How manipulative are messages about political candidates? Do reporters influence our public opinion? Is there an agenda-setting factor within the media, and how accurately does it report events? What role does the news have in shaping our concept of reality?

Do Presidential TV Ads Manipulate Voters?

Does Television News Reflect a Liberal Bias?

Did Television Influence the Outcome of the Vietnam War?

ISSUE 10

Do Presidential TV Ads Manipulate Voters?

YES: Joe McGinniss, from *The Selling of the President, 1968* (Simon & Schuster, 1969)

NO: Thomas E. Patterson and Robert D. McClure, from *The Unseeing Eye: The Myth of Television Power in National Elections* (G. P. Putnam's Son's, 1976)

ISSUE SUMMARY

YES: Author and reporter Joe McGinniss is convinced that political campaigning is merely a matter of projecting the right image on the television screen to sell the politician to the public, and he examines Richard Nixon's 1968 campaign as an example.

NO: Political scientists Thomas Patterson and Robert McClure studied Nixon's 1972 presidential campaign to explore the effects of political ads on television and concluded that the public is better informed and better able to make decisions as a result of exposure to televised political commercials.

Probably nothing has so transformed the American political process as the emergence of television as a force in elections. Many more people see candidates on television than ever hear them in person. Thus it is not surprising that candidates devote substantial time and money to perfecting their "image." Yet what impact do these carefully cultivated images have on the voter? Can a carefully cultivated image sway the voter? Can voters be "conned" into endorsing candidates solely on the basis of their screen image? Or are voters more clever than politicians think at evaluating the many sources of information that inundate them in the midst of a campaign: debates, campaign literature, interactions with friends and with members of their own or other political parties?

Communication researchers have been interested in the political effects of mass media for decades. In principle, public opinion is the basis of democracy. Yet how is public opinion formed, and how stable is it in the face of media's power to alter it? The weight of research suggests that media's power directly to influence voting decisions is limited; however, media may be able to *shape* public political discourse. If media sets the agenda for public discussion or provides the information that opinion leaders disseminate, the candidate who can shape the mediated political discourse—who can control the issues of the campaign through careful media manipulation—can gain an important edge in the campaign.

In the fast-moving world of American campaign politics, we may never know just how much influence an advertising campaign has on a particular election. Certainly, candidates believe that these campaigns are essential and almost certainly will continue to spend large portions of their campaign funds to reach the American people through political advertising.

These authors have dealt with the question of the influence of campaign advertising and come to different conclusions. Joe McGinniss in *The Selling of the President, 1968* details the careful packaging of Richard Nixon in the 1968 presidential campaign. Based on his own observations while he traveled for months with the press corps who were covering Nixon's campaign bid for the presidency, McGinniss came to the conclusions that political campaigning was merely a matter of creating a political image and selling the politician to the public. Two decades later many have repeated that claim, arguing that, for example, President Reagan created an image of power and control that won him two elections and a label of the "Teflon President" because allegations of wrongdoing never seemed to harm his public image.

Political scientists Thomas Patterson and Robert McClure studied the 1972 presidential election campaigns of George McGovern and Richard Nixon. They conclude that the public is informed by political commercials and thus able to make better decisions. Although they acknowledge that voters can be manipulated by the media, they argue that the benefits in increased voter knowledge far outweigh the cost of the small number of voters who will select a candidate based on trivial reasons—and who would probably do so with or without advertising.

YES   Joe McGinniss

POLITICS AS A CON GAME

Politics, in a sense, has always been a con game.

The American voter, insisting upon his belief in a higher order, clings to his religion, which promises another, better life; and defends passionately the illusion that the men he chooses to lead him are of a finer nature than he.

It has been traditional that the successful politician honor this illusion. To succeed today, he must embellish it. Particularly if he wants to be President.

"Potential presidents are measured against an ideal that's a combination of leading man, God, father, hero, pope, king, with maybe just a touch of the avenging Furies thrown in," an adviser to Richard Nixon wrote in a memorandum late in 1967. Then, perhaps aware that Nixon qualified only as father, he discussed improvements that would have to be made—not upon Nixon himself, but upon the image of him which was received by the voter. . . .

Advertising, in many ways, is a con game, too. Human beings do not need new automobiles every third year; a color television set brings little enrichment of the human experience; a higher or lower hemline no expansion of consciousness, no increase in the capacity to love.

It is not surprising, then, that politicians and advertising men should have discovered one another. And, once they recognized that the citizen did not so much vote for a candidate as make a psychological purchase of him, not surprising that they began to work together. . . .

Advertising agencies have tried openly to sell presidents since 1952. When Dwight Eisenhower ran for reelection in 1956, the agency of Batton, Barton, Durstine and Osborn, which had been on a retainer through his first four years, accepted his campaign as a regular account. Leonard Hall, national Republican chairman, said: "You sell your candidates and your programs the way a business sells its products." . . .

With the coming of television, and the knowledge of how it could be used to seduce voters, the old political values disappeared. Something new, murky, undefined started to rise from the mists. "In all countries," Marshall

McLuhan writes, "the party system has folded like the organization chart. Policies and issues are useless for election purposes, since they are too specialized and hot. The shaping of a candidate's integral image has taken the place of discussing conflicting points of view." . . .

The television celebrity is a vessel. An inoffensive container in which someone else's knowledge, insight, compassion, or wit can be presented. And we respond like the child on Christmas morning who ignores the gift to play with the wrapping paper.

Television seems particularly useful to the politician who can be charming but lacks ideas. Print is for ideas. Newspapermen write not about people but policies; the paragraphs can be slid around like blocks. Everyone is colored gray. Columnists—and commentators in the more polysyllabic magazines—concentrate on ideology. They do not care what a man sounds like; only how he thinks. For the candidate who does not, such exposure can be embarrassing. He needs another way to reach the people.

On television it matters less that he does not have ideas. His personality is what the viewers want to share. He need be neither statesman nor crusader; he must only show up on time. Success and failure are easily measured: How often is he invited back? Often enough and he reachs his goal—to advance from "politician" to "celebrity," a status jump bestowed by grateful viewers who feel that finally they have been given the basis for making a choice.

The TV candidate, then, is measured not against his predecessors—not against a standard of performance established by two centuries of democracy—but against Mike Douglas. How well does he handle himself? Does he mumble, does he twitch,

does he make me laugh? Do I feel warm inside?

Style becomes substance. The medium is the message and the masseur gets the votes. . . .

"The success of any TV performer depends on his achieving a low-pressure style of presentation," McLuhan has written. The harder a man tries, the better he must hide it. Television demands gentle wit, irony, understatement: the qualities of Eugene McCarthy. The TV politician cannot make a speech; he must engage in intimate conversation. He must never press. He should suggest, not state; request, not demand. Nonchalance is the key word. Carefully studied nonchalance.

Warmth and sincerity are desirable but must be handled with care. Unfiltered, they can be fatal. Television did great harm to Hubert Humphrey. His excesses—talking too long and too fervently, which were merely annoying in an auditorium—become lethal in a television studio. The performer must talk to one person at a time. He is brought into the living room. He is a guest. It is improper for him to shout. Humphrey vomited on the rug.

It would be extremely unwise for the TV politician to admit such knowledge of his medium. The necessary nonchalance should carry beyond his appearance while *on* the show; it should rule his attitude *toward* it. He should express distaste for television; suspicion that there is something "phony" about it. This guarantees him good press, because newspaper reporters, bitter over their loss of prestige to the television men, are certain to stress antitelevision remarks. Thus, the sophisticated candidate, while analyzing his own on-the-air technique as carefully as a golf pro studies his swing, will state frequently that there is no place for "public relations gimmicks" or "those show business guys" in his campaign. Most of the television men working for him will be unbothered by such remarks. They are willing to accept anonymity, even scorn, as long as the pay is good.

Into this milieu came Richard Nixon: grumpy, cold, and aloof. He would claim privately that he lost elections because the American voter was an adolescent whom he tried to treat as an adult. Perhaps. But if he treated the voter as an adult, it was as an adult he did not want for a neighbor.

This might have been excused had he been a man of genuine vision. An explorer of the spirit. Martin Luther King, for instance, got by without being one of the boys. But Richard Nixon did not strike people that way. He had, in Richard Rovere's words, "an advertising man's approach to his work," acting as if he believed "policies (were) products to be sold the public—this one today, that one tomorrow, depending on the discounts and the state of the market."

So his enemies had him on two counts: his personality, and the convictions—or lack of such—which lay behind. They worked him over heavily on both. . . .

But Nixon survived, despite his flaws, because he was tough and smart, and—some said—dirty when he had to be. Also, because there was nothing else he knew. A man to whom politics is all there is in life will almost always beat one to whom it is only an occupation.

He nearly became President in 1960, and that year it would not have been by default. He failed because he was too few of the things a President had to be—and because he had no press to lie for him and did not know how to use television to lie about himself.

It was just Nixon and John Kennedy and they sat down together in a television studio and a little red light began to glow and Richard Nixon was finished. Television would be blamed but for all the wrong reasons.

They would say it was makeup and lighting, but Nixon's problem went deeper than that. His problem was himself. Not what he said but the man he was. The camera portrayed him clearly. America took its Richard Nixon straight and did not like the taste.

The content of the programs made little difference. Except for startling lapses, content seldom does. What mattered was the image the viewers received, though few observers at the time caught the point. . . .

What the camera showed was Richard Nixon's hunger. He lost, and bitter, confused, he blamed it on his beard. . . .

He was afraid of television. He knew his soul was hard to find. Beyond that, he considered it a gimmick; its use in politics offended him. It had not been part of the game when he had learned to play, he could see no reason to bring it in now. He half suspected it was an eastern liberal trick: one more way to make him look silly. It offended his sense of dignity, one of the truest senses he had.

So his decision to use it to become President in 1968 was not easy. So much of him argued against it. But in his Wall Street years, Richard Nixon had traveled to the darkest places inside himself and come back numbed. He was, as in the Graham Greene title, a burnt-out case. All feeling was behind him; the machine inside had proved his hardiest part. He would run for President again and if he would have to learn television to run well, then he would learn it.

America still saw him as the 1960 Nixon. If he were to come at the people again, as a candidate, it would have to be as something new; not this scarred, discarded figure from their past.

He spoke to men who thought him mellowed. They detected growth, a new stability, a sense of direction that had been lacking. He would return with fresh perspective, a more unselfish urgency.

His problem was how to let the nation know. He could not do it through the press. He knew what to expect from them, which was the same as he had always gotten. He would have to circumvent them. Distract them with coffee and doughnuts and smiles from his staff and tell his story another way.

Television was the only answer, despite its sins against him in the past. But not just any kind of television. An uncommitted camera could do irreparable harm. His television would have to be controlled. He would need experts. They would have to find the proper settings for him, or if they could not be found, manufacture them. These would have to be men of keen judgment and flawless taste. He was, after all, Richard Nixon, and there were certain things he could not do. Wearing love beads was one. He would need men of dignity. Who believed in him and shared his vision. But more importantly, men who knew television as a weapon: from broadest concept to most technical detail. This would be Richard Nixon, the leader, returning from exile. Perhaps not beloved, but respected. Firm but not harsh; just but compassionate. With flashes of warmth spaced evenly throughout.

Nixon gathered about himself a group of young men attuned to the political uses of television. . . .

Harry Treleaven, hired as a creative director of advertising in the fall of 1967, immediately went to work on the more serious of Nixon's personality problems. One was his lack of humor.

"Can be corrected to a degree," Treleaven wrote, "but let's not be too obvious about it. Romney's cornball attempts have hurt him. If we're going to be witty, let a pro write the words."

Treleaven also worried about Nixon's lack of warmth, but decided that "he can be helped greatly in this respect by how he is handled. . . . Give him words to say that will show his *emotional* involvement in the issues. . . . Buchanan wrote about RFK talking about the starving children in Recife. *That's* what we have to inject. . . .

"He should be presented in some kind of 'situation' rather than cold in a studio. The situation should look unstaged even if it's not."

Some of the most effective ideas belonged to Raymond K. Price, a former editorial writer for the *New York Herald Tribune*, who became Nixon's best and most prominent speech writer in the campaign. Price later composed much of the inaugural address.

In 1967, he began with the assumption that "the natural human use of reason is to support prejudice, not to arrive at opinions." Which led to the conclusion that rational arguments would "only be effective if we can get the people to make the *emotional* leap, or what theologians call (the) 'leap of faith.' "

Price suggested attacking the "personal factors" rather than the "historical factors" which were the basis of the low opinion so many people had of Richard Nixon.

"These tend to be more a gut reaction," Price wrote, "unarticulated, nonanalytical, a product of the particular chemistry between the voter and the *image* of the candidate. *We have to be very clear on this point: that the response is to the image, not to the man.* . . . It's not what's *there* that counts, it's what's projected—and carrying it one step further, it's not what *he* projects but rather what the voter receives. It's not the man we have to change, but rather the *received impression.* And this impression often depends more on the medium and its use than it does on the candidate himself."

So there would not have to be a "new Nixon." Simply a new approach to television.

"What, then, does this mean in terms of our uses of time and of media?" Price wrote.

"For one thing, it means investing whatever time RN needs in order to work out firmly in his own mind that vision of the nation's future that he wants to be identified with. This is crucial. . . ."

So, at the age of fifty-four, after twenty years in public life, Richard Nixon was still felt *by his own staff* to be in need of time to "work out firmly in his own mind that vision of the nation's future that he wants to be identified with."

"Secondly," Price wrote, "it suggests that we take the time and the money to experiment, in a controlled manner, with film and television techniques, with particular emphasis on pinpointing those *controlled* uses of the television medium that can *best* convey the *image* we want to get across. . . ."

"The TV medium itself introduces an element of distortion, in terms of its effect on the candidate and of the often subliminal ways in which the image is received. And it inevitably is going to convey a partial image—thus ours is the task of finding how to control its use so

the part that gets across is the part we want to have gotten across. . . .

"Voters are basically lazy, basically uninterested in making an *effort* to understand what we're talking about . . . ," Price wrote. "Reason requires a high degree of discipline, of concentration; impression is easier. Reason pushes the viewer back, it assaults him, it demands that he agree or disagree; impression can envelop him, invite him in, without making an intellectual demand. . . . When we argue with him we demand that he make the effort of replying. We seek to engage his intellect, and for most people this is the most difficult work of all. The emotions are more easily roused, closer to the surface, more malleable. . . ."

So, for the New Hampshire primary, Price recommended "saturation with a film, in which the candidate can be shown better than he can be shown in person because it can be edited, so only the best moments are shown; then a quick parading of the candidate in the flesh so that the guy they've gotten intimately acquainted with on the screen takes on a living presence—not saying anything, just being seen. . . .

"[Nixon] has to come across as a person larger than life, the stuff of legend. People are stirred by the legend, including the living legend, not by the man himself. It's the aura that surrounds the charismatic figure more than it is the figure itself, that draws the followers. Our task is to build that aura. . . .

"So let's not be afraid of television gimmicks. . . . get the voters to like the guy and the battle's two-thirds won."

So this was how they went into it. Trying, with one hand, to build the illusion that Richard Nixon, in addition to his attributes of mind and heart, considered, in the words of Patrick K. Buchanan, a speech writer, "communicating with the people . . . one of the great joys of seeking the Presidency"; while with the other they shielded him, controlled him, and controlled the atmosphere around him. It was as if they were building not a President but an Astrodome, where the wind would never blow, the temperature never rise or fall, and the ball never bounce erratically on the artificial grass.

They could do this, and succeed, because of the special nature of the man. There was, apparently, something in Richard Nixon's character which sought this shelter. Something which craved regulation, which flourished best in the darkness, behind clichés, behind phalanxes of antiseptic advisers. Some part of him that could breathe freely only inside a hotel suite that cost a hundred dollars a day.

And it worked. As he moved serenely though his primary campaign, there was new cadence to Richard Nixon's speech and motion; new confidence in his heart. And, a new image of him on the television screen.

TV both reflected and contributed to his strength. Because he was winning he looked like a winner on the screen. Because he was suddenly projecting well on the medium he had feared, he went about his other tasks with assurance. The one fed upon the other, building to an astonishing peak in August as the Republican convention began and he emerged from his regal isolation, traveling to Miami not so much to be nominated as coronated. On live, but controlled, TV.

NO

Thomas E. Patterson
and Robert D. McClure

THE IMPACT OF TELEVISED
POLITICAL COMMERCIALS

One minute after a product commercial fades from the television screen, most viewers have forgotten what was advertised. They cannot recall whether the ad trumpeted aspirin, shaving cream, or automobiles. A particularly clever or amusing commercial may draw some notice, and linger in their thoughts, but most product ads pass from the mind as quickly as from the screen.[1]

Presidential ads affect viewers differently. On television only a month or two every four years, their novelty attracts attention. Also their subject matter. They picture and discuss men seeking the nation's highest office, and most Americans feel that choosing a President deserves more consideration than selecting a brand of antacid. A clear indication of presidential advertising's attention-getting ability is that most viewers can rather fully recall the message of a presidential spot. When asked to describe a commercial they had seen during the 1972 election, 56 percent of the viewers gave a remarkably full and complete description of one, and only 21 percent were unable to recall anything at all from political ads.[2] In market research, any product whose commercials are recalled with half this accuracy is considered to have had a very successful advertising campaign.[3]

People also evaluate presidential advertising differently than product advertising. A study conducted for the American Association of Advertising Agencies in the 1960s discovered that television viewers judge product commercials more on *how* they communicate their message than on *what* they say about a product.[4] A commercial for a soft drink or a paper towel is regarded as good or bad by the television audience more on whether it is enjoyable to watch than on the truthfulness of its message or the value of the information it contains. People judge presidential ads, on the other hand, primarily on *what* they say, not *how* they say it. Whether the techniques used in presidential spots are visually appealing or unappealing seems to matter little. Viewers seem concerned mainly with whether the advertising message is truthful and worth knowing. Where the American Association of Advertising Agencies' study found that only 46 percent of viewer reactions to product ads related to the information communicated, 74 percent of the viewer reactions to presidential commercials shown in 1972 centered on the information contained in the message.[5]

Thus, presidential spots get noticed, and the attention centers on the message. But to what end? Does the viewer learn anything about the candidates? Does he find out anything about the issues?

For years, most political observers have been certain they knew the answers: Advertising builds false political images and robs the American electorate of important issue information. On both counts, this orthodox view is wrong. In a presidential campaign, spot commercials do much more to educate the public about the issues than they do to manipulate the public about the candidates.

ADVERTISING'S IMAGE IMPACT

In presidential politics, advertising image-making is a wasted effort. All the careful image planning—the coaching, the camera work, the calculated plea—counts for nothing. Just as with network news appearances, people's feelings about the candidate's politics—his party, past actions, and future policies—far outweigh the influence of televised commercials.

Strong evidence for advertising's ineffectiveness comes from a look at *changes* in voters' images during the 1972 campaign. Just before presidential ads began appearing on television and again when the candidates' ad campaigns were concluding, the same people were asked to judge the images of Nixon and McGovern. They evaluated each candidate on seven traits associated with personality and leadership. Because the same people were questioned each time, an exact measure exists of how their images changed during the time when the candidates' ads were appearing on television.

These changes in voters' images indicate that advertising image-making had no effect. . . . Among people who preferred Nixon, his image showed a 35 percent improvement and McGovern's image a 28 percent decline. This happened among people exposed to many of the candidates' ads and to those seeing few commercials, if any. Among people backing McGovern, however, his image made a 20 percent improvement and Nixon's had an 18 percent decline. And again, no significant difference occurred in the image changes of people heavily and lightly exposed to presidential advertising.

Thus, whether people watched television regularly, and constantly saw the advertised images of Nixon and McGovern, had no influence on their impressions of the two candidates. Whatever people were getting from political spots, it was not their image of the candidates. . . .

By projecting their political biases, people see in candidates' commercials pretty much what they want to see. Ads sponsored by the candidate who shares their politics get a good response. They like what he has to say. And they like him. Ads sponsored by the opposing candidate are viewed negatively. They object to what he says. And they object to him.

A sampling of viewers' reactions to the series of image commercials used by George McGovern throughout the general election campaign illustrates how strongly political bias affects viewers. These spots pictured McGovern among small groups of people in natural settings, discussing their problems and promising to help them if elected. The commercials were intended to project an image of McGovern as a man who cared about people. Whether viewers received this image, however, had little to do with what happened on the television screen. It was all in their minds:[6]

He really cares what's happened to disabled vets. They told him how badly they've been treated and he listened. He will help them.
—37-year-old, pro-McGovern viewer

McGovern was talking with these disabled vets. He doesn't really care about them. He's just using them to get sympathy.
—33-year-old, pro-Nixon viewer

It was honest, down-to-earth. People were talking and he was listening.
—57-year-old, pro-McGovern viewer

Those commercials are so phoney. He doesn't care.
—45-year-old, pro-Nixon viewer

McGovern had his coat off and his tie was hanging down. It was so relaxed, and he seemed to really be concerned with those workers.
—31-year-old, pro-McGovern viewer

He is trying hard to look like one of the boys. You know, roll up the shirt sleeves and loosen the tie. It's just too much for me to take.
—49-year-old, pro-Nixon viewer

I have seen many ads where McGovern is talking to common people. You know, like workers and the elderly. He means what he says. He'll help them.
—22-year-old, pro-McGovern viewer

He's with all these groups of people. Always making promises. He's promising more than can be done. Can't do everything for everyone.
—41-year-old, pro-Nixon viewer

These people were watching the same George McGovern, listening to the same words, and yet they were receiving vastly different impressions of the Democratic presidential nominee.

Even undecided voters are not influenced by advertising image-making. Just like partisans, the candidate images of undecided voters fluctuate with vote choice, not advertising exposure. In 1972, undecided voters' images changed very little and fit no definite pattern until *after* they had picked their candidate. Among those choosing Nixon, and only *after* they had done so, his image had a 35 percent improvement and McGovern's a 35 percent decline. This pattern of image change was the rule for those seeing many presidential ads and those seeing few or none. Likewise, for those picking McGovern, his image showed a 40 percent improvement and Nixon's a 55 percent decline. Again, there was no difference in this pattern based on the undecided voter's exposure to televised political commercials.

Spot ads do not mold presidential images because voters are not easily misled.

They recognize that advertising imagery is heavily laden with something that is not intrinsically related to personal character at all—how the candidate looks on camera. This pseudocharacter, to some extent coached, posed, and created by the best media talent money can buy, is a "look" built into spots that is totally unreal. And viewers recognize its meaninglessness. Even the candid portrayals of presidential aspirants that sometimes appear in image appeals are ineffective. People's guards go up when a spot goes on. So no matter the style of presentation, when only 60 seconds are used to say that a candidate is big enough to handle the presidency, voters find the message skimpy, debatable, and unconvincing. They know that the candidate will display his strengths and mask his weaknesses and that a 60-second glimpse does not provide much of an insight into a man's fitness for the nation's highest office.

Symbolic manipulation through televised political advertising simply does not work. Perhaps the overuse of symbols and stereotypes in product advertising has built up an immunity in the television audience. Perhaps the symbols and postures used in political advertising are such patently obvious attempts at manipulation that they appear more ridiculous than reliable. Whatever the precise reason, television viewers effectively protect themselves from manipulation by staged imagery.

ADVERTISING'S ISSUE IMPACT

But where image appeals fail, issue appeals work. Through commercials, presidential candidates actually inform the electorate. In fact, the contribution of advertising campaigns to voter knowledge is truly impressive.

During the 1972 presidential election, people who were heavily exposed to political spots became more informed about the candidates' issue positions. . . . On every single issue emphasized in presidential commercials, persons with high exposure to television advertising showed a greater increase in knowledge than persons with low exposure. And on the typical issue, individuals who happened to see many commercials were nearly half again as likely to become more knowledgeable as people who saw few, if any, televised spots. Issue knowledge among people with considerable advertising exposure achieved a 36 percent increase compared with a 25 percent increase among those with minimal exposure. Persons heavily exposed to advertising were particularly aided in their knowledge about Nixon's position on China and military spending and about McGovern's position on military spending and taxes.

This information gain represents no small achievement. Televised political advertising has been widely maligned for saying nothing of consequence. Although the issue material contained in spots is incomplete and oversimplified, it also is abundant. So abundant in fact, that presidential advertising contributes to an informed electorate.

Advertising also educates voters because of the powerful way it transmits its issue content. Three basic advertising strategies—simplicity, repetition, and sight-sound coordination—combine to make presidential spots good communicators. Ads contain such simple messages that they leave almost no room for misunderstanding. . . .

THE EXTENT OF ADVERTISING MANIPULATION

Precise statistics on advertising's manipulative effects are hard to develop, because advertising, like other forms of media persuasion, works among and through a complex web of other influences. Seldom does a voter make his candidate choice for a single reason, whether the reason be political commercials, party loyalty, or a particular issue. Moreover, most people make up their minds about the candidates prior to the general election campaign, the time when presidential advertising saturates television programming. In 1972, as in previous elections where survey data have been gathered, about 80 percent of the electorate stayed with the choice it had decided upon before the general election began. Without doubt, some of these voters were reinforced in their initial vote choice by what they saw through television advertising. But how does one identify—among the people not changing their minds—those who would have changed their minds were it not for advertising? It is a treacherous task to assess whether people might have done something they did not do. So the effects of advertising on a voting decision are not that easily typed.

But some voters do decide their vote choice during a presidential general election and these people offer the best opportunity for understanding advertising's influence. In three interviews conducted with the same people during the 1972 general election, voters were asked which candidate they planned to support. If they changed their mind between one interview and the next, they were asked the reasons for the change and, if information about the candidates played some part in the change, where that information came from. By looking for advertising themes and sources in the reasons people gave for their vote changes, one way of estimating advertising's effects is provided. . . .

For three in every four people who arrived at their final vote choice during the 1972 general election, televised advertising had *no* discernible influence. . . . Some 42 percent cited important events, such as the Paris peace talks, as the reason why they selected their candidate; 11 percent said they decided to follow party allegiance, as did the factory worker who said, "I've always been a Democrat and McGovern is a Democrat"; 12 percent gave an old maxim, such as "not changing horses" or "it's time for a change," as their reason; 7 percent said they made their choice on the advice of their spouse or a friend or a co-worker; and 5 percent, although unable to provide a specific reason for choosing a candidate, did not watch much, if any, television during the 1972 campaign. In all of these decisions, televised advertising may have played some part, but at most, it was only a contributory influence. Additionally, 7 percent of vote changers present the situation of undetermined advertising effect. These people could give no clear reason for their candidate choice, but they were widely exposed to political ads during the campaign. Televised advertising, then, might have been the reason for their choice although other explanations, such as party loyalty or important political events, are also plausible.

So the first fact that must be recognized is that political advertising competes with other influences for the loyalties of indecisive voters. Before televised spots were used, less-informed voters were choosing candidates because they had a vague feeling that it was time for a change, because their father had pulled the same party lever years before, because an event triggered a reaction, because their spouse or union leader told them what to do. Today, most indecisive voters still select their candidate for such reasons.

Clear cases of advertising influence occurred among only 16 percent of those people making their candidate choice during the general election, or roughly 3 percent of the total electorate, since only one in five voters make up their minds during this time. But not even all these people can be labeled the victims of advertising manipulation. Indeed, the second fact about advertising influence is that simply because spot information helps people make up their minds does not mean manipulation occurs. True manipulation through advertising involves more than voters obtaining information that subsequently guides their vote choice. Spots are truly manipulative only when they convince the voter to act in the candidate's best interests and not the voter's. By this definition, of the 16 percent influenced by advertising, about half (9 percent) *were not* manipulated and about half (7 percent) *were* manipulated. To distinguish between these two types of advertising influence, here are the brief, but actual, voting histories of two people who during the 1972 general election made their vote choice from advertising information.

The first voter is a 74-year-old woman who before she retired worked at an unskilled job. In 1972, she was deeply concerned about having enough income to live on; her social security and small savings forced her to make ends meet on only $3,000 a year. Asked at the begin-

ning of the campaign what one political problem troubled her the most, she replied: "The amount of social security. It is not enough for most people to live on." Asked the same question at the end of the campaign, she said that "taxes were too high for older people on fixed incomes."

This woman called herself an Independent, but her past voting behavior had been strongly Democratic. She claimed to have backed Kennedy, Johnson, and Humphrey in the three previous presidential elections. Her choice for the 1972 Democratic nomination was George Wallace, and when McGovern got the nod, she was undecided about whether to vote for him or Nixon. In late October, she made her choice. She selected McGovern and gave this reason:

I've seen many commercials where George McGovern wants to help older people, to get them more social security and otherwise help them all he could. Nixon has vetoed bills for helping older people and McGovern has shown a definite interest in doing something for us. If Nixon hasn't done anything in the last four years, he probably won't do it now. He looks after big business, not the worker. Nixon's funds are from big business and they'll try to put him in again. I've no use for him.

The second voter is a 30-year-old hospital worker with two years of college. He is married and has one child. At the start of the general election, he was mainly concerned that the United States maintain a flexible foreign policy. At the campaign's end, he labeled unemployment the nation's major problem.

This man called himself a lukewarm Republican and in 1968 had not bothered to vote. But he registered to vote in 1972, and when the general election campaign began, he intended to support McGovern.

By October, he had become undecided about McGovern, and just before the election day he switched to Nixon. He cited one particular commercial as the major reason:

I saw this ad where it says McGovern keeps changing his mind. It said he had first said this and then that. He did this last year and what about next year. It put a question in my mind about whether I wanted to vote for McGovern. He doesn't seem reliable as a person. He seems to be changeable with regard to the issues. So I eliminated him. Actually I guess Nixon has done okay for the last four years. I'm not crazy about either one, but I'm voting for Nixon.

Advertising did not manipulate the first voter. It did the second. The woman used the best information available to her to maximize her political values. Although McGovern was making the same arguments about the elderly in his campaign speeches and they were more fully reported and criticized in newspaper reports, the woman did not depend heavily on the news media. But she received from advertising the information she most needed. It informed her about the candidates' social security and other old-age benefits, and she chose the candidate who promised to do her the most good.

The man, on the other hand, was manipulated. He responded to the candidate's interest, not his own. Through commercials, this man's view of his stake in the political system was replaced by the candidate's view. He was concerned about America's role in world affairs and unemployment, and yet he cast his vote on the basis of an idea placed in his head by advertising and seemingly unrelated to his own political concerns. He was used. He had no strong feelings that the nation needed decisive leadership and

no firm ground for assuming McGovern would not provide it. His view of politics simply came to mimic the view of a Nixon advertisement.

America can tolerate the effect that advertising has on people like this man. Counting for one or perhaps two voters in every hundred that got to the polls, this man and others like him will select a candidate for trivial reasons with or without advertising. (Before being persuaded by the Nixon commercial, the man indicated his vote for McGovern was premised on the fact that "McGovern had got a raw deal because of all the criticism about Eagleton.") And besides, since their reasons for choosing a candidate seem randomly selected, their votes distribute about equally between the candidates.

The benefits provided other voters by televised political advertising far exceed this kind of cost. Not only do more Americans, like the woman who learned which candidate was best for her, obtain information that helps them determine how their self-interest can be served, but many more people acquire information that helps them to validate a prior decision. And then there are people who simply learn a little more from ads than what they would have otherwise been able to learn.

NOTES

1. Leo Bogart, *Strategy in Advertising* (New York: Harcourt Brace & World, 1967), p. 139.
2. Respondents were first asked whether they had seen a Nixon or McGovern commercial. If they indicated seeing an ad, they were then asked: "Would you tell me what you can about the Nixon (McGovern) commercial you remember best?" Those remembering nothing about the ad were classified as "unable to recall." Other replies were classified as partial or full recall depending on whether respondents state

the central message of the commercial they had seen.

3. Bogart, *Strategy in Advertising,* p. 139.

4. Raymond A. Bauer and Stephen A. Greyser, *Advertising in America* (Boston: Harvard University Press, 1968), chap. 7.

5. *Ibid.* Percentages based on a reconstruction of data contained in source.

6. Responses come from interviews conducted with potential voters during the 1972 general election. Responses have been edited to improve readability. Ages and occupations have been changed to protect identities of respondents.

POSTSCRIPT

Do Presidential TV Ads Manipulate Voters?

What accounts for the contradictory conclusions of these two readings? One answer may be in the different perspectives of the authors. McGinniss speaks as an insider in the Nixon campaign, watching the efforts to package him appropriately. Patterson and McClure base their findings on the result of talking to some 2,000 voters during the 1972 campaign.

There are several analyses of campaign advertising. Edwin Diamond and Stephen Bates in *The Spot: The Rise of Political Advertising on Television* (MIT Press, 1984) is a readable analysis of the interaction of marketing and politics. Kathleen Jameison's *Packaging the Presidency: A History and Criticism of Presidential Campaign Advertising* (Oxford, 1984) examines how candidates shape and are shaped by presidential campaign advertising in the television age. Using a similar procedure to that of McGinniss, Timothy Crouse in *The Boys on the Bus* (Random House, 1972) examines the campaign from the perspective of a journalist working the campaign trails of Nixon and

McGovern. The value of this book is that it goes beyond an analysis of these campaigns to become a discussion of political reporting. In a slightly different vein, C. Anthony Broh writes about media coverage of a more recent campaign in *A Horse of a Different Color: Television's Treatment of Jesse Jackson's 1984 Presidential Campaign* (Joint Center for Political Studies, 1987).

ISSUE 11

Does Television News Reflect a Liberal Bias?

YES: William A. Rusher, from *The Coming Battle for the Media: Curbing the Power of the Media Elite* (William Morrow, 1988)

NO: Michael J. Robinson and Maura E. Clancey, from "Network News, 15 Years After Agnew," *Channels* (January/February 1985)

ISSUE SUMMARY

YES: William Rusher, publisher of the *National Review,* says that despite the number of media sources from which we have to choose, most information comes from "the media elite," a small corps reflecting a strongly liberal bias.
NO: Michael Robinson and Maura Clancey, both of the Media Analysis Project at George Washington University, find little partisan bias in news reports but do see a tendency to focus on negative issues.

In the days when most cities had several newspapers, it was not difficult for the public to seek alternative political viewpoints or read a newspaper that confirmed their own political beliefs. Newspapers often reflected the political philosophy of the owner of the paper. But since the decline of the American press, the public has turned to other channels of information, most notably television and radio, to receive political information. Is it possible for broadcast media to provide a plurality of viewpoints? Even though many station managers, news directors, and political reporters may try for objectivity, it is likely that a certain amount of personal bias may influence the writing of stories and their presentation. What's more, when the broadcast media are the purveyors of this type of material, it is unlikely that the number of distribution channels in any locality will reflect the diversity that the print media once had.

Political bias may come through the words used to describe a politician, platform, or policy, or it may be manifested in the placement of a story within a newscast or even the juxtaposition of one story next to another. Most of the charges of bias come from individuals who are on the opposite end of the political spectrum. The first of the following articles has been written by a self-proclaimed conservative whose primary complaint is that the few major news sources in the U.S.—the "media elite"—purport to be giving news but in reality are delivering selected portions of facts that lack the balance necessary to the presentation of the entire story.

The second selection recalls the words of former vice president Spiro Agnew, who sharply cast epithets at reporters and thus contributed to the controversy over whether journalists distorted their news stories. The content analysis of 2 campaigns and 100 days of media coverage found insufficient evidence to conclude that there was political bias in most stories, although if there was to be a liberal bias found, it was centered in the television networks' coverage of domestic issues.

Were Agnew's criticisms valid, and was there a negative cast to news reports? Robinson and Clancey found a 20-to-1 ratio of bad to good news stories. What they also found was that journalists tended to cast individuals into a "good guy/bad guy" role.

These selections examine the content of mediated messages and help us understand what we may glean from the political messages in the media. Do we, though, use selective attention to key into a specific story? Do we use selective retention to remember the story or the cast on the story? Just as in the days of many newspaper options, individuals have choices of what to pay attention to, and we know that we most often seek opinions that favor our own. Perhaps it is interesting to consider who you deem a credible source, and why.

There are various perspectives to consider about the importance of this issue. We must ask these questions if we are to take a stand on the objectivity and validity of the press, and we need to consider the interpersonal impact of newscasters' delivery and print journalists' choices of words. When we examine these elements more closely, we learn not only about the industries themselves but about ourselves and how we use the media. An interesting comment to reflect upon is the last line of the Robinson and Clancey article. Even if their research is wrong—does the decline of liberalism today make a comment upon the aspersions cast by right-wingers?

YES
William A. Rusher

THE TROUBLE WITH THE MEDIA

There are seventeen hundred daily newspapers and thousands of weeklies, plus thousands more weekly, fortnightly, monthly, and quarterly magazines, as well as thirteen hundred television stations and ten thousand radio stations in the United States, all of which are entitled to be included in that broad category called "the media." . . .

Our attention will be confined to those which regularly deal with national and international events and the issues arising from these. That excludes, at the outset, many local newspapers, many "specialty" magazines, and even a good many radio and television stations (for example, those of an exclusively religious nature). It also excludes, for all practical purposes, the many newspapers and radio and television stations whose reportage of national and international events is essentially derivative—i.e., consists of reprinting or broadcasting stories distributed by the major wire services or other primary news sources, or broadcasting "news programs" prepared and produced elsewhere (e.g., by the television networks).

We will also exclude from our discussion those media (the classic example being the relatively small magazines called "journals of opinion") which specialize in commenting editorially on national and international events from a specific political viewpoint. Of course many newspapers and magazines, as well as a good many radio and television stations, reserve specific segments of space or time for editorial comments by management, but we are speaking here of those media, such as the aforesaid journals of opinion (*The Nation, The New Republic, National Review,* etc.), that exist, openly and primarily, to press the case for a particular political viewpoint.

These exclusions reduce the media on which we shall focus our attention to a much more manageable number. A good many newspapers around the country, especially in the larger cities, maintain news bureaus of their own in Washington and even in certain important foreign capitals, and there are a number of "independent" radio and television stations (i.e., not affiliated with a network) which also conduct reportage on national and international events. But with a few important exceptions these individual newspapers

From William A. Rusher, *The Coming Battle for the Media: Curbing the Power of the Media Elite* (William Morrow, 1988). Copyright © 1988 by William A. Rusher. Reprinted by permission of William Morrow & Co., Inc.

and stations do not, either individually or collectively, shape to any great extent the character of the news coverage available today to the average American.

For all practical purposes the typical sentient American receives his or her information on what is happening in the world from a relatively small number of sources, which are often referred to as "the media elite." By fairly common agreement, these include:

• the two major wire services: the Associated Press and United Press International

• the three major commercial television networks: ABC, NBC, and CBS

• the two principle newsmagazines: *Time* and *Newsweek*

• three newspapers, each of which is nationally important for a different reason: the *New York Times*, the *Washington Post*, and the *Wall Street Journal*

In addition, most observers would probably be willing to add to the above select circle a few other contenders:

• the "educational," or at any rate noncommercial, radio and television networks of the Public Broadcasting System

• a third newsmagazine: *U.S. News and World Report*

• A relative new "all-news" network available on cable television: Cable News Network

These do not, of course, by any means exhaust the sources of information on public events available to Americans today. The *Reader's Digest*, for example, if only by virtue of its huge circulation, cannot be disregarded when it ventures into news reportage. But it is perfectly fair to say that *most* people receive *most* of their information from the above sources. Furthermore, these particular sources are the ones which happen to have, broadly speaking, the highest prestige *as* sources—and also, partly because of that fact, the most influential readers and viewers.

The bewildering variety of the American media becomes still less overwhelming when we reflect that the television networks have contrived, for our comfort and convenience, to have their important share of the day's information served up to us by a remarkably small number of familiar faces. Probably only the more careful newspaper readers bother to notice the by-line over a story from Washington or London in the *New York Times*, or would recognize the author's name if they did. The wire services (usually) and the newsmagazines (sometimes) transmit their news stories anonymously. But an astonishingly large proportion of America's daily supply of national and international "news" is received from a tiny handful of familiar television personalities—most notably the anchormen of the three major commercial networks' evening news programs: currently Dan Rather (CBS), Tom Brokaw (NBC), and Peter Jennings (ABC).

The universe of television personalities, dealing with "news," whose faces are familiar to most Americans is, of course, somewhat larger than these three, but not overwhelmingly so. It would include a few network "news desk" types such as NBC's John Palmer and ABC's Jed Duvall, the more prominent White House correspondents like ABC's Sam Donaldson, NBC's Andrea Mitchell, and (formerly) CBS's Lesley Stahl, and those few interviewers and talk-show impresarios (Barbara Walters, Roger Mudd, and Ted Koppel come to mind) who retain enough superficial objectivity, and deal directly enough with news stories, to retain some claim to the title "reporter."

Just outside this inner circle of "news reporters" is a somewhat larger but still relatively small group of television personalities whom the networks present to their viewers for the purpose of "analyzing" the news. These are often recruited from the ranks of Washington reporters—journalists who have retired from the arduous work of gathering the news to the pleasanter and far more lucrative task of commenting on it from the vantage point of their accumulated wisdom. These commentators may be presented individually if their prestige and apparent objectivity warrant it (John Chancellor and Walter Cronkite, for instance), or in groups that purport to represent a spectrum of opinion (Robert Novak, Jack Germond, Carl Rowan, etc.). The ranks may also be fleshed out with former reporters who have established themselves as commentators ("columnists") in the print media (Tom Wicker), or who became columnists without benefit of a reportorial background (William F. Buckley, George Will).

To the extent that such individuals speak frankly from a given viewpoint, or to the extent that groups of such people do in fact represent a reasonably wide spectrum of opinion, the networks, and those print media that follow their example, are of course not open to criticism. But straight news reporters and their editors, in both the print and electronic media, purport to be dealing with news events in a fairly objective or at least a reasonably balanced way.

And it is precisely here—in the presentation of news and news analysis by America's media elite, both print and electronic—that we come upon the quarrel with which [we are] concerned. It is the conviction of a great many people, not all of them conservative by any

means, that news presentation by the media elite is heavily biased in favor of liberal views and attitudes.

It is important, right at the outset, to specify precisely what is being objected to. This is a free country, and journalists are every bit as entitled to their private political opinions as the rest of us. But the average newspaper or television news program, and certainly those we have categorized as the "media elite," purport to be offering us something more than the personal opinions of the reporters, or the chief editor, or even the collective opinions of the journalistic staff. In one way or another, to one extent or another, they all profess to be offering us the "news"—which is to say, an account of as many relevant events and developments, in the period in question, as can be given in the space or time available. Moreover, in offering this account, the media we are discussing implicitly claim to be acting with a reasonable degree of objectivity. Their critics sharply challenge that claim.

But just how much objectivity is it reasonable to expect? The question is more complicated than it may at first appear. There is a school of thought—popular, perhaps naturally, among a certain subcategory of journalists themselves—that a journalist is, or at least ought to be, a sort of vestal virgin: a chalice of total and incorruptible objectivity. But this, of course, is nonsense, and is certainly not expected by any reasonable person.

Journalists too are, after all, sons and daughters of Adam. Their conception was far from immaculate; they share our taint of Original Sin. They were born into our common society, received the same general education we all received, and had roughly the same formative experiences. How likely is it that, simply by choosing to pursue a career in journalism, they underwent some sort of miraculous transformation, to emerge shriven and pure, purged of all bias and dedicated henceforth solely to the pursuit of the unvarnished Truth?

To be sure, a certain amount of detachment is always welcome in a journalist, and sensible reporters are careful to cultivate a reputation for it. Probably the average man or woman in the street would even agree, if questioned, that a reporter ought to be "fair" or "unprejudiced" or something of the sort. Certainly, at a low level, we expect—or anyway hope—that he will at least get the basic facts right: The defendant's name was Jonas, not Jones; he pleaded nolo contendere, not "guilty"; he was sentenced to two years in jail, not twenty; and so on. Questioned further, the average person would probably also agree that a reporter ought not to simply ride his personal hobbyhorses: e.g., "expose" only individuals or organizations that he happens to dislike. But anyone who probes the average American much more deeply than this will start running into very pronounced doubts about exactly how fair or unbiased most journalists are—and also about how unbiased it is reasonable to expect them to be.

Consider, after all, the reporter's dilemma. More often than not he will find, upon investigating a possible story, far more factual material than he can possibly report. His duty, then, becomes to choose among these facts—decide which are important and must be reported, and which are irrelevant or repetitious and can be ignored. By this act of choosing, however, the reporter progresses from being the mere conduit of facts to being the determiner of their relevance. And

that inevitably raises the question: relevance to what?

Against his will, if necessary, the reporter will be forced to answer this question by developing a *theory* of what the story is all about. In so doing, he moves into a brand-new role: Far from merely "reporting the facts," he becomes to some degree the creator of the story.

To take an example, let's suppose that a teenager holds up a delicatessen owner at gunpoint and escapes with eighty-nine dollars from the cash register. What facts might a reporter investigating the story and writing an account of it deem relevant?

Almost certainly, nowadays, if the teenager was black, the reporter will omit that fact, even if he himself privately thinks that the high unemployment rate among teenage blacks is the proximate cause of most crimes committed by individuals in that age category. Beginning about a quarter of a century ago, most of the American media made a conscious decision not to mention, in news stories, the race of accused criminals—the more or less official conclusion of American society being that this was, save in very special circumstances, irrelevant.

Would it be relevant that the store owner was Jewish? Here again, the reporter may feel that the background tensions in the neighborhood in question, between idle black youths and Jewish store owners, very definitely contributed to the choice of the victim in this case. But whether he will raise the point may well depend upon what additional facts he can cite in support of this concept of the story: e.g., other recent attacks by black youngsters on Jewish-owned stores in the neighborhood.

What if it transpires that the robber in this particular case is a drug addict, who committed the crime (and has committed others) to support an expensive habit? Alternatively, what if the youth has hitherto been a model student, and committed the robbery only to obtain money for food or medicine for his widowed mother?

There is, in short, often no way a conscientious reporter can avoid developing, and including in his report by implication or otherwise, some underlying theory regarding a story he is investigating. Certainly the bare bones of the one we have discussed (Youth Robs Delicatessen Owner) are far from the whole story, and any reporter who thought they were enough would be open to legitimate criticism. But if the reporter chooses (as we have argued he usually must) among a wide selection of facts, stressing some and omitting others in obedience to his theory or concept of the story, he cannot then legitimately argue that he is merely "the Fates' lieutenant," passively reporting what is there to be reported. The story he writes is necessarily an act of creation, and therefore an act of will.

Very well, then: *Choice* is inevitable. But is *bias* inevitable? According to the College Edition of *Webster's New World Dictionary of the American Language*, a "bias" in this meaning of the word signifies "a mental leaning or inclination; partiality; prejudice." If we can imagine a reporter making a choice among alternative concepts of a story (and therefore among the available facts) *without* consulting some a priori "mental leaning or inclination" or indulging in "partiality" or personal "prejudice," then bias is, at least theoretically, not inevitable.

But realism forces us to admit that it is also very widespread in journalistic practice, especially if we focus our attention not on such local events as a delicatessen robbery but on the brightly lit and hotly contentious stage of national and international affairs. It is asking a lot of a Washington political reporter, say, to insist that he rigorously exclude his own political biases when formulating the theory upon which a particular news story is to be based and selecting the facts to support it. And if he achieves such godlike objectivity in a particular story, it is asking far more to insist that he achieve it routinely, in story after story. The reporter, being human, will ordinarily be unconscious, or only subliminally aware, of the workings of his own political prejudices. If a story of his casts conservative Senator X as a villain—well, Senator X is a villain, that's all, and in suggesting as much the reporter is merely doing his duty by the facts, which are spelled out in the story. The fact that conservatives regard X fondly, and consider liberal Senator Y a villain, may be noted, but without supporting evidence of any actual villainy on the part of Y and largely as indicative of the conservatives' mind-set. In seeking to keep the biases of individual reporters under control, therefore, any reasonably conscientious editor will edit their stories if necessary.

But the chief editor of one of our elite print or electronic media has yet another and far more effective technique for correcting for bias, and that is the concept of *balance*. This concept is perhaps most familiar to us in the coverage of political campaigns. Even the most biased newspaper or television station will assign reporters to cover the major speeches of rival candidates. And those that cover ongoing controversies, in or out of Washington, will usually make at least some effort to interview people on both sides of the issue. It is not, let us repeat, a matter of achieving, or perhaps even pursuing, some ideal of absolute objectivity. All that can be asked or expected is a reasonable effort to avoid the worse excesses of journalistic ax-grinding in particular stories, coupled with a *balanced* coverage that permits both (or all) sides of controversial issues to be aired.

But that is exactly what the American people are *not* getting, and have not gotten for decades, from their media. On the contrary, the version of events served up by our media elite is, with a relatively few exceptions that merely prove the rule, a steady diet of tendentious "news" stories carefully designed to serve the political purposes of American liberalism. The stories themselves, far from being edited to eliminate the worst consequences of the reporters' own biases, are often timed to maximize their political effect. And the editors, far from trying to moderate the consequences of individual bias in particular stories by providing a balanced selection, frequently seem to be trying to enhance those consequences by cumulating their impact.

It is, therefore, among editors too that we must search for the explanation of the phenomenon of bias, as we see it on display in our major media. They too, of course, are human; they too have their opinions, and their personal biases. But they don't have the reporter's excuse that he is virtually compelled to adopt some theory of the story. Why do they so often turn their backs on the concept of balance?

It seems likely that the mental processes of the editor resemble rather closely those of the reporter because, in most cases, the editor was once a reporter himself. An editor today not only tends to adopt the reporter's theory of a given news story and combine it with others having a similar bias; he will often try to fit the story into a larger conceptual framework of his own: a sort of "super-theory" representing his own personal overview of current history.

Of course, there are wide areas of news reportage to which the above description doesn't apply. Just as there are individual news stories—about fires, auto accidents, the birth of quadruplets—that don't have self-evident political implications, so there are entire areas of news coverage—sports and art, to name only two—where political considerations are comparatively rare. Much of the "news" we read and see, therefore, is relatively free from the sort of political bias we have been discussing. But the rest is simply grist for the mills of the dominant editors in the higher ranks of the media, and these do not hesitate to construct, from the stories fed to them by their reporters, a conspectus of events that conforms to their own private view of the world.

This analysis was expounded brilliantly by Joseph Sobran in an article in the March 27, 1987, issue of *National Review.* His immediate subject was the "Howard Beach incident," in which a black youth was killed by a car on a highway while trying to escape, with two friends, from a gang of white youths who were allegedly attacking them with baseball bats. But Sobran uses this episode to illustrate what he contends are underlying habits of mind on the part of the media. I shall take the liberty of quoting his article extensively, because I have never read a more incisive analysis of the psychological process that results in the media's manifest liberal bias:

Why did Howard Beach get so much media coverage? An indirect answer comes from Thomas Friedman, Jerusalem bureau chief of the *New York Times*, grappling with the question why Israel, a faraway country the size of New Jersey, gets so much media attention. The answer is *not* the number of Jews in the American media, he argues, since the European press gives Israel just about the same amount of coverage. The answer is that Israel has mythic resonance for all Westerners.

"Men have never taken the world just as it comes," [Friedman] observes. "We need to explain the world to ourselves, and, to do so, we have used stories—myths and fables—to record our experiences and shape our values. In most cultures, these narratives are tied together in what has been called a 'super story.' Religions are a super story. Ideologies can be a super story."

Sobran then proceeds to apply the concept of the "superstory" to the Howard Beach incident:

All news is "biased," in that it's the selection of information in accordance with tacit standards of relevance. We notice the bias when the news is chosen to fit a "super story" the audience doesn't necessarily subscribe to. All earthquake stories are biased against earthquakes, but the bias is unanimous, and nobody complains. But the super story behind the Howard Beach story was Racist America. . . .

"News" consists not only of high-impact events, but of local events of low impact that can be assimilated to pet myths. But most journalists are unaware of their commitment to myths, and think of themselves as, in Dan Rather's words, "honest brokers of information." You don't shoot the messenger for bringing bad news! Except that the messenger exercises a lot of discretion as to which news to deliver.

If the mailman did that, he'd lose his job. . . .

The media are so saturated with myth that it's fair to see "news" as an early stage on the assembly line whose final product is a *New York Times* editorial. The Howard Beach incident, of no national importance in itself, offered an occasion to attitudinize. It had less to do with raw "fact" than with *l'art pour l'art*. It achieved the maximum ratio, this side of Janet Cooke, of opinion to datum. . . .

Finally, Sobran generalizes his point:

The super story is Progress, the long view. "Value judgments" of good and evil represent unseemly impulses or old prejudices; they are "simplistic." . . .

In the progressive myth, there is no Good or Evil, as traditionally understood: The ultimate categories are Past and Future. The world is broadly divided into the forces of the Past versus those of the Future, reactionary and progressive, politely termed "conservative" and "liberal" when necessary. Most political conflicts can be typed in these terms and treated journalistically as so many little segments of the super story. . . .

The progressives' own value judgments don't have to be stated. They're built into the form of the stories themselves. The forces of the Past come equipped with a discernible set of traits: bigotry, greed, hate, selfishness, ignorance, zealotry, extremism—terms that by now all have a "right-wing" whiff about them. Ever heard of a liberal or left-wing bigot or hate-group?

By the same token, the forces of the Future can be discerned by their compassion, idealism, hope, intelligence, openness to new ideas. (Who ever heard of being open to *old* ideas?) . . .

The mythology determines the tone of just about any specific story on South Africa, "social" spending, the

Pentagon, "civil rights," disarmament talks, Chile, abortion, and various other perennial topics. . . .

Consciously or unconsciously, most editors go through the process Sobran describes, assembling the news stories that cross their desks into a far larger, more enduring, and more meaningful edifice: the superstory (or supertheory, as we earlier described it) that constitutes their notion of the world. Unlike their reporters, they are not compelled to do so; the impulse is derived from their own reportorial experience, fortified by self-indulgence. It lies within their power to present a more balanced picture of the "news"; but they don't, because they prefer to paint the world in the primary colors of the liberal superstory.

But why do the editors of our elite media display such an overwhelming preference for the *liberal* superstory? In a monograph published by the Media Institute of Washington, John Corry, the nonfiction television critic of the *New York Times*, concedes that "of course" television reflects "a liberal bias." But he argues that this is not so much deliberate as because it necessarily reflects "the dominant culture," which in turn is the product of the opinions and preferences of the country's artists and intellectuals. "This culture," Corry contends, "is rooted firmly in the political left, where it finds its own closed frame of reference. Little dissent is tolerated and little is found."

Corry's proposition that the media elite are heavily influenced by the "dominant" culture is undoubtedly correct. It can, in fact, be argued that the liberal superstory described by Sobran simply reflects the world view of that culture. But that scarcely constitutes, in 1987, much of an excuse for the behavior of the

media elite. The day is long gone when one could say, as Lionel Trilling correctly said in 1950, that "in the United States at this time liberalism is not only the dominant but even the sole intellectual tradition." Liberalism may still be, in a narrow sense, America's "dominant culture"—the overwhelmingly popular viewpoint of intellectuals, especially in the academy. But no profession as closely in contact with its environment as journalism claims to be can seriously contend that conservatism simply doesn't deserve, today, better-balanced coverage than it is receiving.

After all, conservatives took control of the Republican party nearly a quarter of a century ago, since which time the party has won every presidential election except 1976. Even in the purely intellectual realm, William F. Buckley has presided over a discussion program on PBS (its sole concession to conservatism) for more than twenty years. The influence of the "dominant culture"—liberalism—on the media is indisputable; the justification for it, however, is no longer valid.

But there is, in addition, no lack of evidence that at least a great many members of the media elite are far more than merely other-directed fellow travelers of the dominant culture. When we learn from a 1983 *Mother Jones* interview that NBC's Tom Brokaw says Ronald Reagan's values are "simplistic and old-fashioned," that he lives in a "fantasy land," that his supply-side economics policy "was just a disaster," and that human rights in El Salvador are "a sham," or are told by David Blum in a 1986 *New York* profile of the same network's Bryant Gumbel that "the veins in his forehead seem ready to pop as he attacks the [Reagan] administration's policy toward the poor and hungry," we are entitled to assume that these people participate enthusiastically in, rather than merely go along with, the liberal bias that characterizes NBC News.

In the case of Richard M. Cohen, however, we don't have to assume anything. In an article on the Op-Ed page of the *New York Times* on August 31, 1987, Cohen, who is senior producer of foreign news for the *CBS Evening News*, described the thought processes and news-manipulating techniques of a powerful member of the media elite as clearly as it has ever been done, or is ever likely to be done.

What loosened Cohen's tongue, presumably, was the fact that his immediate subject was South Africa, concerning which American public is comfortably monolithic and which therefore exposed him and his network to no danger of a bruising collision with American conservatives on the merits of the particular issue. But Cohen seems not to have realized how much he was revealing, concerning his own attitudes and techniques, that was applicable to a whole spectrum of far more controversial subjects.

Cohen's article was a call for Western news organizations to pull out of South Africa altogether, rather than try to soldier on under the severe restrictions currently being imposed by the white regime. Under the state-of-emergency regulations now in force, both publications and broadcasts concerning events in the black townships and homelands are heavily censored to exclude what the government considers inflammatory or likely to incite violence. With specific regard to television, Cohen complained: "We cannot broadcast or even shoot pictures of any unrest, which is defined by South African authorities. We cannot show police or security forces acting in

their official capacity trying to 'keep the peace.' Our cameras are not supposed to be within telescopic range of such events."

Worse yet, though Cohen doesn't mention it, there is evidence that these regulations have had considerable effect. In late 1985 and early 1986 there were riots, fire bombings, and "necklace" killings of suspected black "collaborators" in many of the black townships of South Africa. A year later Allister Sparks, a liberal South African correspondent, reported in a dispatch to the *Washington Post* that "a mood of battle weariness has settled over [black revolutionaries]. . . . [It] is recognized that a popular insurrection leading to a seizure of power is unlikely." Without the stimulus of intensive press coverage, and especially television coverage, a very substantial measure of calm had returned to the townships.

It was not, however, the impact of the emergency regulations on developments in South Africa but their effect on the formation of American public opinion that chiefly concerned Cohen:

> The American consciousness about South Africa, I believe, was formed and maintained by the constant television images of brutal repression in many forms: the image of the padded, faceless policeman, club raised; the image of a black youth with fear covering every inch of his face as he throws a rock. These were constant and common images, and now they are missing.
>
> One day in October 1985, an innocuous truck, driven by whites, moved ostentatiously through the streets of Cape Town. It was out of place and provocative, and when black kids began throwing rocks, the truck stopped and armed police jumped out of boxes on the back of the truck.

At CBS we always referred to that day as the "Trojan Horse" incident. The surprise attack, the beatings and arrests were captured in frightening detail on videotape by a CBS cameraman who risked great injury to keep his camera rolling. Such were the risks our South African colleagues took daily. Those pictures were broadcast that night on the CBS Evening News and were seen by millions of Americans. By the next morning, they were all over European television.

They are called tight shots. The camera moves in close enough to see the expression on a face, even the look in an eye. In South Africa, they are the narrow, harrowing images of oppression. If a picture is worth a thousand words, television can do what column inch after column inch of newspaper copy cannot. Television can raise the consciousness of a nation.

It is important not to let one's perception of the significance of the above quotation be distorted by a natural sympathy for Cohen's indignation at the situation he found in South Africa. One may wonder, in passing, why Cohen and the CBS Evening News so rarely manage to find and photograph equally compelling evidences of state despotism in the Soviet Union, or Communist China, or Cuba, or Nicaragua—or why, if they are forbidden to photograph such scenes in such places, Cohen doesn't recommend that Western news organizations withdraw from those countries too. But that, also, is beside the point.

The point is that Cohen clearly arrogates to himself, as a passionate and well-positioned liberal, the right—indeed, as he probably conceives it, the obligation—to "form and maintain" the "American consciousness" on foreign political topics about which he cares deeply. To this end, he has no compunction about subjecting viewers of the CBS Evening News to "constant television images," including "tight shots" and similar emotive devices, designed to produce the desired impression. He is acutely aware that these confections will be "seen by millions of Americans," and that within twenty-four hours they will also be spread "all over European television." In this way, he boasts, "television can raise the consciousness of a nation."

There is, of course, nothing in the least new or surprising about this. Every American who has seen a "news" broadcast on one of the TV networks can testify that the technique is used ad nauseam. All that is surprising is to see such a candid and vivid description of it displayed on the Op-Ed page of the New York Times. Verily, the boys are getting careless.

For of course Mr. Cohen and the CBS Evening News—and their opposite numbers at ABC and NBC and PBS—don't limit their consciousness-raising efforts to such relatively unobjectionable targets as the white government of South Africa. They hew wood and carry water for every imaginable liberal propaganda ploy, from denigrating the Nicaraguan resistance to pooh-poohing the Reagan administration's Strategic Defense Initiative, and from denouncing Ronald Reagan's economic policies to caricaturing the American Right.

Was it, do you suppose, Richard Cohen who treated us to those "tight shots" of perspiring fat ladies with straw boaters and palmetto fans at Goldwater rallies back in 1963, and took all those dramatic pictures of Alabama police dogs lunging at conveniently invisible targets during the race riots of the 1960s, or was all that before his time? Was it the CBS

Evening News—I rather think it was—that regaled us with shot after shot of "burning bonzes" in Saigon during the Vietnam War, so that America might at last understand how unwanted our help was in that unhappy country? Was it NBC or ABC, or CBS again, or all three, that deluged us with tendentious stories about soup kitchens and block-long unemployment lines in 1982, and have dwelt ever since, with loving care, on so-called pockets of poverty that still, after five years of the longest economic boom in our postwar history, allegedly testify to the existence of "hunger" and "homelessness" as ineradicable stigmata of the Reagan administration?

But even such examples are not necessarily persuasive. After all, Richard Cohen may be right about all these things, and his critics may be wrong. The real point is: Who is this Richard M. Cohen, and how does he find himself in a position of such power that he can decide, all alone (or more likely with the enthusiastic concurrence of a few similarly minded colleagues), the political issues on which "the American consciousness" is to be "formed and maintained"?

For make no mistake: Cohen is no fluke. He is a stellar example of what is wrong with the American media elite. There are many hundreds and probably thousands of others like him, in positions high and low, visible and not so visible, diligently taking in the laundry of the liberal Left. They are strongly opinionated, highly politicized individuals. They know very well what they are doing, and they are under no illusion that their views represent, or are even close to, the American mainstream. They are merely convinced that they are right, and they are positively delighted that they occupy positions from which they can "form and maintain" the "American consciousness." They have, in addition to jobs that are well paid by almost any standard, the satisfaction of wielding genuine power on behalf of causes in which they deeply believe. Not surprisingly, their typical attitude toward their critics is one of silent arrogance.

But just how inevitable is this state of affairs? Is it right, is it even tolerable, that news organizations pledge to a reasonably balanced presentation of the "news," and claiming all sorts of special constitutional powers and privileges to assist them in achieving that high objective, should be able to use the First Amendment or their federal licenses to shove such loads of biased bushwah down the throats of the American people without contradiction night after night?

NO

Michael J. Robinson
and Maura E. Clancey

NETWORK NEWS, 15 YEARS
AFTER AGNEW

Fifteen years ago Vice President Spiro Agnew introduced some of the most memorable phrases ever hurled at journalism, or at the network news. Reporters were not only "effete snobs" but also "hopeless hypochondriacs of history" and "nattering nabobs of negativism."

In the early 1970s right-wingers also began backing up their complaints about the networks' bias with quantitative research. Media critic Edith Efron concluded that network coverage of Vietnam, civil rights, and the Humphrey and Nixon campaigns was "biased in favor of the liberal, Democratic, left axis of opinion." Rock-ribbed professor Ernest Lefever analyzed defense-related *CBS Evening News* coverage in 1972 and 1973, and said it was slanted in favor of liberalism and détente with the Soviets.

More recently, the politically nonaligned social scientists Stanley Rothman and Robert Lichter reinforced the conservative case against the network news with an eye-opening series of articles profiling the people who report the news. Rothman and Lichter found, for example, that more than 80 percent of the network news corps eligible to vote in 1972 pulled the lever for George McGovern; that a clear majority of network newspeople classify themselves as liberal, and that more than half say they don't believe in God. Their findings were so dramatic that Katharine Graham, queen mother of *The Washington Post*, came away saying that perhaps "Spiro Agnew *had* something with all that media-conspiracy business."

Ronald Reagan's landslide reelection, however, has complicated any simple complaints about liberal media bias. Some critics might say he won 49 states in spite of network hostility; others might conclude that television's superficial, picture-oriented coverage fit perfectly with his masterful media management.

Whatever the networks' impact, they ought to be judged by what they actually reported. Are Agnew's complaints about liberal bias valid today?

From Michael J. Robinson and Maura E. Clancey, "Network News, 15 Years After Agnew," *Channels* (January/February 1985). Copyright © 1985 by Michael J. Robinson and Maura E. Clancey. Reprinted by permission.

Since 1979, the Media Analysis Project at George Washington University has been examining nightly news programs for evidence of bias. In 1980, we analyzed CBS coverage of the Presidential campaigns. In 1984, we did the same thing with all three networks. And in between, we surveyed network "soft news"—feature reports and commentaries on public-policy issues during 100 days early in 1983.

In all three studies we found that most right-wing allegations about the network news just don't hold up. Ideological bias is one of those mistakes that the network news doesn't make. In the 1980 primaries CBS treated "liberal" Ted Kennedy worse than it treated "middle-of-the-roader" Jimmy Carter, and in the general-election campaign CBS treated Carter worse than Reagan.

Our findings on coverage of last year's Reagan-Mondale contest indicate that Reagan got worse press than Mondale, but in the 625 campaign pieces appearing on the network news between Labor Day and Election Day we found issue bias in only 17 stories—3 percent of the networks' campaign reports that were examined. Among those 17, 10 leaned to the left and seven to the right, but overall the biased pieces were so few in number and the bias so weak in implication that real issue bias hardly existed at all.

Campaign coverage, however, can't be used to judge the networks' business-as-usual performance. To do that in our 100-day study, we looked where ideological bias would most likely be—in the "soft" feature reports and commentaries that are allowed by journalistic tradition to display some opinion. The stories we examined also came from the period when liberal bias would be predictable—early in 1983, when the public's approval

HOW THE STUDY WAS DONE

Researchers in the Media Analysis Project at George Washington University examined more than 200 network news features—85,000 words, enough to fill a medium-sized book. They were aired on the evening news programs of the three major networks during the first 100 days of 1983.

Funding for the study was provided by the John and Mary Markle Foundation, of New York.

Included in the study were feature reports (of two-and-a-half minutes or longer) and commentaries that touched directly on domestic policy, the Reagan presidency, political scandals, and international affairs. *Excluded* were pieces about the campaign, about social life and values, about personalities, and about the policy-making process per se (except those linked directly to policy disputes).

Also included in the survey were commentaries from ABC's *This Week with David Brinkley* because at the time the network didn't include commentaries on its nightly show.

Any attempt to measure news bias has the problem of defining standards of bias, liberalism, and conservatism. In this study, two of the three major members of the research team considered themselves conservative, Republican, or Reaganite—anything but secular humanist. Yet, despite our personal ideologies, all those who did the screening and scoring of news reports had little trouble agreeing more than 90 percent of the time as to whether a report showed liberal or conservative bias. M.J.R./M.E.C.

of Reagan and his economic policies had reached its lowest ebb in the polls.

We looked for evidence to support or quash what has developed as the standard three-part indictment of network newspeople and their news: first, that they are too *liberal;* second, that they are too *arrogant,* or "imperial," and third, that they are too *negative,* snide, and cynical. As for the newspeople, we're willing to concede (for the sake of argument) their liberalism, their negativism, and maybe even their arrogance. But as for the most serious charges—that the evening news itself reflects a liberal bias and arrogance—the evidence is too weak to convict the accused.

CHECKING TWICE FOR BIAS

We looked for bias in two ways. First, we examined the words of the reports for "bias per se." Then we looked again for a more subtle form of bias in the news organizations' selection of topics—"bias by agenda."

Network correspondents seldom overtly express political bias. More often it surfaces in their implications. In a two-part feature in February 1983, Dan Rather began by observing that in the Soviet Union war is "by design, an obsession," and correspondent Don McNeill concluded the same series by asserting that the Russians' "morbid indulgence in the memory of war and suffering . . . is one of the greatest dilemmas of the nuclear age." Both comments may be truisms, but they clearly imply a conservative viewpoint on U.S.-Soviet relations.

We checked newscast tapes for implicative statements concerning policy issues, and found first that many don't lend themselves to classification along the traditional left/right spectrum of U.S.

politics. For example, correspondents generally expressed muted joy about the chaos and backbiting among OPEC nations over fluctuating oil prices in winter 1983. Bias there was, but not left/right coloring. We classified those pieces as ambiguous. But on most issues—acid rain, prayer in public schools, support for Nicaraguan *contras,* and the MX missile—there are clear positions left and right, and reports about them can be judged accordingly.

On those fundamental issues that divide liberals and conservatives in the 1980s, the network news contains no consistent left-wing bias of any significance. Of the feature reports and commentaries on national news during the first four months of 1983, 77 percent either gave nearly equal time and treatment to both sides or were ideologically neutral. We classified only 13 percent of the reports as liberal per se, and 10 percent as conservative. But the major finding here was that eight out of 10 "soft" policy-oriented pieces were essentially unbiased, left or right.

We thought the abortion issue would be a perfect trap to snare network bias. Lichter and Rothman found that 90 percent of network newspeople are "pro-choice," liberal on abortion. But in 1983 the networks did a marvelous job of avoiding that trap. For example, it's almost impossible to imagine a more balanced or less partisan report than the one filed by ABC's John Martin on January 21, the eve of the 10th anniversary of the Supreme Court's legalization of abortion:

"It was part of a movement, women wanted the right to decide whether to abort . . . or to bear a child," Martin reported. "But other women had doubts—the feeling that the fetus was alive—too human to abort. . . . By 1972, 17 states had legalized abortion. Then the Supreme Court ruled that the constitutional right of privacy is broad enough to encompass a woman's decision whether or not to terminate her pregnancy, in effect, legalizing abortion. For many, the decision was a welcome victory. . . . But for others it was a defeat for morality."

Unexpectedly, conservative and hawkish pieces were actually more subjective and harder-hitting than the ones we classified as liberal or dovish. Consider David Brinkley's commentary on Muammar el-Qaddafi, the Libyan dictator, which ended, "We have often heard reports that Egypt would invade Libya and dispose of Qaddafi using American weapons. Those of us who think it would be a good idea wonder what they're waiting for." Still, Brinkley's jingoist outburst is very much the exception, not because it's so hard-line but because it's neither neutral nor ambiguous.

Throughout, bias per se is scarce, but there's still the possibility of bias by agenda, in the selection of topics a newscast covers or ignores. We checked for this kind of bias in each report by asking ourselves whether its issue is one that President Reagan likes to discuss, such as crime in the streets, or one that a Walter Mondale prefers, such as the plight of the unemployed.

Once again, wholesale bias in favor of the liberal agenda just doesn't exist on the evening news. Frankly we expected to find more. But as it happened, liberal news topics—the recession, "the new poor," apartheid, Salvadoran death squads—accounted for only 26 percent of air time. And conservative topics—such as unwarranted government regulation and Soviet repression—accounted for only 21 percent of air time.

Admittedly, the networks' agenda is clearly liberal when they address domestic issues. The instances of liberal bias outnumber the conservative 36 percent to 22 percent on the evening news. But their single most-discussed domestic issue was crime in the streets. Moreover, the domestic imbalance coexists with an imbalance in foreign news agendas that lean to the right, 18 percent to 14 percent. Overseas stories are dominated by negative reports on Marxist countries, featuring Soviet repression, corruption, and inefficiency.

ON THE SCENT OF ARROGANCE

If the right and the left agree on anything about network news, it's the arrogance of television newspeople and newscasts. We measured two different aspects of arrogance, or "media imperialism": stridency and judgmentalism. What we termed a "strident" piece ignores or belittles the opposing view, while a "nonstrident" piece suggests there is more than one legitimate position to take. By this measure, more than 99 percent of the feature reports and 80 percent of the commentaries were not strident. When four out of five network commentators stop short of belittling their opponents on an issue, it's hard to convict them of arrogance.

Using the other measure of arrogance, we found that 92 percent of the features were *non*judgmental: The newsperson almost never said explicitly which way a public policy ought to go. In fact, correspondents' conclusions often sound like the all-purpose innocuous tag-line used by newsman Roland Hedley, of the comic strip *Doonesbury,* "Only time will tell."

POSITIVELY NEGATIVIST

Significantly, it was neither political bias nor arrogance that Spiro Agnew emphasized when he went public with his attack on the network news. Whether through accident or acumen, Agnew actually got it right: His major complaint was that the networks had become "nattering nabobs of negativism."

And so it is with today's network news—a constant cacophony of carping and criticism. Sentence by sentence we noted whether the news implied something negative or positive about the world that is related to public policy. Again, most of the statements were merely descriptive and thus neutral. Still, among those that carry a negative or positive message, the ratio of bad to good news was precisely 20 to one. In 100 days, we counted only 47 of those positive statements by correspondents.

We found the same negative tendencies using what we call the good-guy, bad-guy test. When an official or organization was being clearly blamed for a policy problem, we attached the label, "the bad guy." When somebody was being credited for solving or avoiding a problem, he was "the good guy." In all, we found four times as many bad guys as good guys. The worst guy was the Soviet Union and its leadership. Next worst was Reagan and his administration.

Journalists might explain such negativism by saying that it accurately describes the state of the world—bad. But even on topics where good news was available, coverage was decidedly downbeat. The best example is the economic recovery that began during the period we studied: Unemployment fell a full percentage point, inflation stayed low, and interest rates held steady. But that was not how the networks played the recovery. The ratio of bad-news to good-news features and commentaries was more than four to one. For example, in a lead-in to an economics story in February 1983, Dan Rather downplayed the recovery: "While President Reagan was in St. Louis today speaking of an America on the mend, there was another America not far off— an America of 12 million unemployed where the wounds are too fresh and painful to mend."

Two weeks later, Rather was at it again in another lead-in: "At his news conference . . . President Reagan said the recovery is beginning. Recovery may indeed be just around the corner. . . . Tonight we look at some people for whom 'just around the corner' isn't close enough."

There's a real question as to whether Rather's lead-ins were biased leftward, but there is no question whatever as to their mood—negative, in spite of the good news.

In a separate study, the Institute for Applied Economics found that although 95 percent of the nation's economic indicators were *positive* during the last half of 1983, 86 percent of the soft economic news pieces on the network news were negative. We found the same thing during the first half of the year. But the downbeat approach doesn't reveal partisan bias—just negativity of the same kind that colored the news of Carter's economic program three years before.

TO JUDGE WHAT NETWORK NEWS IS AND isn't, consider the kinds of imbalance we found. The number of reports showing bias per se was so small, and the left/right political balance so close, that liberal views have a net advantage of only three percentage points. Comparing air time devoted to items on the liberal and conservative agendas, the liberals again have an advantage, but it's just five points. However, comparing the numbers of bad-news and good-news statements yields a net advantage of 90 points for the critical.

Some media critics consider negativism the most serious bias in broadcast journalism. Adam Clymer of *The New York Times* believes that negativism denies the network news its credentials as serious journalism. Ben Wattenberg goes even further in his new book, *The Good News Is the Bad News Is Wrong*, arguing that network negativism is the major element feeding our collective doubts about the state of the nation. Once we would have agreed with Wattenberg, but now we think the bad-news bias is no big problem. After all, if Americans could feel as optimistic last Election Day, as they apparently did, despite eight million unemployed, despite a very dicey situation in Central America, despite real interest rates approaching 10 percent, and despite a frosty relationship between the world's two nuclear giants, they apparently can handle the negative-news spin from the networks.

The most intriguing question raised by our findings may well be why network news is as politically balanced as it is. One might also ask why the media elite—so secular, so trendy, so bicoastal in their personal values—dress so conservatively, more like the nation's banking elite. In fact, they follow journalistic codes for about the same reasons they follow dress codes. They know that issue bias on the air is about as acceptable as punk hair styles.

Network newsfolk may talk liberal, but that reflects an easy-listening liberalism that's far less leftist than surveys indicate. In private conversation, national correspondents express their liberal values more as catechism than belief. As close witnesses of the self-serving folly common in politics, few of them really expect big government to make the world right. Sensing, as they do, the public apathy and ignorance about politics, correspondents rarely consider the common man a good bet to build a better society. And earning, as they do, salaries in the nation's top 1 percent, network newspeople regard wholesale redistribution of wealth as less than an immediate necessity.

In the end, the only clear network bias seems to be toward bad news. That's consistent with the age-old journalistic penchant for comforting the afflicted and afflicting the comfortable. The comfort of great power tends to spoil your image on the evening news, whether you're left-wing or right. Andropov or Reagan, big government or big business.

Judging by what we found, a liberal is at least as likely to be frustrated with day-to-day network journalism as a conservative. (And any real leftist detests the network news.) If liberals and Democrats had to rely on what political bias actually exists in the news media, liberalism would probably be in the same sad shape it's in today.

POSTSCRIPT

Does Television News Reflect a Liberal Bias?

The nature of the relationship among sources, reporters, and the construction of images in the audience's heads has been a topic of academic debate and professional discourse since the beginning of the print media. So many theoretical claims revolve around the topic of ideological control by the media organizations that this one issue alone could provide enough material for a course worth's of information.

For example, the role of the media in agenda setting is one area for discussion. If the media indeed *give us something to think about,* common sense would dictate that the way information is presented is an important factor in understanding how people use the media. Both the functional uses and the gratifications approaches to media analyses acknowledge that a media presentation will interact with the individual's sense of self to shape meaning. Similarly, gatekeeper studies (i.e., studies of the structures of news organizations and the ideological framing of messages) all inform the *critical* analysis of the relationship of the news apparatus and the messages.

What becomes paramount in any of these studies is the realization that any subjective interpretation of phenomena will reflect (consciously or unconsciously) the researcher's own interpretive bias. Two individuals may view the same thing but create different meanings from the action because each person's experience and psychological composition is different. Such is the complexity of understanding the impact of media and the construction of messages within the self.

Many excellent studies attempt to explore the dynamics behind the range of theoretical interpretations inherent in this issue. Michael Bruce MacKuen and Steven Lane Coobs's *More Than News: Media Power in Public Affairs* (Sage, 1981); Jay G. Blumler and Dennis McQuail's *Television in Politics: Its Uses and Influences* University of Chicago Press, 1969); and *The Idea Invaders* by George N. Gordon, Irving Falk, and William Hodapp (Hastings House, 1963) all take the perspective that the mediated experience is a multifaceted one.

The study of press organizations and the relationships of the journalists to their professions in an international arena is discussed by L. John Martin and Anju Grover Chaudhary in *Comparative Mass Media Systems* (Longman, 1983) and by Oliver Boyd-Barrett in *The International News Agencies* (Sage, 1980).

ISSUE 12

Did Television Influence the Outcome of the Vietnam War?

YES: J. Fred MacDonald, from *Television and the Red Menace: The Video Road to Vietnam* (Praeger, 1985)

NO: T. D. Allman, from "PBS's *Vietnam:* How TV Caught the Unprintable Truth," *Channels* (November/December 1983)

ISSUE SUMMARY

YES: Professor J. Fred MacDonald investigates media content during the Vietnam War and concludes that society was given a war agenda that reduced the struggle to issues of good versus evil.
NO: Author T. D. Allman examines the television documentary that supposedly told the "real" story of Vietnam and concludes that television indeed showed the real story—that Vietnam was about devastation rather than politics.

There is general agreement that television coverage of war focuses on images of death and destruction. The nature of television news is to provide the viewer with the most graphic visual images possible. In war, those images can evoke emotions and capitalize on the human dimensions of military actions. Two areas of controversy, however, concern the impact of these images on personal opinion and the ideology of those who produce and package these images for viewer consumption.

As the first military action to be covered live by electronic news-gathering technologies (ENG) and satellite distribution, media critic Michael Arlen was prompted to call Vietnam the first "living room war." His thesis (which is shared by many critics) is that American viewers were shocked by the grim reality of war when confronted by real blood and mounting casualty rates. The immediate coverage of the actions, therefore, strongly influenced American sentiment about the morality of our involvement in Vietnam as well as our sense of whether or not this war could be won. Many authors speculate on what perceptions could have been formed of other wars that involved American military intervention if television had shared the images "firsthand."

J. Fred MacDonald supports the idea that television played a crucial role in shaping viewer perceptions by offering shallow reporting and propaganda, thereby making the war familiar but increasing viewers' confusion about the reasons for the military action. His analysis of reporters' war coverage and their reliance on messages from the White House suggests that both reporter bias and control of information from political leaders skirted the real issues of war. The events were reduced to typical television entertainment while avoiding the central issues surrounding our involvement in Vietnam. The political ideology of war was shaped to accommodate the biases of the television medium.

With a different perspective on the role of television and Vietnam, T. D. Allman reflects on war coverage fifteen years after the Tet offensive, an event usually credited as turning American sentiment against the war because of the portrayal of stunning U.S. defeat at the hands of the Viet Cong. The vehicle used for analysis was the 13-part documentary on PBS, *Vietnam: How TV Caught the Unprintable Truth*.

In reviewing the PBS documentary, Allman develops the thesis that televised coverage of Vietnam merely showed us what we might have otherwise not seen or heard but that the responsibility for the events of the war were directly attributable to individuals in government and the military who orchestrated the events that even television did not cover. For Allman, the dispute surrounding the outcome of the war reflects questions of political and military intervention—not that of the media. Accordingly, if Vietnam had not been covered by television, Americans would still have questioned the involvement of the U.S. military in such an action.

The positions of the two authors of these selections confirm the two major areas of controversy in televised portrayals of any form of news or information mentioned above. One argument concerns the *content* of media and questions both the impact of iconic representations as well as the ability of any form of media to extend those images to the public.

The other position reflects *structural* issues of the relationship of sources, newsmakers, and their subjective construction of the stories presented to the public. This position argues that images cannot be neutral, so who then determines their meaning? Are meanings constructed by the journalist, the cameraperson, or the editor? Do meanings reflect the philosophies of news organizations, or perhaps are they constructed in the minds of the viewers or listeners? If any part of these questions can be answered "yes," it is possible to develop an argument for ideological bias in the media. The two selections that follow each draw from one of these theoretical positions.

YES

J. Fred MacDonald

TV AND THE COMING
OF THE VIETNAM WAR

It is ironic that while it was silent, even ignorant, about the coming Vietnam War, television had prepared the nation for just such a battle. It was not a conscious brainwashing, but a subtle persuasion acted out over a dozen or more years of programming. TV told Americans the world was black and white, good and bad. TV showed that American virtues always triumphed, that American answers were best for mankind, and that Americans were selfless, wanting only to help others. Simplistic in its anti-Communism, increasingly venerative of national political leaders, and traditionally superficial and biased, TV indicated there was no need for profound analysis or for skepticism. Whether fiction or actuality, child-oriented or intended for adults, video ill served the public. It offered too many distorted images of the non-American world. It provided far too little information with which to assess world affairs. At a time when Americans depended upon the medium for honest diversion and accurate reportage, television offered too much propaganda and shallowness.

At no time in the nation's history did the United States go to war as in Vietnam. There were no cries of "Remember Pearl Harbor!" or "Remember the Maine!" Vietnam was not an openly declared "police action" taken in conjunction with a vote of the United Nations. Kennedy did not go before Congress, as had Woodrow Wilson and other wartime chief executives, to obtain a constitutional declaration of war. The Vietnam War was eased into. Without open debate and without popular comprehension of the issues, motives, or consequences, Americans one day simply found themselves in an Asian land war. The anti-Communist action that under Truman and Eisenhower had been only a holding action in Southeast Asia now became an active American war undertaken on the basis of secret decisions by Kennedy and his advisers.

The first television exposure of the Vietnam War was made by James Robinson, the NBC correspondent stationed in Hong Kong. On "Projection

'62," televised January 5, 1962, Robinson seemed to flabbergast his colleagues when he bluntly declared to anchorman Frank McGee, "Well, Frank, like it or not—admit it or not—we are involved in a shooting war in Southeast Asia." No American broadcast journalist or network had ever described the actions of U.S. advisers in Southeast Asia as did Robinson.

In his analysis Robinson left no doubt that American forces were not just training South Vietnamese troops to resist Communist insurgents:

> American troops in battle uniforms, fully armed, are being killed [by] and killing Communist-led rebels in South Vietnam. American officers are in full command authority of important military operations there. And our active military participation in this war is on the increase. Our involvement stems from the fact that the South Vietnamese are unable, and, in some instances, unwilling to make the necessary sacrifices to save their land from Communist take-over. United States officials there have told me we must win this war, even if we have to militarily attack North Vietnam, the present source of Red infiltration and aggression.

Perhaps the most objective correspondent at NBC, Robinson refused to see the struggle in Vietnam in terms of anti-Communist clichés. Instead, he explained the conflict more realistically:

> The Asian Communist strategy to conquer South Vietnam is not based on ideology. Rather, it's self-survival. The Red regimes in Peking and Hanoi are proved economic failures. They simply can't feed their subjects. They must have the surplus food of South Vietnam in the very near future, and eventually in all Southeast Asia, or they'll collapse.

Robinson recognized that the new Vietnam War was the result of political and military decisions made in Washington. But he warned against overestimating American prowess and underestimating the strength of the enemy. "The presence of American soldiers in this battlefield doesn't necessarily guarantee victory," noted Robinson, "for U.S. involvement will trigger increased efforts for the Asian Communist camp." He added ominously, "Is President Kennedy willing and able to cope with this avalanching military challenge in the Far East? Many there doubt it."

To this date network TV had communicated the battle between Communists and non-Communists in Vietnam as classic Red guerrilla subversion valiantly resisted by freedom-loving, religious South Vietnamese. When Vice-President Johnson visited the South Vietnamese premier in mid-1961, he call Diem "the Winston Churchill of Asia"—this to go along with Diem's other sobriquet, "the Abraham Lincoln of Southeast Asia." As for the American role in Diem's struggle, it had been portrayed as advisory, helping the South Vietnamese to help themselves—and economic, providing financial aid to bolster the South Vietnamese economy. This was the essence, for example, of the two-part CBS documentary "Guerrilla," which aired on "The 20th Century" on November 12 and 19, 1961.

That James Robinson startled his peers on "Projection '62" is apparent from the following discussion of his assessment.

McGee: Now, Jim, let me get this clear. I think it's important. You're saying that we are not simply training South Vietnamese troops over there to fight, but that American soldiers in uniform are carrying guns and shooting at the enemy?

Robinson: That's absolutely right. Also, our Navy is patrolling in South Vietnamese waters to seal off infiltration from the North. We have our Air Force in combat operations there. Rangers and Special Forces are out in hand-to-hand combat in the jungles and in the delta regions of South Vietnam.

Cecil Brown: Jim, a few dozen helicopters and a few thousand troops do not represent a very extensive commitment. . . .

Sander Vanocur: . . . Jim, I think that your evaluation is much too strong. We are not in a war there, we don't consider—a local operation. . . .

Robinson: Well, Sandy, in a sense this is a pretty shocking political morality from Washington. Because we have already promised officially to South Vietnam that we will go to any efforts to save that country from the Communists. And what are we doing? Carrying out an experiment now in American lives there without knowing really what we're going to do?

Bernard Frizell: Well, I think the question, Jim, really is: Is this going to develop into another Korea?

Robinson: It certainly is! It already *has* developed into another Korea! We have many countries anxious to get in there. Many countries already participate in the war there. You have Malaya sending considerable amounts of equipment. England has sent advisers. You have the Philippines and Thailand ready to send troops in there.

The only comment more unnerving than Robinson's revelations of active participation this early in the Vietnam War, was his prophetic final statement on what Americans might expect in Vietnam in 1962: "Tragic news will shock, sadden many American families in 1962—news of deaths of Americans killed in Southeast Asian conflicts."

The Kennedy administration offered television journalists a wide variety of crises and program innovations to fill the evening news and documentary specials. From civil rights at home to the Peace Corps abroad, from Cuba and Berlin to the Alliance for Progress in Latin America and new initiatives in central Africa—there was under JFK a news dynamism absent from politics under Eisenhower. Moreover, with television technologically more mature by the 1960s, visual communication of domestic and international challenges to Kennedy's activism could be more thoroughly presented.

American TV, however, seemed more fascinated with the Kennedy personality than the Kennedy policy. The surprised and defensive reactions of those NBC correspondents to James Robinson's report—essentially a "radio" report with no pictures nor film to enhance his points—reveal the shallowness of TV news when it gravitates to personality instead of thorough, objective analysis. On January 12, 1962, NBC aired its eleventh hour-long "JFK Report" without having fully probed developments in South Vietnam. On February 25, 1962, that network broadcast a "White Paper" entitled "Red China," again without looking at American policy in Southeast Asia. The administration continued to exploit the president's aplomb in short-answer news conferences and succinct statements taped for the nightly news. By late March, Senator William Proxmire, a Wisconsin liberal Democrat, publicly urged Kennedy to use television more responsibly by speaking to the nation in detail about administration policies.

On the matter of South Vietnam, the president at his news conferences was seldom pressed for details when he mentioned American commitments. Without a probative retort, on January 31, 1961, he announced, "The situation in Vietnam is one that's of great concern to us. . . . The United States has increased its help to the government." On February 7 he spoke to U.S. economic aid to Vietnam, and the existence of "training groups out there which have been expanded in recent weeks as the attacks on the government and the people of South Vietnam have increased," but there were no follow-up questions asking for specifics. Nor was there a press reaction to JFK's appeal for caution in reporting on South Vietnam. He told the journalists on February 7:

> Now, this is a danger area where there is a good deal of danger, and it's a matter of information. We don't want to have information which is of assistance to the enemy—and it's a matter which I think will have to be worked out with the government of Vietnam, which bears the primary responsibility.

When asked to explain developments in Vietnam because "We don't have any overall coverage. . . . [and] because the Pentagon won't put out anything," Kennedy on March 7 brushed off his questioner: "I don't think you could make a judgment of the situation," he remarked, adding, "It's very much up and down, as you know, from day to day and week to

week, so it's impossible to draw any long-range conclusions." A month later, in his conference on April 11, the president lamented the death of American soldiers in South Vietnam, but quickly added, "We cannot desist in Vietnam." Again, however, there were no follow-up questions.

As presidential evasion continued, television, by the spring of 1962, finally began to analyze the situation in South Vietnam. On May 8, NBC aired "Viet Nam—Last Chance," an hour-long analysis narrated by Edwin Newman and James Robinson. *Variety* described the program as "at a superficial level . . . a good war story in motion pictures, and at its most profound . . . a balanced, purposeful study of U.S. policies, native politics, and armament in Southeast Asia." More revelatory was the May 23 ABC telecast of "Howard K. Smith with News and Comment." Since leaving CBS in the fall of 1961 and moving to prestige-hungry ABC News, Smith had been given a prime-time commentary program in which to treat issues he felt most pressing. In this installment Smith's topic was "What is Kennedy going to do about the Cold War that past administrations didn't do?" Specifically, he focused on South Vietnam and "one of his conspicuous new approaches, Mr. Kennedy's interest in guerrilla warfare."

Smith opened areas never fully explored on network TV. He told how in one year Kennedy had raised the number of American Special Forces from slightly more than 1,000 to a projected 10,000. While all were volunteers, Kennedy "passed down word that promotion will be faster for regular Army men who . . . volunteer for guerrilla service." Further, Smith reported American "troops pouring into Thailand."

There were administration spokesmen to pronounce the necessity of increased U.S. intervention. Walt Whitman Rostow, chief State Department policy planner, described Communist guerrilla warfare as "a type of war they [Communists] feel they can impose on a transitional society at a certain moment in vulnerability in the course of its movement towards modernization." Roger Hilsman, the director of intelligence for the State Department, likened the Communist guerrillas to the gangsters in Chicago in the 1920s—lacking true popular support, but operating freely because local government was not effective in controlling their terror and retaliation.

Secretary of Defense Robert S. McNamara was both manipulative and forthright when he discussed the Vietnam situation with Howard K. Smith. After Smith had presented strong criticism of Diem's autocratic regime in Saigon, McNamara spoke glowingly of the premier's accomplishment "to move his country toward a democratic structure." When quizzed more specifically by Smith, the secretary of defense admitted that in Vietnam "autocratic methods within a democratic framework were required."

More frankly, McNamara held out little hope for a quick victory over Communism in South Vietnam. When asked to estimate "how long it's going to take to settle this issue in South Vietnam," his answer was not encouraging. "I can't, but I'm certain it isn't a matter of months," McNamara responded, "rather a matter of years. I would guess three to five at a minimum."

It is important to note that throughout this program—in fact, throughout the several years that Howard K. Smith broadcast commentaries for ABC—he was not opposed to the anti-Communist commitment in Southeast Asia. This program was filled with encouragement for the administration to upgrade its performance, militarily and psychologically. Smith also subscribed to the domino theory, which envisioned the collapse of countries like Burma and Thailand should Communism be victorious in Indochina.

Journalistically, Smith was a product of World War II. One of Edward R. Murrow's young protégés covering the war in Europe, Smith gave one of the war's most powerful broadcasts when, in May 1945, he described conditions in bombed-out Berlin—once the fourth largest city in the world, now in ruin because of Allied bombing and occupation. Like so many from that era, words like "appeasement" and "isolation" were to Smith synonymous with the advance of Fascism; and Hitler's policy of conquering one independent country after the other was a political pattern never to be allowed again.

Smith was an anti-Communist, but within a liberal framework. He called for the overthrow of Castro because the Cuban leader was like Hitler. On his program of September 30, 1962, he declared:

> My completely personal view is that Castro's Cuba has become a threat to U.S. security—a more important threat than the Communist invasion of South Korea was. . . . I think Castro's satellite government has to be removed. Cuban patriots, aided by us, should do it. But if Russian guns have made that too difficult, direct American action should be contemplated. . . . For us, this is a little like watching Hitler's march into the Rhineland. He could have been stopped easily then.

Smith also viewed Communist China with values from the Hitler experience.

"In China the need for living space is not out of date," he told his audience on March 7, 1962, "In China, *Lebensraum* may become the sharpest of all issues. . . . the huge Chinese population is way out of control. It's going to have to move somewhere sometime unless Chinese technology improves immensely," Still, he could be pragmatic. He was willing to recognize, for example, that China and the Soviet Union had national interests that differed, and this meant a world of Communisms to be dealt with diplomatically. Thus, on December 12, 1962, he could suggest:

> . . . it is all a rich opportunity for us. . . . If Communism is no longer monolithic, our attitude in dealing with it should cease to be a solid monolithic opposition. The use of Western trade to reward moderate Communist countries and to punish radical, aggressive Communists—this while standing firm on basic commitments—might change the course of history by peaceful action.

In the early years of the American slippage into the Vietnam War, television journalists failed to offer informed rebuttal or even healthy doubt when the government explained the imperatives for a military commitment in Southeast Asia. Smith was the only network newsman regularly editorializing; there were no opposing voices urging a full exposure of the issues in Vietnam, a weighing of all sides, a full national debate of the advisability of the American actions, or an adherence to constitutional processes in the expanding military role of the United States in Southeast Asia.

In many cases, moreover, American TV journalists held political views that matched administration perceptions. Like Kennedy, many newsmen saw Communist China as an aggressive anti-American power threatening to establish hegemony over all of Southeast Asia—and perhaps all Asia. The two CBS correspondents stationed in Asia, Bernard Kalb and Peter Kalisher, saw Chinese Communism behind Asian upheavals. On "Years of Crisis: 1962," Kalb contended the Chinese never made a secret that Communism for all Asia was their goal. "Their objective," said Kalb, "is to brainwash all of Asia, rattle Asia, weaken Asia, and then make Asia ripe for the taking over by the Communists." For Kalisher, "Red China sees world domination for Communism, with Red China at the head of the band."

The principal Chinese weapon, according to Kalisher, was manpower. Because "You can't tell a Chinese from the Vietnamese or from any of the other races—most of them—in Asia," he contended, the Chinese were able to pour "men and enthusiasm into all these trouble spots in Asia." This tactic, he said, allowed the Chinese to feel they "can bring us [the United States] down where the Russians can't with atomic might." Therefore, Kalisher said, the Chinese "think that this nonsense about paying lip service to American atomic might is ridiculous because they've got ways of getting around it."

One of the few newsmen to see weakness and conservatism in Communist China was Marvin Kalb of CBS. On "Years of Crisis: 1963" he argued with Kalisher, contending, "I question very much any marked success either in Chinese internal or external policy." According to the younger Kalb brother, "The only mild success that Communist China has had in several years has been in conveying the impression to the Soviet Union and to many other Communists that they stand for something very revolutionary. But the fact is that Chinese foreign policy has been marked by *great* caution throughout Asia."

While Kalisher, the Far Eastern correspondent, continued to claim Communist China was the disruptive, aggressive force in Asia, Marvin Kalb was the CBS correspondent at the State Department. And Kalb's view seemed less an independent conclusion than a reflection of a "new look at Communist China" he described as taking place at the State Department. Here in the first weeks of the presidency of Lyndon B. Johnson, Kalb suggested that "We are now taking a more pragmatic, less emotional, . . . dispassionate and calm look at China," especially at "the second echelon of authority and power in the Chinese Communist party . . . the younger generation coming up. . . ."

If the opinions of many correspondents might have been affected by Cold War slogans and official government policy, even more questionable were those journalists who worked for the government. Two of the most prominent TV newsmen, Chet Huntley and Walter Cronkite, on more than one occasion lent their talents and prestige to the making of government propaganda films. Specifically, they narrated and appeared in Defense Department motion pictures extolling the anti-Communist goals of the U.S. armed forces.

Early in 1960, while coanchor of the top-rated "Huntley-Brinkley Report," Chet Huntley narrated "The Ramparts We Watch," a propaganda movie lauding the cooperative efforts of the four major branches of the American military. The half-hour motion picture opened with a statement from Secretary of Defense Thomas Gates, Jr. It included footage and voice recordings of President Eisen-

hower and the joint chiefs of staff. The film suggested to its viewers—most likely would-be recruits and trainees—that despite modern technology, the soul of the armed forces remained man. Huntley's narration was accompanied by pictures of American GIs operating machinery, and carrying out human assistance programs in Hong Kong with "refugees from Red China" and with children in a Taiwanese kindergarten. While the modern military carried out missions in outer space, Huntley reminded his viewers, "We still face the need for defending the Free World's ramparts on Earth." What was needed, he suggested, was traditional and human: "The nuclear soldier may look different from today's soldier, but [he] must have the same patriotic fighting spirit and more specialized training."

Even more professionally compromising was Huntley's narration of "The United States Navy in Vietnam." Produced in 1966, this propaganda piece was a 30-minute commendation of the Navy's role in the Vietnam War. Huntley stood dockside and lauded "vertical envelopment," amphibious landings, and the other new techniques the Navy was using "to help the people of Vietnam protect themselves." Viewers saw "civic action" as sailors gave boots to an older villager and clothing to a Vietnamese infant. Here was the latest naval equipment: destroyer-frigate, jets, and helicopters strafing enemy positions, big guns pummeling the Viet Cong enemy from offshore, and the massive aircraft carrier, the U.S.S. *Enterprise*. At a time when millions of Americans watched Chet Huntley weeknights on NBC for a better understanding of the war in Southeast Asia, he was contracting with the Pentagon to appear on camera and narrate its patently propagandistic motion pictures. At a time when his profession needed the utmost in objectivity to report accurately to the American citizenry, with uplifting music in the background Huntley lavished praise on the "Navy man":

Vietnam has already written a new chapter in the annals of naval history. Never before has the potential of the Navy-Marine team been so fully realized. And yet, one important thing remains unchanged: the success of the overall effort will rely, as it always has, upon the acts of the individual man. Whatever credit is due will rest with many thousands of individual men who stand behind the aircraft, the ships, the boats, and the rifles, from the delta to the South China Sea. And whether he serves ashore or in the rivers and coastal waters, at sea or in the skies above, he will shoulder the responsibility for final success or failure. And he will be the one to make the needed sacrifice. And it is important to remember, that no matter what his job or whatever his duty, he is the Navy's greatest single asset: the individual man. This is the American Navy in Vietnam, moving quickly where and when needed, displaying the flexibility of modern sea power, controlling the seas, extending its influence on land, and holding superiority in the air—a three-way force for peace geared to meet aggression at any spot on the globe.

More aggressively anti-Communist were the government films narrated by Walter Cronkite. Although he began working in 1950 for CBS News, in 1953 Cronkite narrated a Defense Department film, "The Price of Liberty." The motion picture dealt with the role of women in the American armed forces. But clearly, from Cronkite's opening words, this 15-minute movie had other purposes: "Liberty is the most expensive commodity in the world today," proclaimed Cronkite while seated at a typewriter. "We have it only because we are willing and able to pay the price for preserving it against Communist aggression." This was a time of "the fight for world freedom," said Cronkite, and "Today armed vigilance must back every truce in the war between freedom and slavery." And, he suggested, "Military strength is still the only practical answer to the menace of Communism."

Throughout his career Cronkite's programs on CBS were marked by their reliance upon the Pentagon for film footage, statistical information, and interviews with prominent military men. This was the case with "The 20th Century," "Air Power," and "The 21st Century." Still, only a few months before he replaced Douglas Edwards as anchorman of the CBS evening news in April 1962, Cronkite narrated "The Eagle's Talon" for the Department of Defense. Ostensibly a report from Secretary McNamara on his first year in office, the film was a paean to the Kennedy administration for strengthening American military power. Cronkite declared the Soviet Union was "the opponent" of America, and all those Polaris, Minuteman, Nike-Hercules, Nike-Zeus, and other rockets were intended to protect the United States from a first strike by the Russians. While he noted that thermonuclear war started by the Soviets "would mean disaster for themselves," Cronkite reminded viewers "that does not mean Communism has curbed its ambition for world conquest." According to him, "Communist China even now has plans to dominate Asia by mass murder as in Tibet, destroying ancient civilizations." On Cuba, he remarked, "Right next door is a nation we freed in 1898, Cuba, as Communist tyranny holds sway and whiskers do not hide the naked face of dictatorship."

This was powerful propaganda. Oversimplified, well-scored, graphically illustrated, and stridently narrated, the Defense Department film described a world in which the U.S. Army "is face to face with Communism around the world." To meet the threat, the film alleged, the Kennedy administration was enhancing the nuclear and nonnuclear potentials of the armed services.

In classic propaganda style, after having frightened viewers with images of thermonuclear war and threats of savage Red aggression, Cronkite reassured them that with Kennedy everything would be fine. "No matter what the future holds, there is no need to fear for America," Cronkite guaranteed, for "The President, as Commander-in-Chief, keeps the decade of decision alert to Washington's advice, still timely today: 'To be prepared for war is one of the most effectual means of preserving peace.' "

There were several significant instances of network news personnel having close ties to government. Edward R. Murrow left CBS to head the United States Information Agency (USIA). He died, however, before returning to broadcast journalism. John Chancellor of NBC left the network in 1965 to become director of the government's chief propaganda outlet, the Voice of America. After several years in that capacity, he returned to NBC. In a reversal of the movement from broadcasting to government service, James C. Hagerty became the head of ABC News in 1961 after having been President Eisenhower's press secretary through most of Ike's two terms.

Corporate executives in the television industry also were closely associated with the partisan political interests of government. While it was common during World War II for broadcasting leaders to work for the Roosevelt administration, the practice was not widespread in the 1960s. Yet, at least two major TV executives were active in the Johnson administration: Frank M. Stanton and Robert E. Kintner. Stanton was president of CBS while also a trustee and chairman of the RAND Corporation, a government-supported think tank that one journalist described as "an annex of the Pentagon." He was also appointed by President Johnson to head the Committee on Information Policy, an advisory group offering advice on government propaganda policy. Stanton, furthermore, was a close friend of the president. He and his wife once considered building a house on LBJ's Texas ranch. Kintner, the president of NBC in the mid-1960s, was also a personal friend of Lyndon Johnson, that relationship extending back to Washington during the New Deal. As he did with Stanton, the president occasionally telephoned Kintner to complain about TV coverage or to seek advice. When Kintner left NBC in 1966, he accepted a Johnson appointment as special assistant to the president.

Government found TV networks and producers eager to assist in U.S. propaganda efforts around the world. By late 1961, according to *Broadcasting*, the USIA was receiving the greatest possible cooperation from commercial TV interests. Whether the agency wanted an hourlong NBC documentary on Ernest Hemingway, a CBS drama about the Berlin wall, or a David M. Wolper documentary production concerning the great black athlete Rafer Johnson, American television was cooperative. To ensure this harmonious relationship, however, President Kennedy and Edward R. Murrow were careful to meet in the fall of 1961 with the network chiefs, impressing upon industry executives that the government wanted easier access to network archives. While there had always been a cooperative relationship between TV and the propaganda agencies of the U.S. government, beginning with the Kennedy administration, access was simplified, streamlined, and generally enhanced. As one USIA official reported in late 1961, "Our arrangements with them are working well. . . . We're in touch almost daily. . . . We're getting material all the time." . . .

At his televised news conference on July 28, 1965, President Johnson read a letter from a Midwestern woman. It was a short note, but it asked a profound question:

Dear Mr. President:
   In my humble way I am writing to you about the crisis in Vietnam. I have a son who is now in Vietnam. My husband served in World War II. Our country was at war, but now, this time, it is just something that I don't understand. Why?

The chief executive responded to the writer with slogans. Rather than a complex, honest answer, Johnson spoke of fighting for freedom, the Chinese desire "to extend the Asiatic dominion of Communism," the lessons of "Hitler at Munich," the honor of the American "word," and the bloodbath that would follow abandonment of "those who believed in us and trusted us." It was a language of clichés and stereotypes that Americans understood. They had learned it on TV. . . .

Television shaped and directed a generation of Americans to accept something as absurd as an inadequately explained, undeclared war halfway around the globe, costing billions of dollars each year, losing thousands of young lives monthly, and ultimately wrenching the moral fiber of American civilization. The war was justified because it was familiar. The images transmitted over all those years offered explanation enough. Americans could answer that quizzical Midwestern mother, for they all had the TV experience of Good versus Evil, freedom against slavery, and moral, manly honor in mortal struggle with the forces of wickedness. A shared common conductor, video spread its monotonous political message and educated the nation. That it was effective was obvious in the reality of the war in Vietnam.

NO

T. D. Allman

PBS'S VIETNAM: HOW TV CAUGHT
THE UNPRINTABLE TRUTH

Fifteen years after the Tet offensive, arguably the turning point of the
Vietnam war, William Westmoreland and North Vietnamese general Vo
Nguyen Giap sit before PBS cameras—separately, of course—to explain the
significance of the bloody struggle. It is the seventh episode of PBS's
monumental 13-hour documentary, *Vietnam: A Television History*, now showing through December 20. Westmoreland argues, as he has argued since
1968, that Tet was not the stunning and humiliating defeat it seemed to most
Americans, whose television sets brought them images of Americans fighting and dying in a ravaged land. No, insists the general, the TV set was
wrong. Far from being a Viet Cong victory, he says, Tet "proved that we were
winning the war."

General Giap, one of the many leading North Vietnamese officials whom
PBS interviewed in Hanoi, sees things quite differently. In the strict military
sense, Giap concedes, the Tet offensive was a failure: American firepower
forced the Viet Cong and North Vietnamese troops who overran South
Vietnam to withdraw. But psychologically and politically, Giap adds, Tet was
a Viet Cong victory of incalculable importance because it demonstrated that
victory as Americans had understood it was simply impossible in Vietnam—
indeed that military defeat itself could be staved off only at an immense, and
unacceptable, military, political, financial, and psychological cost.

Giap of course was entirely correct. His troops held the U.S. Embassy for
only a few hours, but several months later Lyndon Johnson decided to
abandon the White House. The dumb, unblinking television eye had shown
the American people what all the scholarly tomes and earnest editorials
never had completely managed to convey in print, and what Westmoreland,
even now, does not seem to grasp: The only way to "save" Vietnam was to
destroy it. Never again would the American people really believe the war
was a noble endeavor to confer democracy and progress on Vietnam. Up
until Tet, the debate had centered on how the war might be won. Thereafter
there was only one debate—on how to get out.

Vietnam: A Television History tells us almost as much about television as about Vietnam. The narrator of the program reminds us more than once that Vietnam was the first television war. But this conventional observation turns out to mean more than one at first thinks. Throughout the series we witness television's capacity to communicate more than those in front of the camera, or even behind it, intend.

As we watch the two aging generals, we cannot help seeing beyond the facts, memories, judgments, and opinions the two are seeking to convey. Giap's appreciation of the human nature of war animates his every word and gesture. Westmoreland appears as rigid and unrelated to his surroundings as he did during the war. His notion that it is all a matter of technology and hardware runs through even his pieties about hearts and minds.

Giap, we quickly realize, understands that we Americans are human beings, that we need to believe what his own forces never doubted—that our wars are not just winnable, but worth winning. Westmoreland, as he faces the camera, reveals an equally crucial fact about the war: Like so many of our leaders, the poor fellow never managed to grasp what Vietnam was all *about*.

TELEVISION'S INFLUENCE ON THE WAR WAS axiomatic. For the first time, people could *see* a war while it was being fought. But the enormous influence of television was largely unexplored at the time and remains misunderstood. Was television "biased," as the Westmorelands and the Nixons claimed, or was it "objective," as the network executives and elite commentators countered?

Clearly it is disingenuous to argue that television was wholly objective. Yet its significant bias had to do not with the ideology of those who controlled it but with the medium itself. While print lends itself to abstraction—it is far easier for a writer to state what things "mean" than to recreate the events themselves—television craves concreteness. TV's inherent preference for the dramatic image no doubt influenced coverage of the war as strongly as, for example, the tendency of the B-52 bomber to hit "friendly" targets influenced the American conduct of the war.

Even the most experienced students of the war eventually came to precisely the conclusion the TV camera had arrived at without having to think. By the mid-1960s, for example, Bernard Fall, perhaps the reporter respected the most by those of us who covered the war, announced he was no longer bothering to cover Saigon's undulating intrigues and ceaseless prognostications of light at the end of the tunnel. Caligula's horse, he remarked, could be premier of South Vietnam now, and it wouldn't matter.

For the rest of his life Fall went around with the grunts. It had taken him decades of research and reflection to discover the single most important fact, the determinant truth of the war: All that mattered, after a while, was the American destruction. The television camera arrived at the conclusion unconsciously. One realizes, watching this most painstaking documentary, that television was the *idiot savant* of the Vietnam War.

Time and again on *Vietnam* one sees television challenge the abstract with the concrete, and thereby gain a truth. Thus in the eighth episode, "Vietnamizing the War," we learn that President Nixon ordered the number of troops fighting in

Vietnam steadily diminished between 1969 and 1973. The goal of Vietnamization was to allow the United States to win the war while minimizing the American cost in lives—and the Administration's in political standing.

Yet again a major North Vietnamese and Viet Cong offensive unfolded. And yet again it was ultimately turned back by a stupendous expenditure of American firepower. There in fact was only one real difference between the Tet offensive of 1968 and the Spring offensive of 1972: This time it was the South Vietnamese, not the Americans, who were dropping the bombs. This particular battle of the thirty-year Vietnam war ended when troops from Saigon retook the northern province of Quang Tri.

At the end of the episode the camera pans over Quang Tri City. The only thing moving is a South Vietnamese flag, listlessly flapping in a worn-out wind. Everything else is utter devastation. This was a "victory." The Vietnamization program had worked. In mid-September 1972, for the first time in seven years, there were no Americans killed in battle in Vietnam. That same week 5,000 Vietnamese died in combat.

PBS's commentary on the battle for Quang Tri is characteristically terse. We are told that "the fierce and prolonged battle for Quang Tri City provides extraordinary footage of a South Vietnamese army unit in combat, the terror of the civilian population trying to escape, and the destructive force of modern firepower." The sparseness of *Vietnam*'s narrative, its trust in imagery, is one of its strengths. Its calm is a worthy counterpoint to the shrill commentary that surrounded the war itself. Yet what would happen if this modesty were carried to its logical extreme—and one

watched these films of Vietnam with so sound at all?

The force of the images, in fact, simply outstrips any attempt to impose narrative significance on them. Commentary often seems completely superfluous. At the end of the eighth segment, the camera pans across yet another landscape of desolation. This time the ruins are not of a city, but of an abandoned American PX. Air-conditioners and refrigerators litter the scene like archaeological artifacts. Fans, unconnected to electrical outlets, turn listlessly in the wind.

The most explicit tributes to the power of television on *Vietnam* comes not from the stunning images themselves, but from the high-ranking American officials who planned and ran the war. Former presidents, vice presidents, generals, and cabinet members who once believed that nothing was beyond their power—not even conjuring up a viable South Vietnam with the aid of bullets and bombs—now argue that they failed because the TV camera is mightier than the B-52.

We all remember Spiro Agnew's attacks on the media. But perhaps the most revealing vignette of the PBS series involves Hubert Humphrey—supposedly Agnew's liberal antithesis. Humphrey is trying to defend the war, in a speech during the 1968 Presidential campaign, when a group of anti-war protestors starts to heckle him. But Humphrey doesn't turn on his tormentors. Instead he lashes out at the TV crews filming the confrontation. If "you fellows" weren't always broadcasting the protests, he exclaims, protestors wouldn't be on the attack.

Despite Humphrey's accusation, the question of television's influence on the war is not difficult to answer. That the outcome would have been the same,

TV or no, is abundantly clear from those parts of *Vietnam* focusing on what the war did to the Americans who fought in it. The GI's didn't need television to show them the truth about Vietnam. It was all around them. In the fifth episode, "American Takes Charge," an ex-Marine talks about convincing his parents to let him join up, and then about finally arriving in Vietnam to fight for freedom. It took him about a month, he recounts, to discover what it took people like Fall years to discover, and what people like Westmoreland never discovered at all: "What was going on here was nuts." He and other former American soldiers discuss the endless killing and destruction. "She was running away from the Americans who were going to kill her," the Marine says of an old, unarmed Vietnamese woman, "and I killed her, and I didn't think twice about it at the time."

The Marine is crying now and the camera tactfully cuts to some shots of Vietnam. We hear the anguish in his voice; we do not see his face, and it is one of those stunning, terrible Vietnam moments when television, even in looking away, reveals another of the great truths of the war—which was that even the killers were victims.

What were the military implications for the United States of a war that consumed men's souls with the same abandon it used up napalm? The interviews with Vietnam veterans help call attention to one of the most important facts about the war: After a certain point—1970 at the latest—the debate on Vietnam at home became as irrelevant to the actual course of the war as the talk about light at the end of the tunnel in Saigon had become. President Nixon had no choice but to "bring the boys home," because the conduct of the war had so thoroughly de-

moralized the U.S. ground troops that they had become a military liability.

For a lot of U.S. soldiers, the war was not the great crisis of conscience it turned out to be for others. But if gunning down old women didn't get to the GI's, marijuana and heroin and VD and the pervasive reality that the war had no purpose did. By the early 1970s hundreds of American officers were being attacked or killed by their own troops.

In Indochina the TV images seldom flowed in both directions. People in the United States saw Vietnam every night on television, but those of us in Saigon seldom watched the nightly news, even when that was possible. Perhaps that was why the most arresting visual image of the entire series, so far as I was concerned, did not emanate from the devastation of Vietnam, but from the quite different devastation that simultaneously unfolded in the United States. The 11th episode, "Homefront USA," offers a well-known scene—of Vietnam veterans throwing their medals away on the steps of the Capitol in Washington. But it haunted me when I saw it, and it still haunts me, for it involved a degree of repudiation of America's actions in Vietnam that one never saw in Vietnam itself. It is not until the following segment, "The End of the Tunnel," that the U.S. Embassy in Saigon is at last abandoned. But, as the camera shows us those veterans jettisoning their medals the way the helicopters are later jettisoned into the sea, we feel the war might as well be over.

Even a victory in Indochina would not have prevented us from inflicting a terrible defeat on ourselves at home.

DEAN RUSK WAS NEVER ONE OF THE VIETnam war's more perceptive participants, and he is no trove of insight even now. Yet in the course of the PBS series, he raises a valid question.

If the TV cameras had been around in the 1940s, the former secretary of state wonders, and Americans could have seen the carnage then, would the United States also have abandoned the quest for victory during World War II?

Most Americans agree, to an extent they never were able to agree about Vietnam, that World War II was a clear-cut conflict between the forces of good and evil. Yet what if, instead of Movietone News clips of soldiers cheerfully waving as they waded ashore, we had watched, day after day, instantly transmitted footage of the hideous bloodshed at Bataan or Corregidor or the Ardennes? What if we had had, not the universally accepted self-censorship of yesterday's wars, but today's insistence on "objectivity"—an insistence largely brought about by the operation of television in Vietnam?

What really appalled Americans about the images from Vietnam was that they revealed the violence there as pointless, utterly unrelated to any worthwhile goal. The suffering of World War II, on the other hand, could have been accepted because it occurred within a context of shared values and objectives. We would have seen beyond the bloodshed to its purpose. Televising a just war might well increase the national will to fight it.

An even less speculative question remains: Would the Vietnam war have been won had there been no TV cameras? Did television affect, perhaps even determine, the outcome of the war?

The answer, once again, seems clear. No television cameras recorded Lyndon Johnson's clandestine bombing of Laos. Nor did television pay much attention to the gruesome war in Cambodia, provoked first by Richard Nixon's secret bombing of that country, and then by his highly publicized invasion. The two wars were very much the kind that President Nixon had hoped to fight and win in Vietnam. Very few Americans fought, and even fewer died, in either country. Television coverage and congressional oversight of the two conflicts were sporadic. These wars, as Nixon once said of Cambodia, were "the Nixon Doctrine in its purest form." As in Vietnamization, surrogate forces were left to fight the ground war while American planes were given free reign in the skies. Nearly as many tons of bombs were dropped on Laos alone as the United States dropped during the whole of World War II.

But the United States was as utterly defeated in Laos and Cambodia without television as it was in Vietnam with television. Even when the adversary was as truly loathsome as the Khmer Rouge, all that American money and firepower still failed to instill any real fighting spirit in the anti-communist forces. In the end, though the Khmer Rouge knew no television cameras would be awaiting them, they actually overran Phnom Penh before the North Vietnamese and the Viet Cong took Saigon.

In the PBS series, "Cambodia and Laos," the ninth segment, is without doubt the least compelling in the entire production. Laos and Cambodia do not make good television now because they were not televised then. The absence of TV did not "save" Cambodia; in the end it did not save Richard Nixon either. The secret bombing of Cambodia was the military action in Indochina that, more than any other, undid Nixon. The bombing was recorded in the articles of impeachment, along with the Watergate burglary.

Vietnam: A Television History says little explicitly about the interrelationship of the greatest foreign crisis and the greatest domestic crisis of recent American history. Yet as its images cut between Washington and Saigon, the two great melodramas seem only different episodes in the same long-running TV show.

The debates about Vietnam will never end. But *Vietnam* suggests, at least to me, a definitive conclusion to the debate about television and the war. Like the Watergate tapes, the footage from Vietnam allowed Americans to hear what they otherwise might not have heard, to see what they otherwise might not have seen. That is all, immense as it is.

We—like General Westmoreland and President Nixon—have to take responsibility for what we did, and did not do, once we had heard and seen.

POSTSCRIPT

Did Television Influence the Outcome of the Vietnam War?

Much of what informed public debate about Vietnam was not only the media's coverage of the war but also the moral dimensions of U.S. involvement in southeast Asia. It may be difficult to separate issues of the impact of media from the strong personal feelings so many people have about that particular time in history. Because of this, however, we can see that media do play yet one other role in covering something as important as war. Mediated forms of reality can provoke individuals to think about these difficult issues even after the event.

Films such as *Platton, Full Metal Jacket, Apocalypse Now, Casualties of War, Coming Home,* and *Born on the Fourth of July* treat Vietnam with the perspectives gained from history. PBS's television series did the same thing. In this way, many individuals who are troubled by the events in Vietnam can work through important feelings. These films and programs can be cathartic in some ways, but even more importantly, they keep us mindful of these important events of history.

Many critics point out that mediated treatments of war reduce human suffering and tragedy to entertainment, thereby abstracting and trivializing the events. When the highly successful television series "M*A*S*H" was introduced in 1972 while the U.S. was still involved in Vietnam, the series creators said that it portrayed the paradox of war. It focused on doctors who were trying to save lives while the very nature of war is that of taking life. In viewing images of the Korean war while still involved in Vietnam, we can see what McLuhan meant when he said that "we see life (through media) in a rear-view mirror." The horrors of the reality of Vietnam were too difficult to deal with in the evening news, but the historical reflections offered by "M*A*S*H" reinforced the realities of war while calling into question the moral dimensions that would have been too heavy-handed for news or public affairs.

There have been several analyses of the media and war coverage. Gaye Tuckman's *Making News: A Study in the Construction of Reality* (Free Press, 1978) and Edward J. Epstein's *News from Nowhere* (Random House, 1973) are good general overviews. Cases dealing with specific political conflicts include John C. Leggett et al., *Allende: His and Our Times* (New Brunswick Cooperative Press, 1978); Mohamad Tadayon's, "The Image of Iran in the *New York Times*," *Gazette* 26 (1980); John A. Sambe's, "Network Coverage of The Civil War in Nigeria," *Journal of Broadcasting*, 24 (1980); and Jarice Hanson and Christine Miller's, "The Moral Dimensions of Reporting Human Rights Coverage in Central America, 1976–1984," in S. Thomas, ed., *Communication and Culture*, vol. 3 (Ablex, forthcoming).

PART 5

Media Business

This section focuses on the practices of specific media businesses and their impact on methods of measuring audience reaction. In it, we explore media industries from the perspective of manifest and latent content in the messages produced. What do we learn from methods of market segmentation and evaluative feedback? What is the primary function of advertising, and to what extent does it influence our behavior? Are the structures of media industries responsive to the public's desires? How do monopolies in this industry affect media content?

Do Ratings Serve the Viewing Public's Interest?
_____

Is Advertising Ethical?
_____

Media Monopolies: Does Concentration of Ownership Jeopardize Media Content?

ISSUE 13

Do Ratings Serve the Viewing Public's Interest?

YES: Hugh Malcolm Beville, Jr., from *Audience Ratings: Radio, Television, and Cable* (Lawrence Erlbaum Associates, 1985)

NO: Todd Gitlin, from *Inside Prime Time* (Pantheon Books, 1983)

ISSUE SUMMARY

YES: Hugh Malcolm Beville, a ratings pioneer, defends the credibility and utility of ratings and argues that ratings provide networks with the information necessary to make decisions about what the public wants.
NO: Todd Gitlin, professor and popular author, attacks the misuse of ratings data, citing that when high ratings are demanded of all new programs, cancellation decisions are made too quickly and the public suffers.

There may be no institution as unpopular as the ratings services. They are an audience and/or marketing assessment device, but in popular culture imagery, they have become the entertainment equivalent of the voting booth. Audience members are aware and critical of ratings services in a way that they would never be of similar measures used to assess their satisfaction with cars, cornflakes, or even movies and magazines.

Television programming is a highly competitive and incredibly expensive gamble always conducted with one eye on ratings. Obviously, the networks are preoccupied with ratings, and some have described the process of selecting shows as one of finding the least objectionable program—one that does not have to be good, just less objectionable to most people than anything else on television at that moment.

Do ratings serve the public interest? Broadcasters were charged with "serving the public interest" in the 1934 Communications Act. This criterion has been frequently applied to the news and programming functions of broadcast outlets and has in the past led individual stations to air different types of programming (i.e., children's, public affairs, educational, religious, and local-interest programs. Yet what influence should this have on the ratings game? Presumably, ratings are a feedback mechanism allowing programmers to provide shows in which the public is interested. Does providing shows of interest fulfill the requirement to operate in the public interest? Many would argue that it does not and place much of the blame on the ratings services. The major complaints about ratings fall into four broad categories, according to Beville: Ratings are not accurate (small or bad samples, cooperation rates low, viewers change typical viewing patterns or report incorrectly); ratings are biased (rigging, hype during sweeps); ratings are misleading (no information provided on liking, reaction, or effect); and ratings are misused (to make quick and "lowest common demoninator" decisions). It is the final, and both authors agree most important, complaint with which Beville and Gitlin deal.

According to Hugh Beville, ratings are an excellent feedback mechanism. In his book *Audience Ratings*, Beville provides an extensive analysis of the types, uses, and procedures of ratings services. In this excerpt, he argues that much of the criticism of ratings services springs from the desire of critics to be arbiters of taste. Ratings, he further argues, are the scapegoats for decisions that are unpopular with certain audience segments. Whatever our evaluation of the outcome, ratings allow the people to make their own choices about the available entertainment fare.

Todd Gitlin, in this excerpt from his book *Inside Prime Time*, argues that much of the debate over ratings ignores the most important issues. Ratings are statistically sound, although the sampling ignores or underrepresents some groups—typically groups that advertisers do not care about in any case. What is important is that numbers have become the sole criterion by which shows live or die. Letting numbers, and the quick return of numbers, decide the fate of a program curtails artistic quality and does not allow shows to develop audiences over time. Such a decision process assures that we will not be able to select from among good programs but only from among what is least objectionable.

YES

Hugh Malcolm Beville, Jr.

RATINGS: SERVANT OR MASTER?

INTRODUCTION

We have seen by now that ratings are indeed a feedback mechanism to the industry the same way that the human nervous system is to the human body. Advertisers started the first rating system in 1930 to assure themselves of the audience delivery of programs they sponsored. Until that time they were "flying blind," fed a maze of claims, faced with uncertainties. When did people listen? By the day? By the hour? What did they listen to? How many and what stations were received? Only an organized measurement of audience could provide answers. Without such answers, the broadcast media could never move ahead to today's prosperity. The Cooperative Analysis of Broadcasting (CAB) in 1930 established the essential feedback mechanism required to engender advertiser confidence.

Once established, the ratings system provided important decision-making data for advertisers' use of network radio because at that time commercial prime-time programming was largely in their hands. Networks sold time, not programs, and had little control over their own schedules. Advertising agencies, with assistance from talent agencies and some independent consultants, produced the programs in which the sponsor placed the commercials.

With the growth of television, a much more expensive medium, few advertisers could any longer sponsor weekly hours or half-hours but went to alternate-week sponsorship. As that too became unaffordable, the networks gradually took over the programming responsibility, and advertisers bought one-minute (later 30-second) commercial positions. This arrangement made it possible for advertisers to spread their advertising over more programs, networks, and time periods, a move made productive because nonduplicated cumulative ratings figures could be supplied by Nielsen Audimeters. With the networks in charge of their own schedules, no longer could a George Washington Hill (of American Tobacco fame) or a Firestone family dictate program fare for the nation.

From Hugh Malcolm Beville, Jr., *Audience Ratings: Radio, Television, and Cable* (Hillsdale, NJ): Lawrence Erlbaum Associates, 1985), pp. 219-222, 234-241. Copyright © 1985 by Lawrence Erlbaum Associates, Inc. Reprinted by permission. Some notes omitted.

As networks became more in control, they sought more ratings feedback because audience size determined the sale (and the price) of the commercial positions that had to be sold to support the entire structure. The inevitable changes in public taste could be more closely monitored, while ratings use assisted networks in developing audience flow patterns of similar demographic groups and in counterprogramming against strong competition. The net result was the rapid growth of television as the most powerful communications and advertising medium we have seen.

Critics of broadcasting (professional and amateur), as well as our society's elitists, have few kind words for what is broadcast. But generally their most venomous remarks are reserved for broadcast ratings and their so-called tyrannical influence on programming. According to David Halberstam, William S. Paley of CBS created "the modern structure of broadcasting, with its brutal ratings system and its unparalleled profits." Halberstam fails to say in what respect the ratings system is "brutal." Would Halberstam characterize the newspapers' Audit Bureau of Circulation, whose figures are also used by advertisers in decision making, in the same way? Many daily newspapers and dozens of magazines have died because of poor circulation figures. Nor can one ignore the fact that publishers are as keenly concerned that their books appear in *The New York Times* best seller list as any network or advertiser is in the latest top 10.

The sports world is attuned to the effect of individual star performances on team success on the field and at the gate, all measured by statistical data. Moreover, college football and basketball teams are ranked by sportswriters to provide a weekly top 10 list. These are only a few of the parallel examples that may be drawn in related fields of communications, entertainment, and sports.

Insofar as the record of major newspaper failures is concerned, would such an end have come if their editors had had a daily or weekly rating report card on readership of individual stories versus their competition? Effective mass communication requires an efficient feedback system. With it, the medium can meet the needs and interests of its audience. Trial and error is possible because mistakes can be detected quickly. New entertainment and information forms can evolve under systematic oversight of audience response. Without feedback, a medium cannot efficiently serve its audience and sooner or later will fail.

The ratings system looms large in the minds of intellectuals as the black-hatted culprit who wipes quality programming off the air. Clearly, many overall criticisms of the television medium are laid at the door of ratings. Some disparagements of ratings are based on misunderstandings of their nature and function. It is more likely, however, that much of such criticism is really finding fault with the television medium and with the tastes of the American mass audience it serves. Whereas once the targets for the literary elite were the Hollywood "dream merchants," then radio programs' "pandering to the masses," it is now commercial television's "vast wasteland" that debases our culture. Beyond that, it is no doubt a dislike of advertising and a distrust of the competitive market economy that finances the media.

A major problem is that television as a medium, as a business, lives in a goldfish bowl. It is on stage for public viewing 18 to 24 hours daily, seven days a week, 52 weeks a year. Adults (18 and over) watch TV over four hours on an average day. *TV Guide*, with a weekly circulation of 17 million, and every Sunday newspaper, plus most dailies, carry complete program schedules, plus reviews, news, and summaries of ratings reports, including the top 15 shows. Television programming is a major topic of daily conversation in and away from home. When corporate management changes take place, *The New York Times* generally reports them in the business section; when network changes occur they receive front-page news treatment.

Americans are "hung up" on statistics, so the idea of Nielsen ratings intrigues them. At the same time, their lack of sophistication about statistical sampling raises serious doubts in their minds about how good the ratings are. Pseudo-intellectual types find it impossible to believe that "tripe like 'Beverly Hill-billies' or 'Dukes of Hazard' " could indeed have been America's number one show. They never watched them, nor did they know anyone who had.

They would probably be just as surprised to learn that in January 1982, "The current best-selling book on campus, according to the *Chronicle of Higher Education*, was *Garfield Bigger Than Life*, a volume of cartoons about a corpulent housecat." The next 5 of the top 10 were made up of other cartoon anthologies, plus two solution books for Rubik's Cube. Harlequin paperbacks were very popular also. . . .

From the time we got our first report card at school, and Brownie points in Cub Scouts performance, measurement of some type became part of life. The number and precision of the measurements increase as one enters the world of academic and sports competition. High school grade-point averages and SAT scores determine what colleges one can enter, just as college grade levels determine who makes the dean's list or edits the law review. The athlete's "stats" in football or basketball determine his chance for a scholarship or for success in the drafts and free agent market. Accountability and readiness for promotion in most fields are judged in terms of performance according to established criteria—meeting quotas or budgets, increasing sales or profits, decreasing expenses or labor problems, improving corporate image or stock price.

Advertisers, who initiated broadcast ratings in 1930, did so because based on their then limited use, they realized the potential advertising power of radio. They were unwilling, however, to commit increased budgets to the new electronic medium unless they had some tangible measure of the unseen audience they reached by this miraculous medium. That's where ratings started, and that's where they will remain as long as radio, television, and cable are commercial media. Joel Swerdlow is correct when he says, "The key to any real change in the rating system lies with the advertisers. Only they among the players have the incentive to find something better. . . . "[1]

Twenty billion dollars is quite an incentive. That's the total gross amount spent by all advertisers on electronic media in 1983. Narrowing it down to expenditures by national advertisers only on television—network and spot—the total becomes $12 billion. Major spenders are some of America's blue-chip corporations: Procter & Gamble ($577 million), General Foods ($303 million), American Home Products ($197 million), General

Mills ($201 million), General Motors ($191 million), PepsiCo ($163 million), AT&T ($161 million). Why are these well-run, highly regarded business organizations apparently satisfied with the current ratings system? After all, this money is spent to develop more sales—the life-blood of any corporation. If they were being misled or short-changed, would not someone hear about it? Would hundreds of corporate managements and boards of directors sit still for budgets allocated on faulty data?

There are several very good reasons, which, if the industry's critics would listen, they might understand. The advertiser's confidence in ratings starts with his knowledge of surveys and market research. He knows that the ratings figures are estimates, but he also knows that the errors that may accompany an individual figure tend to even out when many programs and spots are purchased. The advertiser also, from the enormous amount of independent survey work conducted on share of market, marketing new products, copy themes, tests of commercials, etc., has available a vast amount of detailed data that enables him to confirm the ratings reports. . . .

RATINGS ARE MISUSED

Here we deal with "ratings tyranny." Ratings, it is charged, so dominate the decision making of networks, stations, and program suppliers that they lead to the cancellation of quality programs and result in programs appealing to the lowest common denominator. It is said that ratings distort news judgment and lead to the scheduling of lurid and sensational news stories and investigative reporting. Such allegations obviously have a factual basis. Ratings are the lingua franca of broadcasting, and little is to be gained by arguing otherwise. As commercial advertising media, with no subscription income (except for PBS stations), the financial health of each broadcasting enterprise must be ensured to maintain the many program services that may not be self-sufficient.

A major misperception in making ratings the scapegoat is the failure to understand that they are only the end result, not the cause. Ratings cancel no programs, sell no spots, revise no schedules, negotiate no make-goods—ratings *users* do. The same can be said for sales and profit figures produced by accountants. They too are a managerial tool to guide decisions directed to maintaining a healthy, profitable enterprise.

The Carnegie Commission on the Future of Public Broadcasting in its report "A Public Trust" quotes Gary Steiner.[2]

> At the end of a concert at Carnegie Hall, Walter Damrosch asked Rachmaninoff what sublime thoughts had passed through his head as he stared out into the audience during the playing of his concerto. "I was counting the house," said Rachmaninoff. The principal test of public broadcasting's accountability to the community is whether anybody is listening or watching.

. . . PBS is a regular subscriber to and user of national and local ratings reports. The BBC had its own rating service for many years. Ratings services operate in scores of countries around the world, from Switzerland to Hong Kong. Many of these broadcasting systems are government operated and/or non-commercial. Broadcasters have to make a greater effort to "count the house" than the concert artist, theater manager, or ball-club owner because of the intangible character of the audience.

The intellectual and cultural level of our society is not what our elitist critics wish it to be. The average American looks to TV primarily for light entertainment, something to take the pressure off, help him or her relax and forget the day's problems. The commercial networks and independent stations (programming similar fare but with greater emphasis on movies and sports) have continued to garner close to 90 percent of all television viewing, despite the "higher-quality" program offerings of public television stations and the variety of cable television originations. With live opera, symphony, and ballet performances, National Geographic specials, the McNeil-Lehrer News Hour, and the best of BBC drama in its schedule, PBS was able to capture only an average audience share of 3 percent in the spring of 1984. Two cable networks, dedicated to supplying subscribers with "quality programs," folded after less than a year's operation. Can Nielsen or network executives be held accountable for the failure of the public to select such programs?

What about people in the television establishment itself? Here we find distrust of ratings greatest among the creative people, who often believe it is an unfair and faulty form of report card.

No one has better analyzed the conflict between program creation and broadcast research than Paul Klein, whose credentials to do so are impeccable. Klein contends.[3]

> ... probably in no area of research other than television is the criterion variable fed back to you so quickly—usually within weeks, maybe even days. TV ratings might well be the fastest dependent variable in research history.

> Why is the rating so important to us? Why do we hold our breath every day when we come to work? Because our pricing, our scheduling, our budgeting, our jobs all are dependent on our ability to predict this number with reasonable accuracy. If we miss in our forecast, it costs us money—either "lost opportunity" money through underpricing, or "makegood" money through overpricing. In both cases these are real dollars. . . .

> The creative people sometimes feel they should have the right to a "quality" program regardless of the ratings. They resent the fact that they are forced to accept audience popularity as part of the standard by which they are to be judged. . . .

> The creative person's concern that "research corrupts" means in part that "research tries to channel me into playing the numbers game. I want to remain true to the standards of my art." Ultimately, of course, there is no option. We are, all of us, in the communications business—and the business of business is making money. . . .

> One factor that is often omitted in discussions of research is that the fact that we *have* the research doesn't mean we have to *use* it—we can choose to ignore it. To have information about viewer attitudes towards a program is not in and of itself a threat to creative integrity. It is the potential of pressure to "do something about it" that is the underlying concern. But that is not *research* pressure (though it may be management pressure, expressed or implied).

One can easily see that Klein is following the stern admonition of Samuel Johnson: "Sir, no man but a blockhead ever wrote except for money."

Perhaps William S. Paley, -longtime CBS chairman and the dean of network programmers, expressed the dilemma best. In early 1980 at age 79 he was having overnight audience ratings phoned to him at home every morning because of the close CBS–ABC rating race. He explained, "I don't think people always understand that television is a mass medium. I care about quality, but I also care about the bottom line."[4]

The pressure for high ratings is alleged to result in local news organizations seeking sensational and lurid topics, especially during sweeps weeks. This is when series on abortion, teen pregnancy, incest, rape, child abuse, and so on are unveiled, it is charged. The accusations are not baseless, but the dimensions of the practice and the extent of its influence on ratings are overblown. Local news ratings and revenue are critical for stations. They can't risk losing any share to competitors during a rating period and therefore present promotable features for the early and late news shows. Journalistic practices and ethics are probably not much different in television than in newspapers. Some take the sensational route, others focus on investigative reporting of local politics and education, suspected chicanery by elected officials, or upcoming city budget crunches. As discussed above, the incentive for such shenanigans would quickly wither if the sweeps weeks were replaced by 52-week surveying.

The print field is not without its exponents of large audience numbers. *Newsweek* has had six top editors and seven presidents in the past 12 years. *Time* magazine, commenting on the January 1984 editor change, states:[5] "One major reason for the frequent turnover, according to company executives," is owner Katherine Graham's "dissatisfaction with the pace of *Newsweek*'s efforts to catch up with *Time*." The 1982–1983 comparisons showed *Time* widening its lead in both

circulation and ad revenue—the "ratings" that count in the magazine business.

The president and chief executive officer of *U.S. News & World Report*, James H. McIlhenny, frankly says; "In the ancient marketplace promoters provided minstrels and jugglers for entertainment to attract people to the market. We provide news, *People* provides gossip, and *Playboy* magazine provides lust to attract people . . . our advertisers come to our market not so much because we sell them but because we deliver a known market of buyers."[6]

The charge that ratings encourage imitation (and by implication discourage "truly creative" efforts) is frequently heard. For example, Eric Barnouw says, "Many executives say their personal preferences would move them in other directions but that their duty is to mass preferences as evidenced by quantifiable trends. Such evidence—as in Nielsen ratings—inevitably encourages imitation of current successes."[7] True enough, but is imitation of current successes a legacy attributable to broadcast ratings alone?

In discussing the phenomenal success of Rupert Murdoch as a multinational publisher, Tom O'Hanlon[8] comments, "Murdoch will give a job to anyone who can make a sales chart move," and quotes Murdoch's view that " . . . the problem with U.S. journalism is that they simply don't know how to compete." O'Hanlon, explaining Murdoch's Fleet Street background, writes:

. . . at a time when many U.S. newspapers are dying and the public is turning to the tube, the British daily press continues to get bought and read. If the American press struggles to advance social justice and to achieve something called responsibility, the British press struggles to be bright and inventive and to be involved with what actually interests ordinary men and women.

Robert Dahlin, a long-time observer of the book field, in discussing publishers' successes and failures, states: "We should remember that nobility of publishing is anchored, however loosely, in the bottom line." In reporting the phenomenal and unexpected success of *In Search of Excellence: Lessons from America's Best Run Companies* by Thomas J. Peters and Robert H. Waterman, Dahlin says: "Now similar books are scheduled from a variety of publishers."[9] A smash hit musical on Broadway is invariably followed by many others (*Chorus Line, Forty-second Street, On Your Toes, Evita,* for example). Hollywood imitative cycles are legendary, ranging from space drama to horror films to single parents to spy pictures. The astonishing success of the Cabbage Patch Kids brought almost instant imitators. Magazine successes featuring female nudity, health and exercise, personal finance, travel, and home computers quickly experienced numerous imitators. Is it somehow more legitimate to imitate on the basis of dollar or unit sales, box-office attendance, or circulation than for higher ratings, which are the prime broadcasting audience gauge?

VIEWING PUBLIC'S INTEREST

In the final analysis, the fundamental question to be answered is, "Do ratings serve the viewing public's interest?" The first answer is that, so far as can be ascertained, no one has proposed an alternative feedback system. A mass medium requires mass audience for success. Broadcast management needs audience response data for programming, selling, promotion, and many other purposes;

advertisers who invest more than $20 billion annually in television, radio, and cable must have vast amounts of detailed audience data, which their agencies analyze, evaluate, and act on in an accountable manner; creative program producing and syndicating organizations need data on audience size and changes in public tastes as indicated by trends in program popularity. Ancillary data, qualitative or otherwise, may be useful, but there is no substitute for a basic quantitative "head count." That's true for every commercial publication, play, movie, professional sport, or concert feature. It seems even to be accepted in radio—it is only in the television medium that critics condemn audience counts as evil instruments.

A root cause of this criticism is the elite's dislike of much television program fare. The intelligentsia would appear to be quite willing to deprive the blue- and white-collar workers of their beer and pretzels if they themselves could have wine and cheese instead. That is the road to disaster for the television medium, as well as for those viewers who would find their favorite programs scratched for entertainment and information they have voted against time and time again. Does this meet what the FCC requires of its licensees—that they operate in the public interest, convenience, and necessity?

Television is an intrusive medium. It is difficult to view it at all without being exposed to programs (or program elements) one may not like. It's not as easy to scan and skip as one does in reading a newspaper or magazine. The all-pervasive power of television as the quintessential mass medium does not encourage the program of highly specialized interest. Perhaps the newer video forms—cable, video cassettes, teletext, and videotex—will be better suited to the narrowcasting mode.

As already stated, ratings are actually a form of taskmaster. That report card, delivered every day to network executives (and to station managers in major markets) represents facts that will not go away. The show that doesn't measure up, that indicates serious audience weakness, must eventually be jettisoned, even though the executives involved in that decision personally like it. Otherwise, a diminished lead-in will damage the audience level of following programs, and that entire evening's schedule is jeopardized. This is the essence of the free competitive broadcasting system.

Faltering program series may be canceled quickly, moved to what may be a less competitive spot, or removed temporarily for further work or for a more favorable environment. Schedules constantly shift, and probes for adversarial weaknesses are made by specials and miniseries. . . .

In [a Roper Poll from 1982], television was chosen by 65 percent of respondents as the source of "most of your news about what's going on in the world today"; newspapers were named by 44 percent, radio 18 percent.

Another national poll on leisure time . . . [from] May 1982 showed television as the most popular leisure activity, with 72 percent saying they watched television every day or almost every day. Respondents estimated that they have an average of 4½ hours of leisure time a day and that they spend about 2 hours 50 minutes (63 percent of the total) watching television. Ratings surveys show that these recall estimates are understatements—Nielsen data for a comparable period showed that the average TV household tunes to television about 6½

hours a day and the average person age 12 + watches about 4 hours daily.

The *TV Guide* circulation of 17 million, the record sale of 20 million TV sets in the United States in 1983 (consistently outpaced in 1984) and the burgeoning sales of home video cassette recorders, which are principally used to record and play back commercial television programs, are tangible testaments to the American public's favorable reaction to and involvement in the output of television and cable.

Every time a network makes a substitution, it is testing a new program that it has reason to believe could do better than its predecessor. The audience gains by constantly getting new choices of programs from the three networks.

William Rubens, NBC vice president for research, recently said:[10]

Let me remind you that we want to present popular entertainment and news to as many people as possible. As far as we know, we reflect society's values, and I think there is more evidence that the media are socialized by the audience than that the audience is socialized by the media. In other words, you viewers out there have much more effect on us than we have on you.

A keen and objective student of mass media, Dr. W. Russell Newman, co-director, Research Program on Communications Policy, Massachusetts Institute of Technology, believes that:[11]

A . . . mechanism of media influence seems to be a pattern of cultural homogenization . . . emphasizing common elements of audience appeal and incorporating cultural strands into the mainstream. . . . The American public is not held hostage by the technology of television. The rating system makes the networks very responsive to changing audience tastes and interest. . . . The elements of adventure, humor, violence, sex and politics have been consistently predominant in the primordial myths, nineteenth-century novels and modern media fare (perhaps in roughly equal proportion).

Dr. Newman concludes: "Those who feel the media stifle and constrain diversity might pause to consider to what extent the media have and will continue to reflect the strong commonalities of human interests and concerns."

Time magazine in an editorial comment[12] following a deep scrutiny of the jury system in 1982, wrote: "TIME observes that trial by jury realizes an essential democratic ideal; that a citizen's security is best protected not by any institutional or intellectual elite, but by the common sense of his fellow citizens . . . " In a meaningful way, ratings are also an expression of democracy in action—viewers and listeners have free choice of a wide variety of free entertainment, news, and information. No other medium anywhere in the world can match the variety and quality of the total output of the programs that weather our ratings system to reach the American public.

NOTES

1. Joel Swerdlow, "The Ratings Game," *Washington Journalism Review*, Washington, D.C., October 1979.
2. Gary Steiner, *The Creative Organization* (Chicago: University of Chicago Press, 1965), p. 207, cited in *A Public Trust: The Report of the Carnegie Commission on the Future of Public Broadcasting* (New York: Bantam Books, Inc., 1979).
3. Paul L. Klein, "*TV Program Creation and Broadcast Research:* Conflict or Harmony?", New York, Chapter/AMA Conference, Waldorf Astoria Hotel, April 13, 1981.
4. Tony Schwartz, "An Intimate Talk with William Paley," *New York Times Magazine*, December 28, 1980.
5. "Newsweek's Outsider Bows Out," *Time*, January 16, 1984.
6. *Marketing News*, October 29, 1982, p. 12.
7. Eric Barnouw, *The Sponsor* (New York: Oxford University Press, 1978), p. 113.
8. Tom O'Hanlon, "What Does This Man Want?", *Forbes*, January 20, 1984.
9. Robert Dahlin, "Commentary on the Unpredictability of Readers," *The Christian Science Monitor*, November 4, 1983.
10. William S. Rubens, "The Role of Media on Democratic Policy," presentation to the National Decisions Program Seminar, Political Science Department, University of Pennsylvania, October 1983.
11. W. Russell Newman, "Communications Technology and Cultural Diversity," paper presented at American Sociological Association annual meeting, San Francisco, California, September 1982.
12. *Time* magazine advertisement in *Advertising Age*, April 1982, p. 39.

NO

Todd Gitlin

BY THE NUMBERS

If program tests are automatically soft, audience ratings might appear hard. Network corridors and production lots hum with talk of last week's, even last night's numbers. Research executives spend hours on the phone with programmers, relaying the numbers that will become the talk of today's lunches: *ratings*, expressed as a percentage of all the television households in the country, and *shares*, expressed as a percentage of all the households that are watching television during one particular period. Numbers are industry gold and executives are the managers waiting for up-to-the-minute reports from their mines. The common obsession is: Which network is number one for the week, the month, the year? Who's up, who's down? One's chances for promotion might hang on the ratings for programs one has developed or defended. In the back of the network's collective mind, everyone knows that company profits hang on the numbers, which become the basis for advertising rates.

Each year the numbers have seemed to come in faster, glory and ignominy becoming virtually instantaneous. By 1973, as the networks grew more competitive and the technology of audience measurement more sophisticated, it became possible to measure major market results overnight, through special samples run by the A. C. Nielsen Company in New York, Chicago, Los Angeles, San Francisco, and, since 1982, Philadelphia and Detroit. Now executives like to say, as CBS's Steve Mills puts it, "We get a daily report card. This is one of the few businesses in the world I know where a guy comes to work every morning and looks to see how he did the day before."

Veterans gaze back fondly at the good old days when ratings weren't much mentioned unless a show did abysmally. "Occasionally we got a really disastrously low rating on *Playhouse 90*, like a seven share," the longtime CBS and NBC executive Ethel Winant remembers, "and someone would mention it to us. But it wasn't like a call from someone saying, 'My God, it's a disaster!' It was just an interesting statistical thing." When Nielsen started its Television Index in 1950, delivery of the national audience ratings took six weeks. In 1961, delivery improved to six-teen days; in 1967, nine days; in 1973, a week. "It used to be a couple of weeks before you knew you were a failure," Winant recalls. "And so it didn't matter anymore. You were on to something else. Now everybody talks about the ratings. Competition has made us crazy."

Competition and measurement tech-nique accelerated in tandem. Indeed, the "overnights" were the fruit of a technol-ogy Nielsen would probably not have developed had competition-crazed net-works not created a market for it. By 1976, when ABC first overtook CBS as the top-rated network, competition had revved to a whine, and the greater the competition, the more public attention was paid to it. By the late seventies, major newspapers were listing the week's top-rated shows, stock market analysts and major investors as well as fans were paying heed, and all this attention was cycling back to the networks in the form of still more intense competition. The drive to keep up with the latest numbers became so intense that abstention seemed odd, requiring explanation. One day, when I asked Grant Tinker, as newly appointed NBC chairman, about the rat-ings of a controversial movie broadcast the night before, he said, "I try not to keep up with the overnights. People in my company are amazed that I don't give a rat's ass about the overnights."

While Tinker may have disdained the fetish of immediate numerical gratifica-tion, he could scarcely afford indif-ference to the overall ratings. I asked him how close to the front of his conscious-ness he kept the price of RCA stock. "Very close," he said. He could not per-mit his idealism about quality "to get in front of the viability, the profitability, of the business. That is my primary man-date, to make sure NBC is healthy." The difference between the more and less enlightened top executives is that the more enlightened try to build schedules for longer-term strength, for next year or the year after that, while the others con-centrate on next week and next month and claim that the farsighted have no choice, since the next week looks so dis-mal for them. Short-term or long-term, network purpose rests on the ratings.

Then how good are the ratings? Most producers and writers are skeptical or downright hostile. Many blacks and His-panics in the industry believe that the Nielsen sample underrepresents minor-ities because Nielsen employees are loath to tread into the ghettoes. Devotees of "quality" think it overrepresents heavy TV watchers, the proverbial beer guzz-lers who wander in and out of the living room, easily satisfied with fluff. More-over, they argue, Nielsen doesn't mea-sure anyone's satisfaction, but only the raw numbers of households and eye-balls. Indisputably, Nielsen's sample is small. In May 1982, 1,260 households were hooked up to Audimeter boxes re-cording the stations tuned to, with 1,121 reporting on the average day.* Common sense, innocent of the theory of statistical sampling, finds it hard to believe that so few households can represent the entire television-viewing population of the United States; each Nielsen household "represents" almost 70,000 actual households!

*The sample runs higher in the winter months. For purposes of demographic breakdown, Nielsen also maintains a separate diary sample in which selected households record who is watch-ing which programs. In May 1982 this sample ran to 2,563 households, of which 1,828 reported on the average day. Late that year, Nielsen an-nounced plans to enlarge its Audimeter sample to provide statistically significant numbers for less-watched cable and satellite channels.

There is no way to explore these suspicions without a certain amount of statistical inquiry, but I shall try to keep it short and sweet. Intuition notwithstanding, the sample-size issue is a red herring. If the sample had been drawn perfectly at random from the national population, it would have been large enough so that the standard error on a rating of 20 would have been 1.2; that is, if a show were actually watched in 20 percent of the nation's households, the odds are 68 percent that the Nielsen rating would fall between 18.8 and 21.2, and 95 percent that it would fall between 17.6 and 22.4. The sample sizes and standard errors fall in the same range as national Gallup and Harris surveys. Network research executives point out that the Nielsen household figures are more rigorous, less a function of interpretation, since they measure an unambiguous fact (television set switched on to a certain channel) rather than a response to a potentially loaded question about attitudes or voting intentions.

If Nielsen has an important flaw, it would have to lie not in the size of the sample but in its representativeness. The Nielsen Company selects its initial sample randomly according to accepted statistical practice. The problem is that not everyone chosen for the sample agrees to install the Nielsen Audimeter devices. Congressional hearings in 1963 brought out the fact that fewer than half of the designated Nielsen sample cooperated. Goaded by congressional scrutiny, Nielsen raised its payments to cooperating households and pushed its staff to solicit more aggressively. By 1966, the cooperation rate had risen to about 75 percent. But although an industry-wide committee urged Nielsen to push on to an 80 percent cooperation rate, the rate

proceeded—as in all other statistical surveys during this age of public suspicion—to slump. By 1979, the Nielsen cooperation rate had sagged to 70 percent; in 1980, to 67 percent. The question is, are people who refuse to sign on different from people who do sign on in a way that affects the patterns of their viewing?

Such questions concern the industry, partly because advertisers rely on the credibility of the Nielsen sample, and partly because sloppy statistics make for bad public relations. The 1963 congressional hearings were brought about by some scandalously sloppy methods. In their wake, therefore, the three networks and the National Association of Broadcasters established a joint research group on the ratings, the Committee on Nationwide Television Audience Measurements, or CONTAM. The big problem was how to tell what noncooperators were doing, since by definition these were the people who refused to allow the Nielsen boxes into their homes. CONTAM decided, reasonably enough, to inquire by telephone. Since Nielsen numbers of cooperators and noncooperators were too small to produce statistically significant results, the 1964 CONTAM study turned to a much larger but similarly selected and solicited population, the 200,000 households picked by the American Research Bureau (ARB) for its November 1963 "sweep." (These large samples, gathered three months each year, give the networks and local stations the circulation figures from which to set new advertising rates.) ARB supplied the phone numbers of some 175,000, of whom more than half, 94,000, were dialed. By the time unreliable interviews were weeded out, 84,302 were available; about one-third were with people who had cooperated with ARB, while the rest had originally refused to keep TV-watching diaries.

The results of this and later studies showed, as critics had charged, that cooperators did indeed watch somewhat more television than noncooperators. The cooperators were also younger, better educated, and lived in larger families. More to the point, their tastes ran, if anything, toward the more ambitious programs. Of forty-two programs checked, five ran at least 20 percent higher in the cooperators' ratings than in the total group. Among them were *East Side, West Side* and *That Was the Week That Was*. (Seven ran lower in the cooperators' ratings, only three of them by as much as 5 percent: *Rawhide, Breaking Point,* and *The Price Is Right,* the last hardly a case of an intelligent show undercounted in the ratings.) But the rankings of shows most popular among cooperators were barely different from rankings in the total sample. Of the ten ranked highest by the cooperators, nine also ranked highest in the total sample; and the same ratio held for the lowest-ranked. In other words, the major difference between the two groups was that the cooperators were disproportionately inclined toward the two most irreverent, politically liberal, and convention-subverting programs on the air: *East Side, West Side,* in which George C. Scott played a social worker trying, and failing, to solve the social problems of the ghetto (later in the series the Scott character concluded that social problems required political solutions, and joined the staff of a reform congressman); and *TW3,* a topical satire softened from its English origin but still genially acerbic. Assuming Nielsen noncooperators were like people who refused to keep ARB diaries—and there was no rea-son not to—the Nielsen ratings were then skewed toward programs favored by the young and better-educated.

Are there then other factors tending to undermine the representativeness of the Nielsen sample? Between them, critics and CONTAM have considered several more conceivable sources of bias: (1) Before 1964, Nielsen excluded the 4 percent of households in the Mountain Time Zone; this was rapidly remedied, although periodically some western stations argue they are still undercounted.* (2) It is conceivable that Nielsen Audimeter signals and ARB diary entries are inaccurate, or could be misread or misinterpreted. (3) Possibly some Nielsen households keep their sets turned on even when not viewing—to vote, in effect, for their favorite shows. (4) As they age, the households also grow less representative of the population, and they differ in the important respect of knowing, after all, that they are Nielsen households. The 1963 hearings revealed that some Nielsen households had been kept in the sample for a dozen years. Beginning in 1966, however, Nielsen responded to criticism by instituting a 20 percent annual turnover in the household sample, and 33 percent in its personal diaries, but even this rate could lock in certain tastes longer than they deserve. (5) Through 1963, the congressional investigators found, Nielsen violated some of its own strictures in choosing counties to sample, and some Nielsen fieldmen departed from acceptable survey practice in choosing households to substitute for noncooperators. (6) Nielsen counts only viewers in

---

*Nielsen still excludes Alaska and Hawaii, which air mainland shows late, but these states include only 0.6 percent of the U.S. population.

houses and apartments. In 1970, 2.9 percent of the population at any given time were living in institutions, military barracks, dormitories, boardinghouses, hotels, and motels. (7) It has also been charged that the Nielsen sample is not properly weighted for demographic factors including age and, most controversially, race.

Random errors cannot, of course, be ruled out. But with the exception of the race and age issues, it is not clear in what systematic direction, if at all, these factors in the aggregate would bias the Nielsen numbers for particular shows. What counts in decision-making, after all, are not absolute Nielsen numbers but their relative positions. To investigate the possible effects of all these confounding factors, CONTAM in 1964 matched Nielsen Audimeter ratings against ARB diary figures, and found they corresponded remarkably well; nineteen of the twenty highest-rated Nielsen shows were also among the ARB top twenty. More to the point, in 1969 and 1970 CONTAM checked Nielsen figures with sophisticated telephone surveys. The telephone and Nielsen figures matched within 1 or 2 percent, well within the limits of sampling error. There remains the logical possibility that Nielsen and ARB share a systematic bias with telephone surveys. People could be systematically lying, for example, about what they watch. Yet there is no particular reason to believe all three populations would be inclined to lie in the same fashion.

If cooperator bias tilts the Nielsen and ARB samples toward the younger and more educated, and the poor also have fewer phones, are the preferences of blacks, Hispanics, older people, and the poor being systematically under-

counted? Advertisers might not mind if this were the case; these people are not big buyers anyway. We do know that blacks and Hispanics are drastically underrepresented in filling out the diaries that record the members of the household (as opposed to total households) who view for Nielsen and ARB. According to one study, only 15 to 20 percent of Hispanics mailed back viewing diaries in English or Spanish, compared with 55 percent of the general population. Blacks and Hispanics might also be under-included in the Nielsen household survey, for two reasons. The first is that Nielsen draws its samples from census data. If the Census Bureau still undercounts the housing units of the poor, as minority groups have charged in the past, then the Nielsen sample, too, would be, as former NBC executive Paul Klein says, "upslanted." The second reason is that, in most surveys, the less educated are less likely to cooperate even if asked and the less educated are still disproportionately black and Hispanic. On the other hand, it is conceivable that since the cooperator studies of the early sixties, the less educated have become more willing to sign on as Nielsen households, whether for pride, money, or the desire to affect the ratings. Feeling some heat from critics, Nielsen began to offer black families $2 a month, twice the regular payment.

Although they still do not disclose the ethnic composition of their samples, Nielsen and ARB also began to change their system for choosing samples and weighting results. As advertisers grew more interested in demographic breakdowns in the seventies, and the networks followed suit, the rating companies set out to produce more precise counts of the audience in general, not just the number of households. It remains true, though, that counts of viewers, which depend on the tenacity, literacy, and veracity of diary-keepers, will always remain less reliable than the automatic, electronically scored Nielsen Audimeter signals.

Plainly the Nielsen system has had its shortcomings, but in the end there are strong pressures to keep it honest. For one thing, advertisers want to get their money's worth, and therefore want a count that is at least internally consistent. If it is in the interest of the networks to overcount their audience—or at least the wealthiest eighteen- to forty-nine-year-old segment that spends the most money—it is assuredly not in their interest to lose credibility with advertisers who pay the networks' way.

In any event, network executives are satisfied that the Nielsens are accurate and reliable; their research executives assure them that it's so. "I think it's among the finest research that is done in the social sciences," Arnold Becker says. "And to the degree that they are somewhat imprecise, in terms of the actual precise number of millions, they are not imprecise in terms of ranking what is most popular to least popular. And that's all that matters." In other words, it remains possible that factors yet undiscovered affect the accuracy of Nielsen numbers as measures of total audience size, but unlikely that such hypothetical factors would affect their use in measuring relative ratings.

Still, in the tumult of everyday figuring and judging, network executives, even research specialists, often commit the standard occupational error of unwarranted precision. When Nielsen publishes its figures every two weeks, it reminds subscribers of the standard errors, but executives functionally forget what they were taught in elementary statistics: that all survey statistics are valid only within predictable margins of error. For example, the 1981–82 series rankings showed *Dynasty* in twentieth place with a 20.4 season rating and *Hill Street Blues* in twenty-ninth place with 18.6. But statistically there was a 10 percent chance the two shows actually drew the same size audience. Once managers agree to accept a measure, they act as if it is precise. They "know" there are standard errors—but what a nuisance it would be to act on that knowledge. And so the number system has an impetus of its own. In the heat of scheduling meetings, researchers don't remind the assembled executives that the numbers are imprecise. Over the long haul, the numbers are "good enough," and the long haul is what statistics are good for. Executives compose schedules, not shows. But shows are renewed or canceled one at a time, and in the short run, so the cancellation of a show like *Lou Grant* may hang on a collective forgetting that its ratings figures are, in fact, imprecise.

Then, too, the intensity and significance of viewing are beyond Nielsen's ken. The numbers measure only sample sets tuned in, not necessarily shows watched, let alone grasped, remembered, loved, learned from, deeply anticipated, or mildly tolerated. The John and Mary Markle Foundation is attempting to work up a system for getting "qualitative ratings," measurements of the intensity of "the viewing experience." The networks are only mildly interested. After all, the current system works toward its intended purpose. Whatever Nielsen measures, it measures consistently. The ratings are like the Gross National Product, Paul Klein once said. They measure something connected with audience size, but exactly what is irrelevant, for they measure the same thing in the same way week after week, year to year, and therefore the relative differences and shifts over time should be taken seriously. The numbers are a currency for transactions. Given their commitments to gross efficiency in time and dollars, what else are networks and advertising companies to use?

The top network executives pride themselves on intuition, experience, and seasoning, on their instinct for the popular; but at each annual scheduling meeting the top research executives are always included among the five to ten people who buy, renew, and drop shows. They are there to be on tap, not on top, advising on the demographics of audiences and the consistency of evening-long blocs; but their voices are strong. They may differ with programmers on tactics and the weight of factors, but many programmers are former researchers and they are marketers all. The limits of numbers are clear: They always have to be interpreted, and of course they measure only the past, not the future. But absent a clear standard of taste or a strong sense of traditional form, absent any clear aesthetic or moral values in the mass market or in the executive suites, the numbers have the great virtue of being there, looking radiantly exact.

Audience measurement looms larger in network tactics, too, as the three-network competition grows more intense and the networks seemingly less adept at reading the public mind. The increasing sophistication of the technology for gathering and distributing the numbers matches the frenzy of short-term thinking that arose in the seventies, when scheduling became a year-round affair. As the numbers came in faster and faster,

the networks began to dump failing series within a month or two, or to take them off the air for a major retooling of tone, or cast, or (as in the case of *Cagney and Lacey*) both. As the psychologist and television-effects researcher Percy Tannenbaum says, you resort to a shotgun when your aim is bad. Gone were the days when a show was ordered in thirty-nine episodes for the year. With rising costs and rising competition, the number sank to twenty-six, then twenty-two, even to thirteen. By 1980, the networks were ordering iffy new shows only four or six episodes at a time. Two or three bad weeks and the show could be banished forever. Producers gaze back nostalgically to the days when unusual shows like *All in the Family*, *The Mary Tyler Moore Show*, *M*A*S*H*, and *Lou Grant* started out slowly but got a chance to build their audience, taking off only late in the season, or even, in the case of *Lou Grant*, during summer reruns. Reliance on numbers, which once promised stability of judgment, plays a part in producing frenetic change. As on Broadway and in the bookstores, a combination of profit pressure, fierce competition, and rising costs gives new goods less and less time to prove themselves. All the more pressure on the medium to cater quickly, unambiguously, to whatever component of audience taste seems to rise to the surface at a given moment and holds out the possibility of being measured simply. But the haste to make investments pay off quickly is no better for art, even for entertainment, than it is for wine.

POSTSCRIPT

Do Ratings Serve the Viewing Public's Interest?

Obviously, the networks are concerned about ratings and use them to help make programming decisions. So they do provide useful information for programmers. Do they, however, reflect public diversity? Are they a useful feedback mechanism for reflecting public taste? If they are flawed or misused, what are the implications for commercial media systems and for the public at large?

Roger Wimmer and Joseph Dominick in *Mass Media Research: An Introduction*, (2nd edition) (Wadsworth, 1987) introduce ratings research, as do Fletcher et al. in *Handbook of Radio and TV Broadcasting: Research Procedures in Audience, Program and Revenues* (Van Nostrand Reinhold, 1981). Probably the most comprehensive book on ratings is the one by Beville from which you have just read an excerpt. It covers radio, television, and cable services; compares methodologies; examines the issue of qualitative versus quantitative ratings; discusses how ratings are used; and examines governmental involvement in investigations of ratings services and systems.

Of course, program ratings are important because they are used to establish the prices for which advertising can be sold. Erik Barnouw talks about the advertising end of the business in *The Sponsor: Notes on a Modern Potentate* (Oxford, 1978).

ISSUE 14

Is Advertising Ethical?

YES: Theodore Levitt, from "The Morality (?) of Advertising," *Harvard Business Review* 48 (July/August 1970)

NO: Raymond Williams, from "Advertising: The Magic System," *Problems in Materialism and Culture* (Verso Publications, 1980)

ISSUE SUMMARY

YES: Harvard Business School professor Theodore Levitt presents a philosophical treatment of the human values of advertising as compared with the values of other "imaginative" disciplines and argues that embellishment is expected by consumers.

NO: Author Raymond Williams, who taught media courses at Open University in London, argues that advertising has surpassed its initial goal of selling goods and services and has become involved with the teaching of social and personal values and exploits the weaknesses of capitalist societies.

Dallas Smythe first described commercial media as a system for delivering audiences to advertisers. This perception of the viewing public as a "market" for products as well as an audience for advertising—a main source of media revenue—reflects the economic orientation of our current media system. The unplanned side effects of advertising, however, concern many critics. For example, socialization into consumption, consumerism, and materialism and high expectations are one set of concerns. Expectation of personal reward is probably the major basis of influence. Many of the questions are very familiar: Is advertising deceptive? Does it create or perpetuate stereotypes? Does it create conformity? Does it create insecurity in order to sell goods? Does it cause people to buy things that they do not really need?

The effects of advertising are highly dependent upon frequency and predominance of exposure, with attention a necessary condition. Involvement in advertising messages tends to be low, but that does not hinder advertising from having an influence. There has been a tremendous amount of proprietary research—research done for a corporation and not available to the general public—on how to increase advertising's effectiveness. Surprisingly, available evidence from research does not indicate that advertising is unusually persuasive in its attempts to influence buying.

Despite the debate on the effectiveness of advertising, many millions of dollars are spent on advertising.

Theodore Levitt undertakes a defense of advertising, arguing that it should be compared to art. It is not intended to be a literal representation of truth in the real world but rather an embellished offering of expected benefits. If products delivers the benefits that consumers expect, then advertising is perfectly acceptable.

Raymond Williams, on the other hand, rejects the claims of advertising as a service and characterizes it instead as a monstrous exploitation of the weaknesses of individuals living in a confused society. (His central criticism is that advertising is the consequence of a social failure to find public information and to make decisions over a wide range of everyday economic choices.)

If advertising is an art—simply a transformation of the mundane by embellishment, which is expected and understood by all—then surely advertising is a harmless addition to our lives. Can it do real harm? What if it offers relief for the pangs of social inferiority—pangs that advertising sometimes creates at the same time it offers solutions. Is advertising a harmless American business practice that helps the economy by keeping goods and services, especially new goods, flowing? Or is it a fundamentally unethical practice that offers false remedies to major and minor social problems? Or is it even more importantly one of the mechanisms by which the organization of the market becomes the organization of the individual?

YES

Theodore Levitt

THE MORALITY (?) OF ADVERTISING

A BROAD VIEWPOINT REQUIRED

Most people spend their money carefully. Understandably, they look out for larcenous attempts to separate them from it. Few men in business will deny the right, perhaps even the wisdom, of people today asking for some restraint on advertising, or at least for more accurate information on the things they buy and for more consumer protection.

Yet, if we speak in the same breath about consumer protection and about advertising's distortions, exaggerations, and deceptions, it is easy to confuse two quite separate things—the legitimate purpose of advertising and the abuses to which it may be put. Rather than deny that distortion and exaggeration exist in advertising, in this article I shall argue that embellishment and distortion are among advertising's legitimate and socially desirable purposes; and that illegitimacy in advertising consists only of falsification with larcenous intent. And while it is difficult, as a practical matter, to draw the line between legitimate distortion and essential falsehood, I want to take a long look at the distinction that exists between the two. This I shall say in advance—the distinction is not as simple, obvious, or great as one might think. . . .

What Is Reality?

What, indeed? Consider poetry. Like advertising, poetry's purpose is to influence an audience; to affect its perceptions and sensibilities; perhaps even to change its mind. Like rhetoric, poetry's intent is to convince and seduce. In the service of that intent, it employs without guilt or fear of criticism all the arcane tools of distortion that the literary mind can devise. Keats does not offer a truthful engineering description of his Grecian urn. He offers, instead, with exquisite attention to the effects of meter, rhyme, allusion, illusion, metaphor, and sound, a lyrical, exaggerated, distorted, and palpably false description. And he is thoroughly applauded for it, as are all other artists, in whatever medium, who do precisely this same thing successfully.

Commerce, it can be said without apology, takes essentially the same liberties with reality and literality as the artist, except that commerce calls its creations advertising, or industrial design, or packaging. As with art, the purpose is to influence the audience by creating illusions, symbols, and implications that promise more than pure functionality. Once, when asked what his company did, Charles Revson of Revlon, Inc. suggested a profound distinction: "In the factory we make cosmetics; in the store we sell hope." He obviously has no illusions. It is not cosmetic chemicals women want, but the seductive charm promised by the alluring symbols with which these chemicals have been surrounded—hence the rich and exotic packages in which they are sold, and the suggestive advertising with which they are promoted.

Commerce usually embellishes its products thrice: first, it designs the product to be pleasing to the eye, to suggest reliability, and so forth; second, it packages the product as attractively as it feasibly can; and then it advertises this attractive package with inviting pictures, slogans, descriptions, songs, and so on. The package and design are as important as the advertising.

The Grecian vessel, for example, was used to carry liquids, but that function does not explain why the potter decorated it with graceful lines and elegant drawings in black and red. A woman's compact carries refined talc, but this does not explain why manufacturers try to make these boxes into works of decorative art.

Neither the poet nor the ad man celebrates the literal functionality of what he produces. Instead, each celebrates a deep and complex emotion which he symbolizes by creative embellishment—a content which cannot be captured by literal description alone. Communication, through advertising or through poetry or any other medium, is a creative conceptualization that implies a vicarious experience through a language of symbolic substitutes. Communication can never be the real thing it talks about. Therefore, all communication is in some inevitable fashion a departure from reality.

Everything Is Changed . . .
Poets, novelists, playwrights, composers, and fashion designers have one thing more in common. They all deal in symbolic communication. None is satisfied with nature in the raw, as it was on the day of creation. None is satisfied to tell it exactly "like it is" to the naked eye, as do the classified ads. It is the purpose of all art to alter nature's surface reality, to reshape, to embellish, and to augment what nature has so crudely fashioned, and then to present it to the same applauding humanity that so eagerly buys Revson's exotically advertised cosmetics.

Few, if any, of us accept the natural state in which God created us. We scrupulously select our clothes to suit a multiplicity of simultaneous purposes, not only for warmth, but manifestly for such other purposes as propriety, status, and seduction. Women modify, embellish, and amplify themselves with colored paste for the lips and powders and lotions for the face; men as well as women use devices to take hair off the face and others to put it on the head. Like the inhabitants of isolated African regions, where not a single whiff of advertising has ever intruded, we all encrust ourselves with rings, pendants, bracelets, neckties, clips, chains, and snaps.

Man lives neither in sackcloth nor in sod huts—although these are not notably inferior to tight clothes and overheated dwellings in congested and polluted cities. Everywhere man rejects nature's uneven blessings. He molds and repackages to his own civilizing specifications an otherwise crude, drab, and generally oppressive reality. He does it so that life may be made for the moment more tolerable than God evidently designed it to be. As T.S. Eliot once remarked, "Human kind cannot bear very much reality."

. . . Into Something Rich and Strange
No line of life is exempt. All the popes of history have countenanced the costly architecture of St. Peter's Basilica and its extravagant interior decoration. All around the globe, nothing typifies man's materialism so much as the temples in which he preaches asceticism. Men of the cloth have not been persuaded that the poetic self-denial of Christ or Buddha—both men of sackcloth and sandals—is enough to inspire, elevate, and hold their flocks together. To amplify the temple in men's eyes, they have, very realistically, systematically sanctioned the embellishment of the houses of the gods with the same kind of luxurious design and expensive decoration that Detroit puts into a Cadillac.

One does not need a doctorate in social anthropology to see that the purposeful transmutation of nature's primeval state occupies all people in all cultures and all societies at all stages of development. Everybody everywhere wants to modify, transform, embellish, enrich, and reconstruct the world around him—to in-

troduce into an otherwise harsh or bland existence some sort of purposeful and distorting alleviation. Civilization is man's attempt to transcend his ancient animality; and this includes both art and advertising. . . .

And by Similar Means . . .
Let us assume for the moment that there is no objective, operational difference between the embellishments and distortions of the artist and those of the ad man—that both men are more concerned with creating images and feelings than with rendering objective, representational, and informational descriptions. The greater virtue of the artist's work must then derive from some subjective element. What is it?

It will be said that art has a higher value for man because it has a higher purpose. True, the artist is interested in philosophic truth or wisdom, and the ad man in selling his goods and services. Michelangelo, when he designed the Sistine chapel ceiling, had some concern with the inspirational elevation of man's spirit, whereas Edward Levy, who designs cosmetics packages, is interested primarily in creating images to help separate the unwary consumer from his loose change.

But this explanation of the difference between the value of art and the value of advertising is not helpful at all. For is the presence of a "higher" purpose all that redeeming?

Perhaps not; perhaps the reverse is closer to the truth. While the ad man and designer seek only to convert the audience to their commercial custom, Michelangelo sought to convert its soul. Which is the greater blasphemy? Who commits the greater affront to life—he who dabbles with man's erotic appetites, or he who meddles with man's soul? Which act is the easier to judge and justify? . . .

Symbol & Substance

As we have seen, man seeks to transcend nature in the raw everywhere. Everywhere, and at all times, he has been attracted by the poetic imagery of some sort of art, literature, music, and mysticism. He obviously wants and needs the promises the imagery, and the symbols of the poet and the priest. He refuses to live a life of primitive barbarism or sterile functionalism.

Consider a sardine can filled with scented powder. Even if the U.S. Bureau of Standards were to certify that the contents of this package are identical with the product sold in a beautiful paisley-printed container, it would not sell. The Boston matron, for example, who has built herself a deserved reputation for pinching every penny until it hurts, would unhesitatingly turn it down. While she may deny it, in self-assured and neatly cadenced accents, she obviously desires and needs the promises, imagery, and symbols produced by hyperbolic advertisements, elaborate packages, and fetching fashions.

The need for embellishment is not confined to personal appearance. A few years ago, an electronics laboratory offered a $700 testing device for sale. The company ordered two different front panels to be designed, one by the engineers who developed the equipment and one by professional industrial designers. When the two models were shown to a sample of laboratory directors with Ph.D.'s, the professional design attracted twice the purchase intentions that the engineer's design did. Obviously, the laboratory director who has been baptized

into science at M.I.T. is quite as responsive to the blandishments of packaging as the Boston matron.

And, obviously, both these customers define the products they buy in much more sophisticated terms than the engineer in the factory. For a woman, dusting powder in a sardine can is not the same product as the identical dusting powder in an exotic paisley package. For the laboratory director, the test equipment behind an engineer-designed panel just isn't as "good" as the identical equipment in a box designed with finesse.

Form Follows the Ideal Function

The consumer refuses to settle for pure operating functionality. "Form follows function" is a resoundingly vacuous cliché which, like all clichés, depends for its memorability more on its alliteration and brevity than on its wisdom. If it has any truth, it is only in the elastic sense that function extends beyond strict mechanical use into the domain of imagination. We do not choose to buy a particular product; we choose to buy the functional expectations that we attach to it, and we buy these expectations as "tools" to help us solve a problem of life.

Under normal circumstances, furthermore, we must judge a product's "non-mechanical" utilities before we actually buy it. It is rare that we choose an object after we have experienced it; nearly always we must make the choice before the fact. We choose on the basis of promises, not experiences.

Whatever symbols convey and *sustain* these promises in our minds are therefore truly functional. The promises and images which imaginative ads and sculptured packages induce in us are as much the product as the physical materials themselves. To put this another way, these ads and packages describe the product's fullness for us: in our minds, the product becomes a complex abstraction which is, as Immanuel Kant might have said, the conception of a perfection which has not yet been experienced.

But all promises and images, almost by their very nature, exceed their capacity to live up to themselves. As every eager lover has ever known, the consummation seldom equals the promises which produced the chase. To forestall and suppress the visceral expectation of disappointment that life has taught us must inevitably come, we use art, architecture, literature, and the rest, and advertising as well, to shield ourselves, in advance of experience, from the stark and plain reality in which we are fated to live. I agree that we wish for unobtainable unrealities, "dream castles." But why promise ourselves reality, which we already possess? What we want is what we do *not* possess! . . .

Symbolism Useful & Necessary

With*out* symbolism, furthermore, life would be even more confusing and anxiety-ridden than it is *with* it. The foot soldier must be able to recognize the general, good or bad, because the general is clothed with power. A general without his stars and suite of aides-de-camp to set him apart from the privates would suffer in authority and credibility as much as perfume packaged by Dracula or a computer designed by Rube Goldberg. Any ordinary soldier or civilian who has ever had the uncommon experience of being in the same shower with a general can testify from the visible unease of the latter how much clothes "make the man."

Similarly, verbal symbols help to make the product—they help us deal with the uncertainties of daily life. "You can be sure . . . if it's Westinghouse" is a decision rule as useful to the man buying a turbine generator as to the man buying an electric shaver. To label all the devices and embellishments companies employ to reassure the prospective customer about a product's quality with the pejorative term "gimmick," as critics tend to do, is simply silly. Worse, it denies, against massive evidence, man's honest needs and values. If religion must be architectured, packaged, lyricized, and musicized to attract and hold its audience, and if sex must be perfumed, powdered, sprayed, and shaped in order to command attention, it is ridiculous to deny the legitimacy of more modest, and similar, embellishments to the world of commerce. . . .

The Question of Deceit

Poetic descriptions of things make no pretense of being the things themselves. Nor do advertisements, even by the most elastic standards. Advertisements are the symbols of man's aspirations. They are not the real things, nor are they intended to be, nor are they accepted as such by the public. A study some years ago by the Center for Research in Marketing, Inc. concluded that deep down inside the consumer understands this perfectly well and has the attitude that an advertisement is an ad, not a factual news story.

Even Professor Galbraith grants the point when he says that " . . . because modern man is exposed to a large volume of information of varying degrees of unreliability . . . he establishes a system of discounts which he applies to various sources almost without thought. . . . The discount becomes nearly total for all forms of advertising. The merest child watching television dismisses the health and status-giving claims of a breakfast cereal as 'a commercial.' "[1]

This is not to say, of course, that Galbraith also discounts advertising's effectiveness. Quite the opposite: "Failure to win belief does not impair the effectiveness of the management of demand for consumer products. Management involves the creation of a compelling image of the product in the mind of the consumer. To this he responds more or less automatically under circumstances where the purchase does not merit a great deal of thought. For building this image, palpable fantasy may be more valuable than circumstantial evidence."[2]

Linguists and other communications specialists will agree with the conclusion of the Center for Research in Marketing that "advertising is a symbol system existing in a world of symbols. Its reality depends upon the fact that it is a symbol . . . the content of an ad can never be real, it can only say something about reality, or create a relationship between itself and an individual which has an effect on the reality life of an individual."

Consumer, Know Thyself!

Consumption is man's most constant activity. It is well that he understands himself as a consumer.

The object of consumption is to solve a problem. Even consumption that is viewed as the creation of an opportunity—like going to medical school or taking a singles-only Caribbean tour—has as its purpose the solving of a problem. At a minimum, the medical student seeks to solve the problem of how to lead a relevant and comfortable life, and the lady on the tour seeks to solve the problem of spinsterhood.

The "purpose" of the product is not what the engineer explicitly says it is, but what the consumer implicitly demands that it shall be. Thus the consumer consumes not things, but expected benefits—not cosmetics, but the satisfactions of the allurements they promise; not quarter-inch drills, but quarter-inch holes; not stock in companies, but capital gains; not numerically controlled milling machines, but trouble-free and accurately smooth metal parts; not low-cal whipped cream, but self-rewarding indulgence combined with sophisticated convenience.

The significance of these distinctions is anything but trivial. Nobody knows this better, for example, than the creators of automobile ads. It is not the generic virtues that they tout, but more likely the car's capacity to enhance its user's status and his access to female prey.

Whether we are aware of it or not, we in effect expect and demand that advertising create these symbols for us to show us what life *might* be, to bring the possibilities that we cannot see before our eyes and screen out the stark reality in which we must live. We insist, as Gilbert put it, that there be added a "touch of artistic verisimilitude to an otherwise bald and unconvincing narrative."

Understanding the Difference

In a world where so many things are either commonplace or standardized, it makes no sense to refer to the rest as false, fraudulent, frivolous, or immaterial. The world works according to the aspirations and needs of its actors, not according to the arcane or moralizing logic of detached critics who pine for another age—an age which, in any case, seems different from today's largely because its observers are no longer children shielded by protective parents from life's implacable harshness.

To understand this is not to condone much of the vulgarity, purposeful duplicity, and scheming half-truths we see in advertising, promotion, packaging, and product design. But before we condemn, it is well to understand the difference between embellishment and duplicity and how extraordinarily uncommon the latter is in our times. The noisy visibility of promotion in our intensely communicating times need not be thoughtlessly equated with malevolence.

Thus the issue is not the prevention of distortion. It is, in the end, to know what kinds of distortions we actually want so that each of our lives is, without apology, duplicity, or rancor, made bearable. This does not mean we must accept out of hand all the commercial propaganda to which we are each day so constantly exposed, or that we must accept out of hand the equation that effluence is the price of affluence, or the simple notion that business cannot and government should not try to alter and improve the position of the consumer vis-à-vis the producer. . . .

Business is caught in the middle. There is hardly a company that would not go down in ruin if it refused to provide fluff, because nobody will buy pure functionality. Yet, if it uses too much fluff and little else, business invites possibly ruinous legislation. The problem therefore is to find a middle way. And in this search, business can do a great deal more than it has been either accustomed or willing to do:

• It can exert pressure to make sure that no single industry "finds reasons" why it should be exempt from legislative restrictions that are reasonable and popular.

• It can work constructively with government to develop reasonable standards and effective sanctions that will assure a more amenable commercial environment.

• It can support legislation to provide the consumer with the information he needs to make easy comparison between products, packages, and prices.

• It can support and help draft improved legislation on quality stabilization.

• It can support legislation that gives consumers easy access to strong legal remedies where justified.

• It can support programs to make local legal aid easily available, especially to the poor and undereducated who know so little about their rights and how to assert them.

• Finally, it can support efforts to moderate and clean up the advertising noise that dulls our senses and assaults our sensibilities.

NOTES

1. John Kenneth Galbraith, *The New Industrial State* (Boston, Houghton Mifflin Company, 1967), pp. 325–326.
2. Ibid., p. 326.

ADVERTISING: THE MAGIC SYSTEM

HISTORY

It is customary to begin even the shortest account of the history of advertising by recalling the three thousand year old papyrus from Thebes, offering a reward for a runaway slave, and to go on to such recollections as the crier in the streets of Athens, the paintings of gladiators, with sentences urging attendance at their combats, in ruined Pompeii, and the fly-bills on the pillars of the Forum in Rome. This pleasant little ritual can be quickly performed, and as quickly forgotten: it is, of course, altogether too modest. If by advertising we mean what was meant by Shakespeare and the translators of the Authorized Version—the processes of taking or giving notice of something—it is as old as human society, and some pleasant recollections from the Stone Age could be quite easily devised.

The real business of the historian of advertising is more difficult: to trace the development from processes of specific attention and information to an institutionalized system of commercial information and persuasion; to relate this to changes in society and in the economy: and to trace changes in method in the context of changing organizations and intentions.

DEVELOPMENT

There is no doubt that the Industrial Revolution, and the associated revolution in communications, fundamentally changed the nature of advertising. But the change was not simple, and must be understood in specific relation to particular developments. It is not true, for example, that with the coming of factory production large-scale advertising became economically necessary. By the 1850s, a century after Johnson's comment, and with Britain already an industrial nation, the advertising pages of the newspapers, whether *The Times* or the *News of the World*, were still basically similar to those in eighteenth-century journals, except that there were more of them, that they were more closely printed, and that there were certain exclusions (lists of whores, for example, were no longer advertised in the *Morning Post*). . . .

TRANSFORMATION

The strange fact is, looking back, that the great bulk of products of the early stages of the factory system had been sold without extensive advertising, which had grown up mainly in relation to fringe products and novelties. Such advertising as there was, of basic articles, was mainly by shopkeepers, drawing attention to the quality and competitive pricing of the goods they stocked. In this comparatively simple phase of competition, large-scale advertising and the brand-naming of goods were necessary only at the margin, or in genuinely new things. The real signs of change began to appear in the 1880s and 1890s, though they can only be correctly interpreted when seen in the light of the fully developed 'new' advertising of the period between the wars.

The formation of modern advertising has to be traced, essentially, to certain characteristics of the new 'monopoly' (corporate) capitalism, first clearly evident in this same period of the end and turn of the nineteenth century. The Great Depression which in general dominated the period from 1875 to the middle 1890s (though broken by occasional recoveries and local strengths) marked the turning point between two modes of industrial organization and two basically different approaches to distribution. After the Depression, and its big falls in prices, there was a more general and growing fear of productive capacity, a marked tendency to reorganize industrial ownership into larger units and combines, and a growing desire, by different methods, to organize and where possible control the market. Among the means of achieving the latter purposes, advertising on a new scale, and applied to an increasing range of products, took an important place.

Modern advertising, that is to say, belongs to the system of market-control which, at its full development, includes the growth of tariffs and privileged areas, cartel-quotas, trade campaigns, price-fixing by manufacturers, and that form of economic imperialism which assured certain markets overseas by political control of their territories. There was a concerted expansion of export advertising, and at home the biggest advertising campaign yet seen accompanied the merger of several tobacco firms into the Imperial Tobacco Company, to resist American competition. In 1901, a 'fabulous sum' was offered for the entire eight pages of *The Star*, by a British tobacco advertiser, and when this was refused four pages were taken, a 'world's record', to print 'the most costly, colossal and convincing advertisement ever used in an evening newspaper the wide world o'er'. Since the American firms retaliated, with larger advertisements of their own, the campaign was both heavy and prolonged. This can be taken as the first major example of a new advertising situation. . . .

THE SYSTEM

In the last hundred years, . . . advertising has developed from the simple announcements of shopkeepers and the persuasive arts of a few marginal dealers into a major part of capitalist business organization. This is important enough, but the place of advertising in society goes far beyond this commercial context. It is increasingly the source of finance for a whole range of general communication, to the extent that in 1960 our majority television service and almost all our newspapers and periodicals could not exist without it. Further, in the last forty years and now at an increasing rate, it has passed the frontier of the selling of goods and services and has become involved with the teaching of social and personal values; it is also rapidly entering the world of politics. Advertising is also, in a sense, the official art of modern capitalist society: it is what 'we' put up in 'our' streets and use to fill up to half of 'our' newspapers and magazines: and it commands the services of perhaps the largest organized body of writers and artists, with their attendant managers and advisers, in the whole society. Since this is the actual social status of advertising, we shall only understand it with any adequacy if we can develop a kind of total analysis in which the economic, social and cultural facts are visibly related. We may then also find, taking advertising as a major form of modern social communication, that we can understand our society itself in new ways.

It is often said that our society is too materialist, and that advertising reflects this. We are in the phase of a relatively rapid distribution of what are called 'consumer goods', and advertising, with its emphasis on 'bringing the good things of life', is taken as central for this reason. But it seems to me that in this respect our society is quite evidently not materialist enough, and that this, paradoxically, is the result of a failure in social meanings, values and ideals.

It is impossible to look at modern advertising without realising that the material object being sold is never enough: this indeed is the crucial cultural quality of its modern forms. If we were sensibly

materialist, in that part of our living in which we use things, we should find most advertising to be of an insane irrelevance. Beer would be enough for us, without the additional promise that in drinking it we show ourselves to be manly, young in heart, or neighbourly. A washing-machine would be a useful machine to wash clothes, rather than an indication that we are forward-looking or an object of envy to our neighbours. But if these associations sell beer and washing-machines, as some of the evidence suggests, it is clear that we have a cultural pattern in which the objects are not enough but must be validated, if only in fantasy, by association with social and personal meanings which in a different cultural pattern might be more directly available. The short description of the pattern we have is *magic*: a highly organized and professional system of magical inducements and satisfactions, functionally very similar to magical systems in simpler societies, but rather strangely coexistent with a highly developed scientific technology.

This contradiction is of the greatest importance in any analysis of modern capitalist society. The coming of large-scale industrial production necessarily raised critical problems of social organization, which in many fields we are still only struggling to solve. In the production of goods for personal use, the critical problem posed by the factory of advanced machines was that of the organization of the market. The modern factory requires not only smooth and steady distributive channels (without which it would suffocate under its own product) but also definite indications of demand without which the expensive processes of capitalization and equipment would be too great a risk. The historical choice posed by the development of industrial production is between different forms of organization and planning in the society to which it is central. In our own century, the choice has been and remains between some form of socialism and a new form of capitalism. In Britain, since the 1890s and with rapidly continuing emphasis, we have had the new capitalism, based on a series of devices for organizing and ensuring the market. Modern advertising, taking on its distinctive features in just this economic phase, is one of the most important of these devices, and it is perfectly true to say that modern capitalism could not function without it.

Yet the essence of capitalism is that the basic means of production are not socially but privately owned, and that decisions about production are therefore in the hands of a group occupying a minority position in the society and in no direct way responsible to it. Obviously, since the capitalist wishes to be successful, he is influenced in his decisions about production by what other members of the society need. But he is influenced also by considerations of industrial convenience and likely profit, and his decisions tend to be a balance of these varying factors. The challenge of socialism, still very powerful elsewhere but in Britain deeply confused by political immaturities and errors, is essentially that decisions about production should be in the hands of the society as a whole, in the sense that control of the means of production is made part of the general system of decision which the society as a whole creates. The conflict between capitalism and socialism is now commonly seen in terms of a competition in productive efficiency, and we need not doubt that much of our future history, on a world scale, will be determined by the results of this competition. Yet the conflict is really much deeper than this, and is also a conflict between different approaches to and forms of socialism. The fundamental choice that emerges, in the problems set to us by modern industrial production, is between man as consumer and man as user. The system of organized magic which is modern advertising is primarily important as a functional obscuring of this choice.

'CONSUMERS'

The popularity of 'consumer', as a way of describing the ordinary member of modern capitalist society in a main part of his economic capacity, is very significant. The description is spreading very rapidly, and is now habitually used by people to whom it ought, logically, to be repugnant. It is not only that, at a simple level, 'consumption' is a very strange description of our ordinary use of goods and services. This metaphor drawn from the stomach or the furnace is only partially relevant even to our use of things. Yet we say 'consumer', rather than 'user', because in the form of society we now have, and in the forms of thinking which it almost imperceptibly fosters, it is as consumers that the majority of people are seen. We are the market, which the system of industrial production has organized. We are the channels along which the product flows and disappears. In every aspect of social communication, and in every version of what we are as a community, the pressure of a system of industrial production is towards these impersonal forms.

Yet it is by no means necessary that these versions should prevail, just because we use advanced productive techniques. It is simply that once these have entered a society, new questions of structure and purpose in social organization are inevitably posed. One set of answers is the development of genuine democracy, in which the human needs of all the people in the society are taken as the central purpose of all social activity, so that politics is not a system of government but of self-government, and the systems of production and communication are rooted in the satisfaction of human needs and the development of human capacities. Another set of answers, of which we have had more experience, retains, often in very subtle forms, a more limited social purpose. In the first phase, loyal subjects, as they were previously seen, became the labour market of industrial 'hands'. Later, as the 'hands' reject this version of themselves, and claim a higher human status, the emphasis is changed. Any real concession of higher status would mean the end of class-society and the coming of socialist democracy. But intermediate concessions are possible, including material concessions. The 'subjects' become the 'electorate', and 'the mob' becomes 'public opinion'.

Decision is still a function of the minority, but a new system of decision, in which the majority can be organized to this end, has to be devised. The majority are seen as 'the masses', whose opinion, *as masses* but not as real individuals or groups, is a factor in the business of governing. In practical terms, this version can succeed for a long time, but it then becomes increasingly difficult to state the nature of the society, since there is a real gap between profession and fact. Moreover, as the governing minority changes in character, and increasingly rests for real power on a modern economic system, older social purposes become vestigial, and whether expressed or implied, the maintenance of the economic system becomes the main factual purpose of all social activity. Politics and culture become deeply affected by this dominant pattern, and ways of thinking derived from the economic market—political parties considering how to sell themselves to the electorate, to create a favourable brand image; education being primarily organized in terms of a graded supply of labour; culture being organized and even evaluated in terms of commercial profit—become increasingly evident.

Still, however, the purposes of the society have to be declared in terms that will command the effort of a majority of its people. It is here that the idea of the 'consumer' has proved so useful. Since consumption is within its limits a satisfactory activity, it can be plausibly offered as a commanding social purpose. At the same time, its ambiguity is such that it ratifies the subjection of society to the operations of the existing economic system. An irresponsible economic system can supply the 'consumption' market, whereas it could only meet the criterion of human use by becoming genuinely responsible: that is to say, shaped in its use of human labour and resources by general social decisions. The consumer asks for an adequate supply of personal 'consumer goods' at a tolerable price: over the last ten years, this has been the primary aim of British government. But users ask for more than this, necessarily. They ask for the satisfaction of human needs which consumption, as such, can never really supply. Since many of these needs are social—roads, hospitals, schools, quiet—they are not only not covered by the consumer ideal: they are even denied by it, because consumption tends always to materialize as an individual activity. And to satisfy this range of needs would involve questioning the autonomy of the economic system, in its actual setting of priorities. This is where the consumption ideal is not only misleading, as a form of defence of the system, but ultimately destructive to the broad general purposes of the society.

Advertising, in its modern forms, then operates to preserve the consumption ideal from the criticism inexorably made of it by experience. If the consumption of individual goods leaves that whole area of human need unsatisfied, the attempt is made, by magic, to associate this consumption with human desires to which it has no real reference. You do not only buy an object: you buy social respect, discrimination, health, beauty, success, power to control your environment. The magic obscures the real sources of general satisfaction because their discovery would involve radical change in the whole common way of life.

Of course, when a magical pattern has become established in a society, it is capable of some real if limited success. Many people will indeed look twice at you, upgrade you, upmarket you, respond to your displayed signals, if you have made the right purchases within a system of meanings to which you are all trained. Thus the fantasy seems to be validated, at a personal level, but only at the cost of preserving the general unreality which it obscures: the real failures of the society which however are not easily traced to this pattern.

It must not be assumed that magicians—in this case, advertising agents—disbelieve their own magic. They may have a limited professional cynicism about it, from knowing how some of the tricks are done. But fundamentally they are involved, with the rest of the society, in the confusion to which the magical gestures are a response. Magic is always an unsuccessful attempt to provide meanings and values, but it is often very difficult to distinguish magic from genuine knowledge and from art. The belief that high consumption is a high standard of living is a general belief of the society. The conversion of numerous objects into sources of sexual or pre-sexual satisfaction is evidently not only a process in the minds of advertisers, but also a deep and general confusion in which much energy is locked.

At one level, the advertisers are people using certain skills and knowledge, created by real art and science, against the public for commercial advantage. This hostile stance is rarely confessed in general propaganda for advertising, where the normal emphasis is the blind consumption ethic ('Advertising brings you the good things of life'), but it is common in advertisers' propaganda to their clients. 'Hunt with the mind of the hunter', one recent announcement begins, and another, under the heading 'Getting any honey from the hive industry?', is rich in the language of attack:

> One of the most important weapons used in successful marketing is advertising.
> Commando Sales Limited, steeped to the nerve ends in the skills of unarmed combat, are ready to move into battle on any sales front at the crack of an accepted estimate. These are the front line troops to call in when your own sales force is hopelessly outnumbered by the forces of sales resistance . . .

This is the structure of feeling in which 'impact' has become the normal description of the effect of successful communication, and 'impact' like 'consumer' is now habitually used by people to whom it ought to be repugnant. What sort of person really wants to 'make an impact' or create a 'smash hit', and what state is a society in when this can be its normal cultural language?

It is indeed monstrous that human advances in psychology, sociology and communication should be used or thought of as powerful techniques *against* people, just as it is rotten to try to reduce the faculty of human choice to 'sales resistance'. In these respects, the claim of advertising to be a service is not particularly plausible. But equally, much of this talk of weapons and impact is the jejune bravado of deeply confused men. It is in the end the language of frustration rather than of power. Most advertising is not the cool creation of skilled professionals, but the confused creation of bad thinkers and artists. If we look at the petrol with the huge clenched fist, the cigarette against loneliness in the deserted street, the puppet facing death with a life-insurance policy (the modern protection, unlike the magical symbols painstakingly listed from earlier societies), or the man in the cradle which is an aeroplane, we are looking at attempts to express and resolve real human tensions which may be crude but which also involve deep feelings of a personal and social kind.

The structural similarity between much advertising and much modern art is not simply copying by the advertisers. It is the result of comparable responses to the contemporary human condition, and the only distinction that matters is between the clarification achieved by some art and the displacement normal in bad art and most advertising. The skilled magicians, the masters of the masses, must

be seen as ultimately involved in the general weakness which they not only exploit but are exploited by. If the meanings and values generally operative in the society give no answers to, no means of negotiating, problems of death, loneliness, frustration, the need for identity and respect, then the magical system must come, mixing its charms and expedients with reality in easily available forms, and binding the weakness to the condition which has created it. Advertising is then no longer merely a way of selling goods, it is a true part of the culture of a confused society.

AFTERWORD (1969): ADVERTISING AND COMMUNICATIONS

A main characteristic of our society is a willed coexistence of very new technology and very old social forms. Advertising is the most visible expression of just this combination. In its main contemporary forms it is the result of a failure to find means of social decision, in matters of production and distribution, relevant to a large-scale and increasingly integrated economy. Classical liberalism ceased to have anything to say about these problems from the period of depression and consequent reorganization of the market in the late nineteenth century. What we now know as advertising takes its origins from that period, in direct relation to the new capitalist corporations. That the same liberalism had produced the idea of a free press, and of a general social policy of public education and enlightenment, is a continuing irony. Before the corporate reorganization, the social ideas of liberalism had been to an important extent compatible with its commercial ideas. Widespread ownership of the means of communication had been sustained by comparable kinds of ownership in the economy as a whole. When the standing enemy of free expression was the state, this diverse commercial world found certain important means to freedom, notably in the newspapers.

What was then called advertising was directly comparable in method and scale. It was mainly specific and local, and though it was often absurd—and had long been recognized as such in its description as puff—it remained a secondary and subordinate activity at the critical point where commercial pressure interacted with free public communication. That early phase is now more than half a century in the past. From the 1890s advertising began to be a major factor in newspaper publishing, and from the same period control began to pass from families and small firms to the new corporations. Ever since that time, and with mounting pressure in each decade, the old institutions of commercial liberalism have been beaten back by the corporations. These sought not so much to supply the market as to organize it.

The consequent crisis has been most visible in newspapers, which have been very sharply reduced in number and variety through a period of expanding readership and the increasing importance of public opinion. But while some of the other liberal ideas seemed to hold, and were even protected as such, as in broadcasting, by the state, it was always possible to believe that the general situation could be held too. Commercial priorities were extending in scale and range, but an entire set of liberal ideas, which in practice the priorities were steadily contradicting, seemed to stay firm in the

mind: indeed, so firm that it was often difficult to describe reality, because the evidence of practice was met so regularly by the complacent response of the ideas.

What is now happening, I believe, is that just enough people, at just enough of the points of decision, are with a certain sadness and bewilderment, and with many backward looks, giving that kind of liberalism up. What used to be an uneasy compromise between commercial pressures and public policy is now seen as at worst a bargain, at best a division of labour. The coexistence of commercial and public-service television, which was planned by nobody but was the result of intense pressure to let in the commercial interest, is now rationalized, after the fact, as a kind of conscious policy of pluralism. The new name for compromise is 'mixed economy', or there is an even grander name: a 'planned diversity of structures'.

What has really happened is that a majority of those formerly dedicated to public policy have decided that the opposing forces are simply too strong. They will fight some delaying actions, they will make reservations, but a political situation, long prepared and anticipated, is coming through with such a force that these are mainly gestures. Public money raised in public ways and subject to public control has been made desperately (but deliberately) short. Public money raised in the margin of other transactions and consequently subject to no public control is at the same time continually on offer. Practical men, puzzling over the accounts in committees, think they have at last glimpsed reality. Either they must join the commercial interests, or they must behave like them as a condition of their temporary survival. And so a mood is created in which all decisions seem inevitable and in which people speaking of different solutions seem remote and impractical. It is a mood of submission, under the pressures of an effectively occupying power.

What must then, of course, be most desperately denied is that anything so crude as submission is in fact occurring. Some people are always ready with talk of a new forward-looking order. But the central sign of this sort of submission is a reluctance, in public, to call the enemy by its real name. I see the form of the enemy as advertising, but what I mean by advertising is rather different from some other versions. Plenty of people still criticize advertising in secondary ways: that it is vulgar or superficial, that it is unreliable, that it is intrusive. Much of this is true, but it is the kind of criticism advertising can learn to take in its stride. Does it not now employ many talented people, does it not set up rules and bodies to control and improve standards, is it not limited to natural breaks? While criticism is discrete in these ways, it has only marginal effects.

So I repeat my own central criticism. Advertising is the consequence of a social failure to find means of public information and decision over a wide range of everyday economic life. This failure, of course, is not abstract. It is the result of allowing control of the means of production and distribution to remain in minority hands, and one might add, for it is of increasing importance in the British economy, into foreign hands, so that some of the minority decisions are not even taken inside the society which they affect.

The most evident contradiction of late capitalism is between this controlling minority and a widely expectant majority. What will eventually happen, if we are

very lucky, is that majority expectations will surpass the minority controls. In a number of areas this is beginning to happen, in small and temporary ways, and it is called, stupidly, indiscipline or greed or perversity or disruption. But the more evident fact, in the years we are living through, is the emergence and elaboration of a social and cultural form—advertising—which responds to the gap between expectation and control by a kind of organized fantasy.

In economic terms this fantasy operates to project the production decisions of the major corporations as 'your' choice, the 'consumer's' selection of priorities, methods and style. Professional and amateur actors, locally directed by people who in a different culture might be writing and producing plays or films, are hired to mime the forms of the only available choices, to display satisfaction and the achievement of their expectations, or to pretend to a linkage of values between quite mundane products and the now generally unattached values of love, respect, significance or fulfilment. What was once the local absurdity of puffing is now a system of mimed celebration of other people's decisions. As such, of course, advertising is very closely related to a whole system of styles in official politics. Indeed some of its adepts have a direct hand in propaganda, in the competition of the parties and in the formation of public opinion.

Seen from any distance—of time, space or intelligence—the system is so obvious, in its fundamental procedures, that one might reasonably expect to be able to break it by describing it. But this is now very doubtful. If advertising is the consequence of a failure to achieve new forms of social information and decision, this failure has been compounded by the development of the Labour government, which in submitting to the organized market of the corporations has paved the way to a more open and more total submission in the seventies. Historically, this may be seen as the last attempt to solve our crisis in liberal terms, but the consequences of the failure go beyond simple political history. For it has led to habits of resignation and deference to the new power: not only among decision-makers but much more widely, I think, among people who now need the system of fantasy to confirm the forms of their immediate satisfaction or to cover the illusion that they are shaping their own lives.

It is in this atmosphere that the crucial decisions about communications are now being taken. Some of them could have been worse. Pressure on the BBC to take advertising money has been held off, though there is still a lobby, of an elitist kind, prepared to admit it to Radio I, where all things vulgar may lie down together. On the contrary, this is just where it must not be admitted, for the pressure to tie the cultural preferences of a young generation to the open exploitation of a 'young market' is the most intense and destructive of them all. Again, the emphasis on the licence, as a means of revenue, is welcome, as a way of preserving the principle of open public money. The fee is still comparatively low in Britain, and could easily be graduated for pensioners and in some cases abolished. In the BBC and in the government, some local stands are being made.

But it is not only that other people are already adjusting to the altered political climate of the seventies, in which the commercial interests expect to take full control. It is also that the decisions possible to this sort of government, or to a public corporation, are marginal to the continuing trend of economic concentration. A newspaper with two and a half million readers is now likely to shut down: not because such a readership is in a general way uneconomic, but because within a structure determined by competitive advertising revenue it is a relative loser. That process of cutting down choices will continue unless met by the most vigorous public intervention. Commercial radio would rapidly accelerate it.

And what then happens, apart from the long-term hedges and options, is that new figures for viability are accepted for almost all communications services. It is absurd that a sale of a million should be too low for a newspaper. But think of other figures. What is called a vast throng—a hundred thousand people—in Wembley Stadium or Hyde Park is called a tiny minority, a negligible percentage, in a radio programme. Content is then increasingly determined, even in a public service, by the law of quick numbers, which advertising revenue has forced on the communications system.

Submission is not always overt. One of its most popular forms is to change as the conqueror appears on the horizon, so that by the time he arrives you are so like him that you may hope to get by. I don't believe we have yet lost but the position is very critical. What was originally a manageable support cost, in the necessary freedom of communications, has been allowed to turn the world upside down, until all other services are dependent, or likely to be dependent, on its quite local, narrow and temporary needs. An out-dated and inefficient kind of information about goods and services has been surpassed by the competitive needs of the corporations, and these increasingly demand not a sector but a world, not a reservation but a whole society, not a break or a column but whole newspapers and broadcasting services in which to operate. Unless they are driven back now, there will be no easy second chance.

POSTSCRIPT

Is Advertising Ethical?

A rare defense of advertising is found in Yale Brozen's *Advertising and Society* (New York University Press, 1974). Michael Schudson in *Advertising, the Uneasy Persuasion: Its Dubious Impact Upon American Society* (Basic Books, 1984) offers a controversial analysis of the influence of advertising that comes to the conclusion that we lack proof of effect.

Stuart and Elizabeth Ewen's *Channels of Desire: Mass Images and the Shaping of American Consciousness* (New York: McGraw-Hill, 1982) is a critique of advertising in Western society, which they feel has become a preeminent consumer society in which mass imagery has a major influence on public consciousness. William Leiss, Stephen Kline, and Sut Jhally in *Social Communication in Advertising: Persons, Products, and Images of Well-Being* (Methuen, 1986) examine advertising as a process of communication with serious consequences beyond the selling of good and services. Richard Adler et al. in *The Effects of Television Advertising on Children: Review and Recommendations* (Lexington, 1980) examine major issues and existing research concerning the effects of advertising on children.

Robert Atwan, Donald McQuade, and John Wright in *Edsels, Luckies, and Frigidaires: Advertising the American Way* (Delta, 1979) use magazine ads to examine changes in American culture. Jim Hall's *Mighty Minutes: An Illustrated History of Television's Best Commercials* (Harmony, 1984) is an entertaining and potentially useful reference.

ISSUE 15

Media Monopolies: Does Concentration of Ownership Jeopardize Media Content?

YES: Ben H. Bagdikian, from *The Media Monopoly*, 3rd edition (Beacon Press, 1983)

NO: Maxwell E. McCombs, from "Concentration, Monopoly, and Content," in Picard, Winter, McCombs, and Lacy, eds., *Press Concentration and Monopoly: New Perspectives on Newspaper Ownership and Operation*, (Ablex Publishing, 1988)

ISSUE SUMMARY

Yes: Ben Bagdikian, Pulitzer Prize-winning journalist and professor, contends that only 23 corporations control America's mass media, with sobering consequences.
NO: Professor Maxwell McCombs questions whether the marketplace of ideas becomes less diverse and responsive to local needs when competition decreases, and he finds little evidence for this argument in his analysis of newspapers in two Canadian cities.

American business—particularly American media businesses—has been experiencing an unprecedented level of restructuring. Each of the major networks has been acquired or merged within the past decade. Mergers, acquisitions, divestitures, and leveraged buyouts have become a part of the industry. Yet the media industry has a special function defined by its journalistic endeavors and protected by the Constitution as freedom of the press. Can the restructuring of the American media industry threaten the ability of that industry to fulfill its surveillance function?

There is a long tradition of private, rather than governmental, ownership of media in the United States. This stems from the legacy of libertarian philosophy, which argued that truth would emerge from a diversity of voices in the communication marketplace. These diverse voices can best provide the public with information on which to base its decisions. Will this restructuring result in a trend toward the concentration of ownership in the hands of fewer corporations and thereby threaten this diversity of voices? Are media chains responsive to local needs? Does a multinational corporation exert influence on editorial decisions? Does a corporation that is determined to profit from its acquisition of media outlets encourage investigative journalism that might threaten major advertisers?

According to Bagdikian, large corporations are gaining control of the media at an alarming rate. Control of media by a few giant corporations is tighter than it was when the first edition of his book came out in 1983. These dominant corporations can, through their control of news and other public information, censor public awareness of the dangers of information control by the corporate elite. When the central interests of controlling corporations are at stake, he further argues, news becomes weighted toward what serves the economic and political interests of the corporations that own the media.

Maxwell McCombs, perhaps best known for his work in developing the concept of agenda setting, distrusts such a bleak view. As monopolies have grown in the newspaper industry (i.e., the disappearance of competing daily newspapers in individual markets), questions have been raised about how this affects the local reader. McCombs analyzed the content of the daily newspapers in Montreal and Winnipeg *before* and *after* the demise of competing dailies. He found little evidence of diminished quality in the surviving newspaper and, therefore, little evidence for the assertion that competition ensures diversity. He concludes that diversity relies instead on the social responsibility and professional competence of those who own and operate newspapers and that market pressure does not strongly and consistently promote diversity.

YES

Ben H. Bagdikian

THE ENDLESS CHAIN

For where your treasure is, there will be your heart also.

Matthew 6:22

George Orwell in his novel, *1984*, fictionalized Big Brother, intruder into privacy and the big owner of all the mass media in his society. Big Brother used his control of news, information, and popular culture to achieve Big Brother's vision of a conforming society. Most critics understandably thought of Communist societies where, indeed, everyone was surrounded by One Big Owner of the mass media. Among the many social ironies of the 1980s is the change in the world's mass media. Many Communist societies have discovered that they are forced to move away from centralized control of information, though the change is slow and tentative. At precisely the same time the developed democracies of the world, including the United States, have begun moving in the opposite direction, toward centralized control of their mass media, this time not by government but by a few private corporations.

No single corporation controls all the mass media in the United States. But the daily newspapers, magazines, broadcasting systems, books, motion pictures, and most other mass media are rapidly moving in the direction of tight control by a handful of huge multinational corporations. If mergers, acquisitions, and takeovers continue at the present rate, one massive firm will be in virtual control of all major media by the 1990s. Given the complexities of social and economic trends, it is unlikely to result in one owner. It is, however, quite possible—and corporate leaders predict—that by the 1990s a half-dozen large corporations will own all of the most powerful media outlets in the United States. Given the striking similarity in the private political and economic goals of all of the owning corporations, and given the extraordinary combined power of all the forms of modern mass media, it is not particularly comforting that the private control consists of two dozen large conglomerates instead of only one.

Predictions of massive consolidation are based on extraordinary changes in recent years. At the end of World War II, for example, 80 percent of the daily newspapers on the United States were independently owned, but by 1989 the proportion was reversed, with 80 percent owned by corporate chains. In 1981 twenty corporations controlled most of the business of the country's 11,000 magazines, but only seven years later that number had shrunk to three corporations.

Today, despite more than 25,000 outlets in the United States, twenty-three corporations control most of the business in daily newspapers, magazines, television, books, and motion pictures.

The same dominant corporations in these major fields appear in other, often newer, media. It is the open strategy of major media owners to own as many different kinds of media as possible—newspapers, magazines, broadcasting, books, movies, cable, recordings, video cassettes, movie houses, and copyright control of the archival libraries of past work in all these fields. . . .

An alarming pattern emerges. On one side is information limited by each individual's own experience and effort; on the other, the unseen affairs of the community, the nation, and the world, information needed by the individual to prevent political powerlessness. What connects the two are the mass media, and that system is being reduced to a small number of closed circuits in which the owners of the conduits—newspapers, magazines, broadcast stations, and all the other mass media—prefer to use material they own or that tends to serve their economic purposes. Because they own so many of the different kinds of outlets, they have that golden commodity they speak of with financial joy, a "guaranteed audience." But the term "guaranteed audience" is another way of saying "captive audience." . . .

Today, the chief executive officers of the twenty-three corporations that control most of what Americans read and see can fit into an ordinary living room. Almost without exception they are economic conservatives. They can, if they wish, use control of their newspapers, broadcast stations, magazines, books, and movies to promote their own corporate values to the exclusion of others. When their corporate interests are at stake—in taxes, regulation, and antitrust action— they use that power, in their selection of news, and in the private lobbying power peculiar to those who control the media image—or non-image—of politicians. . . .

Neither in practical improvement of service to the public nor in added independence from government is the record of corporate ownership of the media sufficiently impressive to counter the dangers of tightening control of public information. . . .

Beginning in the mid-1960s, large corporations suddenly began buying media companies. It did not require a conspiracy. The trigger was Wall Street's discovery of the best-kept secret in American newspapering.

For decades American newspaper publishers cultivated the impression that they presided over an impoverished institution maintained only through sacrificial devotion to the First Amendment. The image helped reduce demands from advertisers for lower rates and agitation by media employees for higher wages. The truth was that most daily papers were highly profitable. But that was easy to conceal when newspapers were privately owned and no public reports were required. . . .

Major papers began offering their stock publicly in the early 1960s. Firms selling stock to the general public are required by the Securities and Exchange Commission to disclose company finances. Furthermore, Wall Street investment houses who make the major investments in such firms dislike mysteries about properties in which they may invest billions, so they demand even more inside information than the SEC. Suddenly in the 1960s the investing world discovered that the newspaper industry, like the legendary Hetty Green, had assiduously presented itself to the public in the mendicant rags, but was now exposed, as Mrs. Green had been, as fabulously rich. The media race was on, and concentrated ownership followed. . . .

By the 1960s, television was already concentrated in ownership. The three networks and their wholly owned and affiliated stations continue to have more than two-thirds of the audience. Broadcasters enjoy a "natural monopoly" in the sense that there is a limited number of frequencies available in each community and the government protects each station's channel from competition.

Concentrated ownership was in broadcasting's corporate genes. The industry began as a private cartel in 1919 when the Radio Corporation of America (RCA) was formed as an umbrella monopoly under which General Electric, Westinghouse, AT&T, and United Fruit Company agreed to divide the newly emerging radio market among themselves. The National Broadcasting Company was their radio network. CBS did not enter the field until 1927, and not until 1943 did an activist Federal Communications Commission force RCA to divest itself of one of its two radio networks, thus creating ABC.

Television, in the jargon of Wall Street, is a "semimonopoly," not only because of the limited number of owners, but because in most cities the dominant stations have virtually guaranteed high profits; the ratings simply determine which company gets the most.

Recent events in broadcasting have further concentrated ownership in television. Initially, no company was permitted to own more than seven radio and seven television stations. Under the political drive for deregulation, the FCC in 1984 permitted each company to expand its holdings to twelve AM and twelve FM radio stations and twelve television stations. . . .

Hollywood studios, long concentrated in ownership, remain so, and with added complexity. Conglomerates came to appreciate the power to create national styles and celebrities (and extra profits) when combinations of different media reinforced each other in unified promotional campaigns. Today, most of the leading movie studios are also owners in other media, and, thanks to the free-market amnesia about antitrust law, have once again started buying up movie houses to guarantee audiences for their own films and keep out competitors' pictures. In 1948 the United States Supreme Court found ownership of movie theaters by the major movie studios a violation of antitrust law. The U.S. Department of Justice in recent years has ignored that finding and by 1988 a few major studios had bought control of more than a third of all the movie screens in the country.

It is possible that large corporations are gaining control of the American media because the public wants it that way. But there is another possibility: the public, almost totally dependent on the media for such things, has seldom seen in their newspapers, magazines, or broadcasts anything to suggest the political and economic dangers of concentrated corporate control. . . .

But there are two kinds of impact on public opinion, one brief and transient, the other prolonged and deep. The first is the single news item, soon obscured by dozens of new ones, each day tending to obliterate the impact of what went before. A compelling study of the ephemeral quality of isolated news accounts is Deborah Lipstadt's book, *Beyond Belief*, which reveals that American newspapers from 1933 to 1945 printed numerous reports showing that something horrendous was happening to European Jews under Hitler. But the news stories were brief, isolated, and seldom on the front page. They were not pursued with continuity, never drawn together to form a coherent picture, and newspapers did not press to discover the difference between official denials and reality. Consequently, the atrocities did not become important in the public mind and, probably as a result, they did not provoke strong government action. Far more effective in creating public opinion is pursuit of events or ideas until they are displayed in depth over a period of time, when they seem to form a coherent picture and therefore become integrated into public thinking. Continuous repetition and emphasis create high priorities in the public mind and in government. It is in that power—to treat some subjects briefly and obscurely but others repetitively and in depth, or to take initiatives unrelated to external events—where ownership interests most effectively influence the news.

In all the media, it is normal and necessary to decide what to include and what to exclude, what to treat with emphasis and what to relegate to minor display, when to treat something in depth and when to keep it superficial. It is the legitimate task of the professional editor. Because these discriminations are normal and necessary, it is difficult for the public, and often for individual journalism professionals, to detect when, among the elements that go into legitimate news selection, private ownership interests become a factor.

Fifty years ago, executive editors spoke openly to their staffs about owners' sensibilities. Today most editors do not—ironic confirmation of raised professional standards. When protection of an owning corporation's private interests intrudes into news decisions, other professionally acceptable reasons are given (such as "Nobody's interested"). The barrier is seldom absolute: there is merely a higher threshold for such stories. News stories that cast doubt on the corporate ethic must be more urgent and melodramatic than stories sustaining that ethic. Gradually, the total news picture of society is skewed in favor of corporate interests.

The central interests of owners are clear to executive editors who know that there are limits to their freedom and who thus perform varying degrees of self-censorship. Periodically, an executive editor takes literally an owner's encouragement to edit "without fear or favor," and periodically the editor is fired or squeezed out. There are always stories that will require the editor to exercise his or her unstated function of applying the second-hand weight of the owner's thumb on the scale of the news.

Some industrialized democracies have more concentrated ownership than the United States, but no other developed country has the peculiar need of the United States for a different pattern. Every other developed country has a national press and a relatively unimportant local press. In those countries the dozen or more national papers, headquartered in the national capital, are the only ones to carry serious political and economic news. They are available in every locality and—crucially important—each competing national paper is different in its political and economic orientation. Readers have a real choice among the differing papers, in which a wide spectrum of public issues is aired and debated and can thus enter the national discourse.

The United States has never had a true national daily press. American politics is more local than in other countries. Major decisions that are left to the national government in other countries— education, police, land use, property taxes, and much else—are voted on by local communities in the United States. No national news medium can, by itself, serve the American voter. Consequently, there are 1,600 local newspapers and no truly national ones. The *Wall Street Journal* comes closest to a national newspaper, but it is a specialized one. The *New York Times* is only slowly expanding toward general availability throughout the country. *USA Today* is a national paper but it is a daily magazine that does not pretend to be a primary carrier of all the serious news.

In the United States, unlike elsewhere, when a handful of corporations gain control of most daily newspapers, they are collecting local monopolies. Television (which does little systematic local reporting of the kind done by local newspapers) is a semimonopoly of the three affiliated stations. There is more competition in magazines, books, and motion

pictures, but as their ownership has become more concentrated over the years, their social and political orientation has become more uniform. . . .

There are fourteen dominant companies that have half or more of the daily newspaper business (seven years ago there were twenty), three in magazines (seven years ago there were twenty), three in television (seven years ago there were three), six in book publishing (seven years ago there were eleven), and four in motion picture production (seven years ago there were four). Today the dominant firms in each medium total thirty. But some corporations are dominant in more than one medium. For example, Newhouse and Thompson are dominant in newspapers, magazines, and books; Paramount Communications, Inc. (until mid-1989 called Gulf + Western) . . . in books and motion pictures; Time Warner in magazines, books, and movies; Murdoch in newspapers, magazines, and movies. Because of the dominance of some firms in more than one medium, the total number of corporations dominating all major media is twenty-three.

If one considers total revenues from all media, including recordings, cable, and videocassettes, seventeen firms receive half or more of all that revenue. That calculation expresses the collective media power of the seventeen firms. But it does not show which corporations dominate each individual medium, which is the basis of this book [i.e., *The Media Monopoly*, 3/e].

The corporations listed in this book [*The Media Monopoly*] as "dominant" have control of half or more of all the activity in their particular medium. A few dominant firms always establish the nature of any market, and universally they do it with advantage to themselves—in pricing and distribution, in promotion, in obtaining sympathetic government policies, in increasing their control of product beyond consumer choice, and in overwhelming or preventing new competition. . . .

In any field, whether the media or detergents, when most of the business is dominated by a few firms and the remainder of the field is left to a scattering of dozens or hundreds of smaller firms, it is the few dominant ones who control that market. With detergents it means higher prices and lowered choice. With the media it means the same thing for the public news, information, ideas, and popular culture.

The measure of half-or-more-of-the-business varies by medium. For daily newspapers, this book [*The Media Monopoly*] has used average daily circulation because the papers are all issued daily and their circulation is carefully audited by an independent agency. (If gross revenues per company were applied to newspaper companies, the dominance of the top corporations would be even more highly concentrated than if listed by circulation alone; but since accurate figures for the revenue for individual newspapers is seldom available, circulation has been used.) Magazines, on the other hand, are used at different intervals, from weekly to quarterly, so varying circulations are not comparable as measures of strength; annual revenues, the standard of that industry, are therefore used. Television dominance is measured by audience reach, which is regularly surveyed by rating agencies; initial possession of revenues is also used for television and radio. Book and motion picture corporations are measured by annual revenues. Only the audiences and

revenues of a particular medium involved are counted, not revenues of the parent firm, which may be in other media or in nonmedia enterprises. Many of the firms listed below are significant players in other media, but unless they are part of a group that has half or more of one medium, they are not listed as "dominant."

In recent years, ever-mounting levels of media conglomeration worldwide have made it more complicated to determine how much absolute equity each large corporation (or its bank and investment house) has in which combination of properties. The large magazine group, Diamandis, until its sale in 1988, was 70 percent owned by Prudential Insurance Company. It was once owned by CBS, which also had other business, including defense. Recently, Diamandis, in turn, was sold to the large French publishing firm, Hachette, whose chairman is also chairman of the largest defense contractor in France.

Some large firms remain private (Hearst, Newhouse, Reader's Digest Association) without legal need to make public financial filings. For them, market share comes from educated guesses by media specialists on Wall Street and by general knowledge of their audited circulation and advertising pages. Other firms, like Rupert Murdoch's News Corp. Ltd., have complex mixtures of private subsidiaries that operate in a number of different nations. More and more the dominant firms exchange properties to fill out their particular domination patterns or cooperate on mutually beneficial ventures. They have participated in the 1980s phenomenon of the creation of ambiguous forms of debt—junk bonds, preferred stocks treated as bonds, and other new forms of Wall Street paper.

The highest levels of world finance have become intertwined with the highest levels of mass media ownership, with the result of tighter control over the systems on which most of the public depends for its news and information.

Narrow control has advanced rapidly. In 1981, forty-six corporations controlled most of the business in daily newspapers, magazines, television, books, and motion pictures. Today, these media generate even larger amounts of money, but the number of giants that get most of the business has shrunk from forty-six to twenty-three.

The dominant twenty-three corporations are:

1. Bertelsmann, A.G. (books)
2. Capital Cities/ABC (newspapers, broadcasting)
3. Cox Communications (newspapers)
4. CBS (broadcasting)
5. Buena Vista Films (Disney; motion pictures)
6. Dow Jones (newspapers)
7. Gannett (newspapers)
8. General Electric (television)
9. Paramount Communications (books, motion pictures)
10. Harcourt Brace Jovanovich (books)
11. Hearst (newspapers, magazines)
12. Ingersoll (newspapers)
13. International Thomson (newspapers)
14. Knight Ridder (newspapers)
15. Media News Group (Singleton; newspapers)
16. Newhouse (newspapers, books)
17. News Corporation Ltd. (Murdoch; newspapers, magazines, motion pictures)
18. New York Times (newspapers)
19. Reader's Digest Association (books)
20. Scripps-Howard (newspapers)
21. Time Warner (magazines, books, motion pictures)
22. Times Mirror (newspapers)
23. Tribune Company (magazines)

Newspapers

Most of the fourteen corporations that dominate the daily newspaper industry have acquired additional daily newspapers (and other media) in the last seven years. The number of daily papers in the country has continued to shrink, from 1,763 in 1960 to 1,643 in 1989, but total national daily circulation has risen slightly from 62 million to 62.9 million and is dominated by a smaller number of firms, from twenty-seven years ago to fourteen today.

The fourteen, in order of their daily circulation as of September 30, 1988, were:

Gannett Company: *USA Today* and 87 other dailies

Knight-Ridder, Inc.: Philadelphia *Inquirer*, Miami *Herald*, and 27 others

Newhouse Newspapers: Staten Island *Advance*, Portland *Oregonian*, and 24 other papers (Newhouse also owns Condé Nast magazines and Random House book publishing)

Tribune Company: *Chicago Tribune, New York Daily News*, and 7 others

Times Mirror; *Los Angeles Times* and 7 others

Dow Jones & Co.: *Wall Street Journal* and 22 Ottaway newspapers

International Thomson; 120 dailies and book publishing

New York Times: *New York Times* and 26 others

Scripps-Howard Newspapers; Denver *Rocky Mountain News* and 22 others

Hearst; *San Francisco Examiner* and 13 others

Cox; *Atlanta Journal* and 19 others

News Corp. Ltd. (Murdoch): *Boston Herald* and 2 others

Media News Group (Singleton): Dallas *Times Herald* and 17 others

Ingersoll Newspapers; New Haven *Register* and 36 others

Magazines

Tightening concentration was most dramatic in magazines, which from 1981 to 1988 went from twenty dominant corporations to three. The chief cause was the further enlargement of Time, Inc., which in mid-1989 merged with Warner to form Time Warner, the largest media firm in the world. Similarly, Rupert Murdoch's purchase of Walter Annenberg's Triangle Publications made him dominant in yet another field, when combined with his existing magazine holdings. The purchase price of $3 billion was a reminder of how the media field has become an arena open only to giants. In 1979 when Gannett Company bought Combined Communications Corporation (billboards, newspapers, and broadcasting) it was the largest amount of money ever involved in a media acquisition up to that time—$340 million.

The three dominant corporations, in order of estimated annual revenues, are:

Time Warner: *Time, People, Sports Illustrated, Fortune,* and others

News Corp. Ltd.: *TV Guide, Seventeen, New York,* and others

Hearst: *Good Housekeeping, Cosmopolitan,* and others

Television

The three television networks—Capital Cities/ABC, CBS, and NBC—despite mergers, attempted takeovers, extreme corporate turbulence, and declining prime-time viewing, still dominate the field. Cable and home ownership of VCRs has grown, but the three networks still have more than two-thirds of the audience. When all radio and television revenues are counted, the three networks still have most of the revenues. ABC is still owned by Capital Cities, a rich but undistinguished newspaper chain. CBS, after incurring massive indebtedness in fighting off hostile takeovers, finished by being controlled by a real estate operator who instituted draconian cost-cutting and reduction of its most distinguished activity, news and documentary units. General Electric, the tenth largest United States corporation and a major defense contractor, bought RCA, owner of the National Broadcasting Company, for $6.3 billion.

Book Publishing

Book publishing, less driven by the commanding force of mass advertising on which newspapers, magazines, and broadcasting depend, is still highly concentrated. The 2,500 companies that regularly issue one or more books a year are dominated in revenues by six corporations that grossed more than half of book revenues.

In books, as in other media, there is a growing presence of corporations that dominate in other media. Of the six largest book publishing firms, five are active in other media.

The six companies are:

Paramount Communications (Simon & Schuster, Ginn & Company, and others)

Harcourt Brace Jovanovich (Academic Press and others)

Time Warner (Little, Brown; Scott, Foresman; and others)

Bertelsmann, A. G. (Doubleday, Bantam Books, and others)

Reader's Digest Association (Condensed Books and others)

Newhouse (Random house and others)

Motion Pictures

The motion picture industry has always been volatile in its corporate convolutions, but through it all the major studios, in one incarnation or another, have remained dominant.

In 1988, in terms of share of box office grosses for their films, there were four firms with most of the business:

Buena Vista Films (Disney)
Paramount Communications (Paramount Pictures)
20th-Century Fox (Murdoch)
Time Warner (Warner Brothers)

Like other large media companies, General Electric brings yet another complication that distinguishes it from small, local companies: it has, through its board of directors, interlocks with still other major industrial and financial sectors of the American economy, in wood products, textiles, automotive supplies, department store chains, and banking.

Under law, the director of a company is obliged to act in the interests of his or her own company. It has always been an unanswered dilemma when an officer of Corporation A, who also sits as a director on the board of Corporation B, has to choose between acting in the best interests of Corporation A or of Corporation B.

Interlocked boards of directors have enormously complicated potential conflicts of interest in the major national and multinational corporations that now control most of the country's media.

A 1979 study by Peter Dreier and Steven Weinberg found interlocked directorates in major newspaper chains. Gannett shared directors with Merrill Lynch (stockbrokers), Standard Oil of Ohio, 20th-Century Fox, Kerr-McGee (oil, gas, nuclear power, aerospace), McDonnell Douglas Aircraft, McGraw-Hill, Eastern Airlines, Phillips Petroleum, Kellogg Company, and New York Telephone Company.

The most influential paper in America, the *New York Times*, interlocked with Merck, Morgan Guaranty Trust, Bristol Myers, Charter Oil, Johns Manville, American Express, Bethlehem Steel, IBM, Scott Paper, Sun Oil, and First Boston Corporation. . . .

Louis Brandeis, before joining the Supreme Court, called this linkage "the endless chain." He wrote: "This practice of interlocking directorates is the root of many evils. It offends laws human and divine. . . . It tends to disloyalty and violation of the fundamental law that no man can serve two masters. . . . It is undemocratic, for it rejects the platform: 'A fair field and no favors.' "

As media conglomerates have become larger, they have been integrated into the higher levels of American banking and industrial life, as subsidiaries and interlocks within their boards of directors. Half the dominant firms are members of the Fortune 500 largest corporations in the country. They are heavy investors in, among other things, agribusiness, airlines, coal and oil, banking, insurance, defense contracts, automobile sales, rocket engineering, nuclear power, and nuclear weapons. Many have heavy foreign investments that are affected by American foreign policy.

It is normal for all large businesses to make serious efforts to influence the news, to avoid embarrassing publicity, and to maximize sympathetic public opinion and government policies. Now they own most of the news media that they wish to influence.

NO

Maxwell E. McCombs

CONCENTRATION, MONOPOLY, AND CONTENT

Some critics contend that the marketplace of news, entertainment, and commentary becomes significantly less diverse when suspension of publication by a competitor leaves a city with only a single daily newspaper. Monopolies, of course, have become the modal situation across North America. The disappearance of competition and the emergence of monopolies in all but a handful of markets is the culmination of an economic trend set in motion well over a half century ago.

Traditionally, the presence of the competing daily newspapers in a market was taken as prima facie evidence of diversity. But traditional assumptions in democratic political theory about competition and the diversity of news and opinion in the marketplace need to be examined more rigorously. An important role of social science is to make explicit and subject to empirical verification the assumptions only partially articulated in our social rhetoric. Even if traditional democratic assumptions about competition and diversity were empirically true in the eighteenth and nineteenth century, they need to be examined in light of the social and economic situation in the late twentieth century. How much difference does the structure of ownership in a local newspaper market make to what is available to local readers?

Or, alternatively, as the more recent literature on the sociology of news asks, how much of what is available to local readers is determined by the traditions, practices, and beliefs of journalists, regardless of the ownership structure? The traditions of journalism center on news values and ethical standards, such as objectivity and fairness. The homogenizing influence of these traditions on news content has been traced back to the 19th century by Schudson (1978), Shaw (1972), and Roshco (1975). Seminal research by Epstein (1973) and Sigal (1973) has documented the impact of work practices

From Maxwell E. McCombs, "Concentration, Monopoly, and Content," in Robert Picard, James Winter, Maxwell McCombs, and Stephen Lacy, eds., *Press Concentration and Monopoly: New Perspectives on Newspaper Ownership and Operation* (Ablex Publishing, 1988), pp. 129-137. Copyright © 1988 by Ablex Publishing. Reprinted by permission of the publisher.

and organizational constraints on the final news product, influences which are more internal to the news organization and profession than to any external competition. The beliefs and social perspectives of journalists as centripetal forces for a centrist convergence also have been detailed for a variety of news organizations by Gans (1979) and Gitlin (1980).

In short, the sociology of news literature collectively creates the expectation that newspapers competing in the same geographic and demographic market will produce highly similar products. For example, a detailed content analysis of competing dailies in 23 U.S. cities found no statistically significant differences between "leaders" and "trailers" across the 22 content categories compared. Nor did Weaver and Mullins (1975) find any differences in the proportion of space devoted to editorial content. This null relationship between competition and message diversity also is reflected in the preponderance of evidence from the accumulated journalism research of the past five decades (see e.g., Nafziger & Barnhart, 1946; Bigman, 1948; Willoughby, 1955; Nixon & Jones, 1956; Donohue & Glasser, 1978).

These assertions and questions about newspaper content and competition became far more than academic considerations when, in 1981, the Canadian government brought antitrust charges against the country's two major newspaper groups, Thomson and Southam. Among the issues in contention were the suspension of the Montreal *Star* in 1979, leaving Southam's *Gazette* as the only English-language daily in that city; and the suspension by Southam of the Winnipeg *Tribune* in 1980, leaving Thomson's *Free Press* as the only daily there.[1]

These suspensions also created a natural experiment for testing hypotheses about competition and diversity through content analysis. With the shift from competition to monopoly occurring in two widely separated markets, it is possible to do a detailed before-and-after study and to build in a replication.[2] Both in Montreal and Winnipeg, pairs of dailies can be examined in a period of vigorous competition, and the surviving daily can be compared before and after the demise of its competitor. In both cities, the "before" period is 2 years prior to the suspension of competition, and the "after" period is 1 year after suspension, a total span of 3 years.[3]

Drawing from the three intellectual traditions— democratic political theory, sociology of news, and journalism research—this content analysis of the daily newspapers in Montreal and Winnipeg framed two broad competing hypotheses to guide the numerous detailed comparisons of these newspapers. One hypothesis, based on traditional assumptions of competition and diversity, predicts differences during the period of competition in each city. As a corollary, the views of at least some critics also would lead to an expectation of major negative changes in the surviving newspaper. The opposing hypothesis, based on the sociology of news and journalism research, predicts no significant differences between the newspapers during the period of competition in each city. This hypothesis also would predict the lack of any significant changes in the surviving newspaper.

COMPARING THE NEWSPAPERS

Newspapers are the epitome of mass communication, with its broad array of messages for a vast audience. To examine the degree of diversity present in the newspapers of cities such as Montreal and Winnipeg, a content analysis should begin with broad comparisons of these newspapers and progressively narrow the scope of these comparisons. For example, the Montreal newspapers in both 1977 and 1980 published a wide range of news, entertainment, and commentary— 200 items or more a day in each newspaper, hundreds of pages a week.[4] But how different were these editorial products?

There were different news/advertising ratios in the competing Montreal newspapers of 1977. The newshole in the *Star* was 36% of its total space, while the *Gazette's* newshole was 48% of its total space. However, close examination of the figures also reveals a "fat" Montreal *Star* (420 pages per week) verses a *Gazette* less than two-thirds its size (256 pages per week). Under such circumstances it is hardly surprising that the "thin" *Gazette* found it necessary to maintain a proportionately larger newshole in order to compete with the *Star's* extensive contents. And after the *Star's* demise, the now "fat" *Gazette* (536 pages per week) displayed a news/advertising ratio identical to that of the *Star* when it dominated the Montreal market.

During the period of competition in Winnipeg, the *Free Press* was a substantially larger daily than the *Tribune*, averaging over 13 pages and over 50 stories a day more than its competitor. This practice of producing a "fat" daily persisted after the suspension of the *Tribune*. During the period of competition, however, the two newspapers in Winnipeg had different news/advertising ratios. While the *Tribune* maintained a 35/65 ratio of news to advertising, the larger *Free Press*

was closer to a 30/70 ratio of news to advertising. However, after the suspension of the *Tribune*, the *Free Press* increased its newshole, both proportionally and in terms of actual news space. The newshole was now 35% of the total space—an increase from 157 pages in 1978 to 165 pages in 1981.

Of course, the design of each day's newspaper does not result from any set of precise calculations or specifications, but rather from a melange of long-term and short-term decisions and judgments applied to the material available that day. Typically, the material published is no more than 10% to 20% of what is available and, of course, a much smaller percentage of the actual day's events.

Under such circumstances one would hardly expect identical editorial products. Some diversity in news and content is inevitable, but there are varying degrees of diversity! To take a nonjournalistic example, the numerous wineries of California's Napa Valley do not produce perfectly identical Cabernet Sauvingnons. But their diversity is diminished in the eye of the observer when Bordeaux clarets are added to the comparison. Add some white Burgundies, and there is yet more diversity. Enough on the diversities of wine. The point is that the range of diversity in any set of comparisons may be minor in scope. Here the notion of diversity in newspaper content is taken to mean some degree of major scope. Some comparisons conform to what the average person would consider diversity.

Beginning with the general character of the Montreal newspapers, how diverse were their packages of news, entertainment, and commentary in 1977 and 1980? The research presents a picture of *rivals in conformity*. Detailed comparisons of the general content categories reveal only a few significant differences between the two newspapers. Most striking is the larger volume of general news in the *Star* when it dominated the market. Interestingly, the other two differences are from the editorial pages. In 1977 the *Star* ran more local editorials and more letters to the editor than did the *Gazette*. To the extent that a strong local editorial voice is indicated by the number of local editorials, the *Star* was the strongest newspaper in 1977. It also was the newspaper which provided more community participation on the editorial page through publication of letters to the editor. Neither the number of local editorials nor letters to the editor in the *Gazette* increased after the disappearance of the *Star*.

The *Gazette* did significantly increase its general news and sports coverage, and the number of comics, from 1977 to 1980. These three categories largely account for the increased number of items appearing in the *Gazette*.

Parallel to the pattern in Montreal, Winnipeg is another portrait of rivals in conformity. With only three exceptions, the rival *Tribune* and *Free Press* produced highly similar products. Detailed comparisons of the general content categories shows only three statistically significant differences in the amount of news published on a typical day: business news (the *Free Press* published more), lifestyle/food news (again, the *Free Press* published more), and nonlocal editorials (the *Tribune* averaged about one a day, while the *Free Press* concentrated exclusively on local editorials).

After the suspension of the *Tribune* in 1980, the *Free Press* remained much the same newspaper. Only one category, letters to the editor, changed significantly. The number of letters published during a typical week more than doubled, so that the *Free Press* of 1981 was running more letters each week than both newspapers together had published back in 1978. To the extent that a strong editorial voice also is indicated by the number of local editorials, the *Free Press* continued its established practice of publishing two or more local editorials daily.

NEWS OF THE DAY

Narrowing the focus of our attention, to take a detailed look at the news of the day, we can consider those items appearing principally on the front page and main news pages of a newspaper. In all four of the newspapers examined here, more than half of the news of the day falls in the category of political news, evidence for the sociology of news view that the sharing of professional news values across news organizations results in highly similar products.[5] In this case we see a high degree of similarity across two cities and across a variety of time periods.

Comparison of the Montreal profiles reveals no difference between the competing *Star* and *Gazette*. There was a statistically significant change over all in the news coverage of the *Gazette* from 1977 to 1980, a substantial decrease in crime news and a modest decrease in human interest material. Modest increases also occurred in the political and banking categories. Emphasis remained much the same from 1977 to 1980 on all the other categories of the news.

Statistical comparison of the three Winnipeg profiles reveal no difference between the *Tribune* and *Free Press* in 1978, or between the 1978 and 1981 editions of the *Free Press* in their emphasis on various categories of news.

GEOGRAPHY OF THE NEWS

Another way of examining the diversity of newspaper content is to consider the geography of the news, the daily map of the world presented in the news pages. Since all but a few American and Canadian newspapers are highly local in their news perspective, differences would be expected between Montreal in the east and Winnipeg to the west. But a sociology of news perspective would predict high similarity in the geographical focus of newspapers in the same city.

The *geography of the news* in the Montreal newspapers before and after the suspension of the *Star* was essentially the same. Examination of the patterns of geographic coverage reveals that about one story of every six was local news. Roughly a similar proportion of stories was news of Quebec province.

After the suspension of the *Star*, the *Gazette* had a more cosmopolitan emphasis. Local news and Quebec news coverage decreased, while news coverage increased for Ottawa, the Maritimes, western Canada, and foreign countries (other than the U.S.).

In Winnipeg there was a statistically significant difference in the geographic perspectives of the *Tribune* and *Free Press* in 1978. *Free Press* coverage placed a heavier emphasis on local news from Winnipeg. While better than one story out of four was local in the *Free Press'* news of the day, local coverage in the *Tribune* was closer to one story in five. The two papers' coverage of Manitoba provincial news was about the same.

Ontario receives major coverage in almost all Canadian newspapers regardless of their location in the country. While this is true in both Montreal and Winnipeg, the *Free Press* coverage of Ontario

in 1978 was approximately double that of the *Tribune*. Interestingly, the *Tribune* placed much heavier emphasis on U.S. news than did the *Free Press* in 1978. Otherwise, all the papers examined here devote about one story in six to U.S. coverage.

With the demise of the *Tribune*, the *Free Press* cut back on the areas where it exceeded *Tribune* coverage (local news and Ontario news) and expanded where it had trailed the *Tribune* (U.S. news).

SOURCES OF NEWS

There were significant differences among the competing Montreal newspapers in their use of sources. The principal difference in 1977 results from the greater diversity in the *Gazette's* wire service sources for the news of the day. While both newspapers used CP and AP, only the *Gazette* also relied upon UPI. The other principal difference is in the use of syndicated material, more extensive in the *Star* than in the *Gazette*. Interestingly, the use of locally produced staff copy is almost identical in the two newspapers. For both it is about two news stories out of every five.

There were extensive, statistically significant changes in the *Gazette* from 1977 to 1980. Use of locally produced staff copy declined from 38.07% to 29.86%. Of course, the substantial increase in the newshole of the *Gazette* must be taken into account in interpreting this finding. In terms of actual stories, there were 122 staff stories published during a typical week in 1977, and 156 staff stories published during a typical week during 1980. Of course, in terms if the sheer number of local staff news stories, Montreal readers were receiving about 100 fewer stories per week after the *Star* closed.

There also were significant differences among the Winnipeg newspapers in their use of sources. The major difference is the much greater volume of staff produced news in the *Free Press*, a level of staff production maintained after the suspension of the *Tribune*. Otherwise, in 1978 the two Winnipeg newspapers were much the same in their relative use of CP, AP, and syndicated material.

There are statistically significant changes in the *Free Press'* use of news sources from 1978 to 1981, but all of these are in the relative use of external material. Use of CP declined and the use of AP increased, bringing the two into approximate parity. Use of other external sources increased substantially. Both before and after the suspension of the *Tribune*, the *Free Press* staff produced about four stories out of every 10 in the news of the day. This was a significantly higher level of staff stories than appeared in the *Tribune*.

SUMMARY

Traditional democratic assumptions about newspaper competition and the diversity of content are not well supported by these content analyses of the Montreal and Winnipeg papers. Comparisons of the general content reveal few significant differences between either pair of competitors; examination of the news of the day reveals no significant differences at all. There were some differences in the geographic emphasis of the Winnipeg competitors, and there were differences in both markets in the sources of news. But these latter differences, geography and sources, are no more than minor variations on a theme. Emphasizing U.S. news more, or local news less, are minor points of differentiations in essentially

similar products. All four of the newspapers examined here represent the mainstream of North American journalism in style and content.

The "critics corollary" that the demise of a competitor will be followed by diminished quality in the survivor is totally rebutted by the evidence of these content analyses. Only a few changes from before to after the end of competition were found, and all of these were positive changes in the quality of the editorial product.

In short, these data support a sociology of news perspective that newspapers competing for the same geographic and demographic market will produce highly similar products due to the similarity of their professional values, beliefs, and practices. The increasing professionalization of journalism during this century has resulted in a convergence of views among journalists about what is the news of the day. For example, a qualitative analysis of the Montreal newspapers' coverage of a regional power blackout indicated that readers of both newspapers received essentially the same facts emanating from the same sources over a 3-day period.

Finally, these empirical findings undermine the notion that vigorous use of the antitrust statutes can insure a diversity of information in the marketplace. The principal conclusion to be drawn from this content analysis of Canadian newspapers during the last decade is one drawn over 25 years ago by Professors Raymond Nixon and Robert Jones after an extensive examination of 420 competitive and noncompetitive U.S. dailies:

> differences in quality seem to hinge upon the "social responsibility and professional competence" of those who own and operate the papers, irrespec-

tive of whether they have competition. (Nixon & Jones, 1956, p. 313).

Professional perspectives on journalism, not the presence or absence of competition, determine the content of the daily newspaper. Competition does not insure diversity.

NOTES

1. As part of the defense against these charges, Thomson funded an extensive content analysis of the newspapers in Montreal and Winnipeg before and after the suspensions. While the study reported here was prepared for that adversarial procedure, it should be emphasized that Thomson maintained an arms-length relationship at all times. All decisions on conceptualization, hypotheses, operational definitions, analyses, etc. were independently made by the author and his research associates, Luis Torres-Bohl and Val Pipps. These details and the findings were revealed to Thomson executives and the defense team only upon delivery of the completed research report.

2. It is important to point out that, following the demise of the *Star*, the *Gazette* was not a monopoly newspaper per se, but a monopoly English-language paper in Montreal. Another important distinction between these papers is that the *Gazette* has been regarded as an elite newspaper, a Montreal equivalent of the *Globe and Mail*. Additionally, in Winnipeg, the *Free Press* did receive competition, albeit minor, from the new tabloid daily, the *Sun*.

3. To yield representative pictures of what these newspapers provided their readers, three criteria were set for selection of the actual months to be sampled before and after the suspensions in Montreal and Winnipeg:

1. Use of a "typical" news and advertising period to avoid special seasons, such as Christmas and the summer vacation period.

2. Selection of observation points far enough removed from the date of suspension to eliminate the perturbation of this change in the market, yet close enough in time to be pertinent.

3. Holding the observation month constant across time (before and after suspension) and across markets (Montreal and Winnipeg). This yields directly comparable replications

and eliminates a major alternative explanation for any differences in the results.

Since the Montreal *Star* closed in September 1979 and the Winnipeg *Tribune* closed in August 1980, the simultaneous application of these criteria suggested observing each surviving newspaper in September of the year after the suspension in its city, September 1980 for the Montreal *Gazette* and September 1981 for the Winnipeg *Free Press*.

Use of an identical interval for the "before" observation period was complicated by an extended strike at the Montreal *Star* from June 1978 to February 1979. Therefore, the "before" interval was extended to 2 years, September 1977 for Montreal and September 1978 for Winnipeg. In short, each market was observed 2 years before and one year after the end of the competition.

For each of these Septembers, six issues of the newspaper(s), were measured in detail. While a full week's sample can adequately represent a much larger span of time, the contents of any particular week's issues of a newspaper are subject to the idiosyncrasies of that week's news events and advertising campaigns. Therefore, a 6-day *constructed week*, consisting of one Monday, one Tuesday, etc., selected at random from the entire month, was used as the sample. During those periods when two newspapers were being published in the same market, the same constructed week was used for both newspapers.

4. The September 10, 1977, issues of the Montreal *Star* and Montreal *Gazette* were analyzed using both frequency counts and space measurement. The correlations between these two sets of measures across the news categories adapted from Bruce (1966) were .97 for the *Gazette* and .99 for the *Star*. This is true whether the amount of space taken up by the headline was included in the space measure or not. Based on these findings, the decision was made to employ frequency counts as the measurement procedure in this study.

To ascertain the reliability of the frequency counts, two coders were employed. After discussion of the coding categories and procedures, each of the coders *independently* coded the September 12, 1977, issues of the *Star* and *Gazette*. At this point, there was substantial agreement between the coders, but, to further check the robustness of the coding procedures, the two coders next independently coded the September 10, 1977, issues of the two Montreal newspapers. Overall, 24 different comparisons were made as the two coders used the various category sets to content analyze the special sections, editorial and op-ed pages, and news of the day. Both the median and modal correlation was +.99, and only three of the 24 correlation coefficients were less than +.90. Comparisons of independent analyses of the September 11, 1978, issues of the

Winnipeg *Free Press* and *Tribune* also revealed a high degree of reliability in the coding of those data.

5. It should be emphasized that this statement is made in the context of the quantitative approach taken in this study. *Amount* of political news may or may not reflect *quality* of that news. If, for example, the *Free Press* supported the Conservatives and the *Tribune*, before its demise, supported the Liberals, this latter perspective is obviously lost.

POSTSCRIPT

Media Monopolies: Does Concentration of Ownership Jeopardize Media Content?

A number of authors have examined the issue of concentration of ownership in the media industry. See particularly the books by Bagdikian and Picard from which the above selections were taken. Additionally, Benjamin Compaine et al. in *Who Owns the Media? Concentration of Ownership in the Media Communications Industry* 2nd edition, (Knowledge Industries, 1982) examine the same issue. Also useful is Christopher Sterling's *Electronic Media: A Guide to Trends in Broadcasting and Newer Technologies, 1920–1983* (Praeger, 1984), particularly in the ownership and economics sections. A special symposium in the *Journal of Communication* (Summer 1985) entitled "The Marketplace of Ideas Revisited" includes articles by a number of authors on topics ranging from cultural production to the First Amendment.

In his Marxist analysis of the economic and political structure of the broadcasting industry, Herbert I. Schiller in *Mass Communication and the American Empire* (Kelley, 1969) finds it organized primarily to serve the military-industrial complex. In his *Who Knows: Information in the Age of the Fortune 500* (Ablex Publishing, 1987), Schiller examines the largest U.S. corporation's involvement in information technology and the national and international ramifications.

Knowledge Industry 200 (1987) is an irregularly issued economic analysis of America's 200 largest media and information companies, including revenue and profit data, recent restructurings, and corporate officers. For the most recent information on corporate changes, consult an industry-oriented publication such as *Broadcasting* magazine.

PART 6

The Information Society

Predictions of a world increasingly reliant upon media and communications technologies have generally provided either utopian or dystopian visions about what our lives will be like. The information age is indeed upon us. It is our responsibility to ensure that it continues to serve us.

What is meant by "information"? Will today's values be sufficient for a more technologized society? If we can communicate more efficiently, will our understanding of issues also improve? Will more technology help society if people are not technologically literate? Is all "progress" good? By such questioning, we establish the proper role new technologies will play both in society and in our individual lives.

Can Communication Technologies
  Increase Political Participation?

Has High Technology Improved the
  Quality of American Life?

Can Modern Mass Communication
  Promote a Better World?

ISSUE 16

Can Communication Technologies Increase Political Participation?

YES: Ted Becker, from "Teledemocracy: Bringing Power Back to the People," *The Futurist* (December 1981)

NO: F. Christopher Arterton, from *Teledemocracy: Can Technology Protect Democracy?* (Sage, 1987)

ISSUE SUMMARY

YES: Media critic Ted Becker cites several studies that have employed interactive technology to increase voter participation and finds public response to be favorable.
NO: F. Christopher Arterton, dean of the Graduate School of Political Management in New York City, also critiques past experiments in using interactive technology to increase participation, but he sees the cost, quality, and nature of participation as primary problems.

It is hard to determine why voter turnout has been decreasing in every presidential election since 1960, but many social critics note that the decline in voting has corresponded to increased political attention by the media. Some authors claim that television provides a vicarious political arena, thereby making the real political event seem less real and more of a staged experience. Others claim that the increasing number of communication channels and the individual's sense of alienation from society have gone hand-in-hand, thereby reducing citizen desire for participation in the electoral process.

These notions and many others have prompted critics to wonder what possibilities new technologies could provide for extending a sense of participation to an individual who does not vote or become involved in political events. How can forms of media *encourage* participation? The term given to using electronic media for this purpose is *teledemocracy,* and in most cases, the actions of the public are monitored by two-way, or *interactive,* services that utilize traditional and new forms of media distribution for message presentation and immediate response.

Surprisingly, there have been many attempts to use traditional broadcast television, cable (particularly with a response panel for immediate reaction), interactive teleconferencing via satellite, and computer networks for the specific purpose of seeing whether or not individuals are more likely to register their opinions without the traditional voting booth. The authors of our two selections cite some of the specific cases, and although each acknowledges a level of increased participation, their predictions for the future differ.

Becker is encouraged by the willingness of individuals in the test cases to use technology as a form of teledemocracy and cites the users' enjoyment, willingness to participate, and level of involvement as indicative of success for this system of voicing opinion. His studies confirm that people of all ages, races, and education and economic levels were equally willing participants in this form of teledemocracy.

Arterton is much more cautious regarding the impact of teledemocracy. Citing the need for a plebiscite (a direct vote by the entire population) for most truly democratic issues, he warns that today's media are too costly to provide input often enough to mean anything significant to elected officials. Even though he feels that different forms of media may be effective on a smaller scale, the current development of newer technologies and their corporate holdings indicate that plebiscites are even less likely to occur via technological means in the future. Even the benefits to the users, such as reducing travel time to polling places, town meetings, or other such alternatives, may be too costly for most purposes.

The positions of these two authors have some similar areas of discussion, but each interprets the data in a different way. Becker endorses using the technology that is already available and finds that people enjoy this type of interaction, but Arterton says that the technology is still too costly to provide the true picture of public opinion. Each of the authors, however, sees the future use of technology for democratic procedures as interesting and inevitable, at least for some purposes.

What these authors, however, do not discuss (although Arterton alludes to the problem) is how individuals make decisions and interact with the technology. Would the possibility of voting from your living room for a candidate promote voting with less thought or with real motivation behind your support of that person or position? Even though the number of votes cast would be greater, would this indicate that the person was voting on whim or on principle? How can the technological systems control for registered voters, one vote per person, or unauthorized voting? Since all people are not technologically literate, nor do some enjoy new uses of technology, would these people be left out and their voices unheard?

We know that politicians engage media consultants to make them appear better in the media—would a system of teledemocracy favor the best-looking candidate or the position that has been supported with the most sophisticated graphics? We have much to learn about the intricacies of teledemocracy, but the use of today's technology for this purpose is, we agree, intriguing and inevitable.

YES

Ted Becker

TELEDEMOCRACY: BRINGING POWER BACK TO THE PEOPLE

These are bad times for democracy. Only half those American citizens eligible to vote did so in the last presidential election, following a trend of declining voter participation in recent years. Many nonvoters in the United States feel powerless and forgotten, ignored by elected representatives and overwhelmed by what they perceive as the power and influence of special and vested interests.

These are good times for democracy. In Europe, there is a trend for national governments to put vital questions directly to the people for them to decide the destiny of their countries:

- England—join the Common Market?
- Spain—adopt a new constitution?
- Italy—allow abortion?

But whether the trend is favorable or not, there is a deep yearning in nations everywhere to increase the democratic essence of their political life.

Fortunately, new technologies and techniques present exciting prospects for involving people directly in governing themselves. Teledemocracy—the term coined for electronically aided, rapid, two-way political communication—could offer the means to help educate voters on issues, to facilitate discussion of important decisions, to register instantaneous polls, and even to allow people to vote directly on public policy.

Experiments in teledemocracy first began in earnest in the 1970s. The first tests were modest in scale, using small groups like apartment complexes and housing communities.

Perhaps the first successful large-scale adventure was Alternatives for Washington (AFW), which ran from 1974 to 1976. The brainchild of Governor Dan Evans, AFW was a state-sponsored project that sought to involve as many of the state's citizens as possible in conceiving and choosing among a number of potential long-range futures for the state.

AFW started with meetings of a wide-based group of citizens in workshops and seminars, then employed several survey methods to involve even

From Ted Becker, "Teledemocracy: Bringing Power Back to the People," *The Futurist* (December 1981). Reprinted by permission of *The Futurist*, published by the World Future Society, 4916 Saint Elmo Avenue, Bethesda, Maryland 20814.

more people. To draw the public-at-large into the process, AFW sponsored programs on public television, then published over a million questionnaires in all the state's major newspapers that presented eleven futures and asked people for their views. Random-sample polls were conducted to determine what a representative group of citizens would choose as well.

As an exercise designed to provide broad-based, long-distance future planning, AFW was a huge success. More than 45,000 citizens answered the newspaper surveys and thousands more cooperated in the telephone random surveys. Perhaps hundreds of thousands of others watched some part of the TV programming. And many thousands participated in a multitude of meetings around the state.

AFW proved that people are eager to get involved in politics when they believe their opinions are valued and see how the decisions directly affect their futures. Despite the great response to the program, however, the state legislature proved recalcitrant in moving on the recommendations AFW developed.

INTERACTIVE TV INVOLVES PUBLIC

Perhaps the most famous teledemocratic experiment is the QUBE interactive cable TV system in Columbus, Ohio. Set up by Warner Communications Corporation in 1977 and still running, it is the most ambitious and glamorous such system in existence.

Each household subscribing to QUBE has a small black box with five buttons connected to its TV set. The viewing public can respond to questions put to it about programs by pushing the buttons as instructed.

The interaction mostly involves various kinds of entertainment (games) or marketing (the viewer as consumer), but QUBE does provide regular public affairs shows. In an interview program called "Columbus Alive" and special affairs programs, the public—the audience—is asked for opinions on selected issues. The results of this flash "polling" register instantaneously on the screen.

QUBE does have its flaws—it is mainly oriented to consumerism, merchandising, and entertainment. The home console, the black box, does cost money: it nearly doubles the cost of the basic service and would, in "real" voting, represent a "poll tax" that poor people might be hard pressed to pay. QUBE has tested in a rather well-to-do suburb that may not be a reliable gauge of how the rest of America would respond.

But look what QUBE proves! Between 80 and 90 percent of the potential pool of users of this system opt to use it. The evidence is clear that these folks truly enjoy using this teledemocratic system: they express avid interest in participating in feedback; they find the use of the system easy and rewarding. And they are willing to pay for the service directly out of their own pockets.

Another future-planning exercise using television considered highly successful by its organizers, and by participating citizens, was conducted in Canada in 1978–79. "Talking Back" was mainly a network television extravaganza of the Canadian Broadcasting Company.

Telephones, television, and computers linked a large number of simultaneous conferences in a series of electronic meetings to generate a nationwide discussion on several topics of national concern.

Although the Canadian Parliament did not crank out relevant policies as a direct result of "Talking Back," the experiment was an enormous success. In large numbers, from coast to coast, people responded with interest, time, energy, and creative thought.

NEW ZEALANDERS PLAN THEIR FUTURE

New Zealand Televote added some new dimensions to teledemocratic experiments. It was conducted in mid-1981 by a permanent government agency, the Commission for the Future, that was created by New Zealand's parliament for the purpose of involving the public in long-range future studies.

The project used a new kind of public opinion survey—televote—that is two parts telephone survey and one part mail survey. Televote organizers do extensive research for the public, then present the best pro and con argumentation on a subject in easy-to-read formats. People phone in their replies, which gives them time to do the poll at their own convenience. The method is capable of obtaining informed and deliberated opinion from representative samples of citizenry on complicated issues.

Televote originated in Hawaii, where it was used to aid the constitutional convention of 1978 and the state legislature from 1978 to 1980. Hawaii Televote operated out of a university, making the college part of the public government decision-making system. This system has also been less costly than comparable efforts by conventional polling organizations.

To cover the entire country, New Zealand Televote used a three-university network of televote centers.

Although confronted with a complex set of philosophical and policy choices, New Zealanders took to teledemocracy like birds to trees.

Thousands of New Zealanders answered a newspaper televote (with the same information and questions as in the "official televote") that was printed in half of New Zealand's major dailies and promoted by a thirty-station community radio network.

New Zealand Televote showed, too, that all segments of the nation's population—all ages, races, economic, and educational levels—were willing to join in teledemocracy.

TWO TELEDEMOCRATIC SYSTEMS

These examples are not the only teledemocratic experiments of recent vintage, nor are they necessarily the most important. Taken together, though, they help reveal two models of teledemocracy—and demonstrate the even greater promise of teledemocracy given the new hardware already on line, waiting to be plugged in.

The first of these two types of teledemocratic systems might be called Television Talkback (TT). The other is a blend of groups (workshops, conferences, task forces, meetings); polling (random and newspaper); and electronic media involvement (radio and TV) that might be called the Public Participation (PP) model.

Improved teledemocratic projects in the not-so-distant future must combine both kinds to overcome shortfalls each has alone.

For example, the TT system tends to balkanize the public by isolating individuals and families in their homes in front of the TV. Also, printed material has greater versatility than material displayed on a TV screen—and perhaps greater staying power.

The PP models have lacked the flair of the TT model. The modernity, novelty, and spontaneity of Television Talkback—whether via home console, the new "votaphone" method, or conventional telephone—inspire great public participation.

Recent innovations in technology will entice even greater mass participation. By way of illustration, the dramatic increase in electronic games that plug into TV sets will recondition people to interact with their sets rather than sit passively in front of the tube.

Other advances that will stimulate teledemocracy are the video recording and playback systems and the personal home computer. The home is on the verge of becoming *the* major educational and informational center.

New electronic interactive systems are on line and ready for everyday use in several countries, including Canada (Teledon), France (Intelmatique), and Japan (Hi-Ovis). Cable television is ready to spread through the United States like wildfire. The forecast is nothing but bright for teledemocracy, thanks to modern science.

All systems are go for more and better teledemocratic experiments: the theory and knowledge are there; the enthusiasm and enthusiasts are there; the public is there; the paraphernalia are there. Future experimentation will bring us closer and closer to implementing pure electronic democracy in a real-life situation and allow us to transform public opinion as developed and measured by teledemocratic means into the law of some lands.

What is missing is a commitment by policymakers and planners to promote and respond to teledemocratically derived opinion. Such a commitment might arise in the business sector when it is understood that teledemocratic systems, combining these hard technologies and soft techniques, have enormous profit-making potential. Millions of people are already willing to "play and pay" for electronic town meetings, just as they are already paying to shoot down space invaders and enjoy ballets. A similar commitment from the political sector may be harder to come by.

Sometime in the near future the degree of alienation may be so great, the amount of social turbulence so distressing, and the threat of chaos so imminent that a drastic political realignment will be the only path open.

We could take the radical detour to the right and march down the iron road to totalitarianism, with a government akin to the Big Brotherism foreseen by George Orwell.

But it may be preferable to embrace greater and purer democracy, to let people in, to divest, diffuse, and decentralize power as never before. At that moment, teledemocracy will be ready for its greatest challenge and responsibility. The public will no longer expect those in power to ignore its will, because the real power will rest in the will of the public itself. With the help of teledemocratic processes, public opinion will become the law of the land, as in all places where referendums and initiatives are used.

NO

F. Christopher Arterton

THE INSTITUTIONAL CONTEXT OF POLITICAL PARTICIPATION

PARTICIPATION IN DECLINE?

Most political observers would readily agree with the proposition that recently participation has been declining in the United States. The evidence most often cited to support this claim is the steady drop in voter turnout in U.S. elections since 1960. Yet joining interest groups, contributing money, phoning public officials, writing letters, knocking on doors, and a myriad of other activities ought to be included in our definition of active citizenship in a democracy. The fabric of democratic politics is woven more reliably by these strands than upon the ability to cast ballots. Because it is the most observable and measurable form of involvement, however, most attention has been paid to the decline in voting.

The Kennedy/Nixon contest drew 62.8% of all voting-age citizens. By contrast, only 52.6% of voting-age residents of the United States cast a ballot in the 1980 presidential election (and 53.3% in 1984). The same trend has occurred in midterm congressional elections. In 1962, 45.4% of the voting-age population turned out as compared to 35.5% in 1982, a slight increase over the 34.9% who voted in 1978.

How can we explain this decline in voting? The largest single drop in turnout for presidential elections occurred between 1968 and 1972 (from 55.1 to 50.7). For congressional elections, the largest drop was between 1970 and 1974 (from 43.5 to 35.8). For this reason, the Watergate events and the inclusion of 18- to 20-year-olds receive most of the blame for decreased turnout. Watergate, so the argument goes, caused massive voter disaffection, increased feelings of voter inefficacy, and raised levels of skepticism toward politics in general. These attitudinal changes continue to manifest themselves in lower turnout rates. Extending the vote to 18- to 20-year-olds reduced turnout rates because 18- to 20-year-olds have the lowest turnout levels of any age group.

Notice that conceptually these are two very different accounts of the same phenomenon. The first is a psychological explanation: Voter confidence in the political system has been eroded. We know from surveys that those disenchanted with the political system are the least likely to vote, so the explanation appears to fit with our understanding of who votes and who does not. The second account relies on demographic changes: The group with the lowest rate of voting has become a larger share of the electorate. In other words, this explanation suggests that contextual elements account for the decline in voting. By this telling, the drop in turnout is a natural by-product of public policy and not a matter of great concern about the legitimacy of the American system.

While these two arguments have some validity, they cannot fully explain the rates of decline seen over the past twenty years. First, neither could have had anything to do with the decline between 1960 and 1970. Watergate was only a minor issue in 1972; it became a visible influence on elections only in 1974. Moreover, if Watergate did have a depressing effect on turnout, that effect should have started to dissipate in 1980 as increasing numbers of younger citizens without memory or knowledge of those events have entered the electorate.

What of the younger voters? Perhaps they constitute an important factor in the explanation quite apart from the psychological effects of events in the early 1970s. Examining turnout as a function of contextual patterns since 1952, Hansen and Rosenstone (1984) found that every 10% increase in the proportion of the electorate under 25 caused a 3.3% drop in voting participation. They argued that nearly all of the decline between 1960 and 1968 and about one-half of the precipitous drop over the next four years was due to the electorate growing younger. While this is certainly a major factor, we must seek alternative explanations: Either other forces are keeping these young voters from voting as they grow older, or something is keeping older voters from voting as much as they used to, or both. Since franchise was extended to 18- to 20-year-olds in 1972, the proportion of the eligible electorate in the 18- to 20-year-old category has been steadily declining. As a result, turnout should be increasing.

Among the many possible alternative or complementary arguments that could possibly explain the decline in turnout, several seem plausible after careful examination. The first alternative is by far the easiest to demonstrate: The decline is not as much the result of a decrease in voter interest since 1960 as it is an artifact of artificially high levels of voter participation in the years leading up to 1960. The trend in voting before 1960 was upward at nearly an identical (but opposite) rate of change for midterm congressional elections, and close to the same change for presidential races. The current decline may be merely the reversal of a trend that peaked during the heated campaign between Kennedy and Nixon, and the early Kennedy years. This explanation, however, leaves much to be desired; it fails to answer the question of why political interest increased so rapidly between 1940 and 1960, as well as why participation dropped so rapidly after 1962. And it fails to explain why the rates of voting in the United States are usually well below those of most European democracies.

A second possibility, similar to the 18-year-old argument, is that the recent decline in turnout is the result of other baseline shifts in the demographic composition of the electorate. According to this argument, different population subgroups have continued to vote at the same rates, but the composition of the electorate has changed in such a way that subgroups with traditionally low turnout are growing, and those with high rates of turnout are shrinking. We know, for example, that rates of participation are related to economic well-being, the better off are more likely to participate. Since 1970, the long-term trend in the national economy has been downward; it is possible that this trend is responsible for a portion of the decline in turnout. Hansen and Rosenstone (1984) found that one-third of the drop in presidential voting over this period could be related to the percentage of citizens who identified the economy as the nation's most pressing problem. While they also found that direct measures of the economy could be related to the decline in voting, their perceptual indicator—those citing economic problems as most pressing—turned out to be a better predictor.

A major stumbling block for the general argument that low turnout subgroups have been expanding, however, can be located in the finding that education is the single largest factor affecting turnout (Wolfinger & Rosenstone, 1980). Since levels of education have been rising over this period, it seems unlikely that growth in lower SES groups would have such a large impact on turnout, especially given that the fastest and largest rise in levels of education is among the lowest SES groups.

Yet another line of argument suggests that the news media have been covering politics in such a way that voters have developed increased feelings of inef-

ficacy or disinterest. While it is beyond the scope of this project to determine the direct impact of the media on voter attitudes, I do feel compelled to make a few observations about media coverage of elections. First, whereas media coverage of presidential elections used to begin in earnest only after Labor Day, the post-1968 party reforms to increase participation in the nomination phase have fostered an expansion of media coverage more than a year before the general election. The presidential contest now becomes a top news story during the fall preceding the presidential election years. Sixteen months of extensive and nearly continuous coverage may exhaust the interest of most citizens. Furthermore, the abundant polls released by news organizations may serve to make the presidential races even less exciting. If there is no secret about who is ahead of whom, some voters may feel that there is no point to their expending the energy to go to the voting booth. Worse still, election night forecasts in 1980 and 1984 told many Western voters the contest was completely over before they had a chance to vote. As the use of exit polls increases, we can expect more and more voters will hear predicted outcomes broadcast before they have even had a chance to cast their ballots. While the evidence is murky and disputed, these predictions may depress turnout.

The increased use of polls and the more saturated media coverage of elections may well lead to the furthering of citizens' feelings of inefficacy. Just as Watergate increased cynicism, media coverage and projections that cast an election as over before it begins make voters feel their participation is meaningless. We should note that the news media are not the sole (or even major) contributors to decreased efficacy, for certainly the actual political events covered by media have an impact. Washington is far away from most people, and elected representatives are kept far too busy for many voters to feel their input is sought, heard, or acted upon. In short, the complexity and size of late twentieth-century government may have led to reduced feelings of citizen efficacy, which in turn results in reduced turnout.

We should also consider the fact that not only has government become very complex, but life in general is growing more hurried and complicated. Voters' lives are getting even more busy, leaving less time to perform the duty of a "good citizen." The workplace itself has become more specialized, requiring better command of technical skills. But more important, perhaps, is the tremendous growth of distractions available during the little leisure time citizens have left. In the days of smoke-filled back rooms, politics was a hobby. Today, there are many more hobbies to compete with politics. For the vast majority of citizens, politics has always been a leisure time concern. Now this interest may be giving way to many newer, perhaps more engaging, leisure activities.

A perplexing aspect to this problems is illuminated by comparisons to other industrial democracies. In recent elections, the United States has ranked near the bottom (twentieth out of twenty-one) in turnout as a percentage of voting-age population (Glass, Squire, & Wolfinger, 1984). While Glass and his coauthors point out that the United States does not do nearly as badly when turnout among registered voters is compared, their analysis is less persuasive on the point of why so few Americans register to vote. Granted our registration laws may be somewhat stiffer, but the burdens of going through the registration process do not seem that great. Moreover, many of the changes in political context we have discussed here—the demographic changes, the increased importance of media, the complexity of contemporary life-styles—are also being felt in most European democracies. We do not have an adequate account of why the United States is different, and until we do, the decline of participation will remain a troublesome problem. . . .

Can communication technologies be used to stimulate political participation? Can we construct political institutions that use modern technology to increase the opportunities to participate, to communicate to citizens their stakes in politics, to reduce the costs and burdens associated with involvement, and to act as an agent mobilizing and catalyzing citizen involvement?. . . .

THE PARTICIPATION PROJECTS

I will analyze . . . different projects in which elites set out to encourage political activity by citizens. Analytically, these projects constitute a degree of tinkering or experimenting with various institutional arrangements for containing political participation. As such, they take a different approach than that employed by most academic writings on participation that gives attention to explanations of the ways individuals behave. By examining the institutional context within which participation occurs, we may gain insights beyond the numerical instance of participation, moving on to investigate the quality and effectiveness of citizen involvement. . . .

Alternatives for Washington. From 1974 to 1976, then Governor Daniel Evans of

Washington organized a planning project to consider future directions across a range of state policy issues. A group of citizens, nominated by political leaders and interest groups, were brought together to discuss future directions in detail. Their work was subsequently submitted to broad public choice in the form of mailed back newspaper ballots. The project also solicited citizen participation in the form of numerous community meetings, questionnaires, and telephone polls. . . .

Choices for '76. Designed in 1973 to facilitate planning in the New York metropolitan region, Choices for '76 consisted of five films aired on 18 stations in the New York area. Citizens returned ballots printed in local newspapers covering five different regional issues. . . .

Des Moines Health Vote '82. Sponsored by the Public Agenda Forum in December 1982, Health Vote '82 involved a substantial proportion of the Des Moines, Iowa, community in a sophisticated campaign combining public relations skills with a detailed presentation of the significant trade-offs in health care service delivery. Citizens returned ballots printed in the Des Moines Register. . . .

Honolulu Electronic Town Meetings. The electronic town meetings in Hawaii combine television shows on the pro's and con's of a particular issue with two forms of voting. Citizens who wish to express an opinion are able to participate by mailing back the ballots from the newspapers or by calling in to register their opinions during and after the broadcast. . . .

Plebiscites demand broad-gauged mass media. For these purposes, the communications media as they currently exist in the United States are less than ideal. Recent events such as the at-

tempted assassination of Ronald Reagan amply demonstrate that the mechanisms do exist to communicate to all our citizens relatively rapidly. But an analogy drawn from times of crisis does not conform to the requirements of a functioning political system. As currently structured, the media available in the United States simply cannot be used to conduct the extensive and more-or-less continuous efforts that would be necessary to allow citizens to express their views of policy questions on a daily basis.

Among the projects examined, competition for the attention of potential voters has been the most persistent problem encountered by project organizers, especially by those who have sought to conduct plebiscites. The plethora of media is the single most difficult institutional barrier they face. The organizers of projects such as the Honolulu Electronic Town Meetings, Alternatives for Washington, Choices for '76, or the Des Moines Health Vote, have commandeered broadcast television because that medium has the most extensive reach to the citizenry. Their experience, however, documents that despite the capabilities of the medium, repetition and the use of multiple channels are necessary to involve anything approaching all the people. The most successful of these plebiscitarian projects, the Des Moines Health Vote, relied upon frequent public service advertisements, newspaper articles, radio talk shows, and even billboards and bus placards in addition to top public affairs broadcast programming. Yet even Health Vote had sharp limitations that circumscribe the degree to which it met the requirements of an effective, ongoing political system. It was a one-time effort staged over a lengthy time interval (to allow more opportunity to reach citizens and stimulate their thinking). It was concentrated upon a single policy area in a definable media market. And it proved to be expensive and taxing. The project amply demonstrated the capacity of technology to involve citizens in policy discussions, but it also documented how costly and extensive are the exertions needed to achieve even a 25% rate of involvement.

Can these projects serve as a model for a fully developed, effective political system? Evidently not. Consider the fact that, at present, broadcast channels require "roadblocking" and considerable repetition, which necessitates either substantial financial expenditures or a level of cooperation from private broadcasters that seems unlikely.

Moreover, the direction of change in the communications industry appears to be in a direction that will complicate the management of effective plebiscites. That is, competition for the communications industry is expanding the number of available channels. A larger number of conduits will aggravate the problems of getting the public's attention.

Perhaps the communications revolution will, as Barber (1984) suggests, allow society to establish a completely separate conduit reserved for political information exchange and voting. The problem then will become whether citizens are interested enough in public affairs to pay attention to this conduit, given all the other streams of information and entertainment available. These projects emphatically illustrate that public life is in a severe, and often losing, competition with other aspects of individual and social activity.

The evolution of the communications industry appears, on the other hand, to be improving the prospects for "pluralist" forms of teledemocracy. For example, in North Carolina* and Reading*, public officials reach out to solicit constituent opinions using semipublic cable channels. While the technology may look much like a plebiscite (television programming out, telephone calls in), the difference is really one of expectation. Since everyone knows that the cable medium reaches a small audience, the organizers cannot pretend that they are receiving back the "voice of the people."

The more innovative experiments involve the political uses of semi-private media. The legislature of Alaska,* for example, holds committee hearings over a voice-only teleconferencing network and citizens who wish to testify must go to one of 71 sites located throughout the vast state where those state-owned facilities are located. Computer conferences have been arranged allowing a congressman to discuss arms control policy with a limited group of citizens. Another congressman held videoconferences with constituents back home in California.

In addition, the evolving mix of communications media appears to be more conducive to the development of stronger interest groups; they will be able to use these narrower, private links to mobilize their membership. For example, several national interest groups now hold strategy sessions with affiliate state-level organizations to map out a lobbying strategy by a videoconference. As a result, any effective mechanism for embracing citizen participation will have to build into its design a positive role for interest groups and pluralist politics.

*References to participation projects not included in this selection.　　　—Eds.

At present, however, there is still a long way to go before we reach the point at which the available media will be ideal for pluralist dialogues. Many of the efforts studied here employed cable television and a call-in format—mechanisms that are not totally satisfactory. The televised call-in has the potential of reaching large numbers of citizens, yet the number who can voice their opinions via the feedback loop is quite small.

If the currently available conduits are inadequate, what of the future? Audio- and videoconferencing hold better prospects for the few-to-few pattern of communication that is needed for a detailed, interactive exchange of views. In the process, they also give citizens much greater agenda-setting powers than does network television. But they impose additional burdens upon citizen participants over the convenience of cable television: They require that those who would become involved travel to a meeting site. The Alaskan example demonstrates that in order to surmount (or reduce) these burdens, systems employing video- or audioconferencing need to be backstopped by a staff specifically responsible for reaching out to potential participants.

Videotex and computer conferencing may become a suitable middle ground. Videotex can certainly convey outward a substantial amount of information about policy matters and can collect inward opinions from a substantial number of participants. The "voice" given participants may range from a simple yes/no choice to the opportunity for an individual citizen to poll the opinions of everyone else. That citizens have greater control over the timing and extent of information provided them is another benefit of these systems. Computer conferencing, moreover, facilitates horizontal exchange of information permitting citizens to organize politically or negotiate a set of common interests.

Videotex and computer conferencing systems, however, will also exhibit limitations as vehicles of political discourse. As a medium of dialogue, each of these vehicles may be conveniently used by modest numbers of communicators; the emerging technologies do not promise that everyone can have his or her individual say in a national dialogue. Another major problem, shared with cable television, is that videotex and computer conferencing carry material pertaining to a wide variety of human activity. As a result, in a single medium, politics comes into direct competition with these other facets of life for the attention of citizens. Many citizens may choose to spend their time in front of the computer screen engaging in commercial activity or being entertained rather than discussing or influencing politics.

At present, moreover, access to these systems is so severely limited by cost that they cannot be considered practical, and this condition will probably last for a substantial period of time (Blomquist, 1984). Yet they do promise a reduction in the inconveniences associated with the present state of audio- and videoconferencing, and, at the same time, they will permit a more extensive amount of feedback than systems employing the telephone. While they may greatly ease the mechanical problems of conducting plebiscites, they provide no solution to the political problems that this research has documented in plebiscites. Instead, they offer the prospect of facilitating genuine government-to-citizen dialogue patterned on the pluralist model of politics generated by self-interest and self-initiative rather than the populist-plebis-citarian perspective.

The principal observed impact of the use of technology for democratic politics is to reduce the costs and burdens of participation for citizens. These costs may be financial or they may be associated with time, travel, and information necessary to participate politically. Technology does not, however, reduce these costs and burdens across the board. In financial terms, communications technology can be very expensive.

Another important point, however, can be gleaned from the relationship between technology and the costs of participation. Across the range of project designs, technology served to distribute the burdens between those who would elicit participation and citizens who might become involved. Generally speaking, the lower the burdens placed on citizens, the greater the demands (both financial and in an obligatory sense) upon project organizers. For example, where the news media are used to "spoon feed[ing]" citizens the information they need to consider a policy matter, the initiators must assume consequentially higher duties of inclusiveness, fairness, and balance in presenting that information. Similarly, through electronic voting systems, a much larger number of citizens can be induced to participate in a plebiscite than will attend a discussion; but the organizers of plebiscites must be held to higher standards of openness in view of their more substantial control over the agenda of policy considered.

I am speaking conceptually of costs and burdens, and accordingly cannot come to any simple additive notion of whether the costs to society as a whole are reduced or simply redistributed by technology. Clearly, if institutions that have functioned quite smoothly through direct human contact now begin employing technology to conduct communications, they may incur additional costs of operation. There is no evidence that technology can open up the political process while saving money.

But since citizen participation has been rather low in these traditional mechanisms and inequitably distributed across social classes, the advantages of using the emerging communications technology to allocate costs and burdens away from citizens appear rather clear. The principal questions involve the nature of participation that can be encouraged and the institutional patterns that are most successful for generating citizen involvement.

POSTSCRIPT

Can Communication Technologies Increase Political Participation?

These two selections question not only the impact and use of technology in today's society but also the changing nature of democracy. As in most studies of media and society, you can never isolate one area from another. Both media technology and society are inevitably intertwined; each effects the other, and each provides impetus for mutual change. Like the study of any form of communication, one side cannot grow without the aid of the other.

Teledemocracy offers many prospects for increasing participation of the handicapped, the isolated, and the individual who has little time away from work or the family. In today's society, we are becoming increasingly reliant upon technology to reduce problems of time, space, and access to specific environments. Likewise, teledemocracy (as a social action) requires new principles for understanding citizen involvement and opinion formation.

One other area for consideration includes the possibility of teledemocracy or any interactive form of technology to extend traditional geographic boundaries. We have already seen the use of satellites to bring entertainment such as the Super Bowl or the Academy Awards to nations around the world. The extension of teledemocracy to the global arena is already a technological possibility. To what uses, then, might global teledemocracy be put?

While there are not yet a great number of books to draw from regarding teledemocracy specifically, some provocative articles provide interesting suggestions for the viability of such a system. Benjamin Barber's article "Voting Is Not Enough," *Atlantic Monthly* (June 1984), addresses the social and technological ties. Other critiques of specific systems include Jean

Bethke Elshtain's "Democracy and the Qube Tube," *The Nation* (August 7–14, 1982); James Carey's "Videotex: The Past as Prologue," *Journal of Communication* 32 (Spring 1982); and "Minerva: An Electronic Town Hall," *Policy Science* 3(4) by A. Etzioni (1972).

Also, the annual Field Guide of *Channels of Communication* (January issue) provides thumbnail descriptions of technologies, services, and uses of many of the new systems available as well as descriptions of several new experiments along these lines.

ISSUE 17

Has High Technology Improved the Quality of American Life?

YES: Everett M. Rogers and Judith K. Larsen, from *Silicon Valley Fever: Growth of High-Technology Culture* (Basic Books, 1984)

NO: Dennis Hayes, from *Behind the Silicon Curtain: The Seductions of Work in a Lonely Era* (South End Press, 1989)

ISSUE SUMMARY

YES: Professor Everett Rogers and Judith Larsen have chronicled the growth and development of the computer capital of Silicon Valley and provide evidence that social values can adapt to the information age.

NO: Dennis Hayes, a free-lance writer for computer and microchip firms and the magazine *Processed World*, points to the problems incurred by Silicon Valley and warns that the information revolution could have disastrous effects.

The information revolution has often been compared to the Industrial Revolution. Many authors have focused on the comparisons between societies in which the main mode of production involves the manufacturing of goods (as in the Industrial Revolution) and in which the primary mode of work involves the processing of information (as in the information revolution). Many of these writers feel that social change is caused by a greater reliance on technologies for the maintenance of society. In reality, however, social change and technological change may go hand-in-hand. The effects of an increasing reliance on computers as the primary medium of communication (often controlling and linking other forms of media) promise much in the way of efficiency, but what do they really deliver?

In the two selections that follow, the authors have focused on Silicon Valley, an area in northern California (San Jose northwest to Palo Alto) that has become one of the "computer capitals" of the United States. When Silicon Valley began to grow in the 1970s, it was hailed as the community of the twenty-first century, a prototype for the life-style and promise of the information revolution. High-paying jobs in the computer and microchip industries drew well-educated electronic engineers to the area, and social programs within the burgeoning new industries were tailored to meet the needs of working couples. Provided were flexible hours, child care, quality schools for children as well as upscale homes, consumer items, and life-styles that were compatible with the entrepreneurial spirit of the information age—in short, a new type of American Dream that promised the good life. In a few short years, Silicon Valley became home to some of the most wealthy individuals in America who had speculated and succeeded in the development of computer software and hardware.

But the new dream in Silicon Valley also brought with it some unexpected changes in social patterns and resulted in an unexpected set of problems for workers, families, environmentalists, and government representatives. The icon of the computer promised faster, more efficient processing of information and a new set of values compatible with the computer culture. But such reliance on the computer industry also produced negative by-products, such as odorless, tasteless toxic pollution that was hard to detect (until it was too late), stress within family interaction, and a new class of migrant workers searching for work in an industry that valued total commitment, concentration, and creativity to the exclusion of job security and a predictable future.

These two selections focus on the promise of the new dream and the reality of the information revolution. As Hayes indicates, "as the dreams came true they entailed something other than fairy-tale endings."

YES

Everett M. Rogers and
Judith K. Larsen

THE IMPACT OF SILICON VALLEY

The information revolution of today is different from the industrial revolution that preceded it. One difference is that the present revolution is happening much faster. Instead of the several generations required for the industrial transformation, the information revolution is occurring in the period of just one generation. Another difference is that we recognize the information revolution as it is happening. A hundred years ago few residents of Manchester or other English industrial towns knew what was occurring in their society, in part because it was such a gradual change.

An indication of the rapid speed of the information revolution is the number of computers in use. By 1984 computers were becoming ubiquitous as Silicon Valley made them increasingly smaller and cheaper. In the decades since ENIAC (the first computer) launched the computer revolution in 1946, the number of computers went from one, to 600 in 1956, to 30,000 in 1966, to 400,000 in 1976. By 1984 there were over 6 million. In 1990, 50 percent of U.S. households are expected to have a microcomputer. By then the computer revolution will have conquered American society.

Microelectronics is such a widescope technology that semiconductor chips and computers can be applied to almost every situation. Consider farming: a modern dairy farm is equipped with microcomputer-controlled feed devices, triggered by a magnetic key worn by each dairy cow on a chain around her neck. The key serves to determine the amount and type of feed given that cow each day. When a particular cow passes through the milking parlor, a minimum-cost ration is instantly computed and fed to her individually. If her milk production drops, the microcomputer notifies the dairy farmer and cuts the cow's ration, giving her less of the higher priced protein supplements and larger amounts of roughage.

In the past we thought of each communication technology as a separate entity—telephones, for instance, and radio and TV. Today this distinction is disappearing. Due to the computer, each of these communication media are being integrated into a single communication network, which some call "compunications." Such integration occurs when a television news program like Ted Turner's 24-hour news is beamed by satellite to your local cable TV system which then sends it to your home. If your system is interactive, you may respond with a signal to the headend of the cable system, indicating your like or dislike of the news program. Your vote and others are tabulated by a computer and the results flashed on the TV screen. This communication system consists of an integrated network of satellite, cable TV, and computer technologies. Similar integration is happening in the modern office, where a computer terminal on your desk provides a word-processing function, and also links you to other offices to which you can send electronic messages. These instantly transmitted messages can be printed out by the receiver or stored in a computer file—thus the paperless office.

Tool technology is an extension of man's physical powers. Communication technology is the extension of perception and knowledge and enlarges our consciousness. In this sense communication technology is basic to all other technology, as the computer is basic to the new communication technologies. It is computing capability that makes the new information technologies interactive. Interactivity in mass communication systems makes them two-way instead of one-way, as were radio and TV broadcasting and the press. Such interactivity of communication changes the nature of who controls a mass medium. Instead of a handful of TV network executives or a few newspaper moguls deciding what you receive, each individual user of an interactive system has a large degree of control in choosing what information to request and what to avoid. Computers make possible interactive communication, allowing the individualization of information systems.

OFFICE AUTOMATION

The "office of the future" is today. At the heart of office automation is the word-processor, essentially a typewriter connected to a computer. The reason so many organizations rush to buy these expensive machines (the average price for a stand-alone word-processor is $12,000) is the jump in productivity they provide. An office secretary can usually raise typing output by about 20 percent with a word-processor, because editing and retyping are so much easier. Text can be corrected without having to retype the parts of a manuscript that are not changed. The more expensive word-processors can justify the right-hand margin of the page, print in a variety of type faces, and generally make the typed page look like a thing of beauty.

By 1984 there were about 800,000 word-processors in operation in the U.S. with 100,000 of these machines sold during 1983. Yet there is more to office automation than just word-processing. Electronic mail transmits memos and letters from computerized office to computerized office, usually via telephone lines. The advantage is that messages are conveyed instantly and correspondence can be "filed" and retrieved in the computer's memory. Not only can the automated office store correspondence, but it can also store reams of data, putting it, on command, into graphic display on the computer screen.

Given the advantages of the computer in the office, one would expect a rapid rate of adoption. On the contrary, even though office automation got off to a fast start, and is the subject of a great deal of discussion among business executives, the actual rate of adoption today has slowed. It's expensive for one thing. Further, the introduction of office systems often has not been carried out smoothly, as problems of implementation have occurred. The extent of anticomputer feeling often was overlooked when computers first came to the office. Honey was poured into computer terminals in the Minneapolis Post Office and a computer at Metropolitan Life Insurance Company was attacked with a screwdriver. In Denver, car keys were fed into a disk drive, and in Bell, California, a police station computer was shot with a revolver by a policeman. Such extreme cases of frustration with computers are rare, but telling.

One reason for resistance to office automation is the effect of computers on employment. If an office computer can improve a typist's efficiency by 20 or 25 percent, that means that an organization can lay off 20 or 25 percent of its typing employees. Secretarial work represents one of the most important occupations for women and about 35 percent of the typical secretary's time is spent typing. Office automation threatens to add to unemployment rates.

There is another effect of office computers on employment. *Deskilling* is a process of job simplification by means of computer technology so that less skilled, lower paid workers can be substituted for more educated, higher paid employees. Office automation can lead to deskilling if secretarial work is broken down into keyboarding on a word-processor versus other duties where shorthand dictation, accurate typing, and editing skills are required. Another example of deskilling by computer occurs

at grocery check-out stands, where the new technologies no longer require that the operator be able to operate a register. Deskilling is obviously an advantage to employers, but not to the skilled workforce.

Office automation can also change the nature of supervision and control in the office. Computers capable of monitoring, for instance, employee lateness or absence records as well as daily productivity information could easily run a company more "efficiently" than a softhearted human boss given to overlooking employee weaknesses.

ROBOTS

The word "robot" brings to mind an anthropomorphic machine that walks about on two legs, talks, and sometimes harbors sinister intentions. In reality, most present-day robots work in factories and most of them work in Japan. Industrial robots bear little resemblance to humans. They look more like exotic insects, somewhat like the oil pumps dotting the Texas countryside. Some industrial robots resemble a human arm, with an elbow and a clamplike hand (called the gripper). A robot possesses intelligence in the form of a computer (usually a microprocessor) programmed to control the robot in a series of repeated activities. The auto industry is the single most important application for industrial robots, where they work on assembly lines doing such tasks as spot welding, drilling, sanding, and cutting. Robots work a 24-hour shift and perform especially monotonous and/or dangerous tasks. A few manufacturing plants in Japan are almost completely robotized. Computerized robots provide a means to replace labor with highly capitalized information technology. Robots may free humans from performing monotonous and dangerous tasks on assembly lines, but unfortunately robots also put people out of work. Of course someone has to design, manufacture, and maintain the industrial robots. These tasks are information occupations—intellectual work that is replacing manual labor in the factory, just as office automation substitutes for typists and secretaries in white-collar occupations. The at-work applications of computers will replace large numbers of lower-skilled workers and create a demand for fewer, but more educated individuals.

The rapidity with which this social transformation is occurring is aptly called a revolution. Like all major social changes this one will benefit certain people, especially educated professionals in high-technology fields like microelectronics, and will harm many others, as the unemployed thousands in Detroit will attest.

Artificial intelligence is the ability of computers to think like humans. Considerable research is now devoted by university scholars and by R&D workers in certain high-technology firms to advance the field of artificial intelligence. Computers can consistently defeat the human chess player of average-to-expert ability. Other applications of computer intelligence are to teach mathematics, diagnose medical problems, serve as skilled chemical laboratory assistants, and to evaluate military tactics. These applications are primarily limited to an experimental basis at present. In the years ahead important breakthroughs are certain to occur in the uses of artificial intelligence and these may have even more impact on our society than the current concern about unemployment caused by office automation and robotics.

MICROCOMPUTERS AND OUR CHILDREN

In no other area of daily life is the potential of the new communication technology having such a powerful impact as with children.

An estimated 25 million Americans are functionally illiterate. They cannot read a want ad or the label on a medicine bottle or a bus schedule. Another 34 million have only a minimum capacity for very simple reading. These two groups make up about one-quarter of the nation's population. They represent a major problem in a nation that is moving rapidly into becoming an information society. The ability to read and write is an even more essential individual skill in a world organized around computer terminals. Until voice recognition ability is much improved and becomes lower in cost, the main way to talk to a computer is through a keyboard.

Obviously the best way to raise the literacy levels of the U.S. population is to prevent additional millions of functional illiterates from being created by our current ineffective educational system. Computers, especially microcomputers, can provide the means to revitalize our schools—the natural affinity of children for computers can be a powerful tool for teaching the information skills needed for life in an information society. An exciting revolution is now underway in U.S. schools and homes to harness the teaching/learning potential of microcomputers. However this revolution has a long way to go.

U.S. schools have 250,000 computers available to students for educational purposes. Little is known yet from scientific study about the introduction, acceptance, and implementation of computers in schools and the impacts of computers on teaching and learning by children in schools and in their homes. But without doubt a kind of learning/teaching revolution is now underway, triggered by microcomputers.

Children learn about computers with much greater ease than adults. Most observers note that boys are attracted to computers more strongly than girls. If children's use of computers and video games teaches them useful skills for living in an information society, males are getting off to a faster start. In the U.S., girls have equal ability to boys in math and science until around age 12 (sixth grade), thereafter girls often develop a negative attitude toward these subjects and avoid them in high school, thus limiting their career opportunities. Perhaps microcomputers will provide a means of keeping girls interested in quantitative and scientific subjects. But this potential is not yet being realized, as boys presently outnumber girls 3 to 1 in learning to use computers.

Home computers are more accessible to socioeconomically advantaged children, thus serving to widen existing gaps between the "information-poor" and the "information-rich." A 1982 survey of grade school children in California illustrates this gap: 41 percent of the children in an upper middle-class school reported that they had a home computer, compared to less than 1 percent in a nearby Spanish-speaking, lower income school.

The current generation of U.S. children will grow up with computers, much as the children of the 1950s grew up with television. What is different and special about computers is that they are interactive. It is this interactive nature of computers, and of related communication technologies based on computers, that marks a cultural turning point from the passivity of viewing television. Whether the instructional potential of the computer will be exploited by schools and teachers, or whether computers will just go the way of instructional television, programmed learning, and language laboratories, is yet to be determined.

Computers are a mass medium, but of a very special kind in that they are highly individualized due to their interactive nature. It is possible that the use of computers may affect how children think; some observers feel that children who grow up with computers will learn to be more logical and to think in linear sequences. We need to find out. Seymour Papert stated: "I believe that the computer presence will enable us to so modify the learning environment outside the classroom that much, if not all, the knowledge schools presently try to teach with such pain and expense and such limited success will be learned as the child learns to talk, painlessly, successfully, and without organized instruction. This obviously implies that schools as we know them today will have no place in the future." . . .

HACKERS

The epitome of the new computer culture is the "hacker," a computer addict who sleeps by day and sits enthralled at a computer keyboard all night, feeding on junk food and the euphoria of computing. Hackers are social isolates who prefer interaction with a machine over talking to people. Hackers are often found in university computer centers. They may be only a few hundred students at a typical university, yet the significance of hackers lies not in their present numbers, but in their representation of a sub-culture that is rapidly expanding and becoming more influential.

A new generation of hackers is now being created in American homes, schools, and video arcades as vast numbers of children learn to use video games and microcomputers. Computing is "a priesthood of the young." It will be only a few years until the several million school children of today who are becoming computer literates reach college age. Those most likely to become hackers are the extremely intelligent but socially inept. Indeed, it is the anti-social nature of hackers that is the basis for concern about them. Will the computer revolution turn large numbers of our youth into alienated hacker-nerds?

A character sketch of hackers is provided by Joseph Weizenbaum of MIT: "Bright young men of disheveled appearance, often with sunken glowing eyes." Beside their computer terminal are stacks of printout, plastic Coke containers, styrofoam coffee cups, and evidence of their junk-food diets. They have rumpled clothes, unshaven faces, and uncombed hair. As one Stanford hacker pointed out: "The first thing to go is other academic interests. . . . The second . . . is a normal living pattern. Eating and sleeping are completely rearranged to fit the addiction. The typical hacker thinks nothing of eating one meal a day, subsisting on junk food, and sleeping from four to noon almost every day of the week. . . . The third thing to go is a balanced social life."

Hackers will become more of a force in the future as America becomes more of an information society. Today's hackers will be writing the computer programs, creating new computer languages, and designing the new information systems to serve us in future decades. The hackers' strange ways may affect us all, as computers become more ubiquitous and the anti-social character of hackers, which seems weird today, may become common at some future time. . . .

HIGH-TECHNOLOGISTS AS POLITICAL LEADERS

One wonders what kind of national political leader a high-technologist would make. Likely the politician would be a conservative Republican with a strong belief in free market forces and faith in government policies that govern least. Most Silicon Valley tycoons are not concerned with issues of social inequality or injustice; to the entrepreneur, the poor and weak in society are poor and weak because they are inferior. It is the poor and the weak's fault that they are downtrodden, rather than the result of an unequal system. The engineer-entrepreneur believes in social evolution, the absolute correctness of competition, and in technological solutions to social problems. The engineer-politician lacks a liberal arts education, is suspicious of liberalism, and represents the ideology of hard-core conservative Republicanism.

As America moves forward as an information society, these values of competition, a faith in technology, and political conservatism are likely to become more widely shared and more strongly held by the public. The entrepreneurial game as it is now played in Silicon Valley will spread and be accepted everywhere. Trends already advanced in Silicon Valley will gradually occur in the other "Silicon Valleys" being created around the nation. The process will take ten, fifteen, or twenty years, maybe less, and will be accompanied by increasing economic and political power for high-technology regions and for the entrepreneurs who lead them. That trend has already begun, and it can only speed up. . . .

Silicon Valley represents a special kind of supercapitalism—it is a system resting on continuous technological innovation, entrepreneurial fever, and vigorous economic competition. The Silicon Valley game is played out by several thousand capitalist technologists involved in a myriad of deals, spin-offs, start-ups, successes, and failures. The role of the federal and state government is close to zero. Unfettered market forces pass final judgment on the boom or bust of firms and of individuals. Silicon Valley is high-technology capitalism run wild. There is nothing quite like it anywhere else in the world.

Quite understandably, Silicon Valley's industry leaders take pride in the system they have created. Their industry has been good to them, making them millionaires. The microelectronics industry also has been good to the local area, with new jobs and taxes. The microelectronics companies did what the people in the local cities and counties wanted them to do: create new jobs. As the cornerstone of the information society, the microelectronics industry has been good for the nation, providing one of the economic bright spots in an otherwise dreary picture of obsolete, smokestack industries and undertrained workers.

NO

Dennis Hayes

MUTATION: THE ELECTRONIC COLONY

DREAM BOOST

Rarely has one location, one industry inspired dreams among so many. In the decade following the American Quarter Century (1950-1975), a Pacific coastal valley on the western shores of San Francisco Bay became the hub of a global industry. The tidings of its prosperity encouraged imitations from Jerusalem to Tierra del Fuego and attracted immigrants from Islamabad to Pittsburgh. More than this, Silicon Valley—or the mythology constructed on its behalf—stirred dreams that the world had come to identify with some essential part of the U.S. character. The most remarkable of these dreams struck transcendent themes: material salvation through migration and work as a spiritual haven. These merged into a grand social vision of a new technology making life better and creating jobs lost to obsolete industry. Like their nocturnal counterparts, the dreams blended less-than-conscious hopes and fears. It should not have been too surprising, then, that as the dreams came true they entailed something other than fairy-tale endings.

The fairy tale had become the stock literary device for the authors and journalists who named this land of enchantment "Silicon Valley" and chronicled its fortunes in articles, interviews, and books that celebrated the entrepreneurs and the technologists. As a result, a sort of truth-by-anecdote had been allowed to accumulate in which social history was quietly suspended. This oversight affected nearly everyone's vision, including that of investigative journalists, whose custom is to disturb the projects of business enterprise. Lulling critics, pushing dissent well off the pages of acceptable inquiry, the fairy tales transformed skepticism into adulation.

In 1983, a prominent investigative-reporting magazine praised the paths taken by the "microchip moguls" of Silicon Valley and urged popular support for them—as if any such urging was needed. Two years later, another investigative reporter balanced his ebullient book on the Valley with anecdotes of drugs and espionage, but continued to recite the now familiar

From Dennis Hayes, *Behind the Silicon Curtain: The Seductions of Work in a Lonely Era* (South End Press, 1989). Copyright © 1989 by Dennis Hayes. Reprinted by permission of South End Press, 116 South Botolph St., Boston, MA 02115. Notes omitted.

litanies: "Sunnyvale . . . has more millionaires per capita than any city its size in the world. The result is the overnight-wealth story played out scores of times every month." The spell cast by the prosperity was such that each new forward twitch of technology appeared as a social advance.

Before long, the dreams assumed a millenarian stature, lifted by the conviction that history was in the making, that a new stage in civilization was at hand. Who would deny that the Information Age moved with the same unyielding destructive sweep of the Industrial Revolution? In the semi-rural communities that began to model themselves on Silicon Valley, enigmatic urban habitats evolved, marking a visual and cultural rupture with the cities and towns that grew up with Industrial America. In Silicon Valley, there occurred a confusing but inexorable transformation from apricot orchards, Main Street, and ranch hospitality to "smart" missile labs, theme malls, and residence hotels. It was reminiscent, in its thoroughness and abruptness, of the enclosures of the English Commons and the rise of the urban "manufactories" that thrust the Industrial Revolution upon the world. But the epochal metaphors were also inspired by an unspoken desire to transcend the bleakness of Industrial America circa 1975.

By 1980, references to the coastal valley evoked the vital categories of adolescent capitalism: entrepreneur, venture capital, technological innovation, upward mobility. Outside corporate fitness centers, underneath the canopies of *al fresco* cafeterias, the computer professionals could be seen eating salads, browsing through survival-gear catalogs, gazing at digital wrist stopwatches, and sporting the most sophisticated running shoes, as if personally embodying the leanness, adaptability, efficiency, and power of the new technologies. Thus conceived, "Silicon Valley" was like a tonic for the muddled—some said geriatric—U.S. capitalism of the times. It consoled and provided dream material for those who still believed the United States was the land of opportunity. By the early 1970s this belief had been thoroughly shaken by the economic "restructuring," oil price scandals, mergers, and financial speculation that marked the end of the post-World War II national prosperity. A "motivation crisis," panels of scholars and consultants agreed, had been weakening the U.S. will to work and cultivating resentment.

Within Silicon Valley, a politics of hope emerged to compete with the resentment. The United States now looked to the electronics entrepreneurs for deliverance. Around them, economists and politicians formed something of a cargo cult. It was within this context of deliverance that the dreams were subjected to the nuance of many interpretations.

The dream boosters championed a populism whose symbols were the computer and the entrepreneur, and whose opportunities were limitless. Management consultants hailed the "practical autonomy" of the Valley's corporate cultures, which were said to thrive like the potted ferns, rhododendrons, and *benjaminus* ficas that appointed the new "employee-centered" workplaces. The computer's capacity to transfix the new worker was becoming legendary: Silicon Valley worked overtime and its professionals found work meaningful at rates that soared far above national averages.

Spokespeople for the young computer hobbyists, whose inventions made electronics commodities accessible and increasingly affordable, espoused a more radical populism, one that viewed personal computers as anti-corporate tools and a franchise for democracy in the Information Age. The disciples of electronic convenience rose up to praise, in advance, every innovation. Futurists, entitling their treatises in the millennial idiom—*Megatrends, The Third Wave,* etc.— competed with each other in predicting the details of the computer's liberation of work, shopping, and homemaking from drudgery. Economists characterized Silicon Valley as an enclave of "flexible specialization" and "yeoman democracy" that would propel U.S. industry into a new Golden Age.

If the dream boosters' interpretations were diverse, even a little preposterous, they shared a vision of computers and electronics as an essentially progressive force. This diversity freighted the dreams with a pluralist appeal, while technological positivism swept aside the critiques that had shadowed the debut of computers in the 1950s and 1960s. Dreams and hopes, however, were grounded in the prosperity of Silicon Valley and that of the other Silicon terrains that had become, by 1980, the featured topics of Chamber of Commerce luncheons and of U.S. urban planners everywhere. Silicon was the modern stake everyone had been waiting to claim. . . .

On the eve of Independence Day, 1986, a local business columnist could observe glibly that "almost every week some Silicon Valley electronics company decides to move its production overseas." The assembly areas, clogged during the prosperity with bench workers, clerks, technicians, and their managers working overtime, were emptying abruptly at the rate of 1,000 employees per month. Against the advice of management consultants, several companies removed the potted ferns, rhododendrons and ficas from cubicles—scorning the plants' production of negative ions that were said to soothe the harried computer worker. It was as if a film recording the years of mass hirings, frantic expansions, and stock-offering celebrations was rewinding at high speed, reeling in frame after frame of prosperity and its pretensions. Few expected it to last forever; but it had been so brief, so quickly undone. . . .

Had commuters begun to wonder at the stillness that fell over the construction sites, at the fading "For Lease" bunting that was draped across evacuated workplaces? The Valley had, without anyone noticing, accumulated the nation's highest industrial vacancy rate; nearly 40 percent of its workspace, new and used, was empty in 1986 (several times that of Houston and Detroit combined). Real estate speculators were sitting on top of 32 million square feet of sheltered Valley air that was depreciating by the minute. One of the nation's largest realtors concluded that filling the Valley's empty buildings would take nearly three and one half years of boom, something no business columnist was predicting. Other electronics industry regions, such as those near Boston and Phoenix, were likewise glutted. The glut was written off as a classic, if extreme, case of overdevelopment. But there were other views.

The vacant office malls and their unblemished asphalt skirts inspired material for a Japanese comic strip which depicted the President of the United States walking steadfastly through a windswept ghost town. *Kudoka,* the Japanese were calling it, the "hollowing out" of the United States by corporations who liquidated their manufacturing core or exported it to sites offshore, leaving behind a shell of lawyers, accountants, marketing specialists, and, in the Silicon Valleys, design, development, and support staff as well. By its example and through its products, the U.S. electronics industry, more than any other, had promoted and accelerated *kudoka*. *Kudoka*, in fact had been at least as crucial to the industry's prosperity as had the technical ingenuity of its entrepreneurs.

During the 1960s and 1970s, U.S. semiconductor firms took full advantage of the lightweight nature of the microchip assembly and packaging to establish more offshore manufacturing operations than domestic ones. By 1987, chip makers had only one-third of their wafer fabrication facilities in Silicon Valley. Inside the United States, the industry filled its clean rooms mainly with Latin Americans, Asian, and Pacific Rim emigrés. With labor gathered from the lands of the least paid, the industry helped create satellites, global inventory networks, robotics software, and all manner of international data links. These established an infrastructure that encouraged other U.S.-based industries to operate their manufacturing from afar. If *kudoka* was luring the electronics industry's production base away from the United States, the Valley's development and design achievements encouraged a different sort of *kudoka* in less developed countries. From Taiwan, China, the Philippines, India, Pakistan, and Iran, middle- and upper-class emigrés came to Silicon Valley to pursue computer occupations, while many more prepared for degrees in U.S. technical schools. . . .

By 1987, the citizens of San Jose spent $500 million each year—or over $700 for each man, woman, and child—on illegal drugs. The San Jose Police Chief estimated that, at some firms, more than eight out of ten employees, from assemblers to top executives, were taking, buying, and/or selling drugs *on the job*. The highest divorce rate in the nation was creating one of the densest concentrations of lawyers west of Manhattan and filling the Valley's apartments, tract homes, and fern bars with a special sadness which no amount of work or shopping could alleviate. With the pause in prosperity, work itself, like drinking untreated Valley tap water, had become an uncertain activity.

Silicon Valley, which, above all, had promised work to all comers, could no longer come across. By 1985, 60,000 people over the age of 50, many of them former middle managers earning between $35,000 and $75,000, had been laid off, fired, or forced into early retirement. These people were now looking—anywhere—for work, their resumes languishing in the files of personnel departments all over the country. "They're not bag ladies and men; they're briefcase ladies and men," quipped a job counselor. Collecting at dusk in shopping mall parking lots and outlying parks, some of the not-quite-elderly jobless were living out of cars and trailer-campers. Other had taken month-to-month leases in mobile homes (with views of vacant office malls). They lived a shabby compromise with the residences many of them were accustomed to, houses (with views of coastal hills) whose median price had risen well above $200,000. It was then painfully recollected that most Valley electronics firms had offered stock options instead of pension plans. Of course, these 60,000 were only one segment of the "new poor." From 1984 through 1987, by several estimates, from 5 to 10 percent of electronics employees had lost their jobs. No one was calculating joblessness among the variously estimated 150,000 to 200,000 undocumented immigrants.

Others pointed out that the electronics industry had been fouling air, soil, water, workplace, and worker all along. With the belated official recognition of these problems, a reservoir of misgiving and grudge was surely building.

The daughters of the migrant farm laborers who once planted, harvested, and packed Valley fruit had taken jobs inside the fluorescent hothouses amid the chemicals that yielded electronic life. The orchards were paved over and the canneries torn down or auctioned off, reminders of the finality with which the new technology entombed the old. The new work, however, was as tedious and often as migratory and poorly paid as the old; it was more dangerous, for its dangers were far more subtle.

The women labored hard and long—up to twelve-hour shifts. They required regular overtime, or other incomes, to make ends meet; the wages were so low, in fact, that working mothers qualified for welfare assistance. The wages reflected the terms set by a global electronics labor market.

The gases and acids, against most of which the firms protected neither worker nor environment, laced the water supply that once nourished the orchards, converting one of North America's most pristine aquifers into one of the nation's most perilous and puzzling contaminations.

Most of the chemicals left no scars, were unseen, unfelt. Unleashed under names and in combinations that workers couldn't understand, the solvents and etching compounds were confusing the immune systems and altering the chromosomes of many of the farm laborers' daughters, who now left the new work

to preserve their health, or, like the mothers in surrounding neighborhoods, miscarried or bore malformed babies in numbers and at rates that could no longer be ignored.

In May 1988, a three-year California Department of Health Services study found that pregnant women who drank tap water in Silicon Valley and environs (Santa Clara, Alameda and San Mateo Counties) had significantly higher rates of miscarriages and birth defects than those who drank filtered or no tap water during their pregnancies. *Up to twice as many miscarriages and nearly four times as many birth defects occurred.* The report was a follow-up to an earlier study that was prompted by the controversial Fairchild-IBM contaminations.

Who would repair the addled immune systems of the many women laid-off, fired, or no longer able to work in the chemically profuse environments of the Valley's misnamed "clean" rooms? The chipmaking firms denied responsibility for workers' injuries, and, when necessary, paid doctors by the hour for their testimony at workers' compensation hearings, "expert" testimony that discounted as "psychosomatic disorders" the workers' seared lungs and enduring bronchitis, the chronic nose-bleeds and headaches, the AIDS-like pan-allergies. Who would repay the women whose babies were delivered to them stillborn, or with impaired hearts, lungs, and livers? Not the State of California, whose industrial hygienists confirmed high rates of miscarriages and birth defects in neighborhoods surrounding IBM and Fairchild Semiconductor, but dismissed the apparent connections. Not the industry, which assisted IBM and Fairchild in contesting the class action suit brought by parents whose grieving had given way to anger.

Although IBM and Fairchild Semiconductor admitted that chemicals, apparently, had leaked, and were still migrating from their storage tanks, IBM and Fairchild purchased releases from liability, settling the suit secretly and out-of-court.

Who would console the survivors of the 57 people each year who, by 1986, were dying as a result of airborne pollution, mainly from the Valley's congested freeways? Not the Valley's county and city planners, who granted subsidy after subsidy for the overdevelopment, apologized for zoning violations, and proposed special taxes to fund widened freeways and more commuting corridors. Not the voice of Silicon Valley, the *San Jose Mercury News*. Although it broke the story with the banner headline "Santa Clara County's Killing Air," its management had secretly exposed the *News'* press operators to PCB-laced ink day in, day out, for months.

Who would comfort the Vietnamese, Laotian, Cambodian, Indian, Filipino, Pakistani, Iranian, and Hispanic refugees and immigrants, harassed by "racial incidents," their car tires slashed at night, their children beaten coming home from school, their parents underpaid and distressed by the threat of deportation. Not the INS (the dream interpreter of last resort for immigrant families), whose agents welcomed Eastern bloc engineers hired by the military electronics firms, denied Latin American emigrés fleeing regimes allied with the West, and collaborated with sweatshop computer entrepreneurs who trafficked in the resulting underground labor market, scheduling pre-payday raids and separating husband and wife, parent and child, unofficially adding immigrants to the Valley's already high family separation statistics.

Who would calm the families of the commuters and bicyclists maimed and killed by cars that swerved as their drivers, bored with weekday and weekend traffic jams, reached for cassette tapes, struggled to open beers, fumbled in ash trays for yesterday's marijuana? Not the mall and condominium developers, whose projects pushed sidewalks onto the streets and made shopping, schooling, dining out, dancing, taking piano lessons, fetching an ice cream, and almost every trip and errand contingent on access to a car. Not the convenience marts, the fast food outlets, or the discount pharmacies whose franchises saturated the Valley in a frenzy of consumer homogenization.

The evaporation of good will and innocence extended even to the entrepreneur. His success—and it was invariably his, which became yet another charge hurled at the fraternity of electronics industry leaders—now required more than perseverance in service of a new product, more than "an idea and a telephone." More than ever, "entrepreneuring" demanded substantial startup funding and a mean-spirited zeal to subdue competitors. A rising Valley entrepreneur, the subject of a 1985 *Esquire* interview, surveyed a competitor thus:

> He'd stick me in five nanoseconds if he could, but he can't—because I've got big guys behind me . . . So he leaves me alone only because he has to, and I leave him alone only because I can't get as close as I'd like to. And that's okay! But one of these days we'll ride into his village, we'll burn his huts, we'll rape his women, and we'll dance on the bones of his children!

So many had seemed so confident of the destination. Careers had been launched, commutes tolerated, consumption patterns altered, personalities adjusted. The artifacts of a less constricted, slower era (lawn mowers, badminton nets, garden tools, extra bedroom sets) had been stowed away in the mini-storage lockers that pocketed Silicon Valley. Others with no such possessions, who instead had risked long, dangerous passages from equatorial hovels and shanty compounds, had arrived only to suffer new risks, unknown exposures, a modern loneliness. So much had been invested, put on hold, even sacrificed to the dreams of work and prosperity. Where were the dreams leading? What, other than the dreams, connected each to all? . . .

Many migrants to Silicon Valley never stopped migrating—from workplace to workplace. Engineers, electronics trade magazines complained, were changing jobs every two years. Production workers and word processors might work overtime on projects for months, then receive furloughs, hire on elsewhere, or sign up for temporary labor through a "job shop." Shrinking product lifetimes and merger-related job relocations eroded the occupational stability of electronics employees. A new group of "business service" entrepreneurs, the largest number of which were in the temporary help and job placement business, capitalized on the mass transience. By 1985, the growth of this industry outpaced that of every electronics industry segment.

Silicon Valley unsettled its settlers with one of the highest job turnover rates in the country. In 1980, electronics workers vacated their jobs at twice the national average. Yearly job turnover rates for production workers approached 50 percent. The rate had declined somewhat by 1986, but it was now supplemented by layoffs and a growing proportion of "permanent" part-time and contract positions. The employee leasing, part-time work, and layoffs reflected the fickleness of electronics capital—capital that had always been transient, in contrast to the relative permanence of capital in steel, coal, auto, rubber, glass, machine tools, and railroads. These were the U.S. industries whose tradition the White House report, James Fallows, and many others expected the upstart electronics industry to carry on.

What was emerging was a less purposeful, and quite new, migrational pattern—the flow into and out of the new electronics jobs. Workers came and went with such frequency that workplace acquaintance was too short-lived to sustain a class bond. The growth of part-time positions, even when these reflected a marriage of convenience between capital and labor, likewise diluted the workplace as a focus for human connection. Many of the "permanent" part-time jobs were temporary arrangements, since, in practice, the partially employed, no matter how satisfied with their positions, were spending non-work hours preparing for a career or caring for infants who would soon be old enough for a childcare center.

A modern heartland was palpitating to new and relentless rhythms, inhabited by an emigré workforce that couldn't seem to settle down. The aimlessness and occupational motion bequeathed fragmented cultures of work, shifting occupational itineraries, and a new isolation. This elicited the labor leaders' instinctive reluctance to organize electronics workers, since even the bureaucratic, dues-broker union relies ultimately on a collective identity that had eluded the electronics workplace.

The new transience was infectious, and the carrier was the insurgent electronics industry. On the one hand, job turnover rates and part-time positions were rising in the information "processing" and point-of-sale jobs that electronics technology made possible. On the other hand, electronics products (robotics stations, global manufacturing systems) helped automate, simplify, and routinize production labor, effectively lowering wages, creating layoffs, and closing plants. These effects combined to create the framework for mass transience among wage workers in goods and service industries.

Childlike and full of wanderlust, the U.S. electronics industry had confused those dream boosters who took the industry's growth for the first tugs of a longer wave of frontier expansion like those that previously had shaped eastern and midwestern America. There, despite wars and depressions, despite "factories . . . closing down and opening up," prosperity had brought more than a semblance of community and stability. The United States, led by its impetuous electronics industry, was becoming a land of transient workers and moveable workplaces. . . .

While management consultants and their critics debated the corporate role in motivating the computer worker, no one bothered to examine a consequence that overshadowed all others in its peculiarity. Amid all the reveling in work, there flourished an equally remarkable indifference to work's products. Computer work was becoming a new enclave—comparable to the fragmented hobby and lifestyle enclaves that British and U.S. sociologists had identified in modern leisure activities. Among computer professionals, work was so self-referential, so thoroughly personalized, that it no longer required a public rationale in order to yield meaning. No one seemed to care about who purchased the product or what purposes it served. What mattered was the product's capacity to provide more interesting work—a capacity that usually dovetailed with the corporate concern for profitability.

The special alienation of electronics workers from their products was not hard to trace. Computer products were baffling, microscopic, and bore mysterious names. They were infinitely more complex than, and at least as ambiguous as, other commodities. Their ambiguity derived from their role as components—chips, boards, kits, and black boxes—that were incorporated into a wide array of commodities from kitchen appliances to missile guidance systems. Where was the engineer who really knew, or cared about, which products would incorporate the microchips he designed? And computer products were also ephemeral. Volatile markets beckoned, were saturated, overrun, made obsolescent, and forgotten as quickly as new product releases, or new markets, were created. In this way computer work became more and more detached from social contexts. A culture of product indifference and ignorance had engulfed the computer sophisticates.

It was not always so. In the 1970s, a visible faction of inventor-entrepreneurs spoke of their brainchildren—various prototype personal computers—as educational tools, as entertainments, as harbingers of household convenience, and as checks on a corporate computer monopoly. Some corporations, including older ones such as Control Data Corporation and younger ones such as Apple, donated computers to schools and community groups. Electronics innovation, however implausibly, was linked to the public good.

By the 1980s, the perceived need for public rationales had all but vanished.

The computer entrepreneurs and technologists advertised computers as productivity- and profit-enhancing tools, appealing to the increasingly nonpublic realm of work. But even this inward, productivist rationale was actively suspect from a public point of view, since computers were in fact displacing workers and heightening instability by facilitating more automation, encouraging *kudoka*, and placing weaponry on an inherently more dangerous footing.

The ideological association of computer innovation with convenience and social progress was, evidently, fallible. How was society using computers? The electronics industry didn't know. Its think tanks described markets as outlets for electronics sales, not as workplaces employing people and creating social goods and services that would be more or less drastically changed by computer technology. No one, in fact, seemed to know much about the broader uses and impacts of the computer.

The electronics industry had made possible financial networks where none had been. Banks and savings and loans now featured automated tellers, innovative consumer credit lines, and rapid access to expanding financial services, but all banks large and small were less stable and their services more expensive for the consumer. Meanwhile, the wages, benefits, and health of banking, telephone, and airline employees were not improved by the introduction of computers into the workplace. In fact, workers' pay, health, workplace productivity, and product and service quality fared poorly in the most heavily computerized industries: services and retail sales.

As the evidence of dubious progress accumulated, the grand social dream was mutating. Just how computers were

enriching civilization became difficult to say unequivocally. All of this inconclusiveness and misgiving made it easier for computer workers not to examine too closely the social impact of their labors. . . .

The automobile and its private commute were phenomena with more than a quarter-century of U.S. history. Unlike the postwar traffic patterns and predictable rush hours between suburb and urban center, however, traffic now flowed from suburb to suburb, from work suite to shopping mall to housing development, so the traffic itself was aimless, the rush hours less distinct. The new patterns, as well as the flexible work arrangements and chronic overtime, extended the commutes and subverted traffic's predictability. The result was the modern commuter's deepening self-absorption, a persona hardened in the powerlessness each experienced, almost daily, in a mobile solitude.

Individuals leased or purchased (on credit) high-performance cars, off-road vehicles, excursion vans, or fuel-efficient compacts. In jammed traffic, these could travel no faster, nor very efficiently, but they constituted evidence of attempts to assert self-control, to surround oneself with comfort, to economize, or simply to exhibit good taste (no matter how obviously taste was commercially derived). To release themselves from the stalls and carbon monoxide, commuters acquired expensive car stereos on which they indulged their musical tastes, "listened" to books, and attempted (or pretended) to learn other languages. Some leased cellular telephones (real and bogus) and thus remained plugged in to work. Others dined in transit. For an untold number, marijuana, cocaine, or alcohol suspended the special pain of not getting somewhere fast. These were the elaborate yet, by unspoken consensus, popular ruses by which commutes were endured. Thus did Silicon Valley announce the triumph of the privatized thoroughfare, the filtered social experience; its inhabitants were predisposed to the therapeutic allure of the fix.

The home also became an increasingly lonely haven. Video cassette outlets and cable television—the consumer electronics services in hottest demand—secured the victory of the living room and the TV (the "monitor") over the public gatherings and cinema screens of the older cities. While Silicon Valley breadwinners spent less time at home, TV viewing time grew longer, and new modes of isolated consumption unfolded. Multiple TV sets per household allowed a division of viewing within families, while the spread of consumer videotaping offered to insulate TV programming itself from the mass culture of coast-to-coast network broadcasting.

Second to TV viewing, strolling in the sealed-off, thematic shopping mall had become the most popular leisure "activity" in the United States. In court rooms (based on an incident in Silicon Valley), the sidewalks and parking lots of the malls were declared private property, sanctuaries in which free speech was suspended, displays of poverty or extreme behavior cause for expulsion at the discretion of the mall's proprietors. In the new habitats, capital was contriving to mediate, and thereby isolate, human contact in unprecedented fashion.

A surrogate social discourse began to revolve around therapy and consumption, the two becoming less distinguishable than ever. From a Silicon Valley think-tank, a pathbreaking series of studies examined unabashedly and minutely the consumption-as-therapy connections. The result—psychographics—became a catechism for marketing and advertising. Psychographics attempted to characterize and order social values, beliefs, fantasies, and dreams to better attach these ideologically to commodities. It reduced people to an amalgam of consumer lifestyles and urged advertising that associated commodities not so much with ideas ("convenience," "economy") as with experiences and emotions that evinced contemporary values and lifestyles.

Like that of any advertising, the success of psychographics depended utterly on execution. It could not settle the misconstrued debate on whether "advertising really works." Psychographics did, however, reflect and reinforce the spirit of the times. It was a dubious alliance of therapy—once restricted to upper and middle classes—for the masses with a credit card-based discretionary consumption.

A therapeutic allure imbued shopping and the lifestyles that shopping supported with new meaning. U.S. shoppers, their embrace widened by an apparently infinite line of credit, showed a practical indifference to price and an absorbing attraction to the baroque abstractions that passed for product usefulness. The urge to purchase overwhelmed the consumer's perception of need. In 1987, a marketing-research firm surveyed 34,000 mall shoppers and found that only 25 percent had come to purchase a specific object. The same year, a *Wall Street Journal* reporter found shoppers in "total fulfillment" even though "they don't even know what they're after."

It was only a matter of time before individuals would explicitly seek out therapy as a surrogate politics. This was the path blazed by a group of electronics businessmen and their wives in Silicon Valley, who disavowed political activism, yet sought to resolve, through "positive thinking," the dilemma of nuclear arms—as well as the equally pressing problems of guilt-ridden military electronics professionals. They found fertile soil in Silicon Valley for their faith that if only humanity changed its outlook, the new technology's manifestly evil application, nuclear weapons, might evaporate (without any loss of income or convenience). The success of this movement in Silicon Valley and beyond marked a growing constituency for therapy as a substitute for the community-based politics that didn't emerge. In the meantime, the new movement proposed no practical alterations to the Valley's essentially political agenda of producing the weapons and tools of social control and financial gimmickry.

By making endurable the social loneliness of Silicon Valley, the fix proved indispensible to the electronics industry. By postponing the confrontation between the isolated creators of powerful technology and society, it did incalculable harm. . . .

These tainted the grand vision; how was the new technology making life better, more convenient, more comfortable? In Silicon Valley, the vision corresponded less and less plausibly to the lengthening traffic commutes, the drinking water advisories, the teenage homicides, the toxic industrial fires, and the budding awareness of the electronics industry's leading role in shredding the ozone. The pursuit of American dreams had become a prelude to nightmares.

POSTSCRIPT

Has High Technology Improved the Quality of American Life?

Whatever our future holds in the age of the information revolution, we are all experiencing *change* faster than did individuals in the Industrial Revolution. We must be conscious that not all technology is progressive or leads to a better world. Rather, all technology may have both positive and negative effects.

In many ways, the questions surrounding the information revolution are reminiscent of those disputing the introduction of earlier forms of media. For example, when radio was introduced to consumers, many people thought it had the potential for mind control. When television was introduced to mass society, many authors wrote that it signaled the breakdown of the American family and was a harbinger of our inability to think for ourselves. Even the telephone was considered by many to reduce the amount of face-to-face communication so that people would tend to become virtual shut-ins. The potential for the computer to change our life-styles and social relations is equally as complex.

We must learn from earlier forms of media that computers also have the potential to change our relationships to the world but that we may be able to minimize the negative effects if we look at their use systematically and with an eye toward using them and controlling their by-products in a responsible manner. We can do so *if* we proceed cautiously.

There are several books that describe Silicon Valley in greater detail. Among them are Thomas Mahon's *Charged Bodies* (New American Library, 1985); Michael Malone's *The Big Score: The Billion Dollar Story of Silicon Valley* (Doubleday, 1985); Paul Freiberger and Michael Swaine's *Fire in the Valley* (Osborne/McGraw Hill, 1984); and Carolyn Caddes's *Portraits of Success* (Tioga, 1986).

The social use of computers is the focus of such books as Sherry Turkle's *The Second Self: Computers and the Human Spirit* (Simon & Schuster, 1984) and Stephen Levy's *Hackers: Heroes of the Computer Revolution* (Anchor/Doubleday, 1984). An increasing number of books have begun to focus on what effects technology has on specific social groups. Two books that particularly focus on technology and women are *Technology and Women's Voices*, edited by

Cheris Kramarae (Routledge and Kegan Paul, 1988) and *Women, Work, and Technology*, edited by Barbara Drygulski Wright (University of Michigan Press, 1987).

Finally, many perspectives on the information revolution can be found in both the academic and the popular press. The highly readable *Megatrends* by John Naisbitt (Warner Communications, 1982) and Alvin Toffler's *Third Wave* (Bantam, 1981) provide an interesting link with past and future trends. More scholarly treatments may be found in Langdon Winner's *Autonomous Technology* (MIT Press, 1977); John Kenneth Galbraith's *The New Industrial State* (Houghton Mifflin, 1967); and Shoshanna Zuboff's *In the Age of the Smart Machine: The Future of Work and Power* (Basic Books, 1984).

ISSUE 18

Can Modern Mass Communication Promote a Better World?

YES: Ithiel de Sola Pool, from *Technologies of Freedom* (Belknap Press, 1983)

NO: Jacques Ellul, from "Preconceived Ideas About Mediated Information," in Rogers and Balle, eds., *The Media Revolution in America and in Western Europe* (Ablex Publishing, 1985)

ISSUE SUMMARY

YES: Professor Ithiel de Sola Pool of MIT argues that the abundance of new technologies allow greater interaction among individuals and nations.
NO: Professor Jacques Ellul warns that real communication may be lost by too great a reliance on these new technologies to do what only humans can do.

Whether technologies of communication are liberating or restrictive is a popular field for discourse today. Of course, many of the technologies we use today for messaging over distances give us options for communication that were too complex for rational speculation just a few lifetimes ago. Before the age of satellites, who would have thought that we would be able to see live-action images of wars being fought on the other side of the globe? The world can now experience (in many cases simultaneously) a royal marriage, the release from prison of South African leader Nelson Mandela, or a global rock concert like that of "Live Aid."

To "reach out and touch someone" is as easy as lifting a telephone receiver. Instant communication through FAX, electronic computerized message boards, or even a telephone answering machine allows us to leave a message even if the person we need to communicate with is not available at the time. We are no longer constrained by wires with remote and cellular telephones, and networks of computers allow us to withdraw money from automatic teller machines (ATMS) in various locations at any hour of the day or night.

What is amazing about these new technologies or systems is that so many have become available to both business and in-home users in almost all industrialized nations and, to some extent, in many other. The speed with which they have been introduced and seized upon by the public is sometimes staggering—in fact, most of the new technologies and uses have been introduced within the past 10 years! Life as it was when you were born is no longer so.

Professor Ithiel de Sola Pool takes the perspective that these new technologies and uses unite individuals and people of the world in a new and exciting way. For him, it is not as much the technologies themselves as it is the networks that allow for sophisticated systems of interaction. If we can remain free from political interruptions and conflicts, our new communication networks can provide unprecedented levels of freedom of expression. In this article, he warns of the potential pitfalls in greater use of technological networks but remains optimistic about a better world of communication in the future.

Taking a somewhat different approach, Professor Ellul digs beyond the obvious "common knowledge" that seems to accompany new communication possibilities due to greater use of technology and information flow, and he examines the preconceived notions, or myths, that surround the "better world" scenario. In the nine ideas he examines, he questions the many popular futuristic phrases we readily accept today and, in so doing, challenges us to think about not just the consequences of technology but also the ways in which we spread our popular beliefs.

Both of these authors project the future. Many of the images they invoke correspond to those of science fiction. In many ways, science fiction is intriguing because we have enough evidence in our daily lives to see that at least some of it may, indeed, *come true!* We can now travel to outer space, have computers "think" for us through artificial intelligence, see the impact of robots on the workplace and the structuring of human organisms through genetic manipulation. Science fiction, popular conceptions of the future, and academic treatises such as these two articles all contain images of the future that are right and wrong, possible and impossible, comforting and frightening. The two articles should make you think of the realities of the future in a different way but still may not suggest any definitive solutions.

YES   Ithiel de Sola Pool

POLICIES FOR FREEDOM

The technologies used for self-expression, human intercourse, and recording
of knowledge are in unprecedented flux. A panoply of electronic devices
puts at everyone's hand capacities far beyond anything that the printing
press could offer. Machines that think, that bring great libraries into anybody's study, that allow discourse among persons a half-world apart, are
expanders of human culture. They allow people to do anything that could be
done with the communications tools of the past, and many more things too.

The first trend to note is that the networks that serve the public are
becoming digital and broadband. Today, the only broadband signal received
by the ordinary household is its television picture. It is sometimes questioned
whether there are any other uses for which an end-to-end broadband digital
network available to every household and workplace will be demanded.
Such a network would allow two-way transmission of high-definition pictures and text in whole volumes at a time, along with voice, videotex, and
other low-speed services, but why should that be wanted? There are, indeed,
good reasons. High-definition pictures are not just fun. As manual mail
service gets less reliable and more expensive, the sending of magazines,
catalogues, videotapes, and videodisks electronically rather than physically
will become an attractive option. Nor is text delivered in whole volumes at a
time just a luxury. Text a page or so at a time, even if it comes faster than one
can read, is satisfactory for electronic mail or for retrieving pages one knows
one wants, but it does not do for browsing. To use a terminal the way one
uses a bookshelf or filing cabinet, one must be able to thumb randomly
through thousands of pages. And when computers talk to computers, even
though the size of the files they flip back and forth may be modest, a second
is too long for them to wait; their bursty traffic requires large bandwidth for
short periods. Millions of offices and homes may have computers and want
bandwidth enough for them. So if people at home or work want high-
definition moving pictures, if they desire two-way video for teleconferencing
or teleshopping, if they wish to browse in libraries rather than just reading

predefined pages, and if they compute, then the demand for end-to-end broadband networks will exist.

To serve the public, there will be networks on networks on networks. Separate nations will have separate networks, as they do now, but these will interconnect. Within nations, the satellite carriers, microwave carriers, and local carriers may be—and in the United States almost certainly will be—in the hands of separate organizations, but again they will interconnect. So even the basic physical network will be a network of networks. And on top of these physical networks will be a pyramid of service networks. Through them will be published or delivered to the public a variety of things: movies, money, education, news, meetings, scientific data, manuscripts, petitions, and editorials.

Another trend to note is toward increasing sophistication of the equipment on the user's own premises. Since the output and input of networks may be either printed on paper, shown on a screen, or declaimed in sound, the equipment needed on the customers' premises will be costly. Although the costs of computer logic, memory, and long-distance communication are falling, the uses that people want to make of them are expanding even faster. A $4000 microcomputer can today do things that would have required a million-dollar computer a few years ago, when few would have predicted that millions of ordinary people would spend $4000 for that home gadget. In the future, many millions of households will similarly desire large-size high-definition screens, cameras to originate video, and large memory devices to retain libraries of information for work and pleasure.

American industry is speculating that the percentage of disposable income spent on information activities will grow. Companies are positioning themselves to be in that industry. Banks like American Express and manufacturers like Westinghouse are investing in cablecasting; companies like Boeing are selling time-sharing services; and storekeepers like Sears Roebuck are experimenting with videodisk catalogues. Investors see the biggest dollar growth not in transmission or its hardware but in software and the equipment located on the customer's premises. This conclusion is what led AT&T to accept divestiture of its local phone companies in exchange for the freedom to sell information services and equipment to final customers. The science fiction version of the information work station of 2001 with beeps and sirens, flashing lights and video screens, may be fantasy, but the point is right: that is where expense will lie.

Paradoxically, big customers and decentralization will both gain from the development of more elaborate terminal equipment. However splendid may be the homeowner's equipment, it will be only a humble version of what will exist in plants and offices. Companies with information service and carrier billings in the millions will invest in their own networks, leased circuits, compression devices, and other marvelous gadgets designed to help them operate efficiently or cut costs. Depending on the structure of the vendors' and carriers' tariffs, different alternatives will pay off. One trade-off will be between buying communications capacity so as to improve management control and buying local processing power so as to cut communication costs. Trends between such centralizing and decentralizing alternatives may zigzag as technological and tariff changes affect relative prices, but the costs of computing equipment used to store data locally, to compress it, and to process it will probably fall farther and faster than the costs of transmission.

This trend favors decentralization. More and more will be done at the distributed nodes of networks to economize on transmission. That dispersion will be pushed farthest by big users, for they have the resources and technical capability to do so. When in large enterprises the competence and autonomy of scattered nodes are thus strengthened and their subservience to a center is thus lessened, the result, paradoxically, may be decentralization.

Another obvious trend is that with the new technologies, the world is shrinking. To talk or send messages across the world is coming to cost little more than communicating in one's own region. The charge for a call from New York to Los Angeles is now little more than for a call from New York to Albany. Both involve identical costs for the local loops and switches, for setting up the call, and for billing. The variable cost of extra microwave links is a minor item. With satellites, distance becomes almost totally unimportant. Patterns of human interaction will, as a result, change. There will be less cost constraint to do business, consult, debate, and socialize within one's own region only. There will be more freedom to do so with anyone anywhere with whom one finds affinity.

This development, along with the development of multiple technologies of communication and of cheap microprocessors, will foster a trend toward pluralistic and competitive communication systems. With hundred-channel cable systems, videocassettes, videodisks, ISDNs, and network links to thousands of on-line information services, there should be a diversity of voices far beyond anything known today. Telephone monopolies are being broken up. Before computers, phone administrations forbade connecting any "foreign attachment" to their network; today in the United States, Japan, Great Britain, and elsewhere, customers are being allowed to buy terminals at will and to attach them. Before microwave and satellite transmission, phone administrations had a monopoly in stringing wires from city to city, but these new nonwire transmission media are often managed by different enterprises. In the United States such competition already prevails in long-distance service, and local exchange service will not long remain completely monopolistic. Digital termination service, cellular radio, and cables carrying voice and data will all compete with the local phone company.

There is no reason to assume that the communications network of the future will be a single large organization with a central brain. It may be so, but it need not be. Having a hierarchical structure governed by a central brain is only one way to organize complex systems. A human being is organized that way; so is a nation-state. But the capitalist economy is not, nor is the complex system of scientific knowledge, nor is the ecological system of the biosphere. For an uncentralized system to function, there must be some established ways of interconnecting the parts other than by command; the interconnections may be managed by conventions, habits, or Darwinian processes. Capitalist property rights are enforced by laws; language is enforced by custom; creatures in the biosphere do not survive if they cannot metabolize other species.

An uncentralized set of communications systems can function as a single system only if traffic on each network can move through interfaces onto the other networks. The critical requirements are three: the right to interconnect, conformity to technical standards that make interfacing possible, and a directory system.

The variety and autonomy of networks for special groups and services may grow rather than decline, though most of them will interconnect with each other. Some of these networks will and others will not have their own central brains. The different kinds of communication—video, voice, and text; informational and emotive; public and personal—are likely to require differently designed networks, even if interconnected.

Digital technology promotes the trend toward distributed processing throughout the system and against a central brain. It is easier to convert one system of 0,1 pulses into another such system than it is to interface the analog memoryless communications systems of the past. A directory search in the absence of a single universal list is more likely to succeed if it uses intelligent digital devices that scan associative data structures at nanosecond speeds and that communicate with all nodes at the speed of light than if it is bound by the slower circuit switching of the past.

Perhaps the most remarkable trend to note is one whereby the artificial intelligence of computers will increasingly create and read many of the messages on the networks of the future. These computer-composed messages sent from computer to computer may mostly never be seen by a person at all. In an electronic funds transfer, only a few bits are needed to say debit an account by $27.50. Most of the traffic involves checking and rechecking to see whether the signature is authentic, whether money is available, and what balance is left.

The future of communications will be radically different from its past because of such artificial intelligence. If media become "demassified" to serve individual wants, it will not be by throwing upon lazy readers the arduous task of searching vast information bases, but by programing computers heuristically to give particular readers more of what they chose last time. Computer-aided instructional programs similarly assess students' past performance before providing the instruction they need. The lines between publication and conversation vanish in this sort of system. Socrates' concern that writing would warp the flow of intelligence can at last be set to rest. Writing can become dialogue.

Such are some technical features of the communications system that is emerging. Technology will not be to blame if Americans fail to encompass this system within the political tradition of free speech. On the contrary, electronic technology is conducive to freedom. The degree of diversity and plenitude of access that mature electronic technology allows fare exceeds what is enjoyed today. Computerized information networks of the twenty-first century need not be any less free for all to use without let or hindrance than was the printing press. Only political errors might make them so. . . .

GUIDELINES FOR FREEDOM

Difficult problems of press freedom, as well as of economics, arise at the intersections of regulatory models. When resource constraints are small and circumstances neatly fit the historical pattern of publishing, or when resource constraints are severe and circumstances fit the historical situation of a common carrier, then norms exist. The difficulties arise in situations that have elements of each. This was the problem in deciding about the broadcasting system in the 1920s; it is also a problem in the regulation of electronic networks today.

Regulators find it convenient to segregate activities and to keep each organization on its own turf. Much of regulatory law consists of specifications as to who may engage in what activities. Frequency allocations are made for particular uses; CBers or amateurs may not broadcast entertainment; public broadcast stations may not carry ads. In the United States, AT&T and Western Union have been largely partitioned, with AT&T kept out of telex and telegraph traffic and Western Union kept out of voice. Deregulation loosens such restrictions and allows companies to move onto each other's turf. But some segmentation persists.

A price is paid for this rigid delimitation of turf, not only in efficiency and innovation but also in freedom of speech. The notion that government may specify which communications entity is allowed to participate in particular parts of the information industry's vertical flow is hard to reconcile with the First Amendment. To research and write, to print or orate, to publish and distribute, is everyone's right. If government licensing of reporters, publishers, or printing presses is anathema, then so also should be the licensing of broadcasters and telecommunications carriers.

Yet the repeated argument has been made, which may be right or wrong in particular cases, that some degree of natural monopoly prevails in particular parts of the communications field. Whether because there were thought to be only 89 broadcasting frequencies, or because having more than one company digging up the streets was intolerable, or because the carrier that reached most persons was the one most worth joining, it seemed likely that a dominant organization would gain control of a communications resource that other citizens also needed. Under these circumstances the best solution seemed to be to define a monopoly's turf narrowly and to require those who had the monopoly to serve all comers without discrimination.

Since the institutions in such strategic positions are usually basic carriers of physical signals, one way to narrow their domain is to separate the carrier from content-related activities. But there are problems in doing this, in terms both of undercutting the economics of the business and, in America, of bending the Constitution. The unfortunate compromise that has often followed is to license and regulate the monopoly.

Such limited franchises have a way of being extended beyond their original rationale. Enfranchised monopolies that at one time are thought simply to reflect in an orderly fashion the natural realities of the market, and are indeed intended to restrict monopoly, get converted into matters of right. Stations and carriers that are licensed simply to ensure good service by carefully selected organizations when monopoly seems inevitable come to see themselves, and to be seen, as having a vested right in their franchise. Regulatory powers assumed by the government to cope with monopoly also acquire a life of their own.

This faces the communications field with a dilemma. Not all parts of the communications system fit well under the preferred print model. Bottlenecks do exit where there are severe resource constraints. And the regulations that in those situations seem to be required have an insidious bent. They acquire legitimacy; they outlive their need; they tend to spread. The camel's nose is under the tent.

Yet when there is severe scarcity, there is an unavoidable need to regulate access. Caught in the tension between the tradition of freedom and the need for some controls, the communications system then tends to become a mix of uncontrolled and common carrier elements— of anarchy, of property, and of enfranchised services. A set of principles must be understood if communications in the electronic era are to hold as fully as possible to the terms of the First Amendment. The technology does not make this hard. Confusion about principles may.

The first principle is that the First Amendment applies fully to all media. It applies to the function of communication, not just to the media that existed in the eighteenth century. It applies to the electronic media as much as to the print ones.

Second, anyone may publish at will. The core of the First Amendment is that government may not prohibit anyone from publishing. There may be no licensing, no scrutiny of who may produce or sell publications or information in any form.

Third, enforcement of the law must be after the fact, not by prior restraint. In the history of communications law this principle has been fundamental. Libel, obscenity, and eavesdropping are punishable, but prior review is anathema. In the electronic media this has not been so, but it should be. Traffic controls may be needed in cases where only one communicator can function at a particular place at a particular time, such as street meetings or use of radio frequencies, but this limited authority over time and place is not the same as power to choose or refuse to issue a license.

Fourth, regulation is a last recourse. In a free society, the burden of proof is for the least possible regulation of communication. If possible, treat a communications situation as free for all rather than as subject to property claims and a market. If resource constraints make this impossible, treat the situation as a free market rather than as a common carrier. But if resources for communication are truly monopolistic, use common carrier regulation rather than direct regulation or public ownership. Common carriage is a default solution when all must share a resource in order to speak or publish.

Under common law in the nineteenth century, vendors could not be made common carriers against their will. If they offered a service to the general public, it had to be without discrimination, but if they chose to serve a limited clientele, that was their right. This philosophy applies well to publishing. One would not require the Roman Catholic *Pilot* to carry ads for birth control or a trade union magazine to carry ads against the closed shop. But these cases assume that diverse magazines exist. A dilemma arises when there is a monopoly medium, as when a monopoly newspaper in a town refuses ads to one party and carries them for another.

In the world of electronic communications some but not all of the basic physical carriers, and only those, seem likely to continue to have significant monopoly power. It is hard to imagine a value-added network having the dominance in a community that a local newspaper has today. Even now the communications monopolies that exist without privileged enforcement by the state are rare. Even basic physical conduits become monopolies precisely because they cannot exist without public favors. They need permissions that only the state can grant. These favors, be they franchises to dig up the city streets or spectrum to transmit through the air, may properly be given to those who choose to serve as common carriers. This is not a new idea. In 1866 telegraph companies were given the right to string wires at will along post roads and across public lands, but only if they became common carriers. Where monopoly exists by public favor, public access is a reasonable condition.

Fifth, interconnection among common carriers may be required. The basic principle of common carriage, namely that all must be served without discrimination, implies that carriers accept interconnection from each other. This principle, established in the days of the telegraph, is incorporated in the 1982 AT&T consent decree. All long-distance carriers have a right to connect to all local phone companies. That is the 1980s outgrowth of the 1968 Carterphone decision which required AT&T to interconnect with an independent radio-telephone service. Universal interconnection implies both adherence to technical standards, without which interconnection can be difficult, and a firm recognition of the right to interconnect.

Carriers may sometimes raise valid objections to interconnection. Some will wish to use novel technologies that are incompatible with generally accepted standards, claiming that they are thereby advancing the state of the art. Also, when they handle highly sensitive traffic, such as funds transfers or intracompany data, they may not wish to be common carriers and bear the risks of having outsiders on their system. Such arguments are often valid, though they may also be used to lock a group of customers out of using the carrier.

An argument in favor of general interconnectivity is that it facilitates market entry by new or small carriers. It also makes universal service easier. It may even be useful for national security, since a highly redundant system is less likely to be brought down. In short, there are conflicting considerations that must be balanced. As a policy, the requirement of interconnection is a reasonable part of a common carriage system.

Sixth, recipients of privilege may be subject to disclosure. The enforcement of nondiscrimination depends critically on information. Without control of accounting methods, regulatory commissions are lost in a swamp. I once asked the head of the Common Carrier Bureau of the FCC what he would ask for if he could rub Aladdin's lamp. "Revelatory books" was his reply.

Yet American lawmakers, who have imposed far more oppressive and dubious kinds of regulation, such as exit, entry, and tariff controls, have never pushed the mild requirement for visibility. Apart from requiring accounts, legislators have been highly considerate of proprietary information. A firm that enjoys the monopoly privileges which lead to being a common carrier should perhaps forgo, like government, some privileges of privacy. Unbundled rates for cable leasing, for example, help reveal who is being charged for what. Disclosure is not a new idea. Patents and copyrights are privileges won only by making their object public. The same principle might well apply to action under franchises too.

Seventh, privileges may have time limits. Patents and copyrights are for finite periods, and then the right expires. Radio and television licenses and cable franchises, though also for fixed periods, are typically renewable. Some monopoly privileges that broadcasters and cablecasters have in their licenses could expire after a fixed period. This is a way to favor infant industries but limit their privileges when they become giants.

Eighth, the government and common carriers should be blind to circuit use. What the facility is used for is not their concern. There may be some broad categories of use. Emergency communications often have priority. Special press rates for telegraph have been permitted, though their legality in the United States has been questioned. But in general, control of the conduit may not become a means for controlling content. What customers transmit on the carrier is no affair of the carrier.

Ninth, bottlenecks should not be used to extend control. Rules on undeliverable mail have been used to control obscene content. Cablecasting, in which there is no spectrum shortage, has been regulated by the FCC as ancillary to broadcasting. Telegraph companies have sought to control news services, and cable franchisees have sought to control the programs on the cable. Under the First Amendment, no government imposition on a carrier should pass muster if it is motivated by concerns beyond common carriage, any more than the carrier should be allowed to use its service to control its customers.

Tenth, and finally, for electronic publishing, copyright enforcement must be adapted to the technology. This exceptional control on communication is specifically allowed by the Constitution as a means of aiding dissemination, not restricting it. Copyright is temporary and

requires publication. It was designed for the specific technology of the printing press. It is in its present form ill adapted to the new technologies. The objective of copyright is beyond dispute. Intellectual effort needs compensation. Without it, effort will wither. But to apply a print scheme of compensation to the fluid dialogue of interactive electronic publishing will not succeed. Given modern technologies, there is no conceivable way that individual copies can be effectively protected from reproduction when they are already either on a sheet of paper or in a computer's memory. The task is to design new forms of market organization that will provide compensation and at the same time reflect the character of the new technology.

The question boils down to what users at a computer terminal will pay for. For one thing, they will pay for a continuing relationship, as they will continue to need maintenance. It may be easy to pirate a single program or some facts from a data base by copying from a friend of a friend of a friend who once bought it. But to get help in adapting it or to get add-on versions or current data, one might pay a fee as a tender for future relations. The magazine subscription model is closer to the kind of charging system that will work for electronic publishing than is the one-time book purchase with a royalty included.

A workable copyright system is never enacted by law alone. Rather it evolves as a social system, which may be bolstered by law. The book and music royalty systems that now exist are very different from each other, reflecting the different structures of the industries. What the law does is to put sanctions behind what the parties already consider right. So too with electronic publishing on computer networks, a normative system must grow out of actual patterns of work. The law may then lend support to those norms.

If language were as fluid as the facts it represents, one would talk in the electronic era of serviceright, not copyright. But as language is used, old words are kept regardless of their derivation, and their meanings are changed. In the seventeenth century reproducing a text by printing was a complex operation that could be monitored. Once the text was printed on paper, however, it required no further servicing, and no one could keep track of it as it passed from reader to reader. In the electronic era copying may become trivially easy at the work stations people use. But both the hardware and the software in which the text is embodied require updating and maintenance. In ways that cannot yet be precisely identified, the bottleneck for effective monitoring and charging is migrating from reproduction to the continuing service function.

Not only in copyright but in all other issues of communications policy, the courts and legislatures will have to respond to a new and puzzling technology. The experience of how American courts have dealt with new nonprint media over the past hundred years is cause for alarm. Forty years ago Zechariah Chafee noted how differently the courts treated the print media from newer ones: "Newspapers, books, pamphlets, and large meetings were for many centuries the only means of public discussion, so that the need for their protection has long been generally realized. On the other hand, when additional methods for spreading facts and ideas were introduced or greatly improved by modern inventions, writers and judges had not got into the habit of being solicitous

about guarding their freedom. And so we have tolerated censorship of the mails, the importation of foreign books, the stage, the motion picture, and the radio." With the still newer electronic media the problem is compounded. A long series of precedents, each based on the last and treating clumsy new technologies in their early forms as specialized business machines, has led to a scholastic set of distinctions that no longer correspond to reality. As new technologies have acquired the functions of the press, they have not acquired the rights of the press. On print, no special excise taxes may be applied; yet every month people pay a special tax on their telephone bill, which would seem hardly different in principle from the old English taxes on newspapers. On print, the court continues to exercise special vigilance for the preferred position of the First Amendment; but other considerations of regulatory convenience and policy are given a preferred position in the common carrier and electronic domains.

Since the lines between publishing, broadcasting, and the telephone network are now being broken, the question arises as to which of these three models will dominate public policy regarding the new media. There is bound to be debate, with sharp divisions between conflicting interests. Will public interest regulation, such as the FCC applies, begin to extend over the conduct of the print media as they increasingly use regulated electronic means of dissemination? Or will concern for the traditional notion of a free press lead to finding ways to free the broadcast media and carriers from the regulation and content-related requirements under which they now operate? Electronic media, as they are coming to be, are dispersed in use and abundant in supply. They allow for more knowledge, easier access, and freer speech that were ever enjoyed before. They fit the free practices of print. The characteristics of media shape what is done with them, so one might anticipate that these technologies of freedom will overwhelm all attempts to control them. Technology, however, shapes the structure of the battle, but not every outcome. While the printing press was without doubt the foundation of modern democracy, the response to the flood of publishing that it brought forth has been censorship as often as press freedom. In some times and places the even more capacious new media will open wider the floodgates for discourse, but in other times and places, in fear of that flood, attempts will be made to shut the gates.

The easy access, low cost, and distributed intelligence of modern means of communication are a prime reason for hope. The democratic impulse to regulate evils, as Tocqueville warned, is ironically a reason for worry. Lack of technical grasp by policy makers and their propensity to solve problems of conflict, privacy, intellectual property, and monopoly by accustomed bureaucratic routines are the main reasons for concern. But as long as the First Amendment stands, backed by courts which take it seriously, the loss of liberty is not foreordained. The commitment of American culture to pluralism and individual rights is reason for optimism, as is the pliancy and profusion of electronic technology.

NO

Jacques Ellul

PRECONCEIVED IDEAS ABOUT MEDIATED INFORMATION

What are preconceived ideas about information and communication? This terminology does not imply a value judgment that these ideas are false or stupid. Some of them are false and stupid, but others are perfectly exact and sensible.

Preconceived ideas are rather different from what we generally call "common knowledge"; it usually is the result of a slow process, a gradual conviction, as it spreads among the public. Common knowledge is an expression of a sort of popular wisdom which says a lot about those who share it. On the contrary, preconceived ideas are not accepted by the general public (although they will probably be exposed to them gradually through repetitive advertising and the omnipresence of the mass media), but rather in intellectual circles, by people who think and by individuals who act, like media professionals. . . .

This phenomenon of forming preconceived ideas deserves special attention by communication scholars. Why are preconceived ideas constructed? The universe of communication and information is an incredibly fluid, uncertain world which is difficult to grasp and in which the human intelligence seems disoriented. Many communication scholars do not agree that such a high degree of uncertainty exists, and remind us of "theorems" about communication. But the rigor of these scientific theorems obtains only through a drastic simplification of reality, as often must be the case in the social sciences. I am convinced that our understanding about human communication is a blurred one in which we are somewhat lost and usually ready to accept formulae which represent a fixed point from which we can understand part of communication behavior.

"Information Is Power"
This preconceived idea, of course, is related to the unchallenged idea that knowledge and power are perfectly reciprocal. It is not wrong to say that the possession of knowledge confers power today, or that power can only be

exercised when based on knowledge, and through knowledge. I think, however, that knowledge and power do not coincide exactly. The acquiring, and the withholding, of information equally confer power. Such power is often based on information unknown to the general public. And, inversely, the diffusion of information seems to coincide with "democracy."

But it is impossible to proceed with a global formula. Information gathered and used by public authorities is often false (or at least incomplete), because those in power do not have the time to digest the necessary quantity of information to properly exert their power. However, in some specific situations, the acquisition of an item of information not available to others can indeed help to exercise power for a while, such as in a military operation or on the stock market. Obviously, individuals who possess great knowledge in a certain field, acquire a certain superiority and exert an unquestionable power. Such expertise is characteristic of the bureaucrat, the technician or consultant appointed to a political council, or professors vis-à-vis students. It is unquestionable. But at the other end of the spectrum is a general public more and more saturated with information and yet increasingly unable to exercise power, to formulate a sensible opinion, or to exert pressure upon the political environment.

Yet another example of the incompatibility of information and power was France's Algerian War. In that case, the more informed one was, the more unable one was to side with either protagonist (that is to make a decision). During the Algerian War, one had to begin by choosing one's position, and then carefully filter out all information about this conflict, keeping such news as was congruent with one's position. This selective behavior amounts to rigorously transforming every element of news into propaganda (the same alchemy that every political adherent does without being told to). All other information was blacked out. Anybody who tried to get as much accurate information about the F.L.N.[1] as about the French in Algeria, about the way Algerians were treated before the war, and about the way the French Army acted, anybody who tried to look impartially at the two opponents and to know the truth, became more and more unable to take a position for one or the other (that is to say, to exercise power).

Today, the same observation can be made of the war in Lebanon. If we want to consider the Israeli viewpoint, or, on the other hand, only the war, with as much information as possible, we become totally unable to side with one party or the other. We become upset witnesses, tossed around in a chaotic universe which information makes us more and more aware of.

We cannot overlook one other relationship between information and power: Individuals in power either control the means of information, or at least try to use the mass media for their own benefit, so we must inevitably deal with the nature of propaganda. On one hand, information overload is a necessary condition for the development and success of propaganda in affecting opinion. On the other hand, propaganda can only be used when based on true information and through normal communication channels. Here we do see the transfer of information to the domain of power.

I tried to show here that the formula "Information is power," accepted as an obvious truth, covers complex, contradictory, and confusing realities.

"The Flow of Information Replaces the Flow of Goods"

Today we live in a new type of society, one where information is very important, where nothing can be done without information, and where communication networks function constantly. But from this viewpoint, we jump to a confused and inconsistent conclusion. Yesterday's society was characterized by the production of material goods, and its functioning was based on the transfer of those goods, or their exchange. Marx founded his theory, in part, on the very exact idea that social injustices come from the transition from a stage of use value of goods to a stage of the exchange value of goods, from the transformation of the good produced by a worker into a commodity (a transferable element of capital). Marx perfectly analyzed the flow of goods and capital.

Now that our world is interconnected through a dense web of communication networks, the essential exchanges are flows of information. The indispensable element for every action is now information. Machines obey people who feed them information.

But the trend toward our becoming an information society does not mean that the flow of information is replacing the flow of goods. What does this preconceived idea really mean? Communication networks indeed cover the world. But the modern world remains based upon material goods. Information is produced, transmitted, gathered, and manipulated by technologies which are material goods. Information is most interesting when it refers to the flow of goods directly (as in advertising commercials) or indirectly (as in political campaigns). This exchange of goods still dominates even in socialist countries. We see how important commodities are when we realize that information itself becomes a commodity. Yes, the world is covered by information flows, but they are necessarily secondary. They convey information *about* something, information which produces effects which affect the world, but which is not an information world. The content of the information necessarily refers to something, to material commodities. This secondary nature of information is obliterated in our preconceived idea, as if information ends up being an object per se, independent from what it refers to.

Our preconceived idea becomes absurd when it is pushed to the limit, as in the all-too-famous book of Servan-Schreiber (1980), where he says that we can develop the Third World through the diffusion of microcomputers. The politician ignores completely the possibilities of real help that the microcomputers can provide. The computer is only a management tool, and that is all. To use a computerized system implies that there is something to be managed: industrial plants, big cities, intensive agriculture, harbor traffic, etc. But the tragedy of the Third World is precisely that there is no useful economic production. There is nothing to be managed with a computer. Using many microcomputers will not resolve any of the problems of the Third World: hunger, domination by the great powers, ferocious dictators, financial deadends. The Servan-Schreiber argument shows the absurdity of the idea of substituting the flow of information for the flow of material goods: Information does not feed a hungry man. It is a supplementary luxury for rich nations.

"An Excess of Information Informs"

I helped spread this preconceived idea (Ellul, 1972). It is obvious that we are often overwhelmed by too much information which is too intense and too invading: commercials, political ads, comics, traffic signs, and instantaneous information, much of which we have to memorize if we are to know the world in which we live. But it is impossible to do so. A qualitative difference in information exists because of the quantitative excess.

Even in a traditional, closed society, without any media other than direct speech, drums, or visual "telegraphs", information was not scarce. I am always surprised by the extreme rapidity with which really essential information spread in ancient times. For example, during the popular uprising against the King of France in November, 1314, the unrest started in Burgundy on November 6 and spread very fast, from province to province, from Lyon to Normandy, from Artois to Dauphine. On November 24, the Federation of the Revolutionary Leagues was created! It could not happen so fast today. Another example: In Spain, a pogrom against the Jews started in Seville on January 6, 1391, and within a few days spread to all the cities in the province: Alcala, Carmina, Olalla. Twenty cities revolted in 10 days! The social unrest spread in less than 1 month, first to all the cities of Northeast Spain, and then it reached Valencia and Salamanca on the one side of Spain, and Barcelona on the other, in less than 4 months.

So information about very important matters circulates very rapidly, and action immediately follows that information. But that was true in a society not yet overloaded with information. Information was therefore memorizable, as evidenced by the many diaries kept in the 16th century. In such an information-poor environment, really decisive news took on an extraordinary importance. For example, the launching of a crusade or of a heresy led to immediate action.

We live now in a completely different universe, with instantaneous information available to everybody (whether they are concerned or not). Most information is generally not very interesting nor very useful, but it is incredibly numerous. We are exposed to a huge mass of information, but we discard most of it soon after; human memory is totally unable to sort out useful information from useless information. Among the crowd of advertisements which left me indifferent, one of them could have interested me. This torpor is a fortunate phenomenon because if I could memorize everything, I would become crazy. Since I have no reference which would enable me to sort out what should be forgotten, I do so randomly; I memorize an absurd detail of no avail, and I discard decisive information that I should have memorized.

Information-blocking is a refusal to recognize the reality of our information society, an unconscious protest against information overload. The overexposure to information destroys our critical and imaginative reactions. It is impossible to critically examine the thousands of bits of information we are exposed to daily. The multiplicity of different media invades our communication capacities, surrounding us with a world of purely fictional information. Our experience of the real world disappears almost completely in a flood of information. The aspects of life which become most important are those transmitted through the magic of the screen. The rest is of little consequence.

But there is a basic ignorance under the cover of the abundance of information bits. Through the media, *everything* can be said, shown, broadcast about China, Russia, war, hunger. Everything, but without any guarantee of proof or coherence. It is fantasy. We know of numerous examples of newsmen who spread thousands of essentially false facts. They are not liars. They obeyed (although not consciously) that fundamental law stated by Einstein: "Theory determines what *must* be observed." At present, in the midst of numerous news reports, I claim we do not know anything about the war in Lebanon. We may know in about ten years, but at that moment, we will be overwhelmed by thousands of news reports about another world tragedy. Because of the proliferation of the media, and its immediateness, there is no trustworthy news. We can state it as a principle.

So, information which invades our defenses and remains in our minds, and which appears as trustworthy, is actually manipulated and scientifically organized to strike our attention (for example, through propaganda techniques), or else it is shocking.

"Modern Information Systems Endlessly Spread Bad News, While Reducing the Depth of the News Through Transparency"

The more crowded our intellectual universe, the more striking we find information that is dangerous. Shocking and upsetting information becomes more striking. It has been repeated a thousand times (and it has become a popular idea) that only bad news is "news." Although we recognize the obvious truth of this

assertion, we do not always comprehend how it is inherent in all media. The media only transmit "transparency," evidence. It is only possible to grasp the surface of an event and to give the audience a film that has been exposed to a transparent picture. The transparency of tragedy, war, death, and sickness is sufficient in a mass communication medium.

But it is impossible to transmit a deeper dimension, even in a long newspaper article (which the reader will not finish reading) or a lengthy speech of TV. Such messages are targeted to an anonymous audience and consequently cannot go beyond the surface events. It is impossible for a journalist, even if he is very clever and honest, to make his audience see what is complex. But everything really human is also inevitably discreet, slow, and spiraling. Information in the media can only be linear, and hence tragically simplified. Because a mass medium transmits instantaneously, by its very nature it can only transmit immediate evidence. The mass media may try to transmit other kinds of news, but they are reduced by the inevitable law of transparency. Thus the picture of the world possessed by the modern human should not be taken as real (Ellul, 1962).

In other words, the modern human lives in a fictional universe of tragedies which he is completely powerless to prevent, and which ignores the positive environment in which he lives.

"Everything Is Possible With the Computer"

We mystify computer systems. The solution to information overload, we are told, is the computer. Obviously, I cannot memorize and use all the mass of information gathered and transmitted throughout the world. I am limited. Fortunately, I can keep this information in the memory of a computer. I feel reassured.

Unfortunately, the computer cannot memorize everything. Computers follow a binary logic, they can only memorize data that are translated and reduced to binary form. Qualitative, moral, spiritual, and cultural information, or that about human or divine relationships, cannot be so translated. Of course, one can enter data concerning the history of religions, or the formulating of dogmas, but it is impossible to enter data concerning the motive and the motor of faith, and of what leads religion from a state of objective knowledge to a subjective experience.

Information traditionally had both a qualitative and a quantitative aspect which were linked. I transmit information, via a computer, in such a way that you change your behavior accordingly. Your new behavior is not the result of some kind of quantitative calculation, but the result of the human relationship between you and me. If Jesus had been a teacher of dogma, nothing would have happened. The calculations of Einstein have been accepted not because they were correct, but because they were Einstein's calculations. It is useless to separate information from the way in which it is transmitted, the person who transmits it, the place were it originates, and the qualities it evokes to the audience. Try to reduce Hitler's speeches into binary language and you get nothing. But these same speeches made by Hitler changed the world.

The way that knowledge is transmitted depends entirely on the personality of the teacher. If a teacher is enthusiastic, strong, and eager to develop intellectual ability, students follow and learn. Pedagogy is much more than the untiring patience and the constant repetition of a computer. Conversely, the teacher must have something to teach. But students are beginning to believe that all learning is useless, since it is already in the computer, and that many basic intellectual operations are now unnecessary since they can be done by a small machine. If the knowledge of the teacher is undermined by the infinite knowledge of the computer, teaching abilities are not useful anymore.

"One becomes a good blacksmith only by forging" is still true even in this time of universal electronic memory. It is impossible to train the mind if there is no formalized content to exercise that mind. Therefore, the handy formula that "It is all in the computer" should not lead us to rely only on the computer. The quantitative and the qualitative in the human being are absolutely inseparable. When we use a data-bank, if the user does not know anything about the subject matter, he is unable to consult the computer. He simply does not know what question to ask. To know completely what to ask the machine, we have to know as much as its memory does. We have to have analyzed the problem, we have to have planned the operation, and we have to know at what point we need more information. To have learned electronics, computer science, how to use a computer is not enough. You could know how to drive a car, but if you didn't know where you wanted to go, if there are no roads to get there, and if you have no motivation to get started, then your knowledge is useless.

There is yet another difficulty. It is incorrect to say that "Once all the information is entered in the computer, I don't have to worry." Data-banks are organized by human beings. So it is impossible for everything to be recorded. Only data which seem important to one individual (or to a group) are entered in the data-bank. Thus a whole category of facts are necessarily obliterated and discarded as unimportant and irrelevant. If Marx had relied on what a computer could have told him about the economic system of his time, he would never have done the analyses of the economic system, as he did. He used facts that he considered important, but which were disregarded by the (then) dominant paradigm (Kuhn, 1970). Only recognized and accepted knowledge is entered in a computer data-bank. So a data-bank only gets information that has been filtered by specialists.

Once I did an experiment with a very good research assistant. Since I was falling behind in reading my journals and magazines, I hired her to update my files. It was a disaster. She gathered much data in which I was not all interested, and she discarded details, objectively insignificant, which nonetheless for me had a lot of meaning. Similarly, individuals in charge of entering data in a computer do not have a "keen nose" for our interests. They cannot. So the computer data-bank is almost useless to help us cope with the information overload.

"The World Is a Global Village"

Another preconceived idea which is very popular but very questionable, concerns McLuhan's famous concept of the global village. He argued that communication technologies would shrink the entire world, so that we will no longer be isolated from one another. Formerly, in a village of two hundred individuals, everybody knew each other. When something happened, it was known immediately; the information system was almost perfect. When we were introduced to the larger universe through exploration and journeys, we became very poorly informed. At first the individual learned about events years later, then months later, and finally only weeks later. Today, thanks to the Marconi galaxy, we immediately know everything happening everywhere in the world. So we come back to the village situation.

What characterized the traditional village was that everyone knew everyone else. It was global person-to-person knowledge. Information was transmitted by an individual and was accepted as more or less serious and important, depending on the way that the individual was perceived. The story of the shepherd boy who pretended to be attacked by a wolf is significant in that respect. There is no global village today because I do not personally know the personality, the nature, and the ideology of the individual who transmits the information to me. In this sense, I know far less today about China than at the time when I was reading Marco Polo's stories. The infinite communication networks do not bring me closer to anything or anyone. Although the telephone allows such personal contact, the human relationship is greatly altered when information is transmitted through that technology.

Information transmitted by a human is not the same as that transmitted by bees or ants, although a risk of the worldwide communication networks is that it is to be reduced to that. We can now separate the code from the language, the information from the spoken words, or reduce information to bytes. We are making the same mistake as economists did in their classical theory, when they created a human model (the homo-economicus) through reductionism, so that it fit their model of economic behavior. Communication scholars should not forget that words cannot be separated from the person who uttered them. The words have the content, the importance, and the pertinence of the person who formulated them. Such was the situation in the original village, but it is not in the world village!

The same sentence uttered by the president of France and by me is not really the same sentence. We dissociate words from the individual who says them in modern communication systems. It is impossible to do otherwise. When I listen to a TV news report, I don't know whether or not the news organization is connected to the political power being described, nor can I establish if the advertising sponsors influenced the way the facts are presented. I have an immediate source, but does that person act independently or not? In the United States and in Europe there is no censorship (in the usual sense of this word). Censorship also exists as the interposition between the source and the receiver of an invisible third party who gives the real meaning of what is said. That tendency is increased with the capacity of the media to instantaneously transmit a multitude of varied, contradictory, and ever-changing news, in a way that rules out control and verification. Try reading a newspaper one month after its publication and you will notice that about 25 percent of its content was not worth reading.

In the real village, information transmitted from one individual to other inhabitants was relevant to their lives (even when the information was a joke, gossip, or slander). Such information caused a change (for example in the relationship between families), and it almost always led to action. On the contrary, the information I receive today through the media is usually not related to my life. I cannot change my behavior because of this information. What can I do against the advance of the desert in the Sahel, against worldwide hunger, against the Pol Pot regime, against the condition of Cambodians in the camps in Thailand, against the invasion of Afghanistan or of Lebanon?

Information may be instantaneous, and bring about a new mode of thinking, but it has not changed our world into a global village. At most, it caused the disappearance of real villages!

"Dialogue Is Possible"
Another preconceived idea is that dialogue is still possible. On the contrary, we argue that dialogue via the media is impossible; a listener cannot instantaneously respond to whomever is on radio or TV. Moreover a response to a newspaper article, often published a month later, no longer makes sense because the first article has already been forgotten. Furthermore, if the audience already made up their mind as the result of the first article, the response is inconsequential. A dialogue implies a continuing exchange, and a reciprocal adaptation.

We do not dialogue anymore in our society, we "communicate." The role assigned to information-communication in our society is that of lubricant or correlator. Information never concerns individuals as such, but the members of a social corps which must function correctly, consequently excluding the possibility of dialogue. There is futility in advocating exchange between an administration and those who it administers, or in seeking to suppress organizational secrecy through the disclosure of administrative files. Because mass communication is a flow, it excludes the possibility of feedback or dialogue. People are not supposed to provide information *to* the system.

Once everything becomes communication the goal is to receive without distortion, to accumulate as much information as possible about everything. When the effort is to create an international order through information and communication, then we have a new conception of the world. It is completely different from that in which we have lived heretofore. When information facilitates everything, every opinion, what confrontation can still exist? The overabundance of information creates a kind of transparency, in that everything is known (everything becomes transparent).

Mass-communicated information alerts the process of thinking, but suppresses dialogue.

"Dialogue Is Impossible"

Our previous preconceived idea has two contradictory aspects; we just looked at the pessimistic side. Now we argue that modern means of communication make everything possible, including the exchanges of information ("dialogues"). Since the media have become less and less expensive, an incredible potential capacity to communicate is offered to everyone. Since we can now communicate with everybody, an endless and universal dialogue is created.

In the two contradictory aspects of "dialogue," the word does not have exactly the same meaning. On one hand, everything can be said, communicated, or exchanged at every level of society. But let us consider what really happens in three cases of increased communication. The French telecommunication services complain that the French do not use their telephones enough. Less than two telephone calls are made per customer per day. The French do not try to communicate, to dialogue through this wonderful tool. Consider Teletel. The French who have it, do not use it; only one-fourth ever use it.

Or take the phenomenon of CB radios in recent years. Here we have enthusiastic, fanatical people. We remember their angry demonstrations when it appeared that the French government might not authorize this marvelous means of "dialogue." But we also notice the worthlessness of the CB conversations, the stupidity of these dialogues, and the nonexistence of a real relationship. The conversation is limited to such exchanges as "How are you buddy?" or "The weather looks great today." There is not one worthwhile dialogue out of a thousand. What can we talk about with a total stranger, about whom we know nothing, and whom we do not even see? The same worthlessness appears with the multiplicity of Free Radios (*Radios Libres*) in France. Now is the time to reconsider Beranos' question: "Freedom to do what?"

It is fascinating that we find nothing to say with these wonderful means of communication. We cannot find a way to provide new and original information. So we give out cooking recipes, advice to housekeepers, answers for worried parents, horseracing prognostications, restaurant locations, and other fascinating trivia. We have nothing to transmit. When we talk to someone we know, the conversation is enhanced by common experience. Conversation with a stranger is reduced to nonexistence. When we say proudly that "everything" is possible with modern media, we talk only about the possibility of the material transference of information. But for everything to really be possible, the human being should be capable of doing "everything." For example, think of the mediocre films or slide shows put together by thousands of amateur photographers after returning from their vacations. The means of communication outweigh the ability of the communicator to use the medium. The result is emptiness.

The proliferation of communication technologies today demonstrates that these tools are only gadgets; they only serve to transmit the absurd.

"The Mass Media Foster Democracy"

Contrast the worthlessness of the information that is transmitted versus the weight, the importance, the immediacy, and the seriousness of the same information when transmitted by the State or by big companies. A division still exists between those who transmit, those who have every possible means to gather, sort out, manipulate, and pass on information, versus the receivers who cannot use these means. "Everything is possible" is not true. There is an aristocracy of transmitters and a plebeian mass of receivers, audiences, and spectators. Great specialists have huge power and cannot be controlled. The division between the information-rich and the information-poor more profoundly divides society than the former social classes. You cannot do anything against individuals who have information power. A writer unfairly treated by important newspapers cannot do anything. If he tries he will simply become a non-person. Nobody will publish his books. He will be thrown into oblivion, as in feudal times.

The plurality of information does not help close the inequality. Nowadays, everything depends on public opinion. And public opinion depends very much on its opinion-makers' roles. Those who use the mass media are technicians, as aristocratic as other, great technicians; it is out-of-the-question to penetrate their domain. The amateur has but his hobby. He is more eager to accept the great information, because he thinks he is taking part in the big game. The proliferation and sophistication of the media make it impossible for the common person to have information worth transmitting through such media. Thus the division between the two classes of the informer and the informed becomes wider.

The belief that anyone can send information is only a wish and a myth; not reality. Thus our traditional conception of democracy is forced to change. So the proliferation of the media seems to be fundamentally anti-democratic.

Conclusion

After having questioned nine preconceived ideas about modern mass communication, I conclude that everything, and its opposite, is said about these communication media. We know everything about microcomputers but we do not know anything about their social impacts and human possibilities. We are in complete doubt about the consequences of the new media. I have examined important studies about the potential of computers, office automation (*bureautique*), artificial intelligence (*robotique*). We are now very uncertain because of the new communications.

I think the first step into wisdom (and also perhaps to knowledge) is to admit that we do not know where we are. We cannot use the research methods of experimentation, analysis, reduction, and deduction heretofore used. We need a different epistemology because of the novelty of the research topic.

My second conclusion is that the incredibly complex and diversified systems of communication technology have the effect of inflating information. We cannot avoid it; so news items have to be produced every hour. You will not pay much attention to your empty television screen. Such inflation is inevitably induced through the existence of communication networks. The famous formula about "The right to be informed" is stupid. Information growth is not the result of a human right, but the industrial product of an apparatus which must transmit it. This highly technical, sophisticated mechanism inevitably produces completely insignificant information. The technological apparatus erases the existence of a significant referent.

The media refer only to themselves.

NOTES

1. *Translators' note:* The F.L.N. was the Front de Liberation Nationale (National Liberation Front), the Algerian freedom fighters' movement during their war of independence 25 years ago.

POSTSCRIPT

Can Modern Mass Communication Promote a Better World?

Both selections ask us to extend common knowledge about the power and impact of communication technologies, but while the first author sees networks facilitating communication, the second believes that the "communicative ability" of the world will stay pretty much the same as it is now. Perhaps a topic for discussion should include whether both of these authors define "communication" and "information" in the same way. An answer to this question might very well provide the seed for further examination of what other authors mean when they use these terms. Perhaps the intellectual baggage and assumptions we bring with us entering into discussions about "communication," "information," and even "technology" prevent us from understanding the true impact of what technologies do to us, or what we do with technology.

There are many recent books and periodicals that discuss various aspects of technology and its use. Popular publications that provide useful data and technological trends include *Technology Review*, a monthly publication of MIT, and *The Economist*, a weekly magazine. Wilson P. Dizard, Jr., in *The Coming Information Age: An Overview of Technology, Economics, and Politics* (Longman, 1982) suggests many ways in which the government's policies influence technological development and use. Jacques Ellul's 1967 book, *The Technological Society* (Free Press), suggests that the importance of "technique" as the metaphor that binds technology and use.

Other texts that examine the impact of trans-border information flow include Anthony Smith's *The Geopolitics of Information: How the Western Culture Dominates the World* (Oxford, 1980) and *Tracing New Orbits: Cooperation and Competition in Global Satellite Development*, edited by Donna A. Demac (Columbia University Press, 1986). The role of information in developing societies and the cultural interpretations of the meaning of information can be found in Jarice Hanson and Uma Narula's *New Communication Technologies in Developing Countries* (Lawrence Erlbaum Associates, 1990).

Several interesting feminist analyses have provided rich information regarding the use of technology by women. Among these sources are Carolyn Marvin's *When Old Technologies Were New: Thinking About Electric Communication in the Late Nineteenth Century* (Oxford University Press, 1988); *Machina Ex Dea: Feminist Perspectives on Technology*, edited by Joan Rothschild (Pergamon, 1983); and *Technology and Women's Voices: Keeping in Touch*, edited by Cheris Kramarae (Routledge and Kegan Paul, 1988).

CONTRIBUTORS TO THIS VOLUME

EDITORS

ALISON ALEXANDER is associate professor in the Department of Communications at the University of Massachusetts at Amherst. She received her B.A. in education from Marshall University in 1971, her M.A. in communication from the University of Kentucky in 1974, and her Ph.D. in communication from Ohio State University in 1979. Her areas of research and publication include television and the family (with particular interest in sibling interaction); the creation of social meaning for media consumption; and children's interpretation of media. Professor Alexander is currently editor of the *Journal of Broadcasting and Electronic Media* and vice president-elect of the Eastern Communication Association.

JARICE HANSON received B.A.s in speech and performing arts and English at Northeastern Illinois University in 1976. She received her M.A. in 1977 and her Ph.D. in 1979 from the Department of Radio-Television-Film at Northwestern University. She is the author of *Understanding Video: Applications, Impact and Theory* (Sage, 1976). She is coauthor, with Dr. Uma Narula, of *New Communication Technologies in Developing Countries* (Lawrence Erlbaum Associates, 1990); and coeditor, with Dr. Indu B. Singh, of *Advances in Telematics* (Ablex, 1990). Her practical media training reflects two years with BBC television in London and seven years at WBBM-TV in Chicago. From 1979 to 1985 she was assistant professor in the Department of Communication at Rutgers University. She is currently associate professor and graduate program director in the Department of Communication at the University of Massachusetts at Amherst.

STAFF

Marguerite L. Egan   Program Manager
Brenda S. Filley   Production Manager
Whit Vye   Designer
Libra Ann Cusack   Typesetting Supervisor
Juliana Arbo   Typesetter
Shawn Callahan and James Filley   Graphics
Diane Barker   Editorial Assistant
David Dean   Administrative Assistant

AUTHORS

T. D. ALLMAN covered the Indochina War for the *Manchester Guardian*. He is the author of *Unmanifest Destiny* (Doubleday, 1984), a book about U.S. intervention in the Third World.

DANIEL R. ANDERSON is a professor of psychology at the University of Massachusetts at Amherst. He has conducted extensive research and has written numerous articles on the television viewing habits of children. He is particularly interested in studying children's attention.

F. CHRISTOPHER ARTERTON is dean of the Graduate School of Political Management in New York City. He is a former research associate at the Institute of Politics at Harvard University.

BEN H. BAGDIKIAN is an award-winning journalist and educator. He is professor emeritus in the Graduate School of Journalism at the University of California at Berkeley. A member of the ACLU, he has been an active supporter of a free and responsible press. His book *In the Midst of Plenty: The Poor in America* (Beacon Press, 1964) had a substantial impact on shaping the public's and the federal government's views on poverty.

TED BECKER has written and reviewed several books about telecommunications. Some of his works have been published in the *American Political Science Review.*

The late **HUGH MALCOLM BEVILLE, JR.,** a writer, college professor, and former executive director of the Broadcast Rating Council, was a staff member of NBC Research for more than 30 years.

DANIEL L. BRENNER is coauthor, with Monroe E. Price, of *Cable Television and Other Nonbroadcast Video Technologies* (Boardman, 1986). He received his J.D. from Stanford in 1976 and was a legal assistant to Mark Fowler during his term as chairman of the Federal Communications Commission.

MAURA E. CLANCEY is a project director at Statistical Research Incorporated in Westfield, New Jersey. She is a former director of the Media Analysis Project at George Washington University in Washington, D.C.

JAMES C. DOBSON is the founder and president of Focus on the Family, an organization dedicated to preserving traditional values. He was a member of the Meese Commission on Pornography, which delivered its final report to the public and to then-president Ronald Reagan in June 1986.

JOHN D. H. DOWNING is chairman of the Department of Radio-Television-Film at the University of Texas at Austin. He is the author of *Film and Politics in the Third World* (Praeger, 1987) and *Third World Cinema: Film, Politics and Aesthetics* (Praeger, 1990).

MICHAEL DYSON teaches ethics and cultural criticism at the Chicago Theological Seminary. He writes the "Black American" column for *Z Magazine*.

FRANK EASTERBROOK is a federal judge in the U.S. Court of Appeals for the Seventh Circuit. He is coauthor, with Richard A. Posner, of *Antitrust: Cases, Economic Notes, and Other Materials*, 2nd ed. (West, 1980).

JACQUES ELLUL, a European communication scholar, is a professor at the Université de Bordeaux in France. Two of his best-known books in the United States are *Technological Society* (Random House, 1967) and *Propaganda: The Formation of Men's Attitudes* (Harper & Row, 1973).

DAVID H. FLAHERTY is a professor of history and law at the University of Western Ontario in London, Ontario. Much of his research and publishing has been in the area of personal privacy.

MARK S. FOWLER is an attorney in the firm of Latham & Watkins in Washington, D.C. He is a former chairman of the Federal Communications Commission.

TODD GITLIN is a professor of sociology at the University of California at Berkeley. He writes for the scholarly and popular press on media, culture, and politics. His publications include *The Whole World Is Watching: Mass Media in the Making and Unmaking of the New Left* (University of California Press, 1980).

MARTIN GOTTLIEB is a projects editor for the *New York Times* and Gannett Visiting Professor at Columbia University's Graduate School of Journalism. He is a past editor in chief of the *Village Voice*.

DENNIS HAYES studied at St. Norbert College and Carleton University. He is a free-lance writer for computer and microchip firms. He resides in California's Silicon Valley, where he has lived since 1979, and is a contributor to the magazine *Processed World*.

The late **WALTER KARP** was a historian and social critic. His publications include *The Politics of War: The Story of Two Wars Which Altered Forever the Political Life of the American Republic* (Harper & Row, 1979) and *Liberty Under Siege* (Holt, 1988).

JUDITH K. LARSEN is affiliated with Cognos Associates of Los Altos, California. *Silicon Valley Fever: Growth of High-Technology Culture* (Basic Books, 1984), which she coauthored with Everett M. Rogers, is her first book.

THEODORE LEVITT is professor emeritus of business administration at the Harvard Business School. His publications include *Marketing for Business Growth* (McGraw-Hill, 1974) and *The Marketing Imagination* (Free Press, 1983).

J. FRED MacDONALD is a professor at Northeastern Illinois University in Chicago. He is the author of several books and articles on radio, television, and racial stereotyping, including *Don't Touch That Dial* (Nelson-Hall, 1979) and *Blacks and White TV: Afro-Americans in Television Since 1948* (Nelson-Hall, 1983).

JANET MALCOLM has been a staff writer at *The New Yorker* since 1965.

ROBERT D. McCLURE is a writer who specializes in national politics. He is coauthor, with Linda Fowler, of *Political Ambition: Who Decides to Run for Congress?* (Yale University Press, 1989).

MAXWELL E. McCOMBS is chairman of the Department of Journalism and the Jesse H. Jones Centennial Professor in Communication at the University of Texas at Austin.

JOE McGINNISS is a widely published nonfiction author and former journalist. He is best known for *The Selling of the President, 1968* (Trident Press, 1968), *Fatal Vision* (Putnam, 1983), and *Blind Faith* (Putnam, 1989).

DIANA M. MEEHAN is a writer and the author of *Ladies of the Evening: Women Characters of Prime-Time Television* (Scarecrow, 1983). She received her Ph.D. from the University of Southern California.

MICHAEL NOVAK directs social and political studies at the American Enterprise Institute in Washington, D.C. His books include *The Spirit of Democratic Capitalism* (Simon & Schuster, 1982) and *Human Rights and the New Realism: Strategic Thinking in a New Age* (Freedom House, 1986).

PARENTS RESOURCE MUSIC CENTER is a non-profit organization based in Washington, D.C., which was formed to educate and inform parents about record lyrics and other issues related to the content of current popular music.

Susan Baker is its president and Tipper Gore its treasurer.

THOMAS E. PATTERSON is chairman of the Political Science Department at Syracuse University's Maxwell School of Citizenship, where he has taught since 1970.

The late **ITHIEL DE SOLA POOL** was the Ruth and Arthur Sloan Professor of Political Science at MIT. His publications include *Technologies of Freedom* (Belknap Press, 1983).

ELAYNE RAPPING teaches in the Department of Communication at the Pittsburgh Center campus of Robert Morris College. She is a frequent reviewer for *The Nation* and the author of *The Looking Glass World of Nonfiction Television* (South End Press, 1987).

MICHAEL J. ROBINSON is a professor in the Department of Government at Georgetown University. He is a former director of the Media Analysis Project at George Washington University in Washington, D.C.

EVERETT M. ROGERS is a professor at the Annenberg School of Communication at the University of Southern California. He is the author of several books and articles on communication, diffusion, and technology, including *Communication Technology* (Free Press, 1986).

JAMES B. RULE is a professor of sociology at the State University of New York at Stony Brook. He is the author of *Private Lives and Public Surveillance: The Politics of Privacy* (Schocken Books, 1974) and *Theories of Civil Violence* (University of California Press, 1988).

WILLIAM A. RUSHER is a senior fellow at the Claremont Institute. He is a former publisher of the *National Review.*

The late **RAYMOND WILLIAMS** taught at the Open University in London until his death in 1988. Among his publications are *Television: Technology and Cultural Form* (Schocken, 1975); *Culture and Society: Seventeen-Eighty to Nineteen-Fifty* (Columbia University Press, 1983); and *The Long Revolution* (Columbia University Press, 1984).

MARIE WINN has written 12 books for parents and children, including *Children Without Childhood* (Pantheon Books, 1983). She has two children and one television set, which is only used on special occasions.

TIMOTHY E. WIRTH is a U.S. senator from Colorado (D). He is a former chairman of the House Subcommittee on Telecommunications, Consumer Protection, and Finance, and is also interested in issues of energy policy and protection of the environment.

FRANK ZAPPA is a musician and a songwriter. He was the creative genius behind the popular music group The Mothers of Invention.

INDEX

ABC, 191, 199, 200, 202, 203, 214, 218, 242, 276, 280, 281
abortion issue, television news coverage of, 203–204
AC/DC, 137, 139
addiction, television as, 49–50
advertising: 39, 205; controversy over ethics of, 252–269; controversy over, in political campaigns, 78–79, 80, 172–185
Agnew, Spiro, and the media, 201–206, 222
alcohol use, mention of, in records, 136
All in the Family, 30, 247
Allman, T. D., on television coverage of the Vietnam War, 220–225
Alternatives for Washington (AFW), 296–297, 303–304
American Research Bureau (ARB), 243, 244, 245
Amos 'n' Andy, 20, 35
Anderson, Daniel R., on television's harmful effect on children, 51–53
androgyne, strong-soft woman as, in popular media, 58–64
Apple, 326
Arterton, F. Christopher, on teledemocracy, 300–307
artificial intelligence, 315, 337, 353
Associated Press (AP), 191, 287, 388
A-Team, The, 20, 28
AT&T, 335, 338, 340
attention span, effect of television on, 5–6, 51
Attorney General's Commission on Pornography, report of, 160–166
automation, office, 313–314, 353

Bagdikian, Ben H., on concentration of ownership and media content, 274–282
balance, in television news programs, 194, 195, 213
banking data, use of, in privacy invasion, 99
Becker, Ted, on teledemocracy, 296–299
Benson, 20, 32
Berle, Milton, 14–15
Beville, Hugh Malcolm, on television ratings, 232–240
Beyond Belief (Lipstadt), 277
blacks, portrayal of, on *The Cosby Show,* 20–40
books, controversy over concentration of publishers of, 274–290
Brenner, Daniel L., on broadcast deregulation, 116–124
Brinkley, David, 202, 204, 216
British Broadcasting Corporation (BBC), 235, 236, 268
Broadcast News, 67, 68–69

broadcasting, controversy over deregulation of, 116–132
Brockett v. Skoken Arcades, Inc., 152
Brokaw, Tom, 191, 197
Buckley, William F., 78, 192, 197
Buckley v. Valeo, 158
Buena Vista Films, 280, 282

cable industry: 127, 131, 236, 238, 239, 278, 281, 303, 306, 313, 335, 336, 340, 341; and privacy regulation, 108–110
Cable News Network (CNN), 191
Carter, Jimmy, 202, 205
CBS, 191, 199, 200, 201, 202, 213, 215, 216, 217, 218, 233, 236, 237, 241, 242, 276, 279, 280, 281
CBS v. Democratic National Committee, 121
CBS v. FCC, 119, 121
censorship: 118, 342, 351; of pornography, controversy over, 152–166; of records, controversy over, 136–148
children: and computers, 315–316; controversy over record censorship for, 136–148; and pornography, 160, 162, 163, 164, 165; television's influence on, 15, 44–53, 128–129, 130, 131
Choices for '76, 304
Cinderella, as female role model, 58
Clancey, Maura E., on liberal bias in television news programs, 201–206
class bias, in television, 4, 8–11, 21, 26, 33, 38
Committee on Nationwide Television Audience Measurements (CONTAM), 243, 244, 245
common carriage, principle of, 340
Common Ground (Lukas), 87, 88
Communications Act, 124
competitor, television as hidden, 45–46
computers: 297, 299, 348–359; use of, in privacy invasion, 98–110; *see also,* Silicon Valley
Constitution, U.S., *see* First Amendment
consumers, and controversy over ethics of advertising, 252–269
Control Data Corporation, 326
Cooper, Barry Michael, on deception in journalism, 91–92
copyright, vs. serviceright, 341–342
corporations, multinational, media control by, 274–290
Cosby Show, The: 46, 62–63; controversy over treatment of racial issues on, 20–40
credit bureau data, use of, in privacy invasion, 99, 100, 101, 108

362